CONTEMPORARY POETS
IN
AMERICAN ANTHOLOGIES
1960-1977

by

Kirby Congdon

The Scarecrow Press, Inc.
Metuchen, N.J. & London
1978

Library of Congress Cataloging in Publication Data

Congdon, Kirby.
    Contemporary poets in American anthologies, 1960-
1977.

    1. American poetry--20th century--Bibliography.
2. Poetry, Modern--20th century--Bibliography.
I. Title.
Z1231. P7C65   [PS323. 5]   016. 811'5'4   78-13772
ISBN 0-8108-1168-5

CONTENTS

iii

INTRODUCTION

This index lists some 6,500 poets whose works are included in about 400 anthologies published during the last 17 years in the United States. While several countries are very active in the publishing and the writing of poetry, I think most readers would agree that the United States is an indicator of what is going on, since this country not only publishes the most books in the most internationally recognized language, but at the same time absorbs Latin American, European and any number of other foreign influences.

Aside from books I could not locate, this index omits the vast and overwhelming area of translations and foreign texts. It also avoids other groups of material that are in themselves subjective--that is, poetry anthologies which are restricted by school or club membership, limited to those paying "dues" for inclusion, or to one age group, historical period, or to song lyrics and the like, where the particular category becomes more important to the book's editor that the art of the poem itself. This limitation, it seems to me, is obvious and sensible rather than arbitrary or prejudiced.

My term "contemporary" in the title refers to poets living in 1960. This omits such key figures as Dylan Thomas (d. 1953), Wallace Stevens (d. 1955), or Edwin Muir who died in 1959, one year before my cut-off date. To many of us, these poets are still "contemporary," but this survey has to begin somewhere, and for many poets 1960 is almost another age. I chose 1960 as a starting point because this was the year the landmark Grove anthology appeared (The New American Poetry: 1945-1960, edited by Donald M. Allen), making an almost tangible and visible beginning for those poets who were affected in their lives and in their work by the bomb on Hiroshima, as well as a distinction between them and other poets whose sensibilities were already defined and active in a previous literary period. The changes in the personality and thinking of poets in this period (1960-1977), not only in their work but in the very names of poets, even has a kind of sociological interest. I think, for example, of the social respectability inherent in the name of Edward A. Uffington Valentine (in Justice and the Law: An Anthology of American Legal Poetry and Verse) of 1960, and by contrast, the many cryptic signatures, only 15 years later, such as that of "Ai" in The American Poetry Anthology of 1975 (edited by Daniel Halpern).

In order to provide a key to new poets, in addition to their well-established elders, I have tried to list every small-press publication I could find. Some such anthologies may be regarded as cliquish, self-serving or "not serious," but almost any anthology can be accused of such prejudices and I feel that an over-all view of anthologies, such as this index tries to present, helps to correct any such perceived imbalance. An anthology, after all, is at best a screening process, and while a friendship, a love affair, or an opportunistic association may lead to a subjective inclusion in one anthology, the same association can not be that dependable a means of entry elsewhere, and so things even out.

A more strenuous judgment is needed to find one's way through the foibles of fashion. Today's star can be tomorrow's has-been; yesterday's naive juvenile may be a future grand old man (or woman) of letters. This is as true for the early and the ancient poets as for our recent contemporaries. I have preferred to err in this compilation by numerical inclusion of the possibly inconsequential rather than by the even greater danger of aesthetic exclusiveness, a criterion that may be well-intentioned, especially for the included, but perilous as a dictum.

In any case, one can easily assume that there is more than one fine and important poet who has never, or hardly ever, been acknowledged by any anthology at all. For him or her this survey is a hateful enterprise and that poet is the one to whom I dedicate this book, because the unknown is always what is most exciting and because it leaves us with still something more to wait upon and to look for in the history of literature. History is a long-legged beast, but the past decade and a half have encapsuled a remarkable period of transformation, equal in interest to that other American literary phenomenon, the twenties. For this reason, I have enjoyed compiling these pages, as though the result were a creative work rather than a mere compilation. I hope I have applied as much care to these listings, nevertheless, as is bibliographically proper. Whatever faults or mistakes remain must be, alas, my own.

Kirby Congdon

Fire Island Pines, N.Y.
Autumn 1977.

ACKNOWLEDGMENTS

The New York Public Library.

The Butler Library and Barnard College Library, Columbia University.

The Schomburg Center for Research in Black Culture, New York City.

The Brooklyn Public Library, Brooklyn, N.Y.

PART I

ANTHOLOGIES

ADAMS, Hazard. Poetry: An Introductory Anthology. Boston:
Little, Brown, 1968.
    W. H. Auden, Elizabeth Bishop, Gregory Corso, E. E. Cum-
mings, J. V. Cunningham, James Dickey, T. S. Eliot, Donald
Finkel, Robert Frost, Allen Ginsberg, Robert Graves, Donald
Justice, X. J. Kennedy, Thomas Kinsella, Carolyn Kizer,
Philip Larkin, Denise Levertov, Robert Lowell, James Mc-
Michael, Jay Macpherson, Robert Mezey, Vassar Miller,
Marianne Moore, Sylvia Plath, Ezra Pound, John Crowe Ran-
som, James Reavey, Theodore Roethke, Delmore Schwartz,
Louis Simpson, W. D. Snodgrass, Stephen Spender, William
Stafford, Allen Tate, James Tate, Theodore Weiss, Richard
Wilbur, W. C. Williams, Charles Wright, James Wright.

*ADOFF, Arnold. I Am the Darker Brother. An Anthology of
Modern Poems by Negro Americans. New York: Macmillan, 1968.
    Samuel Allen, Arna Bontemps, Gwendolyn Brooks, Sterling A.
Brown, Frank Marshall Davis, Robert A. Davis, Owen Dodson,
Ray Durem, Mari Evans, Robert Hayden, Calvin C. Hernton,
Leslie Pinckney Hill, Langston Hughes, Fenton Johnson, LeRoi
Jones, George Love, Myron O'Higgins, Raymond Richard Pat-
terson, Quandra Prettyman, Dudley Randall, Conrad Kent
Rivers, Jean Toomer, Margaret Walker, Joseph White, Rich-
ard Wright.

ADOFF, Arnold. City in All Directions: An Anthology of Modern
Poems. New York: Macmillan, 1969.
    Arnold Adoff, Kofif Awoonor, Christopher Brookhouse, Alan
Brownjohn, David Budbill, Melville Cane, John Pepper Clark,
Leonard Cohen, Julia Fields, Nikki Giovanni, Don L. Lee,
Nicanor Parra, Brian Patten, Raymond Richard Patterson,
Quandra Prettyman, Jacques Prevert, Elaine Schwager, Robert
Paul Smith, Edward S. Spriggs, Yevgeny Yevtushenko.

---

*Where several anthologies are listed under one compiler's name,
they are listed in order of publication, since the index of poets refers only to compiler plus date in such cases.

ADOFF, Arnold. It Is the Poem Singing into Your Eyes: Anthology of New Young Poets. New York: Harper & Row, 1971.
    Kate Ballen, Sydna Bennett, Marc Bergschneider, Jeff Blair, Greg Bowers, Cathy Bresher, Audrey Brooks, S. Marshall Brooks Jr., Nelson (Ameer) Brown, Mary Celinia Bruce, Carrie Burchardt, Karin Carter, Chris Cayer, Stephen R. Comer, M. E. Davison, Mark D'Elia, Gail Dubrow, Jessie Duffey, David R. Dzwonkoski, Bob Frisell, Henry Gordon, Mindy Gorlin, Jeff Heglin, John Heinegg, Ellen Jenkins, Norman Kaplan, Barbara Krasnoff, Paul Layton, Martin Levine, Angelo Lewis, William Alfred McLean Jr., Jude Malouf, Gregg Manin, William Melaney, Susan Meltzer, Susan Mernit, Pam Murtha, Laura Nagan, Jan Oliver, Cleave (Poncho) Reed, Randall Richard, Vivianne Schofer, Elaine Schwager, C. C. Scott, Maureen Sheedy, Jean A. Smith, Jean Streich, Thomas Tammaro, Larry Thompson, Arthur Toegemann, Suzanne Vargus.

ADOFF, Arnold. The Poetry of Black America: Anthology of the 20th Century. New York: Harper, 1973.
    Nanina Alba, Samuel Allen, Johari Amini, S. E. Anderson, Russell Atkins, Imamu Amiri Baraka, Gerald W. Barrax, Gwendolyn B. Bennett, Lerone Bennett, Lebert Bethune, Arna Bontemps, Gwendolyn Brooks, Sterling Brown, F. J. Bryant, John Henrik Clarke, Carole Gregory Clemmons, Lucille Clifton, Charlie Cobb, Conys, Charles Cooper, Sam Cornish, Jayne Cortez, Stanley Crouch, Victor Hernandez Cruz, Margaret Danner, Frank Marshall Davis, Djangatolum, Owen Dodson, William Edward Burghardt Du Bois, Alfred Duckett, Henry Dumas, Ray Durem, Ebon, James Emanuel, Mari Evans, Sarah Webster Fabio, Jessie Redmond Fauset, Julia Fields, Calvin Forbes, Carol Freeman, Hoyt W. Fuller, Carl Gardner, Zack Gilbert, Nikki Giovanni, D. L. Graham, Michael Harper, William J. Harris, De Leon Harrison, Walter Everette Hawkins, Robert Hayden, Donald Jeffrey Hayes, David Henderson, Calvin C. Hernton, Leslie Pinckney Hill, M. Carl Holman, Langston Hughes, Mae Jackson, Lance Jeffers, Ted Joans, Fred Johnson, Georgia Douglas Johnson, Helene Johnson, Joe Johnson, June Jordan, Bob Kaufman, Keorapetse Kgositsile, Etheridge Knight, Bette Darcie Latimer, Don L. Lee, Julius Lester, Angelo Lewis, Elouise Loftin, Pearl Cleage Lomax, Doughtry Long, Audre Lorde, Felipe Luciano, K. Curtis Lyle, Charles Lynch, Lawrence McGough, L. V. Mack, Naomi Long Madgett, Barbara Mahone, Clarence Major, Herbert Martin, Adam David Miller, Wayne Moreland, Pauli Murray, Effie Lee Newsome, Gloria C. Oden, Myron O'Higgins, Raymond R. Patterson, Rob Penny, Julianne Perry, Oliver Pitcher, Sterling Plumpp, Quandra Prettyman, N. H. Pritchard, Dudley Randall, Lennox Raphael, Eugene Redmont, Ishmael Reed, Conrad K. Rivers, Ed Roberson, Carolyn M. Rodgers, Sonia Sanchez, Alvin Saxon (Ojerke), Welton Smith, A. B. Spellman, Anne Spencer, Primus St. John, Lorenzo Thomas, Richard Thomas, James W. Thompson, Larry Thompson, Melvin B. Tolson,

Jean Toomer, Askia Muhammad Toure, Quincy Troupe, Alice
Walker, Margaret Walker, Tom Weatherly, Ron Welburn,
Joseph White, August Wilson, Bruce McM. Wright, Jay Wright,
Richard Wright, Sarah E. Wright, Al Young.

ADOFF, Arnold. My Black Me: A Beginning Book of Black Poetry.
New York: Dutton, 1974.
Imamu A. Baraka, Clucille Clifton, Lloyd Corbin, Jr., Sam
Cornish, Jackie Earley, James Emanuel, Julia Fields, Carol
Freeman, Nikki Giovanni, Kali Grosvenor, William J. Harris,
Vanessa Howard, Langston Hughes, Mae Jackson, Ted Joans,
Norman Jordan, Don L. Lee, Doughtry Long, Barbara Mahone,
Bob O'Meally, Ray Patterson, Rob Penny, Carolyn Rodgers,
Sonia Sanchez, Julius Thompson, Larry Thompson.

AIKEN, Conrad. Twentieth Century American Poetry. New York:
Random House, 1963.
Leonie Adams, John Peale Bishop, R. P. Blackmur, Kenneth
Burke, Horatio Colony, Malcolm Cowley, Edward Doro, John
Gould Fletcher, Horace Gregory, Alfred Kreymborg, Claire
McAllister, Archibald MacLeish, Charles Philbrick, Trumbull
Stickney, Ruth Stone, John L. Sweeney, John Hall Wheelock,
John Wheelwright, Yvor Winters.

ALGARIN, Miguel; Miguel Pinero; Richard August. Nuyorican Po-
etry: An Anthology of Puerto Rican Words and Feelings. New
York: Morrow, 1975.
Miguel Algarin, Angel Berrocales, Bimbo, Shorty Bon Bon,
Americo Casiano, Lucky CienFuegos, Carlos Conde, Sandra
Maria Esteves, Jose-Angel Figueroa, Isidro Garcia, T. C.
Garcia, Jorge Lopez, Archie Martinez, Jesus Papoleto Melen-
dez, Martita Morales, Amina Munoz, Pedro Pietri, Dadi
Pinero, Miguel Pinero, Miguel Luz Rodriguez.

ALLEN, Donald M. The New American Poetry: 1945-1960. New
York: Grove, 1960.
Helen Adam, Brother Antoninus, John Ashbery, Paul Blackburn,
Robin Blaser, Ebbe Borregaard, Bruce Boyd, Ray Bremser,
James Broughton, Paul Carroll, Gregory Corso, Robert Cree-
ley, Edward Dorn, Kirby Doyle, Richard Duerden, Robert
Duncan, Larry Eigner, Lawrence Ferlinghetti, Edward Field,
Allen Ginsberg, Madeline Gleason, Barbara Guest, LeRoi
Jones, Jack Kerouac, Kenneth Koch, Philip Lamantia, Denise
Levertov, Ron Loewinsohn, Michael McClure, Edward Marshall,
David Meltzer, Frank O'Hara, Charles Olson, Joel Oppenheimer,
Peter Orlovsky, Stuart Z. Perkoff, James Schuyler, Gary Sny-
der, Gilbert Sorrentino, Jack Spicer, Lew Welch, Philip Wha-
len, John Wieners, Jonathan Williams.

ALLEN, Donald M. 12 Poets & 1 Painter. San Francisco: Four
Seasons Foundation, 1964.
Bruce Boyd, Robert Creeley, Robert Duncan, Lawrence Fer-
linghetti, Max Finstein, Allen Ginsberg, LeRoi Jones, Joanne

Kyger, Denise Levertov, Charles Olson, Gary Snyder, Lew
Welch.

ALLEN, Gay Wilson; Walter B. Rideout; James K. Robinson. A-
merican Poetry. New York: Harper & Row, 1965.
Conrad Aiken, Wendell Berry, John Berryman, Robert Cree-
ley, E. E. Cummings, James Dickey, Hilda Doolittle, Alan
Dugan, T. S. Eliot, Robert Frost, Randall Jarrell, Denise
Levertov, Robert Lowell, Archibald MacLeish, W. S. Merwin,
Marianne Moore, Ezra Pound, John Crowe Ransom, Theodore
Roethke, Carl Sandburg, Karl Shapiro, W. D. Snodgrass, Al-
len Tate, Richard Wilbur, William Carlos Williams.

ALLEN, John Alexander. Hero's Way: Contemporary Poems in the
Mythic Tradition. Englewood Cliffs, N. J.: Prentice-Hall, 1971.
Conrad Aiken, John Alexander Allen, W. H. Auden, Elizabeth
Bishop, R. P. Blackmur, Louise Bogan, John Ciardi, Eliza-
beth Coatsworth, Robert Creeley, Samuel Daniel, C. Day Lew-
is, Joanne de Longchamps, Babette Deutsch, James Dickey,
R. H. W. Dillard, Clifford Dyment, Richard Eberhart, T. S.
Eliot, Jean Farley, Donald Finkel, Robert Frost, Roy Fuller,
Isabella Gardner, George Garrett, Don Geiger, Jane Gentry,
Brewster Ghiselin, Madeline Gleason, Robert Graves, Thom
Gunn, John Heath-Stubbs, Geoffrey Hill, Robert Hillyer, Daniel
Hoffman, A. D. Hope, Graham Hough, Barbara Howes, Randall
Jarrell, Josephine Jacobsen, Gayle Johnson, Donald Justice,
Chester Kallman, Thomas Kinsella, Stanley Kunitz, Philip Lar-
kin, Denise Levertov, Peter Levi, Ron Loewinsohn, Archibald
MacLeish, Louis MacNeice, E. L. Mayo, James Merrill,
Thomas Merton, W. S. Merwin, Robert Mezey, Josephine
Miles, Howard Nemerov, John Frederick Nims, Robert Pack,
Kenneth Patchen, Kenneth Pitchford, Sylvia Plath, Hyam Plut-
zik, Julia Randall, John Crowe Ransom, Theodore Roethke,
Jerome Rothenberg, Muriel Rukeyser, Carl Sandburg, Ernest
Sandeen, May Sarton, Delmore Schwartz, Winfield Townley
Scott, James Seay, Anne Sexton, William Jay Smith, W. D.
Snodgrass, Gary Snyder, Stephen Spender, William Stafford,
Jon Swan, May Swenson, Henry Taylor, Peter Viereck, David
Wagoner, John Wain, Robert Wallace, J. P. Ward, Robert
Penn Warren, Robert Watson, Richard Wilbur, Richard Wright.

ALLEN, Terry. The Whispering Wind: Poetry by Young American
Indians. Garden City, N. Y.: Doubleday, 1972.
Emerson Blackhorse, Janet Campbell, Ramona Carden, Grey
Cohoe, Phil George, Patricia Irving, King D. Kuka, Alonzo
Lopez, "Barney" Mitchell, Calvin O'John, Ted Palmanteer,
Agnes T. Pratt, Liz Sohappy, Donna Whitewing.

ALOIAN, David. Poems and Poets. St. Louis: McGraw-Hill, 1965.
Conrad Aiken, Richard Armour, W. H. Auden, Robert Beloof,
Elizabeth Bishop, Morris Bishop, Francis Bourdillon, William
Bowles, Sarah Cleghorn, Hilda Conkling, E. E. Cummings,
Hilda Doolittle, Richard Eberhart, T. S. Eliot, Kenneth Fear-

ing, John Gould Fletcher, Robert Frost, Wilfred Wilson Gibson, Arthur Guiterman, John Hay, Randall Jarrell, Robinson Jeffers, Vladislav Khodasevich, James Kirkup, Robert Lowell, David McCord, Phyllis McGinley, Archibald MacLeish, Charles Malam, John Masefield, Florence Ripley Mastin, Marianne Moore, Ogden Nash, Murray Noss, Dorothy Parker, John Crowe Ransom, Theodore Roethke, Carl Sandburg, Siegfried Sassoon, Karl Shapiro, Stephen Spender, Vincent Starrett, Jon Swan, May Swenson, Louis Untermeyer, Peter Viereck, Robert Wallace, W. W. Watt, William Carlos Williams, George Edward Woodberry.

ANANIA, Michael. New Poetry Anthology I. Chicago: The Swallow Press, 1969.
Michael Anania, Charles Doria, Barbara Harr, Richard Lourie, James McMichael, Peter Michelson, William Moebius, Dennis Schmitz.

ARP, Thomas R. The Form of Poetry. New York: Macmillan, 1966.
W. H. Auden, J. V. Cunningham, T. S. Eliot, William Empson, Robert Frost, Robert Graves, Thom Gunn, Ellen Kay, Philip Larkin, Robert Lowell, Marianne Moore, Ezra Pound, John Crowe Ransom, Richard Wilbur, William Carlos Williams.

ARTS FESTIVAL. A Poetry Folio. San Francisco: 1963.
Helen Adam, Robin Blaser, Robert Duncan, Lawrence Ferlinghetti, Allen Ginsberg, Ron Loewinsohn, Lew Welch, Philip Whalen.

ARTS FESTIVAL. A Poetry Folio. San Francisco: 1964.
Richard Brautigan, James Broughton, Max Finstein, Andrew Hoyem, Lenore Kandel, Joanne Kyger, David Meltzer, Gary Snyder, George Stanley.

ASHLAND. Poets on the Platform: Readings from the Second Annual "The Voice and the Word Poetry Festival" Held on the Ashland College Campus April, 1970. Ashland, Ohio: Ashland Poetry Press, 1970.
Grace Butcher, Robert Canzoneri, Hale Chatfield, Cyril A. Dostal, Donald Hassler, James Kilgore, J. R. LeMaster, Robert McGovern, James E. Magner, Jr., James Reiss, Malcolm M. Sedam, Richard Snyder, Hollis Summers, Alberta Turner, Jack Zucker.

BACH, Bert C.; William A. Sessions; William Walling. The Liberating Form: A Handbook-Anthology of English and American Poetry. New York: Dodd, Mead, 1972.
A. R. Ammons, Arna Bontemps, E. E. Cummings, Hilda Doolittle, T. S. Eliot, William Empson, Langston Hughes, Robinson Jeffers, LeRoi Jones, Robert Lowell, Marianne Moore, Ezra Pound, John Crowe Ransom, Theodore Roethke, Carl Sandburg, Karl Shapiro, Allen Tate, Richard Wilbur, William Carlos Williams.

BALAZS, Mary Webber; Nancy Esther James. Touching This Earth.
Poems by Women. New Wilmington, Pa.: Dawn Valley Press,
1977.
Jeannine Dobbs, Anne Hobson Freeman, Barbard Friend, Irene
Haupel Genco, Elizabeth Hewitt, Margaret Honton, Beth Baruch
Joselow, Suzanne Juhasz, Julie Kane, Eleanor Keats, Kathryn
Martin, Judy Neeld, Joan Shapiro, Kathryn Weldy.

BANKER, Lynne. Poets For Peace: Poems from the East. New
York: 1967.
W. H. Auden, Carol Berge, Art Berger, Paul Blackburn, Ed
Blair, Ray M. Carr, Robert David Cohen, Rex Baker Coile,
Maggie Dominic, John Duffy, Annelle Easlic, Helen Engelhardt,
Clayton Eshleman, RobertOh Faber, Dan Georgakas, Ben Gold-
stein, W. E. G., Antoni Gronowicz, Ruth Hamlin, Mike Heller,
David Henderson, C. J. Hinke, Elchanan Ben-Ami, Barbara
Holland, Will Inman, Michael Francis Itkin, Martin A. Wat-
kins, Janice Judson, Hans Juergenson, Allen Katzman, Donald
Katzman, KK, Aaron Kramer, Denise Levertov, Bill Little,
Dick Lourie, Walter Lowenfels, Ken McLaren, Leonore Mar-
shall, George Montgomery, Frank Murphy, James Nash, W.
Oakes, D. Ogilby, Joel Oppenheimer, Paul Prensky, Carol
Rubenstein, Muriel Rukeyser, Cassandre Russell, Ruth Lisa
Schechter, Howard Loeb Schulman, Edith Segal, Judith John-
son Sherwin, Irene Shram, Joel Sloman, Andree Sodenkamp,
Shalom Sperber, Yuri Suhl, Karen Swenson, Harvey Tucker,
Lewis Turco, Beatrice Verne, Martin Wasserman, Hannah
Weiner, Philip Whalen, Verna Woskoff, Leo Young, Gary
Youree, Fred Zappala.

BARAKA, I. A. Afro-Arts Anthology: New Works. Newark:
Jihad, 1967.
Ben Caldwell, O. R. Hand, Yusef Iman, LeRoi Jones, Ed
Spriggs.

BARNES, R. G. Episodes: In Five Poetic Traditions: The Sonnet:
The Pastoral Elegy: The Ballad: The Ode: Masks and Voices.
San Francisco: Chandler, 1972.
John Ashbery, W. H. Auden, Ted Berrigan, John Berryman,
Robin Blaser, Robert Bly, Tom Clark, Gregory Corso, Rob-
ert Creeley, E. E. Cummings, Robert Duncan, T. S. Eliot,
Robert Frost, Allen Ginsberg, LeRoi Jones, Denise Levertov,
Frank O'Hara, Sylvia Plath, Ezra Pound, John Crowe Ransom,
Ishmael Reed, W. R. Rodgers, Theodore Roethke, Jim Rosen-
berg, Gary Snyder, William Stafford, William Carlos Williams,
Ray Youngbear.

BATES, Scott. Poems of War Resistance: From 2300 B. C. to the
Present. New York: Grossman, 1969.
George Abbe, W. H. Auden, Scott Bates, Frank Beddo, Sidney
Bernard, John Betjeman, Ralph Chaplin, Hubert Creekmore,
E. E. Cummings, Richard Eberhart, William G. Eggleston,
Richard Ellison, William Everson, David Ferguson, Florence

Kiper Frank, Nicolas Guillen, Donald Hall, Lindley Williams
Hubbell, Randall Jarrell, Robinson Jeffers, Richard Lattimore,
Denise Levertov, Robert Lowell, Louis MacNeice, Clarence
Major, Marya Mannes, Morton Marcus, Eve Merriam, Pauli
Murray, Howard Nemerov, Kenneth Patchen, Ezra Pound,
Henry Reed, Margaret Rockwell, Carl Sandburg, Siegfried
Sassoon, Karl Shapiro, Stephen Spender, William Stafford,
Adrien Stoutenburg, Richard Tillinghast, Louis Untermeyer,
Reed Whittemore, Oscar Williams.

BATTLE, Sol. Ghetto '68. New York: Panther House, 1968.
Sol Battle, Dale de Nard, Lannon A. Fenner, Jr., Pamela
Gibson, Joey Gonzalvez, Jr., Sandy Grant, William Gray,
Miguel Guzman, Philip S. Hicks, Nellie Holloway, John T.
McRae, Myrna I. C. Maldonado, Carlos Morales.

BAYLOR, Robert; Brenda Stokes. Fine Frenzy: Enduring Themes
in Poetry. New York: McGraw-Hill, 1972.
Brian Aldiss, Kingsley Amis, W. H. Auden, Robert Bagg,
George Barker, Martha Beidler, Lerone Bennett, John Berry-
man, Robert Bly, Alan Bold, Gwendolyn Brooks, Leonard
Cohen, Victor Contoski, Gregory Corso, Henri Coulette, Rob-
ert Creeley, E. E. Cummings, J. V. Cunningham, James
Dickey, Alan Dugan, Richard Eberhart, T. S. Eliot, James
A. Emanuel, William Everson, Kenneth Fearing, David Fer-
guson, Lawrence Ferlinghetti, Robert Frost, Roy Fuller, Dan
Georgakas, Barbara Gibson, Morgan Gibson, Walker Gibson,
Allen Ginsberg, Paul Goodman, Thom Gunn, J. B. S. Haldane,
Michael Hamburger, Anthony Hecht, Calvin C. Hernton, Ruth
Herschberger, Robert Hershon, William M. Hoffman, Robert
Hogan, John Hollander, Langston Hughes, David Ignatow, Ran-
dall Jarrell, Robinson Jeffers, LeRoi Jones, Donald Justice,
X. J. Kennedy, Kenneth Koch, Joseph Langland, Philip Lar-
kin, Carl Larsen, Al Lee, Don L. Lee, Laurence Lerner,
Denise Levertov, Robert Lowell, Annette Lynch, Archibald
MacLeish, Louis MacNeice, Clarence Major, Morton Marcus,
James Merrill, W. S. Merwin, Robert Mezey, Peter Michel-
son, Josephine Miles, Adrian Mitchell, Marianne Moore, Ed-
win Morgan, Ken Noyle, Frank O'Hara, Robert Pack, Brian
Patten, Raymond R. Patterson, Marge Piercy, Sylvia Plath,
Ezra Pound, John Crowe Ransom, Henry Reed, Adrienne Rich,
Theodore Roethke, Alan Ross, Jerry Rubin, Louis B. Salomon,
Arthur M. Sampley, Anne Sexton, Karl Shapiro, Martin Staples
Shockley, Paul Simon, Alan J. Simpson, Robert A. Baker,
William Jay Smith, W. D. Snodgrass, Gary Snyder, Stephen
Spender, William Stafford, George Starbuck, May Swenson,
Allen Tate, James Tate, Peter Viereck, Diane Wakoski, Alice
Walker, John Hall Wheelock, Richard Wilbur, William Carlos
Williams.

BEDIENT, Calvin. Eight Contemporary Poets. New York: Oxford,
1974.
Donald Davie, W. S. Graham, Ted Hughes, Thomas Kinsella,

Philip Larkin, Stevie Smith, R. S. Thomas, Charles Tomlinson.

BEERMAN, Miriam. The Enduring Beast. Garden City, N.Y.: Doubleday, 1972.
Margaret Atwood, Daniel Berrigan, Elizabeth Bishop, John Malcolm Brinnin, Leonard Cohen, Gregory Corso, Isak Dinesen, Robert Frost, Daniel Hoffman, Robert Lowell, Marianne Moore, Ned O'Gorman, Theodore Roethke, Carl Sandburg, Stephan Sandy, May Swenson, Robert Penn Warren, Yvor Winters.

BELL, Bernard W. Modern and Contemporary Afro-American Poetry. Boston: Allyn and Bacon, 1972.
Arna Bontemps, Gwendolyn Brooks, Sterling Brown, Lucille Clifton, Margaret Danner, Frank Marshall Davis, Julia Fields, Nikki Giovanni, Robert Hayden, Langston Hughes, Ted Joans, Bob Kaufman, Keorapetse Kgositsile, Etheridge Knight, Don L. Lee, Audre Lorde, Naomi Long Madgett, Clarence Major, Gloria C. Oden, Dudley Randall, Conrad Kent Rivers, Sonia Sanchez, A. B. Spellman, Melvin B. Tolson, Jean Toomer, Margaret Walker.

BENDER, Eleanor M. Three Tenors, One Vehicle. Columbia, Mo.: Open Places Poets Series, 1975.
James Camp, X. J. Kennedy, Keith Waldrop.

BENDER, Robert M.; Charles L. Squier. The Sonnet: A Comprehensive Anthology of British and American Sonnets from the Renaissance to the Present. New York: Washington Square, 1965.
Conrad Aiken, W. H. Auden, George Barker, Edmund Blunden, Louise Bogan, James Camp, Charles Causley, E. E. Cummings, Robert Frost, Roy Fuller, Robert Graves, Thom Gunn, Donald Hall, John Heath-Stubbs, Robinson Jeffers, X. J. Kennedy, Philip Larkin, Cecil Day Lewis, Robert Lowell, Phyllis McGinley, Archibald MacLeish, Louis MacNeice, John Manifold, John Masefield, Howard Nemerov, John Frederick Nims, Ezra Pound, John Crowe Ransom, Seigfried Sassoon, W. D. Snodgrass, Stephen Spender, Allen Tate, Richard Wilbur, Oscar Williams, Yvor Winters.

BERG, Stephen and Robert Mezey. Naked Poetry: Recent American Poetry in Open Forms. New York: Bobbs-Merrill, 1969.
John Berryman, Robert Bly, Robert Creeley, Allen Ginsberg, Galway Kinnell, Denise Levertov, Philip Levine, Robert Lowell, W. S. Merwin, Kenneth Patchen, Sylvia Plath, Kenneth Rexroth, Theodore Roethke, Gary Snyder, William Stafford, James Wright.

BETTS, William Wilson. Lincoln and the Poets; An Anthology. Pittsburgh: Univ. of Pittsburgh Press, 1965.
Rosemary Benet, Charles Olson, Carl Sandburg.

BLACK HISTORY. Black Poets Write On! An Anthology of Black
Philadelphian Poets. Philadelphia: Black History Museum Commit-
tee, 1970.
    Janet M. Brooks, F. J. Bryant, Jr. , Mincy Cowdery, Greg-
ory Alan Day, Henry Hinton, Mary-Louise Horton, Carol Jeni-
fer, William "Butch" Johnson, Deborah Little, Bruce Lomax,
Carol Luther, Isaac Maefield, Don Mizell, Kuweka Mwandishi,
Richard O'Neill, Roberta Roberts, J. Pamela Saunders, Barry
Smith, James Spady, Tyrone Stephenson, Debra E. Summers,
Bernadine Tinner, Mark Traylor, Rita Whitehead, Sylvia
Young.

BLAZEK, Douglas. Ole Anthology: The Best Poetry as Selected
from All Eight Volumes of Ole Magazine. Glendale, Calif. : Poet-
ry X/Change, 1967.
    Aram Boyajian, John Buckner, Charles Bukowski, Don Cauble,
John Cornillon, Rik Davis, Wally Depew, George Dowden,
Larry Eigner, Dave Etter, Stanley Fisher, Marcus J. Grapes,
Lee Harwood, Robert Head, Shael Herman, Ben Hiatt, Kaja,
Phil Kienholz, Rich Krech, T. L. Kryss, Peter LaRouche, D.
A. Levy, Tom McNamara, Brown Miller, George Montgomery,
Alex Morra, Harold Norse, Barbara O'Connelly, Ron Offen,
Gil Orlovitz, Steve Osterlund, Charles Plymell, Al Purdy,
Steve Richmond, Dennis Saleh, Sid Shapiro, George Sparling,
Kent Taylor, John Turpin, Gerard Van Der Leun, D. R. Wag-
ner, William Wantling, Dennis Williams.

BLY, Robert. The Sea and the Honeycomb: A Book of Poems.
Madison, Minn. : Sixties Press, 1966.
    Werner Aspenstrom, St. Geraud.

BLY, Robert. Forty Poems Touching on Recent American History.
Boston: Beacon, 1970.
    Floyce Alexander, William Burford, Robert Creeley, Ruben
Dario, Robert Duncan, Jacinto Fombona-Pachano, Gene Fowler,
Gene Frumkin, Allen Ginsberg, Donald Hall, David Ignatow,
Robinson Jeffers, Juan Ramon Jiminez, Robert Lowell, Thomas
McGrath, Pablo Neruda, Ezra Pound, Kenneth Rexroth, Theo-
dore Roethke, Louis Simpson, Gary Snyder, William Stafford,
William Carlos Williams, James Wright.

BLY, Robert. The Sea and the Honeycomb. A Book of Tiny Poems.
Boston: Beacon, 1971.
    Saint Geraud, David Ignatow.

BLY, Robert. Leaping Poetry: An Idea with Poems and Transla-
tions. Boston: Beacon, 1975.
    Robert Bly, Russell Edson, Allen Ginsberg, Bill Knott, Greg
Orr, Tom Pickard, Jerome Rothenberg, Gary Snyder, John
Wieners, Marguerite Young, Raymond Zdonek.

BOGAN, Louise; William Jay Smith. The Golden Journey Poems
for Young People. Chicago: Reilly & Lee, 1965.

Leonie Adams, Conrad Aiken, W. H. Auden, Elizabeth Bishop, Edmund Blunden, Louise Bogan, Charles Causley, Frank A. Collymore, Padraic Colum, Frances Cornford, E. E. Cummings, Isak Dinesen, T. S. Eliot, Robert Francis, Robert Frost, Robert Graves, Hilda Doolittle (H. D.), Ralph Hodgson, Barbard Howes, Walt Kelly, X. J. Kennedy, Galway Kinnell, David McCord, Archibald MacLeish, John Manifold, Vassar Miller, Marianne Moore, Ogden Nash, Ezra Pound, Henry Reed, Theodore Roethke, Winfield Townley Scott, Karl Shapiro, William Jay Smith, Stephen Spender, Louis Untermeyer, Derek Walcott, Richard Wilbur, William Carlos Williams, Edmund Wilson, Judith Wright, Andrew Young.

BOGIN, Dennis; Tom Cunningham.   From Out of the Salt Mound: An Anthology of Poetry.   1968.
Dennis Bogin, Michael Culross, Tom Cunningham, Douglas Eichhorn, George P. Elliott, Barbara Feldman, Jaime Ferran, Robert Foster, Dugan Gilman, Ted Hall, Ben Howard, Joan Howard, Walter R. Keller, Don Mager, Roberta Morris, W. D. Snodgrass, John Taggart.

BOLD, Alan.   The Penguin Book of Socialist Verse.   Baltimore: Penguin Books, 1970.
W. H. Auden, David Avidan, Alan Bold, Ian Campbell, Joe Corrie, C. Day Lewis, Langston Hughes, LeRoi Jones, Christopher Logue, Hugh Macdiarmid, Thomas McGrath, Adrian Mitchell, Carl Sandburg, Wole Soyinka.

BONAZZI, Robert.   Toward Winter: Poems for the Last Decade. New York: New Rivers/Latitudes Press, 1972.
Charles Baxter, Robert Bly, Robert Bonazzi, Charlene Chestnut, William F. Claire, Dean Faulwell, George Garrett, Alvin Greenberg, Archibald Henderson, Forrest Ingram, Halvard Johnson, John Knoepfle, Lou Lipsitz, William Matthews, Thomas Merton, Vassar Miller, Roger Mitchell, Richard Morris, H. C. Nash, David Ray, Charles Simic, C. W. Truesdale, Mark Van Doren, James Wright.

BONAZZI, Robert.   Survivors of the Invention: An Ongoing Anthology: Poems 1974.   Austin, Tex.: Latitudes Press, 1974.
William DeVoti, Jeanne Hill, Carlos Isla, Milton Katz, Stephen Keely, Carmella Lane, Robert Joe Stout, George M. Young, Jr.

BONTEMPS, Arna.   American Negro Poetry.   New York: Hill and Wang, 1963.
Samuel Allen, Russell Atkins, Gwendolyn B. Bennett, Horace Julian Bond, Arna Bontemps, William Stanley Braithwaite, Sterling A. Brown, William Browne, Catherine Cater, Marcus B. Christian, Leslie M. Collins, Waring Cuney, Margaret Danner, Frank Marshall Davis, Owen Dodson, Alfred A. Duckett, James A. Emanuel, Mari E. Evans, Julia Fields, Yvonne Gregory, Robert Hayden, Donald Jeffrey Hayes, Carl Wendell

Hines, Jr., M. Carl Holman, Frank Horne, Ted Joans, Georgia Douglas Johnson, Helene Johnson, LeRoi Jones, Clarence Major, Pauli Murray, Effie Lee Newsome, Gloria C. Oden, Myron O'Higgins, Oliver Pitcher, Dudley Randall, Conrad Kent Rivers, Anne Spencer, Melvin B. Tolson, Jean Toomer, James Vaughn, Margaret Walker, Charles Enoch Wheeler, Bruce McM. Wright, Richard Wright, Frank Yerby.

BONTEMPS, Arna. <u>American Negro Poetry</u>. New York: Hill and Wang, 1974.
Samuel Allen, R. Atkins, Gwendolyn B. Bennett, Horace Julian Bond, Arna Bontemps, William Stanley Braithwaite, Gwendolyn Brooks, Sterling A. Brown, William Browne, Catherine Cater, Marcus B. Christian, Lucille Clifton, Leslie M. Collins, Waring Cuney, M. Danner, Frank Marshall Davis, Clarissa Scott Delany, Owen Dodson, Alfred A. Duckett, James A. Emanuel, Mari E. Evans, Julia Fields, Nikki Giovanni, Yvonne Gregory, Angelina W. Grimke, Robert Hayden, Donald Jeffrey Hayes, Calvin Hernton, Carl Wendell Hines, Jr., M. Carl Holman, Frank Horne, Langston Hughes, Ted Joans, Fenton Johnson, Georgia Douglas Johnson, Helen Armstead Johnson, Clarence Major, Pauli Murray, Larry Neal, Effie Lee Newsome, Gloria C. Oden, Myron O'Higgins, Frank Lamont Phillips, Oliver Pitcher, Dudley Randall, Conrad Kent Rivers, Anne Spencer, Melvin B. Tolson, Jean Toomer, James Vaughn, Margaret Walker, Charles Enoch Wheeler, Richard Wright, Marvin Wyche, Frank Yerby.

BOOKER, Merrel Daniel, Sr.; Erma Barbour Booker; Merrel Daniel Booker, Jr.; Sue Booker. <u>Cry at Birth</u>. New York: McGraw-Hill, 1971.
Sherry Blackman, Sue Booker, Ida Boone (Sharon), Gordon Bressack, Daryl Brown, Landa Loretta Brown, Kevin Burrick, Frank Campbell, Josie Campbell, Jimmie Carter, Loleta Carter, Pearl Cleage, Frank Cleveland (Clorox), Jamie Collazo, Gwendolyn Cook, Linda S. Cousins, Deborah Danner, Vincent Dorsett, David Dorsey, Rudolph Douglas, Timothy Engel, Doris Amurr Ezell, Linda Finch, Lawrence Fishbeng, Javita G. Flynn, Wallace Ford, Charles Franklin, Willie Gilbert, Ernestine Graham, Otto Grant, Conrad Graves, Joycelyn Gray, Wiliam Halsey, George Hannah, Ernestine Harris, Howard Harris, Morla V. Harris, Dewey Higgins, Edna Hiner, Evan Hyde, Maurice Shelley Jackson, Robert Jeffrey, Kevin Jennings, Bradlon Johnson, Herschell Johnson, Pamela Jones, Diva Goodfriend Koven, Roger B. Lee, Andrew Lenihan, Nick Levinson, William McCurine, T. P. McGriff, James H. McLemore, Allen Luke Pamela Manning, Lee Marshall, Everett Lee Marshburn, Carmen Martinez, Lydia Martinez, Gloria Morrow, Sharlet Overton, I. L. Owens, Thomas L. Parker, Jerry Peace, Bernard Pearson, Peggy Perry, Linda Porter, A. Warnyenek Pyne, Irvin Ray, Jesse Andrew Raye, Jo Nell Rice, Francille Rusan, Glenn C. Sanders, Eddie Scott, Jr., Sharon, Gerald Shepherd, Juanita Simpson, Wade Spencer, Robert Stall-

worthy, Jerry Taylor, Ella Todd, Christopher Valentine, Mike Walker, John Wesley, Ernest K. Williams, Jr. , Patricia Williams, Susan Young, Yolande Zealy.

BRADY, Frank; Martin Price. Poetry: Past and Present. New York: Harcourt, Brace, Jovanovich, 1974.
 A. R. Ammons, John Ashbery, W. H. Auden, Imamu Amiri Baraka, John Berryman, Elizabeth Bishop, Robert Bly, Gregory Corso, Robert Creeley, E. E. Cummings, James Dickey, Alan Dugan, Robert Duncan, T. S. Eliot, Lawrence Ferlinghetti, Robert Frost, Allen Ginsberg, Thom Gunn, Robert Hayden, Anthony Hecht, John Hollander, A. D. Hope, Langston Hughes, Ted Hughes, Randall Jarrell, Donald Justice, X. J. Kennedy, Kenneth Koch, Philip Larkin, Denise Levertov, Robert Lowell, Archibald MacLeish, James Merrill, W. S. Merwin, Marianne Moore, Gloria C. Oden, Frank O'Hara, Charles Olson, Robert Pack, Sylvia Plath, Ezra Pound, John Crowe Ransom, Adrienne Rich, Theodore Roethke, Anne Sexton, Louis Simpson, Stevie Smith, Gary Snyder, Mark Strand, Charles Tomlinson, Jean Toomer, Robert Penn Warren, Richard Wilbur, William Carlos Williams, James Wright.

BREMAN, Paul. You Better Believe It; Black Verse in English from Africa, the West Indies and the United States. Baltimore: Penguin Books, 1973.
 Peter Abrahams, Chinua Achebe, Lloyd Addison, Christina Ama Ata Aidoo, Frank Aig-Imoukhuede, Ahmed Alhamisi, Samuel W. Allen, Russell Atkins, Kofi Awoonor, Ameer Baraka, Eseoghene Barrett, Vera Bell, Lebert Bethune, Musu Ber, Peter Blackman, Arne Bontemps, Fred Bradford, Dollar Brand, Edward Brathwaite, Kwesi Brew, Gwendolyn Brooks, Sterling Brown, F. J. Bryant, Ed. Bullins, Jon Carew, Martin Carter, John Pepper Clark, Charles Cobb, Sam Cornish, Stanley Crouch, Victor Hernandez Cruz, Waring Cuney, Margaret Danner, Mbella Sonne Dipoko, Owen Dodson, William E. B. Dubois, Henry Dumas, Ray Durem, James A. Emanuel, Yetunde Esan, Julia Fields, Nikki Giovanni, D. L. Graham, Bobb Hamilton, Robert Hayden, David Henderson, Calvin C. Hernton, Carl Wendell Hines, Israel Kafu Hoh, Langston Hughes, Gerald Jackson, Lance Jeffers, Ted Joans, Frank John, Alice H. Jones, Norman Jordan, Bob Kaufman, Ellsworth McG. Keane, Keorapetse Kgositsile, Etheridge Knith, Ellis Ayitey Komey, Mazisi Kunene, John La Rose, Don L. Lee, Julius Lester, Audre Lorde, James Edward McCall, Basil C. McFarlane, Clarence Major, Barbara Malcom, Ezekiel Mphahlele, Mukhtarr Mustapha, Larry Neal, Abioseh Nicol, Arthur K. Nortje, O. T. Ogilvie, Myron O'Higgins, Gabriel Okara, Christopher Okigbo, Dennis C. Osadeboy, Frank Kobina Parkes, Eugene Perkins, Lenrie Peters, N. H. Pritchard, Sun Ra, Dudley Randall, Ishmael Reed, Conrad Kent Rivers, E. M. Roach, Carolyn M. Rodgers, David Rubadiri, Sonia Sanchez, Dennis Scott, Johnie Scott, A. J. Seymour, Philip

M. Sherlock, Leumas Sirrah, 'Wole Soyinka, A. B. Spellman, Ed Spriggs, Harold M. Telemaque, James Washington Thompson, Jean Toomer, Joseph Waiguru, Derek Walcott, Margaret Walker, Ron Welburn, John A. Williams,
Okogbule Wonodi, Jay Wright, Richard Wright, Marvin X,
Al Young.

BREWTON, Sara; John E. Brewton. America Forever New: A
Book of Poems. New York: Crowell, 1968.
    Edith Agnew, John T. Alexander, Mary Austin, Morris Abel
Beer, Helen Bevington, Harriet Gray Blackwell, J. C. Bossidy,
Arthur S. Bourinot, Witter Bynner, Melville Cane, Bruce Cat-
ton, William Childress, Elizabeth Coatsworth, Ann Cobb, Mal-
colm Cowley, James Daugherty, Robert Stiles Davieau, Kather-
ine Edelman, Dave Etter, John Fandel, Roland Flint, Sam
Walter Foss, Doris Frankel, Arthur Guiterman, Oscar Ham-
merstein II, Gwendolen Haste, Roy Helton, Peter J. Henniker-
Heaton, Daniel Whitehead Hicky, John Holmes, Frances Minturn
Howard, Elijah L. Jacobs, Fenton Johnson, Martha Keller,
Reeve Spencer Kelley, Stoddard King, Elizabeth Landeweer,
Ruth Lechlitner, Elizabeth-Ellen Long. Pare Lorentz, David
McCord, Jeanne McGahey, Douglas Malloch, Herbert Merrill,
W. R. Moses, Jessie Wilmore Murton, Berta Hart Nance,
Edith D. Osborne, Albert Bigelow Paine, Elisabeth Peck, Ruth
Delong Peterson, Gerald Raftery, Kenneth Allan Robinson,
Lola Ingres Russo, Lew Sarett, Lydia Huntley Sigourney, J.
C. Squire, Candace Thurber Stevenson, Lionel Stevenson,
James Still, Jan Struther, Jesse Stuart, Hildegarde Hoyt
Swight, Rosemary Thomas, Dorothy Brown Thompson, Nancy
Byrd Turner, Robert Lewis Weeks, James L. Weil, Mildred
Weston, Lillian Zellhoefer White, Vera White, Francis Brett
Young.

BRINDLE, E. S. A Woman's Poetry Anthology. Sherman Oaks,
Calif.: Sherman Oaks, 1975.
    Joanne Abbonizio, L. Kristee Abrahamson, Maureen Mongraw
Aguzin, Jane A. Albrite, Jackie Amerman, Shelley Armitage,
Cherie A. Bagley, Jenni L. Bagley, Joyce M. Bagley, Donna
Batt, Anne Beck, Barbra J. Behm, Sherry Bennett, Lynda
Bernays, Linda S. Bice, Linda L. Bielowski, Bobbi Bocketti,
Ellen Brake, Kay Branine, Susan Bruce, Laurel Brummet,
Pat J. Bushong, Sandra Caltabiano, Nancy Cato, Catherine J.
Cavin, Beth Chase, Miriam Chusid, Linda Climer, Marty
Cohn, Barbard Coryell, Christopher Cottrell, Irene Cullen,
Elaine Dallman, Karen Davis, Sharon N. Delmain, Barbara L.
Dexter, Carol Dine, Mary A. Doll, Nancy Kay Dudek, Leslie
Duremberg, Sandra Dutton, Mary Eastman, Eileen Eliot, M.
Sharon Evans, Thelma P. Fernandez-Yarish, Joan Fiator,
Kathleen Fogarty, Mary Fontaine, Kay Garrett, Joyce Gayles,
Charlotte Fox Ginet, Elaine Goldfeder, Mary Susan Goldman,
Cathy Greene, Florence Greenstein, Madelon Harris, Margot
Henkelmann, Alexandra L. Hickson, Lori Higa, Jo Fredell
Higgins, Carol Hille, Lee Anette Holm, Rona Fogel Holub,

Diane Hottendorf, Blair Ann Hull, Holiday Jackson, Roberta
Jamison, Meg Sims Johnson, Regina Kahney, Fleurette V. O.
Kelley, Holly Knight, Deborah Paulin Lang, Roberta Hickson
Lantz, Carol Ann Lapeyrouse, Sharon Lee Laplante, L.
Lee, Linda Lorraine, Denise Luna, Diane McCarty, Sharon McLeod,
Sally Allen McNall, Linda Macrae, Pat Malcom, Anne Mallon,
Virginia Megeehan Mallon, Elaine Manger, Karen Marke, Marianne Masterson, Helen Menke, Susan Menne, Sally Marlin-Jones, Martha C. Merrill, Patti Mesner, Paula Messina, Patricia Milburn, Kathy Miller, Stevi Minckler, Cynthia Mindell,
Lavonne Mueller, Barbara D. Nazelrod, Jade Nelson, Stephanie J. Olson, Cathy Oltman, Christina V. Pacosz, D. Peacock,
Linda Purrington, Irma Radovsky, Joan G. Riggi, Rebecca L.
Rodes, Zoe Rosenthal, Linda Rzesniowiecki, Becky Sakellariou,
Liz Samuelson, Eileen Sarubbi, Joleene Schan, Teri J.
Schwartz, Ilka Scobie, Linda Preston Scott, Deri Seagull, Edith Shreiner Sharp, Jess Simon, Maurya Simon, Audrey M.
Simurda, Virgie Small, Judith Snyder, Elda Soderquist, Cleo
Soto, Pat Stanton, Catherine Stetson, Jan Sutherland, Margaret
Talbot, Donna Tankersley, Judith Tobin, Joanne Tramonte,
Adriana Tredanari, Suzanne Vaught, Sara Walbridge, Constance
Waldron, Mary S. Weinkauf, Cora J. Weller, Deborah Wheeler,
Jayne D. White, Ruth Anne Wilson, Elsebeth Wulff, Lyle York,
Virginia Dale Zamor.

BRINNIN, John Malcolm. The Modern Poets: An American-British
Anthology. New York: McGraw-Hill, 1963.
Dannie Abse, Conrad Aiken, Kingsley Amis, W. H. Auden,
Robert Bagg, George Barker, John Berryman, John Betjeman,
Elizabeth Bishop, Louise Bogan, Philip Booth, John Malcolm
Brinnin, John Ciardi, Tram Combs, Hilary Corke, E. E.
Cummings, Cecil Day Lewis, Alan Dugan, Richard Eberhart,
T. S. Eliot, D. J. Enright, Irving Feldman, Robert Fitzgerald, Jean Carrigue, David Gascoyne, W. S. Graham, Thom
Gunn, Donald Hall, Michael Hamburger, John Heath-Stubbs,
Anthony Hecht, Daniel Hoffman, John Hollander, Barbara
Howes, Ted Hughes, Randall Jarrell, Elizabeth Jennings, Galway Kinnell, Stanley Kunitz, Joseph Langland, Philip Larkin,
John Lehmann, Robert Lowell, Archibald MacLeish, Louis
MacNeice, James Merrill, W. S. Merwin, Marianne Moore,
Howard Moss, Howard Nemerov, Sylvia Plath, William Plomer,
Henry Reed, Alastair Reid, Anne Ridler, Muriel Rukeyser,
Winfield Townley Scott, James Scully, Karl Shapiro, Louis
Simpson, William Jay Smith, W. D. Snodgrass, Stephen Spender, George Starbuck, May Swenson, Allen Tate, John Wain,
Robert Penn Warren, Vernon Watkins, Richard Wilbur, David
Wright.

BRINNIN, John Malcolm; Bill Read. Twentieth Century Poetry:
American and British (1900-1970). New York: McGraw-Hill, 1970.
Dannie Abse, Conrad Aiken, A. R. Ammons, John Ashbery,
W. H. Auden, George Barker, Michael Benedikt, John Berryman, John Betjeman, Elizabeth Bishop, Louise Bogan, Philip

Booth, John Malcolm Brinnin, John Ciardi, Lucille Clifton, Tram Combs, E. E. Cummings, Peter Davison, James Dickey, Alan Dugan, Richard Eberhart, T. S. Eliot, D. J. Enright, Irving Feldman, Robert Fitzgerald, Arthur Freeman, Robert Frost, Jean Garrigue, David Gascoyne, Allen Ginsberg, Robert Graves, Thom Gunn, Donald Hall, Robert Hayden, Seamus Heaney, John Heath-Stubbs, Anthony Hecht, Daryl Hine, Daniel G. Hoffman, John Hollander, Richard Howard, Barbara Howes, Ted Hughes, David Ignatow, Randall Jarrell, Donald Justice, Bob Kaufman, X. J. Kennedy, Galway Kinnell, Thomas Kinsella, Stanley Kunitz, Philip Larkin, Denise Levertov, Philip Levine, Cecil Day Lewis, Robert Lowell, Edward Lucie-Smith, Archibald MacLeish, Louis MacNeice, James Merrill, W. S. Merwin, Christopher Middleton, Marianne Moore, Howard Moss, Howard Nemerov, Marge Piercy, Sylvia Plath, Ezra Pound, John Crowe Ransom, Alastair Reid, Theodore Roethke, Muriel Rukeyser, Delmore Schwartz, James Scully, Anne Sexton, Karl Shapiro, Jon Silkin, Louis Simpson, L. E. Sissman, Edith Sitwell, William J. Smith, W. D. Snodgrass, Stephen Spender, George Starbuck, Mark Strand, May Swenson, Allen Tate, James Tate, Charles Tomlinson, Derek Walcott, Robert Penn Warren, Vernon Watkins, Theodore Weiss, David Wevill, Richard Wilbur, William Carlos Williams, James Wright.

BROOKS, Cleanth; Robert Penn Warren. Understanding Poetry. New York: Holt, Rinehart and Winston, 1960.
Leonie Adams, W. H. Auden, Elizabeth Bishop, E. E. Cummings, Donald Davidson, Richard Eberhart, T. S. Eliot, William Empson, Robert Frost, Robert Graves, Thom Gunn, H. D., Donald Hall, Randall Jarrell, Robinson Jeffers, Archibald MacLeish, William Meredith, Marianne Moore, Ogden Nash, Ruth Pitter, Exra Pound, John Crowe Ransom, Theodore Roethke, Delmore Schwartz, Karl Shapiro, W. D. Snodgrass, Allen Tate, Vernon Watkins, Richard Wilbur, William Carlos Williams, Yvor Winters, James Wright.

BROOKS, Gwendolyn. A Broadside Treasury. Detroit: Broadside Press, 1971.
Samuel Allen, Imamu Amiri Baraka, Walter Bradford, Gwendolyn Brooks, Margaret Danner, Ronda M. Davis, Ebon Dooley (Ebon), Jon Eckels, James Emanuel, Sarah Webster Fabio, B. Felton, Kent Foreman, Nikki Giovanni, Bobb Hamilton, Umar Abd Rahim Hasson, Robert Hayden, Everett Hoagland, Lance Jeffers, Ted Joans, Alicia L. Johnson, LeRoi Jones, Keorapetse Wm. Kgositsile, Carl Killibrew, Etheridge Knight, Joyce Whitsitt Lawrence, Don L. Lee, David Llorens, Doughtry Long, Naomi Long Madgett, Lawrence P. Neal, Raymond Patterson, Arthur Pfister, Dudley Randall, James Randall, John Raven, S. Carolyn Reese, Conrad Kent Rivers, Carolyn M. Rodgers, Tony Rutherford, Sonia Sanchez, Roland Snelling, Edward S. Spriggs, Stephany, Askia Muhammad Toure, Margaret Walker, Malaika Wangara (Joyce Whitsitt Lawrence), Joyce Whitsitt (J. Lawrence), Marvin X.

BROOKS, Gwendolyn. Jump Bad: A Chicago Anthology. Detroit: Broadside Press, 1971.
 Amini Johari, Walter Bradford, Gwendolyn Brooks, Carl Clark, Mike Cook, James Cunningham, Ronda Davis, Peggy Kenner, Don L. Lee, Linyatta, Carolyn Rodgers, Sharon Scott, Sigmonde Wimberli (Kharlos Tucker).

BROWER, Reuben A.; Anne D. Ferry; David Kalstone. Beginning with Poems: An Anthology. New York: Norton, 1966.
 W. H. Auden, T. S. Eliot, Robert Frost, Marianne Moore, John Crowe Ransom, William Carlos Williams.

BROWN, Patricia L.; Don L. Lee; Francis Ward. To Gwen with Love: An Anthology Dedicated to Gwendolyn Brooks. Chicago: Johnson, 1971.
 Ahmed Akinwole Alhamisi, Samuel Allen, Johari Amini, Gus Bertha, Nora Blakely, W. Bradford, F. J. Bryant, Jr., John Chenault, Carole Gregory Clemmons, Francois Clemmons, Cynthia M. Conley, James Cunningham, Margaret Danner, R. M. Dennis, Alfred Diggs, Jon Eckels, Maxine Hall Elliston, Sarah Webster Fabio, Hoyt W. Fuller, Zack Gilbert, Nikki Giovanni, Joe Goncalves, Michael S. Harper, Alicia L. Johnson, Paulette Jones, Raymond A. Joseph, Delores Kendrick, Keorapetse W. Kgositsile, Helen H. King, Etheridge Knight, Pinkie Gordon Lane, Don L. Lee, David Llohrens, James C. Morris, Rukudzo Murapa, Larry Neal, Tejumola Ologboni, Eugene Perkins, Sterling D. Plumpp, Dudley Randall, Barbara A. Reynolds, Carolyn M. Rodgers, Sonia Sanchez, Sharon Scott, Linwood Smith, A. B. Spellman, Prentiss Taylor, Jr., Joe Todd, Margaret Walker, Bruce Walton (Mtu Weusi), W. D. Wandick, Val Gray Ward, Sigemonde Kharlos Wimberli.

BUKOWSKI, Charles; Neeli Cherry; Paul Vangelisti. Anthology of L. A. Poets. Los Angeles: Laugh Literary/The Red Hill Press, 1972.
 Ameen Alwan, Charles Bukowski, Neeli Cherry, Jack Hirschman, Linda King, Ronald Koertge, Gerald Locklin, Rosella Pace, Gerda Penfold, Stuart Z. Perkoff, Robert Peters, William Pillin, Holly Prado, Steve Richmond, A. P. Russo, Charles Stetler, John Thomas, Paul Vangelisti.

BULKIN, Elly; Joan Larkin. Amazon Poetry. An Anthology of Lesbian Poetry. New York: Out & Out Books, 1975.
 Sharon Barba, Ellen Bass, Robin Becker, Bobbie Bishop, Ellen Marie Bissert, Rita Mae Brown, Elly Bulkin, Ruthe D. Canter, Georgette Cerrutti, Jan Clausen, Martha Courtot, Carol Dine, Sukey Durham, Elsa Gidlow, Judy Grahn, Susan Griffin, Marcie Hershman, Frankie Hucklenbroich, Polly Joan, Willyce Kim, Irena Klepfisz, Ana Kowalkowsky, Jacqueline Lapidus, Joan Larkin, Eleanor Lerman, Audre Lorde, Felice Newman, Pat Parker, Mary Patten, Adrienne Rich, Nine Sabaroff, May Sarton, Martha Shelley, Susan Sherman, Wendy Stevens, Lynn Strongin, May Swenson, Fran Winant, Elsie Young.

CADY, Edwin H. The American Poets. Scott, Foresman, 1966.
Robert Frost.

CALDERWOOD, James L.; Harold F. Toliver. Forms of Poetry.
Prentice-Hall, 1968.
 W. H. Auden, John Betjeman, E. E. Cummings, T. S. Eliot,
Robert Frost, Robert Graves, Archibald MacLeish, John Mase-
field, Ezra Pound, John Crowe Ransom, Theodore Roethke,
Stephen Spender, Richard Wilbur, William Carlos Williams.

CAMP, James E. Pegasus Descending: A Book of the Best Bad
Verse. New York: Macmillan, 1971.
 A. Rasheed Ghazi, X. J. Kennedy, Ali Sedat Hilmi Torel,
Grace Treasone, Stephen Tropp.

CARROLL, Paul. The Poem in Its Skin. Chicago: Follett, 1968.
John Ashbery, Robert Creeley, James Dickey, Isabella Gard-
ner, Allen Ginsberg, John Logan, W. S. Merwin, Frank
O'Hara, W. D. Snodgrass, James Wright.

CARROLL, Paul. The Young American Poets. Chicago: Follett,
1968.
 Vito Hannibal Acconci, George Amabile, Jon Anderson, Roger
Aplon, James Applewhite, Gerard William Barrax, Marvin
Bell, Michael Benedikt, Bill Berkson, Ted Berrigan, Randy
Blasing, Harold Bond, Michael Brownstein, Tom Clark, Clark
Coolidge, Jonathan Cott, Kenward Elmslie, Kathleen Fraser,
Louis Gluck, Robert Hass, Philip Hey, William Hunt, Ronald
Johnson, Robert Kelly, Richard Kostelanetz, John L. Heureux,
Lou Lipsitz, Lewis MacAdams, Howard McCord, Gerald Ma-
langa, Morton Marcus, Jack Marshall, John Morgan, David
Mus, Ron Padgett, John Perreault, Saint Geraud, Aram Saroy-
an, Peter Schjeldahl, Dennis Schmitz, Charles Simic, Kathleen
Spivack, Mark Strand, James Tate, Sotere Torregian, Tony
Towle, Alden Van Buskirk, Allen Van Newkirk, Julia Vinograd,
Diane Wakoski, Anne Waldman, Lewis Warsh, James Welch,
Tyner White.

CARRUTH, Hayden. The Voice That Is Great Within Us: American
Poetry of the Twentieth Century. New York: Bantam, 1970.
 Conrad Aiken, A. R. Ammons, Bill Anderson, Brother Anton-
inus, John Ashbery, Wendell Berry, John Berryman, Elizabeth
Bishop, Paul Blackburn, Robert Bly. Louise Bogan, Philip
Booth, William Bronk, Hayden Carruth, Cid Corman, Gregory
Corso, Robert Creeley, E. E. Cummings, J. V. Cunningham,
James Dickey, Owen Dodson, Edward Dorn, Robert Duncan,
Richard Eberhart, Larry Eigner, T. S. Eliot, Clayton Eshle-
man, Kenneth Fearing, Lawrence Ferlinghetti, Thomas Horns-
by Ferril, Robert Fitzgerald, Robert Francis, Robert Frost,
Jean Garrigue, Allen Ginsberg, Mitchell Goodman, Paul Good-
man, Arthur Gregor, Horace Gregory, Jim Harrison, Robert
Hayden, H. D., Anthony Hecht, George Hitchcock, Daniel G.
Hoffman, Langston Hughes, David Ignatow, Randall Jarrell,

Robinson Jeffers, Ronald Johnson, LeRoi Jones, Donald Justice, Bob Kaufman, Robert Kelly, Galway Kinnell, Carolyn Kizer, Kenneth Koch, Stanley Kunitz, Philip Lamantia, Richard Lattimore, James Laughlin, David Lawson, Denise Levertov, Philip Levine, Lou Lipsitz, Patricia Low, Robert Lowell, Mina Loy, Thomas McGrath, Archibald MacLeish, James Merrill, Thomas Merton, W. S. Merwin, Josephine Miles, Marianne Moore, Stanley Moss, Lorine Niedecker, Frank O'Hara, Charles Olson, Joel Oppenheimer, Kenneth Patchen, Sylvia Plath, Hyam Plutzik, Marie Ponsot, Ezra Pound, Henry Rago, John Crowe Ransom, David Ray, Kenneth Rexroth, Charles Reznikoff, Adrienne Rich, Theodore Roethke, Muriel Rukeyser, Delmore Schwartz, Winfield Townley Scott, Anne Sexton, Harvey Shapiro, Karl Shapiro, Louis Simpson, Joel Sloman, Gary Snyder, Hyman Sobiloff, Jack Spicer, William Stafford, George Starbuck, Robert Sward, May Swenson, Genevieve Taggard, Allen Tate, Jean Valentine, Mark Van Doren, David Wagoner, Diane Wakoski, Robert Penn Warren, Theodore Weiss, Philip Whalen, John Wieners, Richard Wilbur, Jonathan Williams, William Carlos Williams, Yvor Winters, James Wright, Paul Zimmer, Louis Zukofsky.

CARRUTH, Hayden. The Bird/Poem Book: Poems on the Wild Birds of North America. New York: McCall, 1970.
Brother Antoninus, Wendell Berry, Hayden Carruth, Thomas Hornsby Ferril, Robert Francis, George Hitchcock, Robinson Jeffers, Galway Kinnell, Denise Levertov, W. S. Merwin, Bert Meyers, Vassar Miller, Howard Nemerov, Paul Baker Newman, Michael Ondaatje, Kenneth Patchen, Kenneth Rexroth, Theodore Roethke, May Swenson, Mark Van Doren, David Wagoner, William Carlos Williams.

CHACE, JoAn E.; William M. Chace. Making It New. San Francisco: Canfield, 1973.
John Balaban, Imamu Amiri Baraka (LeRoi Jones), Chuck Berry, Robert Bly, Gwendolyn Brooks, Lucille Clifton, Sam Cooke, Gregory Corso, Robert Creeley, Victor Hernandez Cruz, E. E. Cummings, James Dickey, Robert Duncan, Bob Dylan, Florence Elon, Lawrence Ferlinghetti, Edward Field, Allen Ginsberg, Robert Hayden, Randall Jarrell, Bob Kaufman, Kenneth Koch, Don L. Lee, Denise Levertov, Robert Lowell, W. S. Merwin, Josephine Miles, Marianne Moore, Jim Morrison, Frank O'Hara, Charles Olson, Sylvia Plath, Ezra Pound, Otis Redding, Ishmael Reed, Adrienne Rich, Theodore Roethke, Sonia Sanchez, Zel Sanders, James Schuyler, Anne Sexton, Pete Seeger, Charles Simic, Paul Simon, Grace Slick, Bessie Smith, Gary Snyder, William Stafford, Lona Stevens, Diane Wakoski, James Welch, Jonathan Williams, William Carlos Williams, James Wright.

CHATMAN, Seymour. An Introduction to the Language of Poetry. Boston: Houghton Mifflin, 1968.
W. H. Auden, T. S. Eliot, Robert Frost, Robert Lowell, Richard Wilbur.

CHESTER, Laura; Sharon Barba. Rising Tides: 20th Century A-
merican Women Poets. New York: Washington Square, 1973.
Daisy Aldan, Sharon Barba, Anita Barrows, Louise Bogan,
Kay Boyle, Summer Brenner, Besmilr Brigham, Grace Butch-
er, Laura Chester, Lucille Clifton, Madeline De Frees, Bab-
ette Deutsch, Diane Di Prima, Hilda Doolittle, Sonya Dorman,
Leatrice Emeruwa, Siv Cedering Fox, Kathleen Fraser, Isa-
bella Gardner, Daniella Gioseffi, Nikki Giovanni, Judy Grahn,
Barbara Greenberg, Susan Griffin, Barbara Guest, Sandra
Hochman, Barbara Howes, Colette Inez, Erica Jong, June
Jordan, Lenore Kandel, Shirley Kaufman, Carolyn Kizer, Max-
ine Kumin, Joanne Kyger, Denise Levertov, Lyn Lifshin,
Sandra McPherson, Denna Metzger, Josephine Miles, Vassar
Miller, Marianne Moore, Rosalie Moore, Lisel Mueller, Jean-
ette Nichols, Lorine Niedecker, Rochelle Owens, Miriam Pal-
mer, Linda Pastan, Marge Piercy, Sylvia Plath, Adrienne
Rich, Muriel Rukeyser, Sonia Sanchez, May Sarton, Ruth Lisa
Schechter, Anne Sexton, Gertrude Stein, Carolyn Stoloff, Lynn
Strongin, Lynn Sukenick, May Swenson, Mona Van Duyn, Anne
Waldman, Ruth Whitman, Nancy Willard, Helen Wolfert.

CHILGREN, Delia; Melanie De Maria. Wayfaring. San Francisco:
Judas Tree, 1972.
Delia Chilgren, Lily Chilgren, Stephanie De Maria, James Lee
Hubert, Mursalin Machado, Maureen O'Neill, Anthony Salinaro,
Paul Shuttleworth, Steve Showers, Martin De Parres Walsh,
Steve Wilson.

CLARK, Tom. All Stars. New York: Grossman; Sante Fe:
Goliard, 1972.
Ted Berrigan, Tom Clark, Clark Coolidge, Robert Creeley,
Ed Dorn, Dick Gallup, Michael McClure, Alice Notley, Ron
Padgett, Ed Sanders, Aram Saroyan, James Schuyler, Philip
Whalen.

CLAY, Buriel, II; Janet Campbell Hale; Janice Mirikitani; Alejandro
Murgia; Luis Syquia; Roberto Vargas. Time To Greeze! San Fran-
cisco: Glide, 1975.
Fernando Alegria, Donald Alexander, Alurista, Avotcja, Fran-
cis Becenti, Barbara Blackwell, Valerie Jo Bradley, C.
Breeze, Richard Brown, Ed Bullins, Laurena Cabanero, Emily
Cachapero, Graciela Carrillo, John Chenault, Curtis Choy,
Buriel Clay II, K. Coaston, Janice C. Cobb, Victor Hernandez
Cruz, Pamela Donegan, Jim Dong, Dolores S. Feria, David
Fong, Joan Fuentes, Joan Castanon Garcia, Rupert Garcia,
Jessica Tarahata Hagedorn, Janet Campbell Hale, Charles
Hamilton, David Henderson, Ena Hernandez, Roy George Hop-
kins, Elias Hruska-Cortes, Lawson Fusao Inada, Orvy Jundis,
Chris Kobayashi, Geraldine Kudaka, Beryle La Rose, Jean
LeMarr, Kenneth Lee, George Leong, Abbey Lincoln (Aminata
Moseka), Reginald Lockett, Wing Tek Lum, Irwin L. McJunk-
ins, Bayani J. Mariano, Consuelo Mendez, Alison Mills, Jan-
ice Merikitani, Arthur Monroe, Jose Montoya, Dorinda Moreno,

Aminata Moseka, Alejandro Murguia, Lane Nishikawa, Nitama-
yo, Thulani Nkabinde, Carolyn Ogletree, O. V. , Dorothy C.
Parrish, Oscar Penaranda, Teresinha Alves Pereira, Jim
Potts, Ishmael Reed, Evelyn Joyce Reingold, Alfred Robles,
Wendy Rose, Omar Salinas, Raul Salinas, Nina Serrano,
Ntozake Shange, Paula X. James St. Martin, Brenda Paik
Sunoo, Luis Syquia Jr. , Serafin Malay Syquia, Sam Togotac,
William H. Taylor, III, Thank Hai, Marcela Trujillo, Tsui
Kit-fan, Roberto Vargas, Xavier Viramontes, J. Stephen Whit-
ney, Donald Williams, John A. Williams, Nanying Stella Wong,
Doug Yamamoto, Mitsu Yashima, M. Yee, Cyn Zarco.

COLE, William. The Birds and the Beasts Were There. Cleveland:
World, 1963.
Kate Barnes, Patrick Barrington, Vasily Bashkin, John Becker,
Harry Behn, Fyodor Belkin, Peggy Benett, Elizabeth Bishop,
Milton Bracker, John Ciardi, Elizabeth Coatsworth, Padraic
Colum, Hilda Conkling, Frances Cornford, Louis O. Coxe, E.
E. Cummings, Roald Dahl, Charles Dalman, Geoffrey Dear-
mer, Peter Kane Dufault, Clifford Dyment, T. S. Eliot, Elea-
nor Farjeon, Bruce Fearing, Robert Finch, Donald Finkel,
Hugh Finn, Robert Frost, Isabella Gardner, Stella Gibbons,
Lydia Gibson, Wilfrid Gibson, Mary Gilmore, W. T. Goodge,
Paul Goodman, Robert Graves, Robert Beverly Hale, F. W.
Harvey, A. P. Herbert, Pati Hill, Robert Hillyer, Gertrude
Hind, Ralph Hodgson, Robert Horan, Barbara Howes, Ted
Hughes, Robinson Jeffers, Mary Kennedy, Louis Kent, Eugene
F. Kinhead, Vadim Korostylev, Alfred Kreymborg, Ernest
Kroll, Stanley Kunitz, Dilys Laing, Fred Lape, Irving Layton,
W. M. Letts, Denise Levertov, J. T. Lillie, R. P. Lister,
David McCord, Patrick MacDonogh, Albert D. Mackie, Irene
Rutherford McLeod, Winona McClintic, Bert Meyers, Mary
Britton Miller, Ewart Milne, A. Muir, Ogden Nash, Paul
Petrie, Daniel Pettiward, Ruth Pitter, Marnie Pomeroy, Ber-
nard Raymund, James Reeves, E. V. Rieu, Theodore Roethke,
W. E. Ross, Ian Serraillier, Elizabeth Shane, Shelley Silver-
stein, Osbert Sitwell, William Jay Smith, Raymond Souster,
Ruth Stone, May Swenson, R. S. Thomas, John Wain, Robert
Wallace, Rex Warner, William Carlos Williams, Yvor Winters,
Ralph Wotherspoon, Andrew Young.

COLE, William. A Book of Love Poems. New York: Viking,
1965.
Conrad Aiken, Robert Bly, Leonard Cohen, Frances Cornford,
Robert Creeley, E. E. Cummings, Edwin Denby, George Dil-
lon, Lloyd Frankenberg, Robert Frost, Ira Gershwin, Robert
Graves, Donald Hall, A. P. Herbert, Sara Jackson, Robinson
Jeffers, Mary Kennedy, Alfred Kreymborg, John Logan, Pat-
rick MacDonough, John Manifold, Bob Merrill, Ann Morrissett,
Dorothy Parker, Ezra Pound, Herbert Read, Byron Herbert
Reece, Theodore Roethke, Ian Serraillier, Shel Silverstein,
Louis Simpson, A. J. M. Smith, William Jay Smith, Mark
Van Doren, John Francis Waller, Wilfred Watson, John Hall
Wheelock, Sheila Wingfield, William Wood.

COLE, William. Eight Lines and Under. Macmillan, 1967.
John Arden, W. H. Auden, George Barker, Peggy Bennett,
John Betjeman, Paul Blackburn, Robert Bly, Edgar Bowers,
Patrick Bridgewater, G. F. Cayley, Austin Clarke, Leonard
Cohen, William Cole, Frances Cornford, Robert Creeley, J.
V. Cunningham, John Davidson, William M. Davis, Babette
Deutsch, William Dickey, Alan Dugan, Martin Esslin, Donald
Finkel, Robert Francis, Robert Frost, Roy Fuller, Norman
Gale, Menna Gallie, Isabella Gardner, Jean Garrigue, Walker
Gibson, Wilfred Gibson, Robert Graves, Donald Hall, Samuel
Hazo, Annie Higgins, Samuel Hoffenstein, Daniel Hoffman, Ed-
ward Newman Horn, R. G. Howarth, Richard Highes, Randall
Jarrell, Robinson Jeffers, B. S. Johnson, Walta Karsner,
Patrick Kavanagh, Richard Kell, John Kelleher, X. J. Ken-
nedy, Galway Kinnell, Thomas Kinsella, Max Knight, Alden A.
Knowlan, Alfred Kreymborg, Stanley Kunitz, Dilys Laing,
Philip Larkin, Alun Lewis, Hugh MacDiarmid, Norman Mailer,
William H. Matchett, Donald Mattam, T. S. Matthews, Bert
Meyers, E. H. W. Meyerstein, Robert Mezey, Josephine
Miles, E. V. Milner, Adrian Mitchell, Ernest G. Moll, Mari-
anne Moore, Howard Nemerov, William Plomer, Ralph Pome-
roy, J. R. Pope, Peter Porter, Ezra Pound. Justin Richard-
son, Theodore Roethke, Jerome Rothenberg, Siegfried Sassoon,
Delmore Schwartz, Winfield Townley Scott, Ian Serraillier, Eli
Siegel, Philip Silver, Shel Silverstein, Michael Silverton, John
Simon, Louis Simpson, A. J. M. Smith, Stevie Smith, Ray-
mound Souster, William Stafford, Jon Stallworthy, Robert
Sward, John Tagliabue, R. S. Thomas, C. A. Trypanis, John
Updike, Mark Van Doren, Mildred Weston, Richard Wilbur,
William Carlos Williams, Yvor Winters, William Wood, James
Wright, Andrew Young.

COLE, William. The Sea, Ships and Sailors: Poems, Songs and
Shanties. New York: Viking, 1967.
Tom Buchan, Abe Burrows, William Cole, Crosbie Garstin,
Walter Gibson, Wilfrid Gibson, Aldous Huxley, M. La Rue,
R. P. Lister, John Masefield, James Reeves, Ian Serraillier,
Shel Silverstein, William Jay Smith, John Updike, Pat Wilson,
David Wright.

COLE, William. Poetry Brief: An Anthology of Short, Short Poems.
New York: Macmillan, 1971.
Yehuda Amichai, Edmond Ashton, Robert Bagg, Coleman Barks,
Aphra Behn, Gerard Benson, Earle Birney, Robert Bly, Tom
Buchan, Basil Bunting, Tony Buzan, David Calder, Roy Camp-
bell, Lucille Clifton, Leonard Cohen, William Cole, Alex Com-
fort, Frances Cornford, Robert Creeley, J. V. Cunningham,
Charles Dalmon, Paul Dehn, Alan Sixon, Celia Dropkin, Law-
rence Durrell, Richard Eberhart, Gunnar Ekelof, Colin Ellis,
Thomas Erskine, Gavin Ewart, Jake Falstaff, Donald Finkel,
Robert Frost, Roy Fuller, Isabelle Gardner, Gary Gildner,
Louise Gluck, Ryah Tumarkin Goodman, Harry Graham, Cor-
ney Grain, Robert Graves, Richard Leighton Greene, Geoffrey

Grigson, Bernard Gutteridge, John Haines, Donald Hall, Paul
Hannigan, William Hart-Smith, H. R. Hays, Seamus Heaney,
Geof Hewitt, William Heyen, John Heywood, Russell Hoban,
Ralph Hodgson, Molly Holden, John Hollander, John Horder,
Edward Newman Horn, R. G. Howarth, Reuben Iceland, David
Ignatow, Elizabeth Jennings, Gerald Jones, Donald Justice,
Patrick Kavanagh, Mary Kennedy, X. J. Kennedy, Edgar
Klauber, Philip Larkin, Laurie Lee, Christopher Levenson,
C. S. Lewis, Janet Lewis, John L'Heureux, Ron Loewinsohn,
John Logan, Edward Lucie-Smith, Lewis MacAdams, Hugh
MacDiarmid, Donagh MacDonagh, Roger McGough, Louis Mac-
Niece, Jay MacPherson, John Manifold, William H. Matchett,
T. S. Matthews, William Matthews, William Meredith, W. S.
Merwin, Bert Meyers, Thomas Middleton, Josephine Miles,
Marianne Moore, Lisel Mueller, Ogden Nash, Leonard Nathan,
Robert Nichols, Alden Nowlan, Geoffrey O'Brien, Joel Oppen-
heimer, Elio Pagliarani, Nicanor Parra, Linda Pastan, Brian
Patten, Mark Perlberg, Marnie Pomeroy, Ezra Pound, Jacques
Prevert, John Pudney, Paul Ramsey, Herbert Read, Anne Rid-
ler, Charles G. D. Roberts, W. R. Rogers, Theodore Roethke,
William Pitt Root, Alan Ross, Muriel Rukeyser, Siegfried
Sassoon, Winfield Townley Scott, Anne Sexton, Harvey Shapiro,
Shel Silverstein, Michael Silverton, Charles Simic, Louis
Simpson, L. E. Sissman, Stevie Smith, Sydney Goodsir Smith,
William Jay Smith, Gary Snyder, Bernard Spencer, Raymond
Souster, William Stafford, Jon Stallworthy, David Steinglass,
J. K. Stephen, Anne Stevenson, Trumbull Stickney, Hal Sum-
mers, Robert Tannahill, R. S. Thomas, Anthony Thwaite,
Eric Torgersen, Gael Turnbull, John Updike, Robert Vas Dias,
William Wantling, John Webster, Mildred Weston, William
Whewell, Richard Wilbur, Jonathan Williams, Pete Winslow,
William Woods, Judith Wright, William Wycherley, Andrew
Young, Paul Zimmer.

COLE, William. Pick Me Up: A Book of Short Short Poems.
New York: Macmillan, 1972.
Conrad Aiken, Dorothy Aldis, A. R. Ammons, Harry Behn,
Edmund Blunden, Pete Brown, G. J. Cayley, Elizabeth Coats-
worth, Leonard Cohen, Frances Cornford, Robert Creeley,
Paul Dehn, Henry Dumas, Abbie Huston Evans, David Ferry,
Jean Follain, Colin Francis, Robert Frost, Robin Fulton,
Wlaker Gibson, Paul T. Gilbert, Robert Graves, John Haines,
Donald Hall, William J. Harris, W. Hart-Smith, Russell
Hoban, Sandra Hochman, Edward Newman Horn, Michael
Horovitz, Langston Hughes, Richard Hughes, David Ignatow,
Robinson Jeffers, Walta Karsner, X. J. Kennedy, Galway
Kinnell, Alfred Kreymborg, Dilys Laing, Fred Lape, Philip
Larkin, Ernest Leverett, Newman Levy, Edward Lucie-Smith,
Norman McCaig, Eugene McCarthy, Ronald McCuaig, Sandra
McPherson, Donald Mattam, W. S. Merwin, Spike Milligan,
J. B. Morton, Ogden Nash, Howard Nemerov, Mary Neville,
Robert Nye, Mark Perlberg, "Pink," Marnie Pomeroy, Ezra
Pound, Glenn Pritchard, Herbert Read, James Reeves, Naomi

Replansky, Charles Reznikoff, Theodore Roethke, Siegfried Sassoon, Eli Siegel, Shel Silverstein, Michael Silverton, Stevie Smith, Sydney Goodsir Smith, Robert Sund, R. S. Thomas, John Updike, John Hall Wheelock, Yvor Winters, William Wood, James Wright, Andrew Young, Douglas Young.

COLLEY, Ann C.; Judith K. Moore. Starting with Poetry. New York: Harcourt, Brace, Jovanovich, 1973.
    Margaret Atwood, W. H. Auden, Coleman Barks, Elizabeth Bishop, D. M. Black, Robert Bly, Gwendolyn Brooks, Lucille Clifton, Victor Hernandez Cruz, E. E. Cummings, Samuel Daniel, Gerald Duff, Randy Dunagan, Ray Durem, Jaci Earley, Richard Eberhart, Margaret Eckman, T. S. Eliot, Edward Field, Roy Fisher, Kathleen Fraser, Carol Freeman, Robert Frost, Phil George, Nikki Giovanni, Joe Goncalves, Donald Hall, Michael S. Harper, William J. Harris, Robert Hayden, David Henderson, Robert Hershon, Hyachinthe Hill, Langston Hughes, LeRoi Jones, Etheridge Knight, John Knoepfle, John Lacks, David Lawson, Don L. Lee, Julius Lester, Denise Levertov, Audre Lorde, Dick Lourie, Edward Lucie-Smith, Eugene McCarthy, Frances McConnel, Derek Mahon, Clarence Major, Eve Merriam, Judith Moore, Merrill Moore, John N. Morris, Ted Olson, Patricia Parker, Kenneth Patchen, Ray Patterson, Frank Lamont Phillips, Marge Piercy, Tom Poole, Burton Raffel, Ishmael Reed, Theodore Roethke, Vern Rutsala, Therl Ryan, James Seay, James Shirley, Louis Simpson, Gary Snyder, Edward S. Spriggs, James Tate, Richard W. Thomas, John Updike, Robert Vas Dias, Chad Walsh, Patricia Watson, James Welch, Donna Whitewing, Nancy Willard, William Carlos Williams, Al Young.

COLUM, Padraic. Roofs of Gold. Poems to Read Aloud. New York: Macmillan, 1964.
    William Allingham, Padraic Colum, E. E. Cummings, Wilfrid Wilson Gibson, Stephen Spender.

COOMBS, Orde. We Speak as Liberators: Young Black Poets: An Anthology. New York: Dodd, Mead, 1970.
    S. E. Anderson, Desiree A. Barnwell, Joseph Bevans Bush, Pearl Cleage, Jayne Cortez, Stanley Crouch, Lawrence S. Cumberbatch, Walter E. Dancy, Jackie Earley, Mari Evans, Lanon A. Fenner, Wally Ford, Janice Marie Gadsden, Paula Giddings, Nikki Giovanni, Clay Goss, Linda Goss, Donald Green, R. Ernest Holmes, Alicia L. Johnson, Charles Johnson, Herschell Johnson, Alice H. Jones, Arnold Kemp, Jewel C. Lattimore (Johari Amini), Don L. Lee, Tena Lockett, James R. Lucas, Bob Maxey, Don A. Mizell, A. X. Nicholas, Raymond R. Patterson, Arthur Pfister, Herbert Lee Pitts, Timothy L. Porter, Eric Priestley, T. L. Robinson, Carolyn M. Rodgers (Imani), Sonia Sanchez, Ruby C. Saunder, Johnie Scott, Saundra Sharp, Dan Simmons, Shirley Staples, Glenn Stokes, Robert L. Terrell, Charles Thomas, James W. Thompson, Quincy Troupe, Raymond Turner, Jacques Wakefield, Dell Washington, Alan Weeks, Michyle White, Art Wilson, Al Young.

CORBETT, Thomas. Modern American Poetry. New York: Macmillan, 1961.
E. E. Cummings, Robert Frost, John Holmes, Randall Jarrell, Robinson Jeffers, Thomas Merton, John Frederick Nims, Jessica Powers, Carl Sandburg, Delmore Schwartz, Maris Stella, A. M. Sullivan, William Carlos Williams.

CRAFTS, Gretchen B. Our Own Thing. Contemporary Thought in Poetry. Englewood Cliffs, N.J.: Prentice-Hall, 1973.
Blair H. Allen, Bert Almon, W. H. Auden, George Barker, Daniel Berrigan, Morris Bishop, Paul Blackburn, Arna Bontemps, Augustine Bowe, Bonnie Buchanan, Sharon Buck, Gerald Butler, John Ciardi, Leonard Cohen, Judy Collins, Gretch Crafts, Robert Creeley, E. E. Cummings, Peter Davison, Mary Lou Denman, Reuel Denney, Bob Dylan, T. S. Eliot, James Emanuel, Mari E. Evans, Lawrence Ferlinghetti, T. J. Freeman, Robert Frost, Jack Gilbert, Eliot Glassheim, Robert Graves, George Harrison, Frank Horne, Langston Hughes, Scott Kinney, George Lanston, John Lennon, Paul McCartney, Frank Mezta, Barbara Miles, Bill Miller, Susan Murray, Karen Nurmi, Anthony Ostroff, Kenneth Patchen, Michael Pogliano, Stuart Kent Polzin, Ralph Pomeroy, Ezra Pound, Kenneth Rexroth, Betsy Richards, Theodore Roethke, Harvey Shapiro, Karl Shapiro, Robert Shepard, Sharon Sosna, Anne Spencer, D. A. Stahl, Miles Weaver, Alfred K. Weber, John Hall Wheelock, Richard Wilbur, William Carlos Williams.

CRANE, Milton. Fifty Great Poets. New York: Bantam, 1961.
W. H. Auden, E. E. Cummings, Robert Frost, Marianne Moore.

CRANG, Alan. Tunes on a Tin Whistle: Some Real-life Poetry. Oxford, New York: Pergamon, 1967.
W. H. Auden, Leo Aylen, Michael Baldwin, George Barker, Patricia Beer, John Betjeman, A. C. Boyd, Edwin Brock, Alan Brownjohn, Jim Burns, Roy Campbell, Charles Causley, Austin Clarke, Tony Connor, Alan Crang, E. E. Cummings, Keith Douglas, T. S. Eliot, D. J. Enright, Lawrence Ferlinghetti, Robert Frost, Karen Gershon, Zulfikar Ghose, Robert Graves, Thom Gunn, Seamus Heaney, Anthony Hecht, David Holbrook, Michael Horovitz, Ted Hughes, Elizabeth Jennings, B. S. Johnson, Philip Larkin, Laurie Lee, Laurence Lerner, John Logan, Ewan McColl, Archibald MacLeish, Christopher Middleton, Timothy Palmer, Peter Porter, Jonathan Price, Henry Reed, Adrienne Rich, Vernon Scannell, Stephen Spender, William Stafford, Edward Storey, R. S. Thomas, Anthony Thwaite, Charles Tomlinson, Shirley Toulson, Rex Warner.

CROFT, P. J. Autograph Poetry of the English Language: Facsimiles of Original Manuscripts from the Fourteenth to the Twentieth Century. 2 vols. New York: McGraw-Hill, 1973.
W. H. Auden, John Betjeman, Edmund Blunden, E. E. Cummings, Cecil Day Lewis, T. S. Eliot, Robert Frost, Robert

Graves, Louis MacNeice, Marianne Moore, Ezra Pound, Carl Sandburg, Siegfried Sassoon, Edith Sitwell, Stephen Spender.

CROMIE, Robert. Where Steel Winds Blow. New York: David McKay, 1968.
Keith Barnes, Wlater Benton, Robert Beum, Jaime Torres Bodet, John Malcolm Brinnin, Edwin Brock, Witter Bynner, Ralph Chaplin, John Ciardi, Alex Comfort, Hilary Corke, E. E. Cummings, Donald Davidson, Bruce Dawe, Babette Deutsch, Colin Ellis, Maurice English, Dave Etter, William Everson, Robert Churchill Francis, Arthur Freeman, David Gascoyne, Karen Gershon, Wilfrid Wilson Gibson, Richard Gillman, Robert Graves, Mary Hacker, Donald Hall, Alan Patrick Herbert, Sophie Himmel, Daniel G. Hoffman, Kenneth Hopkins, Paul Horgan, Lindley Williams Hubbell, Langston Hughes, Randall Jarrell, Robinson Jeffers, Cho Sung Kyun, Geoffrey Lehmann, Winifred M. Letts, Denise Levertov, Patrick MacGill, Phyllis McGinley, Thomas McGrath, Frederick Louis MacNeice, Marcel Martinet, Stanley Moss, Paul Scott Mowrer, Helene Mullins, Charles Norman, Dorothy Parker, Edith Lovejoy Pierce, Merle Price, Herbert Read, Henry Reed, Kenneth Rexroth, Edgell Rickword, Norman Rosten, Carl Sandburg, Siegfried Sassoon, Louis Simpson, Kenneth Slessor, George Starbuck, Vincent Starrett, Adrien Stoutenberg, Lucien Stryk, Henry Treece, A. Constantine Trypanis, Louis Untermeyer, Peter Viereck, John Wain, John Hall Wheelock, Reed Whittemore, Richard Wilbur, Mance Williams, Tom Wright, Samuel Yellen.

DEE, Ruby. Glowchild, and Other Poems. New York: Joseph Okpaku, 1972.
Calvin Anderson, Linda Baron, Constance E. Berkley, Robert T. Bowen, Daryl Branche, Elaine Brown, Pam Brown, Carl F. Burke, Margaret Burroughs, John Henrik Clarke, Frederick Crawley, Donald S. C. Davis, Guy Davis, Laverne Davis, Nora Davis, Ossie Davis, Alfred Duckett, Jim Estrin, Gary Feldman, E. Y. Harburg, Glenn Hines, Beth Hollender, Yusef Iman, Frank S. Jenkins, Norman Jordan, Robert Kaufman, James R. Lucas, Lisa McCann, Othello Mahome, Efrein Matos, Rhonda Metz, David Nelson, Gordon Nelson, Abiodun Oyewole, Blossom Powe, Rakeman, Dorothy Randall, Joe Nell Rice, Ridhiana, Susan Robbins, Greg Russell, Billy Sipser, Ricky Smith, Linda Thomas, Ann Wallace, Emett "Babe" Wallace, Debbie Whitely, Gwendolyn Williams.

DeLOACH, Allen. The East Side Scene: American Poetry, 1960-1965. Buffalo, N.Y.: State Univ. of N.Y., 1968; Doubleday, 1972.
Carol Berge, Ted Berrigan, Paul Blackburn, Kirby Congdon, Allen De Loach, Harold Dicker, Diane Di Prima, George Economou, Ted Enslin, Allen Ginsberg, Marguerite Harris, David Henderson, Barbara Holland, David Ignatow, Will Inman, Allen Katzman, Robert Kelly, Tuli Kupferberg, Walter Lowenfels, Gerard Malanga, Clive Matson, George Montgomery, Joel Oppenheimer, Peter Orlovsky, Rochelle Owens, Allen Planz,

Jerome Rotherberg, Ed Sanders, Dan Saxon, Armand Schwerner, Susan Sherman, Jay Socin, Diane Wakoski, John Wieners, Louis Zukofsky.

DeLOACH, Allen. A Decade & Then Some. Contemporary Literature. 1976. Buffalo, N. Y.: Intrepid, 1976.
Mindy Aloff, Paule Barton-Haiti, Ted Berrigan, Bonnie Bremser, Ray Bremser, Charles Bukowski, William Cirocco, Marty Cohen, Cid Corman, Gregory Corso, Robert Creeley, Victor Hernandez Cruz, John Daley, Allen DeLoach, Joan DeLoach, Diane di Prima, Charles Doria, Edward Dorn, Theodore Enslin, Allen Ginsberg, Louis Ginsberg, John Giorno, Roberta Gould, James Grauerholz, Tony Harrison, Lee Harwood, Lyn Hejinian, Will Inman, Allen Katzman, Robert Kelly, Judith Kerman, Martha King, Robert La Vigne, Peter Levitt, Lyn Lifshin, Lomawywesa (Michael Kabotie), Hugh MacDiarmid, Clarence Major, David Meltzer, Jack Micheline, Ann Mikolowski, Ken Mikolowski, Eric Mottram, Bud Navero, Harold Norse, Jeffrey Nuttall, Toby Olson, Joel Oppenheimer, Peter Orlovsky, Simon Ortiz, Rochelle Owens, Kevin Power, Bernetta Quinn, Susan Quist, Carl Rakosi, Jerome Rothenberg, Kathy Rudi, Ron Schreiber, Armand Schwerner, Nancy Scott, Walt Shepperd, Miro Silvera, Nathaniel Tarn, Jun K. Tukita, Robert Vas Dias, Ann Waldman, Tom Weatherly, John Weiners, Carl Weissner, Neal Wing.

DERLETH, August William. Fire and Sleet and Candlelight. Sauk City, Wisc.: Arkham, 1961.
George Abbe, Helen Adam, Ethan Ayer, William D. Barney, Gene Baro, Lorna Beers Chambers, Laura Benet, John Betjeman, Robert Bloch, Sam Bradley, Joseph Payne Brennan, Julian Brown, Winifred Adams Burr, Sara King Carleton, Lin Carter, Mabel MacDonald Carver, Gertrude Claytor, Elizabeth Coatsworth, Stanton A. Coblentz, Grant Code, Beverly Connelly, Mary Elizabeth Counselman, Margaret Stanion Darling, Gustav Davidson, August Derleth, Alfred Dorn, Leah Bodine Drake, Dorothy Burnham Eaton, Charles Edward Eaton, Norma Farber, Marguerite George, Ryah Tumarkin Goodman, Frances Angevine Gray, Lisa Grenelle, R. H. Grenville, Amy Groesbeck, Aletha Humphreys, Leslie Nelson Jennings, Geoffrey Johnson, Joseph Joel Keith, Martha Keller Rowland, Mary Kennedy, Walter H. Kerr, Herman Stowell King, Vera Bishop Konrick, Frank Belknap Long, Lilith Lorraine, Stanley McNail, Rosa Zagnoni Marinoni, Anne Marx, Edna Meudt, H. S. Neill, Alden M. Nowlan, Edith Ogutsch, Jennie M. Palen, Conrad Pendleton, Hyam Plutzik, Tom Poots, Dorothy Quick, Katherine Reeves, Alastair Reid, Liboria E. Romano, Raymond Roseliep, Larry Rubin, Sydney King Russell, Antonia Y. Schwab, Walter Shedlofsky, Ruth Forbes Sherry, Jon Silkin, Louis Simpson, Jocelyn Macy Sloan, Clark Ashton Smith, Vincent Starrett, Felix Stefanile, Jane Stuart, Lucia Trent, Lewis Turco, Mark Van Doren, Harold Vinal, Donald Wandrei, Wade Wellman, James L. Weil, Margaret Widdemar, Loring Williams, James Wright.

DE ROCHE, Joseph. The Heath Introduction to Poetry with a Pref-
ace on Poetry and a Brief History. Lexington, Mass. : D. C.
Heath, 1975.
    Margaret Atwood, W. H. Auden, Margaret Avison, Amiri
    Baraka, Wendell Berry, John Berryman, Earle Birney, Eliza-
    beth Bishop, Louise Bogan, Gwendolyn Brooks, Robert Clayton
    Casto, Leonard Cohen, E. E. Cummings, Joseph De Roche,
    James Dickey, Hilda Doolittle, Robert Duncan, Richard Eber-
    hart, T. S. Eliot, Kenneth Fearing, Lawrence Ferlinghetti,
    Edward Field, Robert Frost, Allen Ginsberg, Robert Graves,
    Thom Gunn, John Haines, Langston Hughes, Ted Hughes, Rob-
    inson Jeffers, LeRoi Jones, Donald Justice, X. J. Kennedy,
    Galway Kinnell, Philip Larkin, Denise Levertov, Robert Low-
    ell, Archibald MacLeish, Louis MacNeice, George Meredith,
    W. S. Merwin, Marianne Moore, Howard Nemerov, Donald
    Peterson, Sylvia Plath, Ezra Pound, Alfred Purdy, John
    Crowe Ransom, Henry Reed, Adrienne Rich, Theodore Roethke,
    Carl Sandburg, Seigfried Sassoon, Anne Sexton, Louis Simpson,
    Stevie Smith, W. D. Snodgrass, Gary Snyder, William Staf-
    ford, Mark Strand, Allen Tate, Richard Wilbur, William Car-
    los Williams, Yvor Winters, Al Young.

DI PRIMA, Diane. War Poems. New York: Poets Press, 1968.
    Gregory Croso, Robert Creekely, Diane Di Prima, Robert
    Duncan, Allen Ginsberg, LeRoi Jones, Michael McClure,
    Charles Olson, Joel Oppenheimer, Gary Snyder, Philip Whalen.

DODGE, Robert K. ; Joseph B. McCullough. Voices from Wah'Kon-
tah: Contemporary Poetry of Native Americans. New York: International, 1974.
    Paula Gunn Allen, Charles G. Ballard, Ted Berrigan, Janet
    Campbell, Ramona Carden, Martha Chosa, Gery Cohoe, Phil
    George, Patty Harjo, Bruce Ignacio, King D. Kuka, Littlebird,
    Charles C. Long, Alonzo Lopez, Duane W. McGinnis, David
    Martinez, Emerson Blackhorse Mitchell, N. Scott Momaday,
    Calvin O'John, Simon Ortiz, Agnes Pratt, Fred Red Cloud,
    Ronald Rogers, Norman H. Russell, Bruce Severy, Loyal
    Shegonee, Liz Sohappy, Soge Track, Marnie Walsh, Winifred
    Fields Walters, Archie Washburn, James Welsh, Donna White-
    wing, Ray Young Bear.

DREW, Elizabeth; George Connor. Discovering Modern Poetry.
New York: Holt, Rinehart and Winston, 1961.
    W. H. Auden, Richard Eberhart, T. S. Eliot, Robert Frost,
    Randall Jarrell, Robert Lowell, Archibald MacLeish, Louis
    MacNeice, Marianne Moore, John Crowe Ransom, Theodore
    Roethke, Karl Shapiro, Stephen Spender, Richard Wilbur.

DRIVER, Tom F. ; Robert Pack. Poems of Doubt and Belief: An
Anthology of Modern Religious Poetry. New York: Macmillan,
1964.
    Leonie Adams, Conrad Aiken, W. H. Auden, Gene Baro, E-
    lizabeth Bishop, John Ciardi, E. E. Cummings, Richard Eber-

hart, T. S. Eliot, Robert Frost, Cecil Hemley, Ted Hughes, Robinson Jeffers, Elizabeth Jennings, Galway Kinnell, Philip Larkin, C. Day Lewis, Robert Lowell, Louis MacNeice, W. S. Merwin, Vassar Miller, Marianne Moore, Howard Nemerov, Robert Pack, Sylvia Plath, Theodore Roethke, Delmore Schwartz, Anne Sexton, Jon Silkin, George Starbuck, Allen Tate, Robert Penn Warren, John Hall Wheelock, Richard Wilbur, William Carlos Williams.

DUNNING, Stephen; Edward Lueders; Hugh Smith. Reflections on a Gift of Watermelon Pickle. Glenview, Ill.: Scott, Foresman, 1966.
Sally Andresen, Richard Armour, Eleanor Averitt, William Beyer, Philip Booth, John Ciardi, Elizabeth Coatsworth, Robert P. Tristram Coffin, Gregory Corso, E. E. Cummings, Paul Dehn, Babette Deutsch, Leah Bodine Drake, John Fandel, Bruce Fearing, Lawrence Ferlinghetti, Thomas Hornsby Ferril, Donald Finkel, Roland Flint, Robert Francis, Robert Frost, Walker Gibson, Lyle Glazier, H. J. Gottlieb, A. B. Gutherie, Jr., Donald Hall, Marcie Hans, Sara Henderson Hay, Curtis Heath, Oliver Herford, Ruth Herschberger, Miriam Hershenson, Robert Hillyer, Carl W. Hines, Jr., Edwin A. Hoey, Langston Hughes, Don Jaffee, Beatrice Janosco, Brooks Jenkins, Judson Jerome, Donald Justice, Sy Kahn, Lenore Kandel, Gustave Keyser, Naoshi Koriyama, Maxine Kumin, Ruth Lechlitner, Edward Lueders, Gertrude May Lutz, Margaret Phyllis MacSweeney, David McCord, Jeanne McGahey, Phyllis McGinley, Charles Malam, Marcia Masters, Eve Merriam, Barriss Mills, John Moffitt, Harold Monroe, Rosalie Moore, Richard Kendall Munkittrick, Ezra Pound, Burton Raffel, Gerald Raftery, Theodore Roethke, Dan Roth, Sydney King Russell, Arthur M. Sampley, Carl Sandburg, Lew Sarett, Winfield Townley Scott, Karl Shapiro, William Jay Smith, William Stafford, May Swenson, Genevieve Taggard, James S. Tippett, John Tobias, Robert L. Tyler, John Updike, James L. Weil, Mildred Weston, John Hall Wheelock, William Carlos Williams, Ivor Winters.

DURAND, Robert. The Yes! Press Anthology. Santa Barbara, Calif.: Christopher's Books, 1972.
Diane Di Prima, Robert Durand, Phil Garrison, Walter Hall, Jack Hirschman, Dick Kennedy, Jack Kerouac, Zig Knoll, James Laughlin, Maria D. Mascaro, David Meltzer, Carlos Reyes, Gary Snyder, Lew Welch, Michael Wiater.

EFROS, Susan. This Is Women's Work: An Anthology of Prose and Poetry. San Francisco: Panjandrum Press, 1974.
Alta, Laura Beausoleil, Rena Blauner, Sandy Boucher, Grace Butcher, Dorothy Ann Brown, Susan Calhoun, Lynda Efros, Susan Efros, Cheri Fein, Kathleen Fraser, Heidi Gitterman, Susan Griffin, Jana Harris, Honor Johnson, Thalia Kilrilakis, Fanchon Lewis, Rachel Loden, Adrianne Marcus, Rochelle Nameroff, Tillie Olsen, Marge Piercy, Jeanne Sirotkin, Julia

Vinograd, Julia Vose, Grace Wade, Ruth Weiss, Nancy Willard, Sybil Wood, Jan Zaleski, Alison Zier.

ELLMANN, Richard. The Norton Anthology of Modern Poetry. New York: Norton, 1973.
Dannie Abse, Conrad Aiken, Kingsley Amis, A. R. Ammons, Brother Antoninus, John Ashbery, W. H. Auden, Margaret Avison, Imamu Amiri Baraka, Samuel Beckett, Ted Berrigan, John Berryman, John Betjeman, Elizabeth Bishop, Paul Blackburn, Robert Bly, Richard Emil Braun, John Malcolm Brinnin, Gwendolyn Brooks, Basil Bunting, Austin Clarke, Leonard Cohen, Robert Conquest, Gregory Corso, Robert Creeley, E. E. Cummings, J. V. Cunningham, C. Day Lewis, James Dickey, Hilda Doolittle, Edward Dorn, Alan Dugan, Robert Duncan, Richard Eberhart, T. S. Eliot, William Empson, Irving Feldman, Lawrence Ferlinghetti, Robert Frost, Roy Fuller, Allen Ginsberg, Nikki Giovanni, Robert Graves, Thom Gunn, Ian Hamilton, Jim Harrison, Robert Hayden, Seamus Heaney, Anthony Hecht, Geoffrey Hill, Daryl Hine, John Hollander, Edwin Honig, A. D. Hope, Richard Howard, Langston Hughes, Ted Hughes, Randall Jarrell, Robinson Jeffers, David Jones, Patrick Kavanagh, Thomas Kinsella, Lincoln Kirstein, Etheridge Knight, Kenneth Koch, Stanley Kunitz, Philip Larkin, Don L. Lee, Denise Levertov, Philip Levine, Robert Lowell, George MacBeth, Hugh MacDiarmid, Roger McGough, Archibald MacLeish, Louis MacNeice, John Masefield, William Meredith, James Merrill, W. S. Merwin, Josephine Miles, Marianne Moore, Dom Moraes, Howard Nemerov, Desmond O'Grady, Frank O'Hara, Charles Olson, Sylvia Plath, William Plomer, Ezra Pound, E. J. Pratt, A. W. Purdy, Dudley Randall, John Crowe Ransom, Herbert Read, Kenneth Rexroth, Adrienne Rich, Laura Riding, W. R. Rodgers, Theodore Roethke, Carl Sandburg, Siegfried Sassoon, James Schuyler, Delmore Schwartz, Anne Sexton, Karl Shapiro, Judith Johnson Sherwin, Jon Silkin, Louis Simpson, Edith Sitwell, Stevie Smith, W. D. Snodgrass, Gary Snyder, Ann Spencer, Stephen Spender, Jon Stallworthy, Mark Strand, Allen Tate, James Tate, Charles Tomlinson, Jean Toomer, Diane Wakoski, Derek Walcott, Robert Penn Warren, Vernon Watkins, Theodore Weiss, Richard Wilbur, William Carlos Williams, Yvor Winters, David Wright, James Wright, Richard Wright, Louis Zukofsky.

ELLMANN, Richard. The New Oxford Book of American Verse. New York: Oxford, 1976.
Conrad Aiken, A. R. Ammons, John Berryman, Elizabeth Bishop, Robert Bly, Gwendolyn Brooks, Robert Creeley, E. E. Cummings, James Dickey, Richard Dorn, Robert Duncan, T. S. Eliot, Jean Garrigue, Allen Ginsberg, Anthony Hecht, Langston Hughes, Randall Jarrell, Robinson Jeffers, Galway Kinnell, Denise Levertov, Philip Levine, Robert Lowell, Archibald MacLeish, James Merrill, W. S. Merwin, Frank O'Hara, Sylvia Plath, Ezra Pound, J. C. Ransom, Adrienne Rich, Theodore Roethke, Delmore Schwartz, Louis Simpson, Gary

Snyder, Allen Tate, Robert Penn Warren, Richard Wilbur, William Carlos Williams, Yvor Winters, James Wright.

ENGELBERG, Edward. The Symbolist Poem: The Development of the English Tradition. New York: Dutton, 1967.
W. H. Auden, T. S. Eliot, Robert Lowell, Edith Sitwell.

ENGLE, Paul; Joseph Langland. Poet's Choice. New York: Dial, 1962.
Leonie Adams, Conrad Aiken, Kingsley Amis, George Barker, John Berryman, John Betjeman, Earle Birney, Elizabeth Bishop, Edmund Blunden, Louise Bogan, Edgar Bowers, John Malcolm Brinnin, Gwendolyn Brooks, Charles Causley, John Ciardi, Leonard Cohen, Henri Coulette, E. E. Cummings, J. V. Cunningham, Donald Davie, C. Day Lewis, Richard Eberhart, William Empson, Paul Engle, Lawrence Ferlinghetti, Robert Francis, Robert Frost, Roy Fuller, Brewster Ghiselin, Allen Ginsberg, Robert Graves, Thom Gunn, Donald Hall, Michael Hamburger, Anthony Hecht, Daniel G. Hoffman, John Hollander, John Holmes, Barbara Howes, Langston Hughes, Ted Hughes, Randall Jarrell, Robinson Jeffers, Elizabeth Jennings, Donald Justice, Patrick Kavanagh, X. J. Kennedy, Galway Finnell, Thomas Kinsella, Stanley Kunitz, Joseph Langland, Philip Larkin, Richard Lattimore, Irving Layton, Denise Levertov, Stephen Levine, Robert Lowell, Phyllis McGinley, Archibald MacLeish, Jay MacPherson, E. L. Mayo, William Meredith, James Merrill, W. S. Merwin, Josephine Miles, Marianne Moore, Howard Moss, Ogden Nash, Howard Nemerov, John Frederick Nims, Kenneth Patchen, E. J. Pratt, Henry Rago, John Crowe Ransom, Alastair Reed, Theodore Roethke, James Schevill, Delmore Schwartz, Karl Shapiro, Louis Simpson, William Jay Smith, Stephen Spender, William Stafford, Allen Tate, Charles Tomlinson, Mark Van Doren, Peter Viereck, David Wagoner, John Wain, Robert Penn Warren, Vernon Watkins, Phyllis Webb, John Hall Wheelock, Reed Whittemore, Richard Wilbur, Oscar Williams, William Carlos Williams.

EVANS, David Allan. New Voices in American Poetry: An Anthology. Cambridge, Mass.: Winthrop, 1973.
James Applewhite, Coleman Barks, Marvin Bell, Harold Bond, Van K. Brock, Thomas Brush, Raymond Carver, Peter Cooley, Sam Cornish, Tom Crawford, Philip Dacey, Stephen Dunn, David Allan Evans, Siv Cedering Fox, Virginia Gilbert, Robert Gillespie, Elton Glaser, Louise Gluck, Albert Goldbarth, Michael S. Harper, Philip Hey, Ron Ikan, Erica Jong, R. P. Kingston, Maxine Kumin, Greg Kuzma, Larry Evis, Thomas Lux, Tom McKeown, Morton Marcus, William Matthews, William Pitt Root, Gary Sange, Dennis Schmitz, Mary Shumway, Charles Simic, David Smith, David Steingass, Leon Stokesbury, Mark Strand, Dabney Stuart, Dennis Trudell, Alice Walker, J. D. Whitney, Al Young.

FAGIN, Larry.   Adventures in Poetry: Number Seven.   New York:
The Poetry Project (St. Mark's Church), 1971.
  Joe Brainard, Clark Coolidge, John Giorno, Byrd Hoffman,
  Vincent Katz, Bernadette Mayer, Aram Saroyan.

FELVER, Charles S.; Martin K. Nurmi.   Poetry: An Introduction
and Anthology.   Columbus, Ohio: Charles E. Merrill, 1967.
  W. H. Auden, E. E. Cummings, T. S. Eliot, Robert Frost,
  Robert Graves, Hugh Hartman, Donald Junkins, George Keith-
  ley, Jacob Leed, Archibald MacLeish, Josephine Miles, Mari-
  anne Moore, Ned O'Gorman, Hyam Plutzik, Theodore Roethke,
  James Schevill, Delmore Schwartz, Winfield Townley Scott,
  Karl Shapiro, Allen Tate, Paul Zimmer.

FERLINGHETTI, Lawrence.   City Lights Anthology.   San Francisco:
City Lights Books, 1974.
  Richard Baker-roshi, Richard Brautigan, Charles Bukowski,
  Ed Bullins, Thom Burns, Lucy Catlett, Gail Chiarrello, Rob-
  ert Creeley, Judson Crews, Tom Cuson, Diane di Prima,
  Lawrence Ferlinghetti, Dennis Fritzinger, Allen Ginsberg,
  Barbara Guest, Bobbie Louise Hawkins, Thomas Head, Ericka
  Huggins, Jerry Kamstra, Jack Kerouac, Linda King, Jocelyn
  Koslofsky, Philip Lamantia, Reinhard Lettau, Michael McClure,
  Kay McDonough, Peter Manti, Herbert Marcuse, Diane Meucci,
  Jack Micheline, Patrick Mullins, Huey P. Newton, Harold
  Norse, Nancy Peters, Penelope Rosemont, Michael Rumaker,
  Gary Snyder, Kathleen Teague, Charles Upton, Andre Voznesen-
  sky, Richard Waara, Laurence Weisberg.

FIRMAGE, George J.; Oscar Williams.   A Garland for Dylan Thom-
as.   New York: Clarke & Way, 1963.
  Dannie Abse, Patrick Anderson, Eric Barker, George Barker,
  Helen Bevington, Ronald Bottrall, John Malcolm Brinnin, Wit-
  ter Bynner, John Ciardi, John W. Clark, Sister Claude of
  Jesus, Alex Comfort, Anthony Conran, Stanley Cooperman,
  Allen Curnow, C. Day Lewis, Babette Deutsch, Jane Esty,
  Kendrick Etheridge, Gavin Ewart, Lloyd Frankenberg, Isabella
  Gardner, Jean Garrigue, John Gawsworth, Eliot Glassheim,
  Francis Golffing, John Guenther, T. H. Jones, T. James
  Jones, Elizabeth Lambert, Jack Lindsay, Emanuel Litvinoff,
  John Logan, Hugh MacDiarmid, Louis MacNeice, Sister M.
  Maura, E. L. Mayo, Thomas Merton, Stanley Moss, John
  Nist, Leslie Norris, Elder Olson, Robert Pack, Katherine Jo
  Privett, George Reavey, Kenneth Rexroth, Theodore Roethke,
  Vernon Scannell, Tom Scott, Eli Siegel, Burns Singer, Edith
  Sitwell, Stephen Spender, Felix Stefanile, John Thompson,
  Ruthven Todd, Jose Garcia Villa, Vernon Watkins, Wilfred
  Watson, Phyllis Webb, Oscar Williams.

FOSTER, Dorothy.   In Praise of Cats.   New York: Crown, 1974.
  T. S. Eliot, William E. Harrold, Evelyn Hickman, Ted Hughes,
  Oliver Ingersoll, Randall Jarrell, Louis MacNeice, Martha

Osterso, E. J. Pratt, W. W. E. Ross, Carl Sandburg, Edith
Sitwell, A. S. J. Tessimond, William Carlos Williams.

FOX, Hugh. The Living Underground: An Anthology of Contempo-
rary American Poetry. Troy, N. Y. : Whitson, 1973.
Sharon Asselin, Steve Barfield, John Bennett, James Bertolino,
Douglas Blazek, Robert Bly, Alan Britt, Don Cauble, Richard
Collier, Kirby Congdon, Sam Cornish, Bill Costley, Hollace
Cross, Doug Craw, Joel Deutsch, Gerard Dombrowsky, Albert
Drake, Helen Duberstein, Paul Dyer, Darlene Fife, Thomas
Fitzsimmons, Hugh Fox, Glen Frank, Len Gasparini, Alex
Gildzen, Daniela Gioseffi, Don Gray, Charles Haseloff, Robert
Head, Dick Higgins, George Hitchcock, Will Inman, John Ja-
cob, Margie Johnson, Hugh Knox, Ronald B. Koertge, Allan
Kornblum, Richard Krech, Silvia Krohn, Diane Kruchkow, T.
L. Kryss, Greg Kuzma, D. A. Levy, Duane Locke, Gerry
Locklin, Lynn Lonidier, Marvin Malone, Adrianne Marcus,
Brown Miller, Robert Nelson Moore, Richard Morris, Norm
Moser, Stanley Nelson, Barbara O'Connelly, Claude Pelieu,
Charles Plymell, Dudley Randall, Pat Reh, Ottone Riccio,
Paul Roth, Roger Sauls, Scotty, John Oliver Simon, James
Soric, Terry Stokes, Bob Stout, Kent Taylor, Tom Taylor,
James S. Tipton, Mike Trudeau, H. L. Van Brunt, D. R.
Wagner, William Wantling, Phil Weidman, Paul Wildermann,
The Willie, A. D. Winans, Warren Woessner, Fred Wolver.

FREED, Ray. Doctor Generosity's Almanac: 17 Poets. New York:
Doctor Generosity Press, 1970.
Suzanne Berger-Rioff, Paul Blackburn, Robert Flanagan, John
Harris, C. H. Hejinian, Bill Little, Dan Murray, E. M. Nee,
Sanford Pinsker, D. M. Rosenberg, Howard Schwartz, Chris-
topher Smargie, Peter Van Toorn, Diane Wakoski, Barry Wal-
lenstein, Roger Weaver, G. Yavorsky.

FRIEDMAN, Richard; Peter Kostakis; Darlene Pearlstein. 15 Chi-
cago Pets. Chicago: Yellow Press, 1976.
Ted Berrigan, Walter Bradford, Gwendolyn Brooks, Paul
Carroll, Maxine Chernoff, Richard Friedman, Paul Hoover,
Angela Jackson, Henry Kanabus, Peter Kostakis, Art Lange,
Haki R. Madhubuti (Don L. Lee), Alice Notley, Darlene Pearl-
stein, Barry Schechter.

GALLERY SERIES III. Levitations & Observations. Chicago: Har-
per Square, 1970.
Gerald Adams, Michael Anania, Georgia Axtell, Carey Bacalar,
Etta Bearden, Estelle D. Broadrick, Art Cuelho, Kim Dam-
mers, Irene Dayton, Jack Donahue, J. B. Fiji, Phyllis Ford,
Gretchn Fraelick, Leonard Grilley, Emilie Glen, Christine
Gora, James Hagood, Fritz Hamilton, C. J. Jejinian, M. G.
Jacobs, John Judson, Jessie Kachmar, Nancy Lenau, S. John
Mary Lippert, Jane McCoy, Jeffrey Marienthal, Marcia Muth
Miller, G. R. Morgan, Helen Mullins, Neil Myers, Joyce
Odam, Felix Pollak, Harvey Plotnick, William Rosenfeld,

Sarah Ryder, Eileen Sarubbi, Marion Schoeberlein, Lynne
Slasor, Harold L. Simon, Pat Small, Richard Snyder, Stuart
Steckler, Anthony M. Stelmok, Walt Stevens, W. Allen Taylor,
Richard Charles Thayer, Francine Winant, Helen Winter, Mar-
tha Woodward.

GALLERY SERIES IV/POETS. I Am Talking About Revolution.
Chicago: Harper Square, 1973.
　　Mark Amen, Myrtle Archer, Ronald Baatz, June Brindel,
Alan Britt, randimeridithbrown, S. John Buttaci, Richard W.
Calisch, Martin Neil Charet, Art Cuelho, Irene Dayton, Susan
Lee Dickinson, John Dolan, Jack Donahue, Kimberly Dunham,
Morton Felix, Ross Figgins, Randolph Fingland, Ted Fleisch-
man, George Flynn, Phyllis Ford, Hugh Fox, Martha Fried-
berg, Philip Allan Friedman, Farren Gainer, Philip Gallo,
Tom Galt, Leonard Gilley, Emilie Glen, Lloyd Gold, Walter
Griffin, James Hagood, Fritz Hamilton, Lee Richard Hayman,
Archibald Henderson, Sandi Herschel, Barbara A. Holland,
Colette Inez, David Jaffin, Donald Farnham Johnson, John
Judson, James Koenig, L. N. Krause, Ann Krischon, Clara
Laster, Richard Latta, Esther M. Leiper, Don Levering,
Duane Locke, Lennart Lundh, Frederic Matteson, Ann Mene-
broker, Marcia Muth Miller, James Minor, Douglas Musella,
Joyce Odam, Enid Rhodes Peschel, Harvey M. Plotnick, Rob-
ert Roripaugh, Raymond Roseliep, Don Roscher, Norman H.
Russell, W. E. Ryan, Sarah Ryder, Marion Schoeberlein,
Barbara Kitterman Shepherd, Eve Siegel, Harold Simon, Diane
Stein, Robert Joe Stout, James W. Templeton, Hole Thatcher,
Richard Charles Thayer, Everard Thomson, Henrietta Weigel,
Helen Winter, Helen Gee Woods.

GANNETT, Lewis Stiles. The Family Book of Verse. New York:
Harper, 1961.
　　Rosemary Benet, Polly Chase Boyden, E. E. Cummings, T.
S. Eliot, Robert Frost, Langston Hughes, Robinson Jeffers,
Phyllis McGinley, Archibald MacLeish, John Masefield, Ogden
Nash, Carl Sandburg, James Thurber, Mark Van Doren, Peter
Viereck.

GARDNER, Helen. A Book of Religious Verse. New York: Ox-
ford, 1972.
　　W. H. Auden, John Betjeman, T. S. Eliot, David Gascoyne,
Louis MacNeice, Siegfried Sassoon, Edith Sitwell, Ronald
Stuart Thomas.

GAY, Reggie. Living Theatre Poems. New York: Boss, 1968.
　　Pamela Badyk, Cal Barber, Julian Beck, Rufus Collins,
Echnaton, Saul Gottlieb, Jenny Hecht, Birgit Knabe, Judith
Malina, Gianfranco Mantegna, Mary Mary, Gunter Pannewitz,
Bill Shari, Luke Theodore, Jim Tiroff, Leonardo Treviglio,
Diana Van Tosh, Petra Vogt.

GEORGAKAS, Dan. Z--An Anthology of Revolutionary Poetry. New York: Smyrna Press/Ikon Press, 1969.

Julian Beck, Doug Blazek, Charles Bukowski, Jim Burns, A. D. Clegg, Kirby Congdon, Dave Cunliffe, Madelina Davis, Diane Di Prima, George Dowden, Russel Edson, Dan Georgakas, Morgan Gibson, Saul Gottlieb, Marcus J. Grapes, Thanh Hai, Alex Hand, Shael Herman, David Herreshoff, Will Inman, Abdeen Jabara, LeRoi Jones, Etheridge Knight, T. L. Kryss, Gordon Arthur Lasslet, Walter Lowenfels, Dick Lourie, Alexis Lykiard, Judith Malina, Thanasis Maskaleris, Tina Morris, Harold Norse, Christopher Perret, Dudley Randall, Margaret Randall, Yannis Ritsos, Jeremy Robson, Sonia Sanchez, Minos Savvas, Fed Shaw, Yoshiko Shimizu, Vassilis Vasilikos, Carol Verlaan, William Wantling, Phil Weidman.

GERSMEHL, Glen. Words Among America. New York: Glen Gersmehl, 1971.

Maya Angelou, Austin, Leila Berg, Dan Berrigan, William Burford, Cesar Chavez, John Ciardi, Henry Dumas, William Eastlake, Richard Eberhart, Gene Fowler, Glen Gersmehl, Dottie Gittleson, Paul Goodman, Langston Hughes, LeRoi Jones, Jonathan Kaplan, Jo Kenney, Judith Kroll, Etheridge Knight, Don Lee, Morton Marcus, Eve Merriam, Thich Nhat-Hanh, Dudley Randall, Eugene Redmond, Theodore Roethke, Jean Tepperman, Quincy Troupe, Ngo Vinh Long, Jerry Wexler, Charles Wright.

GIBSON, James. Poetry & Song: An Anthology Chosen by James Gibson. New York: St. Martin's Press, 1967.

W. H. Auden, P. D. Bullock, Richard Church, Elizabeth J. Coatsworth, Geoffrey Dearmer, Elizabeth du Preez, T. S. Eliot, H. A. Field, John Fletcher, Robert Frost, Wilfrid Gibson, Harry Graham, Christopher Hassall, Lee Hays, Ted Hughes, Charles Kingsley, J. A. Lindon, Ewan MacColl, John Masefield, David Mowbray, Ogden Nash, Ruth Pitter, J. Redwood-Anderson, James Reeves, C. G. D. Roberts, Clive Sansom, Pete Seeger, Ian Serraillier, Edith Sitwell, Christopher Smart, Stevie Smith, Hal Summers, A. S. J. Tessimond, Michael Thompson, Gillian Wallington, Elizabeth Worraker, Andrew Young.

GIBSON, James. Poetry & Song. Book Two. New York: St. Martin's Press, 1967.

W. H. Auden, W. Bridges-Adams, Charles Causley, Elizabeth Coatsworth, Kevin Crossley-Holland, Cecil Day Lewis, Elizabeth du Preez, Clifford Dyment, T. S. Eliot, David Eva, Robert Frost, Robert Graves, Alexander Gray, Thom Gunn, Woody Guthrie, Edward Harrington, Linda Hughes, Ted Hughes, John Jeffers, Laurie Lee, Roger Lindley, J. A. Lindon, F. L. Lucas, Ewan MacColl, William McGonagall, Charles Martin, John Masefield, William Morris, Ogden Nash, Norman Nicholson, Ruth Pitter, James Reeves, Edwin Meade Robinson, Clive

Sansom, Siegfried Sassoon, Ian Serraillier, Edith Sitwell, Stevie Smith, Michael Thompson, Rex Warner, Andrew Young.

GIBSON, Margaret; Richard McCann. Landscape and Distance: Contemporary Poets from Virginia. Charlottesville: Univ. Press of Virginia, 1975.
John Alexander Allen, Amanda Bullins, Annie Dillard, R. H. W. Dillard, James Everhard, Jean Farley, Peter Fellowes, Joseph Garrison, Margaret Gibson, Bruce Guernsey, Kate Jennings, Richard McCann, Julia Randall, Gary Sange, Rudy Shackleford, David Jeddie Smith, William Jay Smith, Dabney Stuart, Eleanor Ross Taylor, Henry Taylor, Quentin Vest, Alan Williamson, Anne Winters.

GILDNER, Gary; Judith Gildner. Out of This World: Poems from the Hawkeye State. Ames: The Iowa State Univ. Press, 1975.
Joe David Bellamy, Richard Bissell, Josephine Edith Brown, Michael Dennis Brown, Raymond Carver, G. S. Sharat Chandra, Josephine Clare, Izora Corpman, R. R. Cuscaden, Ann Dara, Stephen Dobyns, Mark Doty, Ruth Doty, Paul Engle, Dave Etter, David Allan Evans, Donald Finkel, Gary Gildner, Daniel Halpern, Curtis Harnack, James Hearst, Carol Hebald, Philip Hey, Jim Heyen, Anselm Hollo, Mark Johnson, John Judson, Donald Justice, Bernard Kaplan, George Keithley, Dave Kelly, X. J. Kennedy, Bertha Kirkendall, Peter Klappert, John Knoepfle, Ted Kooser, Lawrence Kramer, Ernest Kroll, Joseph Langland, John Logan, Victoria McCabe, E. L. Mayo, Myra Mayo, Robert Mezey, Jack Musgrove, Nancy Price, David Ray, Ed Roberson, Raymond Roseliep, Kenneth Rosen, Ralph J. Salisbury, Dennis Schmitz, Jane Shore, Robert Slater, W. D. Snodgrass, William Stafford, Terry Stokes, Ann Struthers, Robert Sward, Dennis Trudell, Robley Wilson, Jr., David Young, Ray A. Young Bear, Susan Zwinger.

GILL, Elaine. Mountain Moving Day: Poems by Women. Trumansburg, N. Y.: Crossing Press, 1973.
Alta, Margaret Atwood, Carol Berge, Elizabeth Brewster, Carol Cox, Susan Griffin, Jessica Tarahata Hagedorn, Marie Harris, Erica Jong, Lyn Lifshin, Pat Lowther, Gwendolyn MacEwen, Marge Piercy, Cathleen Quirk, Phyllis Webb, Kathleen Wiegner, Fran Winant.

GILL, John. New American and Canadian Poetry. Boston: Beacon Press, 1971.
Milton Acorn, Margaret Atwood, Ken Belford, George Bowering, Aram Boyajian, Harley Elliott, Doug Fetherling, Ray Fraser, Len Gasparini, John Gill, Robert Hershon, Geof Hewitt, Emmett Jarrett, George Jonas, Etheridge Knight, Tom Kryss, Patric Lane, Irving Layton, Don L. Lee, Lyn Lifshin, Dick Lourie, David McFadden, Larry Mollin, John Newlove, Alden Nowlan, Robert Peterson, David Phillips, Marge Piercy, J. D. Reed, Dennis Saleh, Tom Schmidt, John Oliver Simon, Stephen Vincent, Ian Young.

GIOVANNI, Nikki. Night Comes Softly. Newark, N. J.: 1970.
Cecilia Africa, Karen Y. Amos (Adesina Ogunelese Akinwanile),
Claudia Anderson, Desiree A. Barnwell, Constance E. Berk-
ley, Diane Bogus, Gwendolyn Brooks, Ann Brown, Ellen M.
Brown, Margaret Burroughs, Carole Gregory Clemmons,
Beverly E. Coleman, Fran Collins (Fatema), Cynthia M. Con-
ley (Zubena), Emma Reno Connor, Priscilla L. Conway,
Jayne Cortez, Linda Cousins, Barbara Crosby, Doris Derby,
Vicky Donaldson, Jacqueline Earley, R. Early, Ethna, Mari
Evans, Carol Freeman, Nikki Giovanni, Bernette Golden,
Linda Goss, Naomi Grimes, Joyce Hansen, Frances Hartwell,
Gwendolyn Holmes, Mae Jackson, Sarah Jarvis, Bessie Jig-
getts, Alicia Johnson, Paulette Jones, June Jordan, Doris
Kemp, Jewel Lattimore, C. A. Lofton, Ruth Rambo McClain,
Arona L. McNeill, Jean M. McNeill, Barbara Mahone, Jean
Denise Mason, Sharon Bell Mathis, Jeannie Douglas Moore,
B. Omalade, Cuba Parks, Jean A. Parrish, Viola Parrish,
Marie M. Pitts, Joan Poe, Marcella Polk, Blossom E. Powe,
Susan Ramm, Isetta Crawford Rawls, Geinge Reed, Barbara
A. Reynolds, Carolyn Rodgers, Ann Sams, Sonia Sanchez,
Sherry Santifer, Carrie Simpson, Diana Teresa Slaughter,
Linda Snorton, Susan Soward, Rose Stewart, Lynn Suruma,
Margaret Walker, Ruth Jones Watson, Joyce Wheeler, Hilda
H. Whitaker, Cleo Williams, Deborah Williams, Sandra Wil-
liams, A. R. M. Woods. Romani Wordlaw, Roxy Lavizzo
Wright.

GITLIN, Todd. Campfires of the Resistance: Poetry from the
Movement. New York: Bobbs-Merrill, 1971.
R. H. Atkinson, Alan Austin, Dubjinsky Barefoot, Lee Baxand-
all, John Beecher, Charlie Bordin, Terry Cannon, Charlie
Cobb, Max Crawford, George Paul Csicsery, Tom Cuson,
Diane Di Prima, Charles Fager, Fred Gardner, Dan Georga-
kas, Allen Ginsberg, David Gitlin, Martin Glass, Paul Good-
man, Tim Hall, Casey Hayden, Christopher Z. Hobson, Will
Inman, Martha Kearns, Richard Krech, T. L. Kryss, Tuli
Kupferberg, Michael Lally, Philip Levine, Stephen Levine, D.
A. Levy, Lou Lipsitz, Dick Lourie, Marilyn Lowen, Marianne
Malley, Paul Mann, Robert Mezey, Robin Morgan, Robert No-
vick, Marge Piercy, Kenneth Pitchford, Craig Randolph Pyes,
Margaret Randall, Edward Romano, Liz Farrell Rose, Michael
Rossman, Danny Schechter, John Oliver Simon, David Sinclair,
John Sinclair, Gary Snyder, David Standish, Jane Stembridge,
Jean Tepperman, Maria Varela, Burton Ira Weiss, Doug
Youngblood.

GLIKES, Erwin A.; Paul Schwaber. Of Poetry and Power: Poems
Occasioned by the Presidency and by the Death of John F. Kennedy.
New York: Basic Books, 1964.
A. R. Ammons, Alan Ansen, W. H. Auden, Richard Barker,
Carol Berge, John Berryman, Roy Fuller, Dorothy Gilbert,
Allen Ginsberg, Michael Goldman, Paul Goodman, Ralph Gor-
don, Barbara Guest, Donald Hall, Robert Hazel, George Hitch-

cock, Robert Hollander, Anselm Hollo, Barbara Howes, Richard F. Hugo, David Ignatow, Will Inman, Donald L. Jones, Walter Kaufmann, X. J. Kennedy, Stanley Koehler, Myron Levoy, Audren McGaffin, Oscar Mandel, Jack Marshall, Josephine Miles, Marjorie Mir, Howard Moss, H. L. Mountzoures, Neil Myers, Richard O'Connell, Anthony Ostraff, Cynthia Ozick, Edward Pols, David Ray, Alastair Reid, Raymond Roseliep, Jerome G. Rothenberg, Harvey Shapiro, Robin Skelton, Marvin Solomon, Barry Spacks, Adrien Stoutenburg, Dabney Stuart, Robert Sward, May Swenson, John Tagliabue, Lorenzo Thomas, Robert G. Tucker, Lewis Turco, Florence Victor, Vernon Watkins, Robert Watson, James L. Weil, Thomas Whitbread, Reed Whittemore, Jonathan Williams, Charles Wright, George T. Wright, Ruth Landshoff Yorck, Louis Zukofsky.

GREAVES, Griselda. The Burning Thorn: An Anthology of Poetry. New York: Macmillan, 1971.
Dannie Abse, John Allcock, Samuel Allen, W. H. Auden, Gaston Bart-Williams, Andrew Baster, John Bennett, John Birkby, Peter Black, William Box, Edwin Brock, Gwendolyn Brooks, Alan Brownjohn, Charles Causley, Tony Connor, Gregory Corso, E. E. Cummings, P. D. Cummins, C. Day Lewis, Alan Dugan, T. S. Eliot, Ross Falconer, Joan Finnigan, Robert Frost, Roland Gant, Alan Garner, Robert Graves, Seamus Heaney, Adrian Henri, Francis Hope, Langston Hughes, Elizabeth Jennings, Joseph Kariuki, Philip Larkin, Laurie Lee, L. Paul Lloyd, Edward Lucie-Smith, Roger McGough, Louis MacNeice, Adrian Mitchell, Ian Mudie, Brian Patten, Mervyn Peake, Kathleen Raine, Flavien Ranaivo, Peter Redgrove, Elizabeth Riddell, Anne Ridler, Theodore Roethke, Colin Rowbotham, Clive Sansom, Siegfried Sassoon, Pradip Sen, Jack Simcock, Stevie Smith, Wole Soyinka, James O. Taylor, R. S. Thomas, John Wain, Richard Wilbur.

GREGORY, Horace; Marya Zaturenska. The Crystal Cabinet. An Invitation to Poetry. New York: Holt, Rinehart and Winston, 1962.
Leonie Adams, Thomas Bateson, Basil Bunting, E. E. Cummings, Hilda Doolittle, Robert Duncan, T. S. Eliot, Dudley Fitts, Robert Fitzgerald, Robert Frost, Robert Graves, Arthur Gregor, Horace Gregory, Robert Hillyer, Hugh MacDiarmid, Archibald MacLeish, Marianne Moore, Ruth Pitter, Ezra Pound, Carl Sandburg, Winfield Townley Scott, Edith Sitwell, Sacheverell Sitwell, William Carlos Williams, Marya Zaturenska.

GREGORY, Horace; Marya Zaturenska. The Silver Swan: Poems of Romance and Mystery. New York: Holt, Rinehart, and Winston, 1966.
Conrad Aiken, Marion Angus, W. H. Auden, Elizabeth Bishop, Stanley Burnshaw, E. E. Cummings, Hilda Doolittle, T. S. Eliot, Dudley Fitts, Robert Fitzgerald, Robert Frost, Robert Graves, Arthur Gregor, Horace Gregory, Ted Hughes, Robinson Jeffers, Robert Lowell, Claire McAllastair, C. F. Mac-

Intyre, Archibald MacLeish, Louis MacNeice, Ernst Morwitz, Ruth Pitter, John Crowe Ransom, Charles Reznikoff, Geoffrey Scott, Edith Sitwell, Sacheverell Sitwell, Rachel Annand Taylor, Carol Valhope, Geoffrey Wagner, Theodore Weiss, Marya Zaturenska.

GROSS, Ronald; George Quasha; Emmett Williams; John Robert Colombo; Walter Lowenfels. Open Poetry: Four Anthologies of Expanded Poems. New York: Simon and Schuster, 1973.
Helen Adams, David Antin, Eleanor Antin, Jerry Badanes, Michael Benedikt, Lawrence Benford, George Bowering, George Brecht, Claus Bremer, Edwin Brooks, David Bromige, Norman O. Brown, Charles Bukowski, Olga Cabral, John Cage, Terry Cannon, Harold Carrington, Len Chandler, John Robert Colombo, Kirby Congdon, Philip Corner, Bobbie L. Creeley, John Daniel, Richard Davidson, Augusto de Campos, Haroldo de Campos, Alvaro de Sa, Harold Dicker, George Dowden, Harold Dull, Henry Dumas, Denis Dunn, George Economou, Russell Edson, Larry Eigner, Clayton Eshleman, Carl Fernbach-Flarsheim, Robert Filliou, Ian Hamilton Finlay, John Giorno, Nikki Giovanni, Eugen Gomringer, Ronald Gross, Jim Harrison, Michael Heller, David Henderson, Calvin C. Hernton, Dick Higgins, Elton Hill-Abu Ishak, Anselm Hollo, Gerald Jackson, Lance Jeffers, Alicia L. Johnson, Halvard Johnson, Joe Johnson, David Jones, Allan Kaprow, Bob Kaufman, Robert Kelly, Etheridge Knight, Bill Knott, Alison Knowles, Joel Kohut, Ferdinand Kriwet, T. L. Kryss, Frank Kuenstler, Markus Kutter, Joanne Kyger, Robert Lax, Don L. Lee, Walter Lowenfels, Edward Lucie-Smith, Jackson Mac Low, Clarence Major, Hansjorg Mayer, Ifeanyi Menkiti, Thomas Merton, John Montague, Edwin Morgan, Peter G. Neumann, Lorine Niedecker, Geoffrey O'Brien, Richard O'Connell, Claes Oldenburg, George Oppen, Anne Oswald, Rochelle Owens, Nicanor Parra, Benjamin Patterson, John Perreault, Robert L. Peters, Dom Robert Petitpierre, Decio Pignatari, Felix Pollak, Bern Porter, George Quasha, Lennox Raphael, Eugene Redmond, Carolyn Rodgers, Diter Rot, Jerome Rothenberg, Gerhard Ruhm, Frank Samperi, Sonia Sanchez, Armand Schwerner, Hugh Seidman, Charles Simic, Thurmond Snyder, Mary Ellen Solt, George Stanley, Charles Stein, Tar Lee Sun, Nathaniel Tarn, James Tenney, Harvey Tucker, Robert Vas Dias, Diane Wakoski, William Wantling, Eliot Weinberger, Hannah Weiner, Nancy Willard, Emmett Williams, Louis Zukofsky.

GWYNN, Frederick L.; Ralph W. Condee; Arthur O. Lewis, Jr. The Case for Poetry: A Critical Anthology. Englewood Cliffs, N.J.: Prentice-Hall, 1965.
Conrad Aiken, W. H. Auden, John Betjeman, Philip Booth, John Ciardi, E. E. Cummings, Carl De Suze, Alan Dugan, Richard Eberhart, T. S. Eliot, Kenneth Fearing, Robert Francis, Robert Frost, Thom Gunn, Donald Hall, Randall Jarrell, X. J. Kennedy, Denise Levertov, Archibald MacLeish, Ogden

Nash, Howard Nemerov, Ezra Pound, John Crowe Ransom, Henry Reed, Theodore Roethke, Carl Shapiro, Stephen Spender, George Starbuck, Richard Wilbur.

HAAS, Russ. Tarzan and Shane Meet the Toad. Long Beach, Calif.: Russ Haas Press, 1975.
Ronald Koertge, Gerald Locklin, Charles Stetler.

HADASSAH. The End. San Francisco: 1965.
C. V. J. Anderson, Harold Bann, Jerry Bloedow, Robert Bloom, Jerry Coonley, Bruce Grund, Hadassah, Tim S. Holt, Charles Kamp, Leo Kartman, Amrit Lal, Thea Marcus, Leland S. Meyerzone, C. J. Newman, B. A. Uronovitz, Alex Van Gelder, Omer Wilson, Yampolsky.

HALL, Donald. Contemporary American Poetry. Baltimore: Penguin, 1962.
John Ashbery, Robert Bly, Edgar Bowers, Robert Creeley, James Dickey, Robert Duncan, Anthony Hecht, Donald Justice, X. J. Kennedy, Galway Kinnell, Denise Levertov, John Logan, Robert Lowell, James Merrill, W. S. Merwin, Robert Mezey, Howard Nemerov, Adrienne Rich, Louis Simpson, W. D. Snodgrass, Gary Snyder, William Stafford, Reed Whittemore, Richard Wilbur, James Wright.

HALL, Donald. A Poetry Sampler. New York: Franklin Watts, 1962.
W. H. Auden, Elizabeth Bishop, Charles Causley, E. E. Cummings, J. V. Cunningham, Richard Eberhart, T. S. Eliot, Kenneth Fearing, Robert Francis, Robert Frost, Robert Graves, Ralph Hodgson, Barbara Howes, Robert Lowell, Archibald MacLeish, Louis MacNeice, Vassar Miller, Marianne Moore, Ezra Pound, John Crowe Ransom, Theodore Roethke, Karl Shapiro, Louis Simpson, Stephen Spender, Richard Wilbur, William Carlos Williams, Yvor Winters.

HALL, Donald. New Poets of England and America: Second Selection. Cleveland: World, 1962.
Kingsley Amis, Gene Baro, Philip Booth, Arthur Boyars, George Mackay Brown, Jane Cooper, Henri Coulette, Donald Davie, James Dickey, Donald Finkel, John Fuller, S. S. Gardons, Thom Gunn, Donald Hall, Michael Hamburger, Anthony Hecht, Geoffrey Hill, David Holbrook, John Hollander, Robert Huff, Ted Hughes, Elizabeth Jennings, Donald Justice, X. J. Kennedy, Galway Kinnell, Carolyn Kizer, Melvin Walker La Follette, Philip Larkin, Laurence Lerner, Denise Levertov, Peter Levi, Philip Levine, John Logan, Edward Lucie-Smith, George Macbeth, James Merrill, W. S. Merwin, Robert Mezey, James Michie, Christopher Middleton, Vassar Miller, Dom Moraes, Howard Moss, Robert Pack, Ronald Perry, Donald Petersen, Sylvia Plath, David Ray, Peter Redgrove, Alastair Reid, Adrienne Rich, Anne Sexton, Jon Silkin, Louis Simpson,

Burns Singer, Iain Crichton Smith, W. D. Snodgrass, George Starbuck, Anthony Thwaite, Charles Tomlinson, David Wagoner, John Wain.

HALLMARK. Poems 1966: Prize Selections in the Third Annual Kansas City Poetry Contest. Kansas City: Hallmark Cards, 1966.
Tom Anderson, Laurel E. Bird, Carol Bosworth, Amarette Callaway, R. P. Dickey, Douglas Flaherty, Lynn Graznak, Del Hilyard, Paul Hopper, Geoffrey A. Oelsner, Jr., Molly Mattfield, Saul Touster, Joe Wittich, Ko Won.

HALPERN, Daniel. The American Poetry Anthology. Boulder, Colo.: Westview, 1975.
Ai, Jon Anderson, Marvin Bell, Michael Benedikt, Frank Bidart, Michael Dennis Browne, Lucille Clifton, Conyus, Peter Cooley, Philip Dacey, Rita Dove, Philip Dow, Norman Dubie, Stephen Dunn, Russell Edson, Susan Feldman, Carolyn Forche, Kathleen Fraser, Tess Gallagher, Gary Gildner, Louise Gluck, Linda Gregg, Marilyn Hacker, Daniel Halpern, Michael S. Harper, Jim Harrison, Robert Hass, William Heyen, Lawson Fusao Inada, Thomas James, Laura Jensen, Erica Jong, Peter Klappert, Judith Kroll, Greg Kuzma, Al Lee, Fred Levinson, Larry Levis, Elizabeth Libbey, Thomas Lux, Angela McCabe, David McElroy, Heather McHugh, James McMichael, Sandra McPherson, William Matthews, Robert Mezey, Paul Monette, Carol Muske, Jack Myers, Gregory Orr, Greg Pape, John Peck, Stanley Plumly, Lawrence Raab, James Reiss, Kenneth Rosen, Michael Ryan, Ira Sadoff, David St. John, Dennis Schmitz, Hugh Seidman, Charles Simic, Roberta Spear, Kathleen Spivack, Maura Stanton, Terry Stokes, Brian Swann, James Tate, Diane Wakoski, Alice Walker, Roger Weingarten, James Welch, Peter Wild, Charles Wright, David Young.

HANNA, Charles. New Poets. Allentown, Pa.: 1960.
Carl Alexy, George Allen, William Brobst, Frederick Busch, William Countess, Richard David, James Ginnegan, Charles Hanna, Elliot Puritz, Marlene Rachmeil, Martin Ruoss, Richard Williams, Bill Wingell, Edith Zimmerman.

HANNUM, Sara; John Terry Chase. To Play Man Number One. New York: Atheneum, 1969.
W. H. Auden, Wendell Berry, Robert Bly, Philip Booth, Shirley Bridges, Gwendolyn Brooks, Charles Causley, Robert Creeley, E. E. Cummings, C. Day Lewis, Babette Deutsch, James Dickey, Alan Dugan, Lawrence Durrell, Richard Eberhart, Robert Frost, Robert Graves, Horace Gregory, Thom Gunn, Donald Hall, Phyllis Masek Harris, Lawrence Hetrick, Barbara Howes, Langston Hughes, David Ignatow, Randall Jarrell, Donald Justice, Jack Kerouac, Crystal Kilgore, Galway Kinnell, Joseph Langland, Richmond Lattimore, Denise Levertov, Robert Lowell, Rod McKuen, Archibald MacLeish, Louis MacNeice, William H. Matchett, Jack Mathews, William

Meredith, Vassar Miller, Marianne Moore, Lisel Mueller, Howard Nemerov, Kenneth Patchen, Sylvia Plath, John Crowe Ransom, Alastair Reid, Adrienne Rich, Theodore Roethke, Carl Sandburg, James Scully, Anne Sexton, Karl Shapiro, Louis Simpson, Stephen Spender, William Stafford, Jon Stallworthy, Ann Stanford, May Swenson, John Updike, Jean Valentine, Mark Van Doren, David Wagoner, John Hall Wheelock, Richard Wilbur, Keith Wilson, James Wright, Marya Zaturenska.

HANNUM, Sara; John Terry Chase. The Wind Is Round. New York: Atheneum, 1970.
Elizabeth Bishop, Robert Bly, Philip Booth, Babette Deutsch, James Dickey, Peter Kane Dufault, Richard Eberhart, Robert Frost, Michael Goldman, Robert Graves, Thom Gunn, Donald Hall, Jim Harrison, Ted Hughes, Galway Kinnell, Joseph Langland, Philip Larkin, Denise Levertov, William H. Matchett, Jack Matthews, Howard Moss, Howard Nemerov, Kenneth Patchen, Alastair Reid, Adrienne Rich, Theodore Roethke, Muriel Rukeyser, Carl Sandburg, Delmore Schwartz, James Scully, Anne Sexton, Ann Stanford, Adrien Stoutenburg, Jon Swan, May Swenson, Mark Van Doren, Ted Walker, John Hall Wheelock, Richard Wilbur, William Carlos Williams, Keith Wilson.

HARLAN, William K. Probes: An Introduction to Poetry. New York: Macmillan, 1973.
Conrad Aiken, Richard Albert, A. R. Ammons, John Ashbery, W. H. Auden, Kathryn Baer, Ted Berrigan, Helen Berryhill, John Berryman, Richard Brautigan, Gwendolyn Brooks, Damian Brown, Joanne Busby, John Cage, Margaret Cesa, Tom Clark, Leonard Cohen, Clark Coolidge, Gregory Corso, Mike Cortes, Robert Creeley, E. E. Cummings, J. V. Cunningham, Ann Debban, James Dickey, Sally Ann Drucker, Robert Duncan, Richard Eberhart, T. S. Eliot, Chana Faerstein, Lawrence Ferlinghetti, Andrew Flege, Paul Foreman, Stephen Formby, Gene Fowler, Kathleen Fraser, Robert Frost, Lloyd George, Allen Ginsberg, Marty Glaberman, Eugene Gomringer, Janice Gould, Don Graham, Robert Graves, J. W. Hackett, Debbie Halpin, Mary Harlan, Mike Harper, Barbara Harr, Christopher Harvey, Robert Hayden, Thomas Head, Anne Hedley, David Henderson, C. R. Hoffman, Heinrich Hoffman, Bernadette Holthius, Langston Hughes, J. Huizinga, David Ignatow, Colette Inez, Randall Jarrell, Robinson Jeffers, Bruce C. Johnson, LeRoi Jones, Shirley Kaufman, Paul Keller, Jimmy Kelso, Galway Kinnell, Carolyn Kizer, Mimi Klimesh, Kenneth Koch, James Koller, Richard Kostelanetz, Philip Lamantia, Lonnie Leard, Denise Levertov, John L'Heureux, Lipsitz, Robert Lowell, Michael McClure, Archibald MacLeish, Morton Marcus, Jack Marion, Laura Mead, Josephine Miles, John Miller, Marianne Moore, Anne Morken, Kelly Mullins, Leonard Nathan, G. C. Oden, Frank O'Hara, Charles Olson, Jonathan Palley, Kenneth Patchen, Benjamin Peret, Sylvia

Plath, Ezra Pound, Sharon O. Ramirez, John Crowe Ransom, Greg Rathjen, Henry Reed, Kenneth Rexroth, Foster Robertson, Theodore Roethke, Pamela Rogers, R-P-O-P-H-E-S-S-A-G-R, Vern Rutsala, Carl Sandburg, Aram Saroyan, James Schevill, Allan J. Schurr, Delmore Schwartz, Paul Secic, Harvey Shapiro, Karl Shapiro, John Showalter, T. S. Shulgin, Charles Simic, John Simonitch, W. D. Snodgrass, Gary Snyder, O. M. B. Southard, Stephen Spender, Gary Stark, Charles Stillwell, Robert J. Stout, Lynn Strongin, Arthur Sze, Charles C. Thomas, Mike Tuggle, Stephen Vincent, David Wagoner, Diane Wakoski, Karla Wallis, Ann Walsh, John A. Ward, Lew Welch, Philip Whalen, Thomas Whitbread, Geoff White, Richard Wilbur, William Carlos Williams, Allen Wisner, James Wright, Frederic Young, Louis Zukofsky.

HARRIS, Marguerite. Emily Dickinson: Letters from the World. New York: Cymric Press, 1970.
Charles Angoff, Jack Anderson, Sam Bradley, Marion Buchman, David Burns, Joseph Cohen, Gregory Corso, Wesley Day, Peter M. Desy, Ree Dargonette, Richard Eberhart, Dave Etter, Allen Ginsberg, Louis Ginsberg, Marguerite Harris, William Heyen, Robert Huff, Constance Hunting, Allen Katzman, Louise Mally, Parm Mayer, Ralph Moss, Violette Newton, Thomas Orr, Bill Porter, George Quasha, Adrienne Rich, Rose Rosberg, Raymond Rosliep, Larry Rubin, Stuart Silverman, Ted Simmons, Peter L. Simpson, William Stafford, Stephen Stepanchev, John Tytell, Eve Triem, J. Unland, John Wheatcroft, Theodore Weiss, Peter Wild, Yvor Winters, Harold Witt, Honora M. Zimmer.

HARRIS, Marguerite. Loves, Etc. Garden City, N. Y.: Doubleday, 1973.
Helen Adam, Carol Berge, John Berryman, Paul Blackburn, Robert Bly, Louise Bogan, Michael Dennis Browne, Doreen Caraher, Marvin Cohen, Robert Cohen, Cid Corman, Robert Creeley, J. V. Cunningham, Robert Duncan, George Economou, Ted Enslin, Isabella Gardner, Allen Ginsberg, Andrew Glaze, Marguerite Harris, Barbara Holland, David Ignatow, Colette Inez, Gloria Kaplan, Allen Katzman, X. J. Kennedy, Galway Kinnell, Bill Knott, Kenneth Koch, Richard Kostelanetz, William Lane, Denise Levertov, John Logan, Walter Lowenfels, Dick Lourie, Jackson Mac Low, Clive Matson, W. S. Merwin, Sergio Mondragon, Violette Newton, Bob Nichols, Gloria Oden, Charles Olson, Toby Olson, George Oppen, Joel Oppenheimer, Zylvia Plath, Margaret Randall, Rochelle Ratner, Gomer Rees, Adrienne Rich, Ed Sanders, Armand Schwerner, Hugh Seidman, Stevie Smith, William Stafford, Mark Strand, R. S. Thomas, Jean Valentine, Diane Wakoski, Frances Whyatt, Jonathan Williams, William Carlos Williams, James Wright, Al Young, Louis Zukofsky.

HARRIS, Marguerite. A Tumult for John Berryman. San Francisco: Dryad Press, 1976.

Jim Barnes, Ted Benttinen, Bruce Berlind, Michael Berryhill, Michael Dennis Browne, Evans Chigounis, William F. Claire, Catherine Coleman, Donald Davie, Peter Davison, R. H. Deutsch, Stuart Dischell, Maureen Duffy, Roy Fisher, Doug Flaherty, Robert Forrey, William Harmon, Marguerite Harris, Charles Haseloff, Roger Hecht, Michael Heffernan, Anita Heller, Barbara A. Holland, David Ignatow, Dennis Johnson, David Keller, Ted Kooser, Peter L. Kazik, Ernest Kroll, Richard Lattimore, Paris Leary, Barbara F. Lefcowitz, Merrill Leffler, Jack Litewka, Michael Lopes, Robert Lowell, Michael Lynch, Arthur Marx, Richard Mathews, Williams Matthews, John Matthias, Peter Meinke, William Meredith, Judity Minty, Herbert Morris, Ralph Palma, Rodney Pybus, Percival Roberts, Raymond Roseliep, Richard Ryan, Stephen Stepanchev, Ruthven Todd, Ed Zahniser.

HARVEY, Nick. Mark in Time. San Francisco: Glide Publications, 1971.
Wilder Bentley, Jeff Berner, Harvey Bialy, Kay Boyle, Richard Brautigan, David Bromige, James Broughton, Lennart Bruce, Victor Hernandez Cruz, Alan Dienstag, Philip Dow, William Everson, Lawrence Ferlinghetti, Gene Fowler, Luis Garcia, Allen Ginsberg, David Gitin, Madeline Gleason, Rafael Jesus Gonzalez, Thom Gunn, Michael S. Harper, John Hart, David Henderson, Jan Herman, George Hitchcock, Andrew Hoyem, Jeanetta L. Jones, Bob Kaufman, Shirley Kaufman, Dan Kenney, Mary Norbert Korte, C. H. Kwock, Joanne Kyger, Daniel J. Langton, Robert Leverant, Amilcar Lobos, Jeanne McGahey, Vincent McHugh, Adrianne Marcus, Morton Marcus, Michael McClure, David Meltzer, Josephine Miles, Wayne Miller, Janice Mirikitani, Jose Montoya, Daniel Moore, Rosalie Moore, Norman Ogue Mustill, Leonard Nathan, George Oppen, Fred Ostrander, Anthony Ostroff, Patricia A. Parker, Thomas Parkinson, Claude Pelieu, Robert Peterson, Charles Plymell, Ishmael Reed, Kenneth Rexroth, Stan Rice, Eugene Ruggles, David Schaff, James Schevill, Nina Serrano, John Oliver Simon, Patrick Smith, Gary Snyder, George Stanley, Lynn Strongin, Kathleen Teague, Sotere Torregian, Charles Upton, Nanos Valsoritis, Lewis Warsh, Ruth Weiss, Lew Welch, John Wieners, Pete Winslow, Al Young.

HAUGE, Bob. Pandemonium: Poems. New York: Pandemonium, 1960.
Mark Di Suvero, Bob Hauge, Landes Lewitin, Donna Miller, Pat Passlof, Hank Raleigh, Milton Resnick, Beate Wheeler, Lyn Williams.

HAUSMAN, Gerald; David Silverstein. The Berkshire Anthology. Lenox, Mass.: Bookstore Press, 1972.
Ron Atkinson, Clark Coolidge, Sam Cornish, Halsey Davis, William DeVoti, Jack Driscoll, Gerald Hausman, Donald Junkins, David Kherdian, Ruth Krauss, Gerard Malanga, Sushil

Mukherjee, Charles Parriott, Lawrence Raab, Aaron Schneider, Benjamin Steele, William Touponce, Ruth Whitman, S. P. Wonder.

HAYDEN, Robert. Kaleidoscope: Poems by American Negro Poets. New York: Harcourt, Brace & World, 1967.
Samuel Allen, Gerald William Barrax, Arna Bontemps, Gwendolyn Brooks, Sterling A. Brown, Margaret Danner, Frank Marshall Davis, Owen Dodson, James A. Emanuel, Mari Evans, Julia Fields, D. L. Graham, Robert Jayden, David Henderson, Calvin C. Hernton, Carl Wendell Hines, Jr., M. Carl Holman, Frank Horne, Ted Joans, LeRoi Jones, Bob Kaufman, Julius Lester, Naomi Long Madgett, G. C. Oden, Myron O'Higgins, Oliver Pitcher, Dudley Randall, Conrad Kent Rivers, Anne Spencer, Melvin B. Tolson, Jean Toomer, Margaret Abigail Walker.

HEAD, Thomas; Paul Foreman. The San Francisco Bark. A Gathering of Bay Area Poets. Berkeley, Calif.: Thorp Springs Press, 1972.
Hilary Ayer, Layeh Bock, Bill Boydstun, Francis Carlet, Margaret Cesa, Wendy Crooks, Tom Flusty, Paul Foreman, Gene Fowler, Carmen Fraser, David Gitlin, Morton Grinker, Thomas Head, Anne Hedley, Judith Hogan, Bruce Johnson, Helena Knox, Dennis Koran, Lonnie Leard, Ken McKeon, Paul Mariah, Daniel Marlin, Josephine Miles, M. Scott Momaday, William Morgan, Richard Morris, Drew Nash, Leonard Nathan, Morton Paley, David Plumb, David Riley, Foster Robertson, Alice Rogoff, Floyd Salas, T. A. Shulgin, John Simon, Ginny Staley, Robert Stock, Hester Storm, J. Anthony Stowers, Lynn Strongin, Arthur Sze, Julia Vinograd.

HEARSE PRESS. Nine by Three. Eureka, Calif.: Hearse Press, 1962.
Robert Beum, Maxine Cassin, Felix Stefanile.

HECHT, Anthony; John Hollander. Jiggery-Pokery. A Compendium of Double Dactyls. New York: Atheneum, 1967.
Sally Belfrage, Irma Brandeis, Donald Hall, Anthony Hecht, John Hollander, Richard Howard, James Merrill, Arthur W. Monks, Paul Pascal, Eric Salzman, E. William Seaman, Nancy L. Stark, Christopher Wallace-Crabbe.

HENDERSON, Stephen. Understanding the New Black Poetry: Black Speech and Black Music as Poetic References. New York: Morrow, 1973.
Margaret Walker Alexander, Samuel Allen, Johari Amini, I. A. Baraka, Gerald W. Barrax, Lillie Kate Walker Benitez, Lebert Bethune, Sharon Bourke, Gwendolyn Brooks, H. Rap Brown, Sterling A. Brown, Karl Carter, Walter Dancy, Margaret Danner, Frank Marshall Davis, Walter De Legall, Owen Dodson, Henry Dumas, Ebon, James A. Emanuel, Mari Evans, Sarah Webster Fabio, Betty Gates, Nikki Giovanni, Oswald

Govan, Donald L. Graham, Gregor Hannibal, Michael Harper, Robert Hayden, David Henderson, Pamela Woodruff Hill, Langston Hughes, Ted Hunt, Lance Jeffers, Ted Joans, Percy E. Johnston, Bob Kaufman, W. Keorapetse Kgositsile, Etheridge Knight, Ladele X (Leslie Powell), Don L. Lee, Audre Lorde, Leo J. Mason, Larry Neal, Daphne Diane Page, Dudley Randall, Eugene Redmond, Nathan A. Richards, Conrad Kent Rivers, Carolyn M. Rogers, Sonia Sanchez, Judy Dothard Simmons, A. B. Spellman, Le Roy Stone, Melvin B. Tolson, Askia Muhammad Toure, Jay Wright.

HEWITT, Geof. Quickly Aging Here: Some Poets of the 1970's. Garden City, N. Y.: Anchor, 1969.
Susan Axelrod, Floyce Alexander, Coleman Barks, William Brown, Gerald Butler, Joseph Cardarelli, Sophi Castro-Leon, Raymond Di Palma, Philip Dow, Peter Fellowes, Dan Gillespie, Barbara L. Greenberg, Alfred Starr Hamilton, Thomas Hanna, William Harmon, William Hathaway, David Hilton, Fanny Howe, Colette Inez, Denis Johnson, Shirley Kaufman, luke (Joseph Brown), Sandford Lyne, Gregory Orr, Edgar Paiewonsky, Stuart Peterfreund, Rochelle Ratner, Stan Rice, Don Shea, Stephen Shrader, Mary Ellen Solt, Craig Sterry, Eric Torgersen, Dennis Trudell, William Witherup.

HEYEN, William. American Poets in 1976. Indianapolis: Bobbs-Merrill, 1976.
Robert Bly, John Malcolm Brinnin, Robert Creeley, John Haines, John Haislip, William Heyen, Richard Hugo, David Ignatow, John Logan, William Mathews, Jerome Mazzaro, William Meredith, Joyce Carol Oates, Linda Pastan, Raymond R. Patterson, John Peck, Stanley Plumly, Ishmael Reed, Adrienne Rich, M. L. Rosenthal, Anne Sexton, Louis Simpson, Dave Smith, William Stafford, Primus St. John, Lucien Stryke, Lewis Turco, James Wright, Paul Zimmer.

HIEATT, A. Kent; William Park. The College Anthology of British and American Verse. Boston: Allyn and Bacon, 1964.
W. H. Auden, Gregory Corso, E. E. Cummings, Richard Eberhart, T. S. Eliot, Robert Frost, Robert Graves, Philip Larkin, Robert Lowell, Archibald MacLeish, Robert Mezey, Marianne Moore, John Morris, Ezra Pound, Theodore Roethke, Anne Sexton, W. D. Snodgrass, Allen Tate, Richard Wilbur, William Carlos Williams, James Wright.

HINE, Al. This Land Is Mine: An Anthology of American Verse. Philadelphia: J. B. Lippincott, 1965.
John Ciardi, E. E. Cummings, Fredrick Ebright, Kenneth Fearing, Robert Frost, Joe Glazer, Al Hine, Robert Lowell, Ernest McGaffey, Phyllis McGinley, Archibald MacLeish, William Tucker Meredith, Howard Nemerov, Ezra Pound, Innes Randolph, Claude Reeves, Edwin Rolfe, Delmore Schwartz, Karl Shapiro, Louis Simpson, Adrien Stoutenburg, Peter Viereck.

HITCHCOCK, George. Losers, Weepers: Poems Found Practically
Everywhere. San Francisco: Kayak Books, 1969.
>Robert Berner, John Robert Columbo, Wayne Dodd, Albert
Drake, Darrell Gray, Ronald Gross, H. R. Hays, Jacob Her-
man, Tim Hildebrand, George Hitchcock, Donald Justice,
Shirley Kaufman, Daniel Langton, Jacqueline McFarland, Thom-
as Merton, Sasha Nejgebauer, Robert Peters, Robert Peterson,
John Ridland, Lee Rudolph, R. E. Seibert, James Tate, James
Sherwood Tipton, Eric Torgersen, Hannah Weiner.

HOFFMAN, Daniel. University & College Poetry Prizes 1967-72.
The Academy of American Poets, 1974.
>Jill Kelsey Aeschbacher, Susan Roe Anthony, Jody Bolz, Cin
Bourgeault, Romola Brady, Jerald Bullis, Noel Callow, Criss
Ellen Cannady, Marty Cohen, Richard Cohen, Richard Duffee,
Stephen Dunn, Hugo Ekback, Florence Elon, Tess Gallagher,
Daniel Allen Gray, Daniel Guillory, Annette Hammer, Marcia
Hastie, Jamie James, Rodney Jones, William Keens, Greg
Kuzma, Larry Levis, A. J. Litwinio, Lawrence Locke, Heath-
er McHugh, Leonard Marcus, Eugene Minard, Judith Moffett,
William A. Nelson, Sallie Nixon, Gregory Orr, Robert Paw-
lowski, Richard Preston, Lawrence Raab, Jean A. Reeve,
Mark Rudman, Michael Rush, Robert B. Shaw, Alex Silber-
man, Judith Soucek, Susan Squier, Joan Stone, Stephen Tap-
scott, Rod Taylor, Rod Townley, Michael Wolfe.

HOLLANDER, John. Poems of Our Moment. New York: Pegasus,
1968.
>A. R. Ammons, John Ashbery, Gregory Corso, Donald Davie,
Robert Dawson, James Dickey, Alvin Feinman, Allen Ginsberg,
Allen Grossman, Thom Gunn, Anthony Hecht, Daryl Hine, John
Hollander, A. D. Hope, Richard Howard, Ted Hughes, Kenneth
Koch, Jay MacPherson, James Merrill, W. S. Merwin, Frank
O'Hara, Sylvia Plath, Adrienne Rich, Frederick Seidel, David
Shapiro, Jon Silkin, Louis Simpson, W. D. Snodgrass, Gary
Snyder, Mark Strand, May Swenson, Charles Tomlinson, Chris
Wallace-Crabbe, James Wright.

HOLMES, Paul C.; Anita J. Lehman. Keys to Understanding: Re-
ceiving and Sending the Poem. New York: Harper & Row, 1969.
>Conrad Aiken, W. H. Auden, Helen Berryhill, Beth Biderman,
Paul Blackburn, Philip Booth, Robert P. Tristram Coffin,
Frances Cornford, E. E. Cummings, Waring Cuney, Frank
Marshall Davis, Mari Evans, Lawrence Ferlinghetti, Edward
Field, Robert Francis, Kahlil Gibran, Thom Gunn, Geroge
Harrison, Richard Hovey, Langston Hughes, Randall Jarrell,
Ted Joans, Donald Justice, Hannah Kahn, X. J. Kennedy,
John Lennon, Paul McCartney, Phyllis McGinley, Rod McKuen,
Josephine Miles, Merrill Moore, Bonaro W. Overstreet, Dor-
othy Parker, Kenneth Patchen, Raymond Patterson, Ralph
Pomeroy, Henry Reed, Theodore Roethke, Karl Shapiro,
Stephan Taugher, Mildred Weston, Richard Wright.

HOPE, D. C. The Wolgamot Interstice. Ann Arbor, Mich. :
Burning Deck, 1961.
James Camp, Donald Hall, John Heath-Stubbs, D. C. Hope,
Bernard Keith, X. J. Kennedy, W. D. Snodgrass, Dallas
Wiebe.

HOPKINS, Lee Bennett. On Our Way: Poems of Pride and Love.
New York: Knopf, 1974.
Peter Abrahams, Gwendolyn Brooks, Lucille Clifton, Linda
Curry, Mari Evans, Nikki Giovanni, Michael S. Harper, David
Henderson, Langston Hughes, Maurice Shelley Jackson, Kojo
Gyinaye Kyei, Don L. Lee, Naomi Long Madgett, Raymond
Richard Patterson, Linda Porter, Quandra Prettyman, Dudley
Randall, Jo Nell Rice, Richard Rive, Yolande Zealy.

HOPKINS, Lee Bennett. Take Hold! An Anthology of Pulitzer Prize
Winning Poems. New York: Thomas Nelson, 1974.
Elizabeth Bishop, Gwendolyn Brooks, Robert P. Tristram Cof-
fin, Richard Eberhart, Robert Frost, Robert Hillyer, Phyllis
McGinley, Archibald MacLeish, W. S. Merwin, Carl Sandburg,
Louis Simpson, Leonora Speyer, Mark Van Doren, Richard
Wilbur, William Carlos Williams, James Wright.

HOWARD, Richard. Preferences: 51 American Poets Choose Po-
ems from Their Own Work and from the Past. New York: Viking,
1974.
A. R. Ammons, John Ashbery, W. H. Auden, Marvin Bell,
Elizabeth Bishop, John Malcolm Brinnin, Robert Creeley, J.
V. Cunningham, Hames Dickey, Alan Dugan, Irving Feldman,
Edward Field, Donald Finkel, Allen Ginsberg, Anthony Hecht,
Daryl Hine, Daniel Hoffman, John Hollander, Richard Howard,
Richard Hugo, Donald Justice, Galway Kinnell, Carolyn Kizer,
Stanley Kunitz, Denise Levertov, Philip Levine, John Logan,
Robert Lowell, William Meredith, James Merrill, W. S. Mer-
win, Howard Moss, Howard Nemerov, Adrienne Rich, Jerome
Rothenberg, Muriel Rukeyser, Anne Sexton, Louis Simpson,
L. E. Sissman, Gary Snyder, Mark Strand, May Swenson,
Allen Tate, Mark Van Doren, Mona Van Duyn, Diane Wakoski,
Robert Penn Warren, Theodore Weiss, John Hall Wheelock,
Richard Wilbur, James Wright.

HOWE, Florence; Ellen Bass. No More Masks! An Anthology of
Poems by Women. Garden City, N. Y. : Doubleday, 1973.
Helen Adam, Alta, Margaret Atwood, Susan Axelrod, Anita
Barrows, Ellen Bass, Phyllis Beauvais, Louise Bogan, Kay
Boyle, Gwendolyn Brooks, Rita Mae Brown, Helen Chasin,
Carole Gregory Clemmons, Lucille Clifton, Jane Cooper,
Ranice Henderson Crosby, Hilda Doolittle, Diane Di Prima,
Madeline DeFrees, Mari Evans, Ruth Fainlight, Elizabeth
Fenton, Nicole Forman, Kathleen Fraser, Carole Freeman,
Nikki Giovanni, Ann Gottlieb, Judy Grahn, Susan Griffin, Anne
Halley, Peggy Henderson, Sandra Hochman, Colette Inez, June
Jordan, Lenore Kandel, Shirley Kaufman, Faye Kicknosway,

Carolyn Kizer, Maxine Kumin, Denise Levertov, Audre Lorde, Cynthia Macdonald, Phyllis McGinley, Sandra McPherson, Marge Magid, Eve Merriam, Vassar Miller, Marianne Moore, Robin Morgan, Pauli Murray, Rochelle Owens, Grace Paley, Miriam Palmer, Marge Piercy, Sylvia Plath, Cathleen Quirk, Julia Randall, Judith Rechter, Naomi Replansky, Adrienne Rich, Wendy G. Rickert, Suzanne Berger Rioff, Carolyn M. Rodgers, Muriel Rukeyser, Anne Stevenson, Ruth Stone, Lynn Strongin, Lynn Sukenick, Susan Sutheim, May Swenson, Margo Taft, Jean Tepperman, Mona Van Duyn, Alice Walker, Margaret Walker, Beatrice Walter, Ingrid Wendt, Wendy Wieber.

HUGHES, Langston. Poems from Black Africa. Bloomington: Indiana Univ. Press, 1963.
Peter Abrahams, G. Adali-Mortti, Frank Aig-Imoukhuede, Edwin Barclay, Kwesi Brew, John Pepper Clark, Peter Clarke, Michael F. Dei-Anang, Roland Tombekai Dempster, Adebayo Faleti, F. K. Fiawoo, Marina Gashe, K. B. Jones-Quartey, A. C. Jordan, Ellis Ayitey Komey, Kojo Gyinaya Kyei, Aqush Laluah, A. L. Milner-Brown, Bloke Modisane, Ezekiel Mphahlele, Abioseh Nicol, Chuba Nweke, Gabriel Okara, Christopher Okigbo, Andrew Amankwa Opoku, Dennis C. Osadebay, Francis Ernest Kobina Parkes, Francesca Yetunde Pereira, Richard Rive, James D. Rubadiri, Wole Soyinka.

HUGHES, Langston; Arna Bontemps. The Poetry of the Negro: 1746-1970. Garden City, N. Y.: Doubleday, 1970.
Nanina Alba, Sidney Alexander, Samuel Allen, Russell Atkins, Gwendolyn B. Bennett, Lebert Bethune, Elizabeth Bishop, Julian Bond, Arna Bontemps, Kay Boyle, William Stanley Braithwaite, Gwendolyn Brooks, Helen Morgan Brooks, Frank London Brown, Isabella Maria Brown, Sterling A. Brown, Witter Bynner, Hodding Carter, Catharine Cater, Marcus B. Christian, Helen John Collins, Leslie Morgan Collins, Alice Corbin, Gregory Corso, Joseph R. Cowen, Wesley Curtright, Margaret Danner, Frank Marshall Davis, Ossie Davis, Babette Deutsch, James Dickey, Owen Dodson, W. E. B. Du Bois, Alfred A. Duckett, Rea Lubar Duncan, Ray Durem, Solomon Edwards, James A. Emanuel, Robert E. Hayden, Donald Jeffrey Hayes, David Henderson, Calvin C. Hernton, Leslie Pinckney Hill, Lucy Ariel Williams Holloway, Moses Carl Holman, Frank Horne, Langston Hughes, Randall Jarrell, Ted Joans, Don Allen Johnson, Norman Jordan, Bob Kaufman, Oliver LaGrone, Hazel Washington LaMarre, Bette Darcie Latimer, Florence Becker Lennan, Frank Lima, Walter Lowenfels, St. Clair McKelway, Naomi Long Madgett, A. B. Magil, Eguene T. Maleska, Maurice M. Martinez, Mason Jordan Mason (Judson Crews), Josephine Miles, Marianne Moore, Beatrice M. Murphy, Pauli Murray, Louis Newman, Effie Lee Newsome, G. C. Oden, Frank O'Hara, Myron O'Higgins, Kenneth Patchen, Raymond Patterson, Kenneth Porter, Dudley Randall, Ishmael Reed, Sarah Carolyn Reese, Conrad Kent Rivers, Ed Roberson, Walter Adolphe Roberts,

Selden Rodman, Dorothy Rosenberg, Muriel Rukeyser, Carl
Sandburg, Karl Shapiro, Lucy Smith, Mary Carter Smith,
Welton Smith, Anne Spencer, Allen Tate, Richard Thomas,
Melvin Beaunearus Tolson, Jean Toomer, Askia Muhammad
Toure, Perient Trott, Darwin T. Turner, James P. Vaughn,
Margaret Abigail Walker, Irma Wassall, Don West, Charles
Enoch Wheeler, Ernest J. Wilson, Jr., Bruce McM. Wright,
Sarah E. Wright, Frank Yerby.

HUNTING, Constance. A Suit of Four. West Lafayette, Ind. :
Purdue Univ., 1973.
 A. L. Lazarus, Barriss Mills, Felix Stefanile, Bruce Wood-
 ford.

HURTIK, Emil; Robert Yarber. An Introduction to Poetry and Crit-
icism. Lexington, Mass. : Xerox College, 1972.
 A. R. Ammons, W. H. Auden, Philip Booth, John Ciardi,
 Gregory Corso, Robert Creeley, James Dickey, Richard Eber-
 hart, T. S. Eliot, William Empson, Paul Engle, Kenneth
 Fearing, Lawrence Ferlinghetti, Robert Frost, George Garrett,
 Allen Ginsberg, Thom Gunn, Langston Hughes, Ted Hughes,
 Randall Jarrell, Robinson Jeffers, LeRoi Jones, Philip Larkin,
 C. Day Lewis, Robert Lowell, Hugh MacDiarmid, Rod McKuen,
 Archibald MacLeish, Louis MacNeice, Marianne Moore, Sylvia
 Plath, Ezra Pound, John Crowe Ransom, Henry Reed, Theo-
 dore Roethke, Carl Sandburg, Delmore Schwartz, Anne Sexton,
 Karl Shapiro, Stephen Spender, May Swenson, John Updike,
 Peter Viereck, John Wain, Richard Wilbur, William Carlos
 Williams.

IMMACULATE, Sister Mary. The Cry of Rachel: An Anthology of
Elegies on Children. New York: Random House, 1966.
 Brother Antoninus, E. E. Cummings, Babette Deutsch, Rich-
 ard Eberhart, Sister M. Emanuel, Robert Frost, Josephine
 Jacobsen, Randall Jarrell, Donald Justice, X. J. Kennedy, J.
 Morley Kinports, Robert Lowell, James McAuley, Samuel
 French Morse, Howard Nemerov, John Frederick Nims, Mary
 Oliver, Alan Paton, John Crowe Ransom, Theodore Roethke,
 Muriel Rukeyser, Dennis Schmitz, Edith Sitwell, Stephen
 Spender, Allen Tate, Mark Van Doren, Peter Viereck, Vernon
 Watkins.

JACKSON, Percival E. Justice and the Law: An Anthology of A-
merican Legal Poetry and Verse. Charlottesville, Va. : Michie,
1960.
 Will W. Ackerly, Austin Adams, Charles Follen Adam, James
 Barton Adams, Conrad Aiken, Bailey Aldrich, Paul Allen,
 Charlton A. Alexander, Taylor Alexander, Nathanael Ames,
 W. M. Ampt, Maxwell Anderson, Mrs. George Archibald,
 Margaret Ashman, W. H. Auden, A. A. Bablitz, Peggy Bacon,
 J. Q. Ballingham, John Kendrick Bangs, Sheppard Barclay,
 David Barker, Walton W. Battershall, Joseph Warren Beach,
 J. H. Beale, Jr., R. C. Berresford, George Birdseye, Fran-

cis C. Blair, Logon E. Bleckley, Harry A. Bloomberg, Harry
R. Blythe, Curtis Bok, Hugh Henry Brackenridge, John G. C.
Brainard, Berton Braley, Marshall Brown, Willard L. Brown,
Irving Browne, Henry Howard Brownell, Dana Burnet, G. Bur-
net, Amelia Josephine Burr, Witter Bynner, Daniel L. Cady,
Malcolm Campbell, Melville Cane, William Howard Carpenter,
William Herbert Carruth, M. L. Carter, Robert W. Chambers,
H. Gerald Chapin, Arthur Chapman, Charles Badger Clark,
Jr., Sarah N. Cleghorn, F. H. Cogswell, John Collins, Rose
Cooke, Parke Cummings, Francis Dana, Pegram Dargan, Hale
K. Darling, Russell W. Davenport, J. D. Davidson, Mitchell
Dawson, Voltarine De Cleyre, Miriam DeFord, Leona McC.
De Mere, August Derleth, Lee Wilson Dodd, Joseph Rodman
Drake, Max Eastman, Leta M. Edwards, Kenneth Fearing,
Thomas Greene Fessenden, David Dudley Field, Morris D.
Forkosch, Sam Walter Foss, Richard H. Fries, Wilfred J.
Funk, Albert W. Gaines, Alfred Gans, William Lloyd Garri-
son, E. K. Giblin, Richard Watson Gilder, Charlotte Perkins
Gilman, Theodore D. Gottlieb, R. D. Gray, Jack Greenberg,
David Greenhood, C. P. Greenough, A. Oakley Hall, Eugene
J. Hall, Prescott F. Hall, Tom Hall, Fitz Greene Halleck,
Charles G. Halpine, Walter Hard, Julian Hawthorne, John
Hay, Susan Henderson Hay, William Herschell, Samuel Hoffen-
stein, John Jarvis Holden, Raymond P. Holden, St. John
Honeywood, Woolsey R. Hopkins, Earl E. Howard, John Hub-
bard, George Huddleston, Dorothy Cope Hulse, Rolfe Humph-
ries, Wallace Irwin, Abraham C. Isaacson, Percival E. Jack-
son, Robinson Jeffers, Henry A. Jeffries, W. H. Johnson,
Elwood S. Jones, Ira Joyce, Reginald Wright Kauffman, George
Klingle, Stillman F. Kneeland, Arthur (Axiphilis) Kramer, Al-
fred Kreymborg, Sid La Cholter, Louis Lande, W. Livingston
Larned, Van Ness Lawless, William V. Lawrence, Mildred B.
Lee, Francis E. Leupp, Emmanuel Lewin, Elias Lieberman,
Karl N. Llewellyn, R. J. Locke, Michael S. Loeb, Archibald
MacLeish, J. M. McNair, Donald G. McNeil, A. Maconochie,
John Albert Macy, Walter Malone, Rosa Zagnoni Marinoni, T.
Dabney Marshall, Edward S. Martin, John W. May, Welburn
Mayock, Alex B. Meek, Josephine Miles, Ruth Comfort Mitch-
ell, James J. Montague, George P. Morris, Helene Mullins,
R. K. Munkittrick, Ogden Nash, Robert Henry Newell (Orpheus
C. Kerr), Starr Hoyt Nichols, J. M. Nolte, George Rapall
Noyes, Charles O'Conor, Ilo Orleans, Frances Sargent Osgood,
Robertson Palmer, Frank J. Parmenter, J. M. Patterson,
Samuel Minturn Peck, Richard Peters, S. B. Pettingill, Jr.,
Casper C. Phillips, Donn Piatt, Francis T. P. Plimpton,
John Poda, Ray Porter, Daniel H. Prior, Joseph M. Pros-
kauer, Harold Trowbridge Pulsifer, Frank Putnam, Louise
Crenshaw Ray, George Lansing Raymond, Ivy Kellerman Reed,
Cale Young Rice, Donald R. Richberg, James Jeffrey Roche,
Arthur E. Rosenberg, Margaret Wheeler Ross, Muriel Rukey-
ser, Damon Runyon, Carl Sandburg, Minot J. Savage, John
Godfrey Saxe, William A. Schmitt, John Seccombe, Jonathan
M. Sewall, Karl Shapiro, H. D. Shedd, Jr., John F. Sherwood,

Louis Sills, J. Lundie Smith, Jr., Lincoln B. Smith, William
R. Smith, Robert O. Spengler, Wendell P. Stafford, Henry T.
Stanton, Chauncey C. Starkweather, Otto M. Sternfeld, James
Still, Joseph Story, Jesse Stuart, Frank G. Swain, M. M.
Teager, John D. Teller, Rose Cooke Terry, J. H. Thacher,
John R. Thompson, William H. Tompkins, William D. Totten,
George A. Townsend, John T. Trowbridge, George F. Tucker,
Nancy Byrd Turner, Ernest Tyler, Louis Untermeyer, Edward
A. Uffington Valentine, Mark Van Doren, Alexis Von Adelung,
Franklin Waldheim, Beecher W. Waltermeier, Darwin E. Ware,
Eugene Fitch Ware, Robert Penn Warren, George H. Westley,
John Weymouth, W. M. Wherry, Jr., Edgar White, Seymour
W. Whiting, Samuel Z. Wicks, Hiram Ozias Wiley, Bartimeus
Willard, E. V. Wilson, Edmund Wilson, John Augustus Wil-
stack, Josh Wink, Henry Winter, Yvor Winters, Albert A.
Woldman, Charles Erskine Wood, D. C. Woods, Frederick A.
Wright, Audrey Wurdemann, A. U. Zinke.

JACOBUS, Lee A.; William T. Moynihan. Poems in Context. New
York: Harcourt Brace Jovanovich, 1974.
Leonie Adams, Richard Aldington, W. H. Auden, Robert Bagg,
Imamu Amiri Baraka, John Berryman, Elizabeth Bishop,
Kwesi Brew, Gwendolyn Brooks, Michael Dennis Browne, John
Pepper Clark, John William Corrington, E. E. Cummings,
Bernard B. Dadie, David Daiches, Birago Diop, Owen Dodson,
Ray Durem, T. S. Eliot, Kenneth Fearing, Robert Francis,
Robert Frost, Allen Ginsberg, Robert Graves, Hilda Doolittle,
Sandra Hochman, Langston Hughes, Ted Hughes, Donald Jus-
tice, Bob Kaufman, X. J. Kennedy, Etheridge Knight, Joseph
Langland, Don L. Lee, Laurie Lee, Denise Levertov, Taban
Lo Liyong, Robert Lowell, Archibald MacLeish, Vassar Miller,
Marianne Moore, Ezekiel Mphahlele, Ogden Nash, J. D.
O'Hara, Gabriel Okara, Kenneth Patchen, Brian Patten, Ray-
mond R. Patterson, Marge Piercy, Sylvia Plath, Ezra Pound,
John Crowe Ransom, Ishmael Reed, Adrienne Rich, Theodore
Roethke, John M. Ruganda, Siegfried Sassoon, Anne Sexton,
Stephen Spender, Allen Tate, Mona Van Duyn, Keith Waldrop,
Jonathan Williams, William Carlos Williams, Richard Wright,
Boevi Zankli.

JAMES Books. Three Some Poems. Cambridge: Alice James
Books, 1976.
Jeannine Dobbs, Kin Gensler, Eliz Knies.

JIHAD. Soul Session: Anthology of the B. C. D. Newark, N. J.:
Jihad, 1969.
Alma, Amani, Ameena, Anasa, Azizi, Saidi Mwanafunzi Chuma,
Jaledi Damu, Mwanafunzi Dhati, Fuhara, Mwanafunzi Juba,
Kicheko, Mwanafunzi Mfolme, Mwanafunzi Mjanja, Mwana-
funzi Moyo Msemaji, Nyenyecka, Salimu, Saidi Sharifu,
Tazamisha.

JONES, Hettie. Poems Now. New York: Kulchur Press, 1966.

Sam Abrams, Carole Berge, Ray Bremser, Ronald Caplan,
Diane DiPrima, Larry Eigner, David Henderson, Kenneth Irby,
Allan Kaplan, Robert Kelly, K. William Kgositsile, Gerrit
Lansing, Gerard Malanga, Joel Oppenheimer, John Sinclair,
Gilbert Sorrentino, A. B. Spellman, Roger Taus, Lorenzo
Thomas, Tony Towle, John Weiners (Wieners).

JORDAN, June. Soulscript: Afro-American Poetry. Garden City,
N. Y.: Doubleday, 1970.
Lewis Alexander, Julia Alvarez, Russell Atkins, Gwendolyn
Brooks, Sterling A. Brown, Katherine L. Cuestas, Linda
Curry, Djangatolum (Lloyd M. Corbin, Jr.), Owen Dodson,
Alfred Duckett, Ray Durem, Jacquelyn Harley, Nikki Giovanni,
Michael Goode, Robert Hayden, David Henderson, Calvin
Henrton, M. Carl Holman, Vanessa Howard, Langston Hughes,
Gayl Jones, LeRoi Jones, June Jordan, Bob Kaufman, Stephen
Kwartler, Don L. Lee, Julius Lester, Audre Lorde, Naomi
Long Madgett, Clarence Major, Larry Neal, Raymond R. Pat-
terson, Ishmael Reed, Sonia Sanchez, Phillip Solomon, Glenn
Thompson, Jean Toomer, Paul Vesey, Margaret Walker, Jay
Wright, Richard Wright.

JOSELOFF, Samuel Hart. A Time to Seek: An Anthology of Con-
temporary Jewish American Poets. New York: Union of American
Hebrew Congregations, 1975.
Marvin Bell, Leonard Cohen, Stanley Cooperman, Irving Feld-
man, Jacob Glatstein, David Ignatow, A. M. Klein, Stanley
Kunitz, Denise Levertov, Eve Merriam, Robert Mezey, Kadia
Molodowsky-Lew, Howard Nemerov, Hyam Plutzik, Charles
Reznikoff, Muriel Rukeyser, Karl Shapiro, Nathaniel Tarn,
Jules Alan Wein, Aaron Zeitlin.

KALLICH, Martin; Jack C. Gray; Robert M. Rodney. A Book of
the Sonnet. Poems and Criticism. New York: Twayne, 1973.
W. H. Auden, George Barker, E. E. Cummings, Richard
Eberhart, Robert Frost, Robinson Jeffers, Robert Lowell,
Archibald MacLeish, Ezra Pound, John Crowe Ransom, Sieg-
fried Sassoon, Karl Shapiro, Stephen Spender, Lucien Stryk,
Allen Tate.

KAPLAN, Cora. Salt and Bitter and Good: Three Centuries of
English and American Women Poets. New York: Paddington, 1975.
Louise Bogan, Hilda Doolittle, Marianne Moore, Dorothy Park-
er, Sylvia Plath, Vita Sackville-West, Stevie Smith.

KATZMAN, Don. Seventh Street: An Anthology of Poems from Les
Deux Megots. New York: Argentina Press, 1961.
Howard Ant, Richard Barker, Carol Berge, Jerry Bloedow,
John Harriman, Marguerite Harris, Phil Havey, Don Katzman,
John Keys, Robert Lima, Jackson Mac Low, Mary E. Mayo,
Robert Nichols, Philip Reys, Thomas D. Segall, Betty E. Taub,
Diane Wakoski.

KAUFFMAN, Donald T. Favorite Christian Poems. Old Tappan,
N. J. : Fleming H. Revell, 1969.
 Sybil Leonard Armes, Margaret D. Armstrong, Maltbie D.
Babcock, Richard Baxter, E. H. Bickersteth, Horatius Bonar,
Mary Gardner Brainard, Madeline S. Bridges, Phillips Brooks,
Hezekiah Butterworth, John Byrom, Amy Carmichael, Eliza-
beth Cheney, James Freeman Clarke, Elizabeth C. Clephane,
John Clifford, Florence Earle Coates, Catherine Cate Coblentz,
Dan Crawford, Jane Crewdson, Fanny J. Crosby, Ralph Spauld-
ing Cushman, William Davenant, Mrs. Donald A. Day, Mary
Mapes Dodge, Digby M. Dolben, Doran, Will Allen Dromgoole,
Mary S. Edgar, W. M. L. Fay, Michael Field, Giles Fletcher,
Annie Johnson Flint, Lona M. Fowler, Ethel Romig Fuller,
C. F. Gellert, T. H. Gill, Andrew Gillies, Washington Glad-
den, Mrs. D. R. H. Goodale, Elizabeth Porter Gould, Jeanne
Marie Guyon, Edward Everett Hale, Minnie Louise Haskins,
Frances Ridley Havergal, Marianne Hearn, Reginald Heber,
Leslie Pinckney Hill, Josiah G. Holland, William Walsham
How, Adoniram Judson, John Keble, Thomas Kelly, Harriet
McEwen Kimball, Frederic Lawrence Knowles, Frances Stoak-
ley Lankford, Edith Willis Linn, Samuel Longfellow, George
Macdonald, Charlotte Grant MacIntyre, Robert McIntyre, Emily
Huntington Miller, Theodore Monod, James Montgomery,
Frances McKinnon Morton, Frederic W. H. Myers, N. P.
Neilson, John Newton, J. W. H. Nichols, Martha Snell Nichol-
son, Johnson Oatman, Jr. , John Oxenham, Jean Sophia Pigott,
Albert G. Pike, Adelaide A. Pollard, Adelaide A. Procter,
Maude Louise Ray, A. A. Rees, Martin Rinkart, William M.
Runyan, Barbara C. Ryberg, Charles Sandford, Margaret E.
Sangster, R. L. Sharpe, A. B. Simpson, Carl J. O. Spitta,
Henry Jerome Stockard, John Banister Tabb, Miriam Teichner,
Anna Temple, Gerhard Tersteegen, Gilbert Thomas, Richard
C. Trench, Grace E. Troy, Ellen H. Underwood, Jones Very,
Lila V. Walters, Myra Brooks Welch, Amos R. Wells, Ruth
Winant Wheeler, Florence Wilkinson, Edith L. Young.

KENNEDY, X. J. Messages: A Thematic Anthology of Poetry.
Boston: Little, Brown, 1973.
 Helen Adam, A. R. Ammons, W. H. Auden, Daniel Berrigan,
Elizabeth Bishop, Robert Bly, Louise Bogan, Philip Booth,
Richard Brautigan, John Michael Brennan, Gwendolyn Brooks,
Charles Bukowski, James Camp, Hodding Carter, William
Childress, John Ciardi, Lucille Clifton, Gregory Corso, Henri
Coulette, Robert Creeley, Victor Hernandez Cruz, E. E.
Cummings, Waring Cuney, J. V. Cunningham, James Den
Boer, Bob Dylan, Richard Eberhart, T. S. Eliot, George P.
Elliott, John Engels, Clayton Eshleman, Dave Etter, Donald
Finkel, Calvin Forbes, Robert Frost, Allen Ginsberg, Paul
Goodman, Donald Hall, John Hartford, Robert Hayden, Anthony
Hecht, David Henderson, Robert Hershon, Daniel Hoffman, A.
D. Hope, Ted Hughes, Richard Hugo, David Ignatow, Randall
Jarrell, Robinson Jeffers, B. B. King, Galway Kinnell, Caro-
lyn Kizer, John Knoepfle, Bill Knott, Maxine Kumin, Stanley

Kunitz, Greg Kuzma, Peter La Farge, Philip Larkin, Irving
Layton, Jay Leifer, Denise Levertov, Philip Levine, Lou Lip-
sitz, Robert Lowell, Roger McGough, Archibald MacLeish,
William Meredith, James Merrill, W. S. Merwin, Bert Meyers,
Richard Moore, Howard Moss, Geoffrey Movius, Howard Nem-
erov, John Frederick Nims, Bink Noll, Gregory Orr, Robert
Pack, Patrice Phillips, Marge Piercy, Sylvia Plath, David Ray,
Thomas Dillon Redshaw, Tim Reynolds, Adrienne Rich, John
Ridland, Martin Robbins, Theodore Roethke, Gibbons Ruark,
Raphael Rudnik, Norman H. Russell, Dennis Saleh, Stephen
Sandy, Aram Saroyan, James Schuyler, Anne Sexton, Harvey
Shapiro, Charles Simic, Nina Simone, Louis Simpson, L. E.
Sissman, Knute Skinner, William Jay Smith, W. D. Snodgrass,
Gary Snyder, Barry Spacks, Skip (Alexander) Spence, William
Stafford, George Starbuck, Mark Strand, Marcia Stubbs, May
Swenson, James Tate, Henry Taylor, John Thompson, Anthony
Thwaite, Walasse Ting, Constance Urdang, David Wagoner,
Diane Wakoski, Keith Waldrop, Rosmarie Waldrop, Robert
Watson, James Welch, Ruth Whitman, Dallas E. Wiebe, Rich-
ard Wilbur, Peter Wild, Miller Williams, William Carlos
Williams, Bruce P. Woodford, James Wright, Al Young, Paul
Zimmer.

KENNEDY, X. J. An Introduction to Poetry. Boston: Little,
Brown, 1974.
Edward Allen, Ern Alpaugh, A. R. Ammons, Imamu Amiri
Baraka, John Berryman, John Betjeman, Elizabeth Bishop,
Robert Bly, Richard Brautigan, Gwendolyn Brooks, Dorthi
Charles, John Ciardi, Lucille Clifton, Leonard Cohen, Eliza
Cook, Cid Corman, Frances Cornford, Robert Creeley, E. E.
Cummings, J. V. Cunningham, Peter Davison, James Dickey,
Emanuel di Pasquale, Hilda Doolittle, Alan Dugan, Bob Dylan,
Richard Eberhart, T. S. Eliot, William Empson, Kenneth
Fearing, Donald Finkel, Ian Hamilton Finlay, Robert Francis,
Robert Frost, Gary Gildner, Allen Ginsberg, Nikki Giovanni,
Robert Graves, Ronald Gross, Woody Guthrie, John Haines,
Donald Hall, John Heath-Stubbs, Anthony Hecht, John Hollander,
Langston Hughes, Ted Hughes, David Ignatow, Mick Jagger,
Randall Jarrell, Elizabeth Jennings, Donald Justice, Alexander
Kerr, James C. Kilgore, Galway Kinnell, Kenneth Koch, Greg
Kuzma, Philip Larkin, Irving Layton, John Lennon, Denise
Levertov, Philip Levine, J. A. Lindon, Robert Lowell, Mina
Loy, Paul McCartney, Hugh MacDiarmid, Rod McKuen, Archi-
bald MacLeish, T. O. Maglow, James Merrill, W. S. Merwin,
Josephine Miles, Marianne Moore, Edwin Morgan, Emanuel
Morgan, Ogden Nash, Howard Nemerov, John Frederick Nims,
Charles Olson, Guy Owen, Dorothy Parker, Dewey G. Pell,
Marge Piercy, Sylvia Plath, Ezra Pound, Dudley Randall,
John Crowe Ransom, Ishmael Reed, Charles Reznikoff, Adri-
enne Rich, Keith Richard, Theodore Roethke, Muriel Rukeyser,
Bill Knott, Carl Sandburg, Anne Sexton, Karl Shapiro, James
Simmons, Paul Simon, Knute Skinner, Stevie Smith, William
Jay Smith, W. D. Snodgrass, Gary Snyder, Barry Spacks,

William Stafford, Timothy Steele, May Swenson, James Tate, Henry Taylor, Grace Treasone, Jean Toomer, Stephen Tropp, John Updike, Keith Waldrop, Ruth Whitman, Reed Whittemore, Richard Wilbur, C. K. Williams, William Carlos Williams, Yvor Winters, James Wright.

KENSETH, Arnold. Poems of Protest: Old and New: A Selection of Poetry. New York: Macmillan, 1968.
    Kingsley Amis, W. H. Auden, Sterling Brown, Olga Cabral, Charles Causley, David Clark, E. E. Cummings, Ray Durem, Lawrence Ferlinghetti, Edward Field, Donald Finkel, Charles Henri Ford, Robert Francis, David Henderson, Ralph Hodgson, Herschel Horn, Donald Justice, Galway Kinnell, Stanley Kunitz, Aaron Kurtz, Joseph Langland, Carl Larsen, Denise Levertov, Walter Lowenfels, Archibald MacLeish, Thomas McGrath, Thich Nhat-Hanh, Tom Paxton, Robert Peterson, Peter Porter, Ezra Pound, John Crowe Ransom, Herbert Read, Margaret Rockwell, W. R. Rodgers, Theodore Roethke, Edwin Rolfe, Siegfried Sassoon, F. R. Scott, Stevie Smith, William Jay Smith, Stephen Spender, George Starbuck, Yuri Suhl, Robert Tucker, Chad Walsh, Richard Weber, Reed Whittemore.

KESSLER, Jascha. American Poems: A Contemporary Collection. Carbondale: Southern Illinois Univ. Press, 1964.
    Jane Cooper, Henri Coulette, Robert Creeley, Irving Feldman, S. S. Gardons, Allen Ginsberg, Barbara Guest, John Hollander, Jascha Kessler, Kenneth Koch, Philip Levine, John Logan, W. S. Merwin, Robert Mezey, W. D. Snodgrass, James Wright.

KGOSITSILE, Keorapetse. The Word Is Here: Poetry from Modern Africa. Garden City, N. Y.: Doubleday, 1973.
    Ama Ata Aidoo, Kofi Awoonor, Dennis Brutus, J. P. Clark, Solomon Deressa, David Diop, Zweli ed Dladla, Keorapetse Kgositsile, Mazisi Kunene, Burns B. Machobane, Mouloud Mammeri, Edouard Maunick, Ifeanyi Menkiti, Guy C. Z. Mhone, Antonio Agostinho Neto, Stella Ngatho, Gabriel Okara, Christopher Okigbo, Okot p'Bitek, David Rudadiri, Wole Soyinka, Tchikaya U Tam'si, Kateb Yacine.

KHERDIAN, David; James Baloian. Down at the Santa Fe Depot: 20 Fresno Poets. Fresno, Calif.: Gilgia Press, 1970.
    James Baloian, B. H. Boston, William Childress, Michael Clifton, Glover Davis, Peter Everwine, C. G. Hanzlicek, Lawson Inada, Gary Johnson, Robert L. Jones, David Kherdian, Philip Levine, Larry Levis, Robert Mezey, Khatchik Minasian, DeWayne Rail, Dennis Saleh, Luis Omar Salinas, Herbert Scott, Roberta Spear.

KHERDIAN, David. Visions of America by the Poets. New York: Macmillan, 1973.
    A. R. Ammons, Imamu Ameer Baraka, Paul Blackburn, Richard Brautigan, Charles Bukowski, Gregory Corso, Robert Creeley, Diane DiPrima, James Dickey, Edward Dorn, Ray

Drew, Lawrence Ferlinghetti, Allen Ginsberg, David Ignatow, Emmett Jarrett, Bob Kaufman, Jack Kerouac, David Kherdian, Kenneth Koch, Denise Levertov, Ron Loewinsohn, Michael McClure, David Meltzer, Frank O'Hara, Kenneth Patchen, Charles Reznikoff, Jerome Rothenberg, Kenneth Rexroth, Gary Snyder, William Stafford, Diane Wakoski, Lew Welch, Philip Whalen, William Carlos Williams, James Wright.

KHERDIAN, David. Settling America: The Ethnic Expression of 14 Contemporary Poets. New York: Macmillan, 1974.
    Mel Berssenbrugge, Gregory Corso, Victor Hernandez Cruz, Nicholas Flocos, Sam Hamod, Joy Harjo, Lawson Fusao Inada, David Kherdian, Charles Reznikoff, Carolyn M. Rodgers, Luis Omar Salinas, Stephen Stepanchev, James Welch, Al Young.

KILEY, Frederick T.; Tony Dater. Listen: The War. Colorado Springs, Colo.: Air Force Academy Association of Graduates, 1973.
    Forrest D. Bachtel, Tom Batson, George Berke, Martin Berkovitz, Whitney I. Blair, Nancy Jo Boggs, Boyd G. Burd, Patrick R. Burke, Craig L. Champion, Eugene Cirillo, Don Clelland, Richard M. Coffman, Anne Cox, Donald R. Crozier, Tony Dater, Gene H. Davis, P. L. Delano, Jean Ebbert, W. D. Ehrhart, Robert J. Eichenberg, Jerry P. Faulkenberry, Robert W. Fett, Robert Francoviglia, Barbara French, Sharon Fuhrman, John P. Gallagher, Tom Gates, David S. Gauntlett, Robert M. Glover, Mary S. Gould, John Harris, Marlene Harris, Mary Hendler, Roland Herwig, Eileen Jackson, Linnie E. Jackson, Winslow David Jones, Frederick Kiley, Philip G. Kivett, James T. Knight III, Richard I. Koeteeuw, John J. Kowalski, Earl E. LaClair, Hollis T. Landrum, Kenneth M. Lloyd, Timothy C. Lockley, Eileen Lundin, Don Mace, C. Marshall McLean, L. Dean Minze, Richard D. Ness, Lawrence E. Olson, Ronald E. Pedro, H. W. Powers, John Clarke Pratt, James G. Ramsay, Jr., Robert Raymond, Jesse C. Rider, James L. Schrarkel, Frank J. Serl, Edward Silverbush, David J. Smith, Robert J. Smith, Clayton Snedeker, Maureen Stuart, James E. Summers, David Sylva, James H. Tiller III, Neal Trent, Dorothy J. Valerlan, David K. Vaughan, Donald E. V. Walker, Edd Wheeler, Franklin C. White, Jr., Franklin C. Whitwell, Linda Williamson, Ebi Wood.

KING, Woodie; Imamu Amiri Baraka. Black Spirits: A Festival of New Black Poets in America. New York: Random House, 1972.
    Johari Amini, S. E. Anderson, Imamu Amiri Baraka, Ed Bullins, Stanley Crouch, Ronda Davis, Jackie Earley, Mari Evans, Nikki Giovanni, David Henderson, Mae Jackson, Norman Jordan, Gylan Kain, Kali, Keorapetse Kgositsile, Don L. Lee, Felipe Luciano, Clarence Major, Amus Mor, Larry Neal, David Nelson, Arthur Pfister, Clarence Reed, Carolyn Rodgers, Sonia Sanchez, Welton Smith, Richard W. Thomas, James W. Thompson, Askia Mohammed Toure, Quincy Troupe.

KING, Woodie, Jr.   The Forerunners: Black Poets in America.
Washington, D. C. :   Howard Univ. , 1975.
Samuel Allen, Russell Atkins, Arna Bontemps, Gwendolyn
Brooks, Sterling A. Brown, Margaret Burroughs, Margaret
Danner, Frank Marshall Davis, Owen Dodson, Robert Hayden,
Lance Jeffers, Oliver La Grone, Naomi Long Madgett, Dudley
Randall, Margaret Walker, Jay Wright.

KING Publications.   Bound and Free: The Poetry of Warriors Be-
hind Bars.   Washington, D. C. :   King Publications, 1976.
Mtendaji Seitu Kamau (Gregory Williams), Imani Kujichagulia
(Charles A. Buchanan), Gomvi Malik (James Jackson), Akili
Sekou Moyo (Corrie L. Lee), Tonbora (Henry J. B. Johnson).

KLONSKY, Milton.   Speaking Pictures: A Gallery of Pictorial Poetry from the Sixteenth Century to the Present.   New York: Crown,
1975.
Jane Augustine, Ronaldo Azeredo, Carol Bankerd, Claus
Bremer, Kenneth Burke, Thomas A. Clark, E. E. Cummings,
Simon Cutts, Robert De Niro, Russell Edson, Kathleen Ferguson, Ian Hamilton Finlay, Charles Henri Ford, John Furnival, Reuben Lucius Goldberg, Dick Higgins, John Hollander,
Ronald Johnson, Richard Kostelanetz, Ferdinand Kriwet, Hansjorg Mayer, Thomas Merton, Christopher Middleton, Edwin
Morgan, Tom Ockerse, Kenneth Patchen, Ezra Pound, Robert
Reisner, Kathy Scherkel, Stevie Smith, Mary Ellen Solt, Jordan Steckel, May Swenson, Emmett Williams, Jonathan Williams, Pedro Xisto.

KNOWLES, Susanne.   Chorus: An Anthology of Bird Poems.   New
York: Funk & Wagnalls, 1969.
Valentine Ackland, Gwyneth Anderson, John Redwood Anderson,
A. J. Arberry, Martin Armstrong, Audrey Beecham, John
Blight, Eileen Brennan, David Campbell, Nevill Coghill,
Padraic Colum, Frances Cornford, Patrick Greagh, Geoffrey
Dearmer, Paul Dehn, Lynn Doyle, Clifford Dyment, Richard
Eberhart, T. S. Eliot, William Empson, Eleanor Farjeon,
Robert Frost, Roy Fuller, W. W. Gibson, Robert Gittings,
A. C. Graham, Robert Graves, Michael Hamburger, William
Hart-Smith, C. Hatakeyama, Seamus Heaney, John Heath-
Stubbs, Philip Henderson, John Hewitt, Ralph Hodgson, Ray-
mond Holden, John Holloway, Flexmore Hudson, Ted Hughes,
M. M. Johnson, Jean Kenward, James Kirkup, Susanne Knowles,
B. C. Leale, Peter Levi, Edward Lucie-Smith, Sylvia Lynd,
James McAuley, Norman MacCaig, Roy McFadden, John Mase-
field, Ernest G. Moll, Ogden Nash, Anthony Naumann, Wilfrid
Noyce, T. O'Donoghue, Ruth Pitter, William Plomer, Peter
Quennell, Herbert Read, Theodore Roethke, Alan Ross, Anth-
ony Rye, V. Sackville-West, Carl Sandburg, Siegfried Sassoon,
E. J. Scovell, Robin Skelton, Stanley Snaith, Douglas Stewart,
R. S. Thomas, Michael Thwaites, Geoffrey Tillotson, Charles
Tomlinson, James Turner, John Updike, Derek Walcott, Arthur
Waley, Ted Walker, Arnold Wall, Rex Warner, C. Henry War-

ren, Vernon Watkins, Marie de L. Welch, John Hall Wheelock, Lawrence Whistler, Richard Wilbur, David Wright, Judith Wright, Andrew Young.

KOHL, Herbert; Victor Hernandez Cruz. Stuff: A Collection of Poems, Visions and Imaginative Happenings from Young Writers in Schools--Opened and Closed. New York: World, 1970.

Sharon Boone, Juanita Bradley, Jesse Burnett, Yvonne Caraballo, Sean Chappell, Steve Clendaniel, Bonnie Cooper, Philip Crowder, Alvin Lewis Curry, Jr., Mike Davis, Jim Denton, Randy Dunagan, Margaret Eckman, Joyce Edwards, Christopher Gamble, Irma Gonzalez, Ida Ruth Griffin, Gary Hall, Phillip Harris, Julie Hendon, Kalen Hendon, Sarah Hendon, Susie Hendon, Robert George Jackson, Laurie Koel, Kathy Koledin, Heidi Lucas, Michaele Lundberg, Sioux McHargue, William McLean, Lucia Martin, Lydia Martinez, Maurya Metal, Lynwood Middleton, John Miller, Wayne Moreland, Donald Morgan, Orlando Ortiz, Dorothy Patterson, Frederick Douglas Perry, Ellie Mae Powell, Renee, Alice Schilz, Barbara Snead, Gloria Truvido, Arthur Williams, Philip Wilson, Jonathan Withers.

KONEK, Carol; Dorothy Walters. I Hear My Sisters Saying: Poems by Twentieth-Century Women. New York: Crowell, 1976.

Lucile Adler, Alta, Maya Angelou, Lila Arnold, Margaret Atwood, Phyllis Beauvais, Louise Bogan, besmilr brigham, Gwendolyn Brooks, Rita Mae Brown, Lynn Butler, Jane Chambers, Helen Chasin, Laura Chester, Jane Cooper, Vinnie-Marie D'Ambrosio, Diane DiPrima, Elaine Edelman, Marie E. Evans, Mary Fabilli, Gena Ford, Gail Fox, Kathleen Fraser, Elsa Gidlow, Virginia Gilbert, Nikki Giovanni, Mary Gordon, Geraldine Hammond, Jeanine Hathaway, Anne Hazlewood-Brady, Margery Himel, Lindy Hough, Barbara Howes, Colette Inez, Phyllis Janik, Erica Jong, June Jordan, Suzanne Juhasz, Hannah Kahn, Faye Kicknosway, Carolyn Kizer, Carol Konek, Mary Norbert Korte, Maxine Kumin, Jacqueline Lapidus, Lynn Lawner, Denise Levertov, Sharon Mayer Libera, Lyn Lifshin, Judith McCombs, Susan MacDonald, Naomi Long Madgett, Carolyn Maisel, Ann Menebroker, Eve Merriam, Josephine Miles, Vassar Miller, Barbara Moraff, Robin Morgan, Lisel Mueller, Deborah Munro, Kathleen Norris, Joyce Carol Oates, Gloria Oden, Ellen Pearce, Marge Piercy, Sylvia Plath, Nancy Price, Paula Reingold, Adrienne Rich, Muriel Rukeyser, Sonia Sanchez, Helga Sandburg, Susan Fromberg Schaeffer, Anne Sexton, Clarice Short, Anita Skeen, Helen Sorrells, Kathleen Spivack, Ann Stanford, Lynn Strongin, May Swenson, Velma West Sykes, Constance Urdang, Mona Van Duyn, Julia Vinograd, Diane Wakoski, Alice Walker, Kath Walker, Margaret Walker, Dorothy Walters, Ruth Whitman, Nancy Willard, Sarah Youngblood.

KOSTELANETZ, Richard. Possibilities of Poetry: An Anthology of American Contemporaries. New York: Dell, 1970.

A. R. Ammons, Brother Antoninus, J. V. Cunningham, S.
Foster Damon, James Dickey, Alan Dugan, Gail Dusenbery,
Allen Ginsberg, John Giorno, Dan Graham, Daniel Hoffman,
John Hollander, Richard Kostelanetz, Stanley Kunitz, Philip
Lamantia, John Logan, Robert Lowell, pbNichol, Liam O'Gal-
lagher, Charles Olson, Sylvia Plath, Kenneth Rexroth, Theo-
dore Roethke, Delmore Schwartz, Armand Schwerner, David
Shapiro, Harvey Shapiro, Mary Ellen Solt, W. D. Snodgrass,
Gary Snyder, Gerd Stern, Melvin B. Tolson, David Wagoner,
James Wright, Louis Zukofsky.

KRAMER, Aaron.　On Freedom's Side: An Anthology of American
Poems of Protest.　New York:　Macmillan, 1972.
　　　Laurence Benford, Alexander F. Bergman, Berton Braley,
Dana Burnet, Olga Cabral, Ralph Chaplin, E. E. Cummings,
John R. Dos Passos, William E. DuBois, Ray Durem, Mich-
ael Gold, Woody Guthrie, Alfred Hayes, Lee Hays, Leslie
Woolf Hedley, Langston Hughes, Aunt Molly Jackson, Norman
Jordan, Denis Knight, Aaron Kramer, Alfred Kreymborg,
Peter La Farge, Denise Levertov, Anne Lifschutz, Archibald
MacLeish, Naomi Long Madgett, Abraham B. Magil, Myron
O'Higgins, Kenneth Patchen, Raymond R. Patterson, Robert
Peterson, Norman Rosten, Muriel Rukeyser, RJS (Robert
Joseph Sigmund), Carl Sandburg, Isidor Schneider, Bertrand
Shadwell, Evelyn Thorne, Quincy Troupe, Louis Untermeyer,
Richard Wright.

KRECH, Richard; John Oliver Simon.　The Anthology of Poems Read
at COSMEP, the CONFERENCE of Small-Magazine Editors & Press-
men, in Berkeley California May 23-26, 1968.　Berkeley, Calif.:
Noh Directions Press, 1968.
　　　John Q. Adams, Harold Adler, Alta, David Hueschke Argo,
Harvey Bialy, John Melville Bishop III, Douglas Blazek, Char-
lie Bordin, Marilyn Cadogan, Andy Clausen, Bob Dawson,
Susan Efros, Hilary Ayer Fowler, Hugh Fox, David Gitin,
Morton Grinker, John Grube, Steven A. Hagerth, Ben L. Hi-
att, Johnthomason, Richard Krech, Lowell Levant, Ron Mc-
Nicoll, Michael Makowsky, Paul Mariah, David Melnick,
Patricia Parker, Charles Potts, Ronald Silliman, John Oliver
Simon, Hester G. Storm, Sunshine, Michael Upton, Vanish,
D. R. Wagner, Joel Waldman, Pete Winslow, Carl Woideck,
Paul Xavier, Al Young.

LANE, Ronnie M.　Face the Whirlwind.　Grand Rapids, Mich.:
Pilot Press, 1973.
　　　Stella Crews, Robert Hayden, Naomi Long Madgett, Herbert
Woodward Martin, Dudley Randall, James Randall, John Ran-
dall, Richard Thomas, June D. Whaley, Jill Witherspoon-
Boyer.

LARRICK, Nancy.　Room for Me and a Mountain Lion: Poetry of
Open Space.　New York: M. Evans, 1974.
　　　Lucius Beebe, Robert Bly, John Dimoff, Isak Dineson, Glenn

W. Dresbach, Thomas Hornsby Ferril, Robert Francis, Robert Frost, Felice Holman, Ted Hughes, Randall Jarrell, Judson Jerome, Donald Justice, Galway Kinnell, Maxine Kumin, Denise Levertov, Myra Cohn Livingston, David McCord, Eve Merriam, John Moffitt, Theodore Roethke, Carl Sandburg, William Jay Smith, Daniel Smythe, William Stafford, Adrien Stoutenburg, Jon Swan, May Swenson, R. S. Thomas, Margaret Tsuda, David Wagoner, Kim Williams, Yvor Winters, Nancy Woods, Al Young.

LARSON, Clinton F.; William Stafford. Modern Poetry of Western America. Provo, Utah: Brigham Young Univ., 1975.
Earle Birney, J. V. Cunningham, Madeline DeFrees, Thomas Hornsby Ferril, Brewster Ghiselin, Thom Gunn, John Haines, Kenneth O. Hanson, John Sterling Harris, Richard Hugo, Lawson Fusao Inada, Robinson Jeffers, Clinton F. Larson, Philip Levine, Edward Lueders, Sandra McPherson, Josephine Miles, Veneta Nielsen, Anthony Ostroff, Kenneth Rexroth, Theodore Roethke, Vern Rutsala, Primus St. John, Ralph Salisbury, Karl Shapiro, Richard Shelton, Clarice Short, Robin Skelton, Gary Snyder, Radcliffe Squires, William Stafford, Ann Stanford, A. Wilber Stevens, May Swenson, Emma Lou Thayne, David Wagoner, James Welch, Peter Wild, John Williams, Keith Wilson, Yvor Winters.

LASK, Thomas. The New York Times Book of Verse. New York: Macmillan, 1970.
George Abbe, Lucile Adler, Vonna Hicks Adrian, Daisy Aldan, Richard Aldridge, Sidney Alexander, David Atamian, Donald C. Babcock, Eleanor Baldwin, Eric Barker, Taner Baybars, Margaret Benaya, John Bennett, Helen Bevington, John Biram, Thomas Blackburn, Frederick Bock, Rosalie Boyle, Milton Bracker, Millen Brand, Edward Brathwaite, Eugene Brooks, Alan Brownjohn, Richard Burns, Witter Bynner, Melville Cane, John Randell Carpenter, Brenda Chamberlain, Katherine Garrison Chapin, J. K. Clark, Walter Clark, Austin Clarke, Elizabeth Chesley, Kirby Congdon, Sidney Cooksley, Cyril Cusack, Louise Darcy, Gustav Davidson, Donald Davie, Joanne De Longchamps, Carleton Drewry, Mark Dunster, Frederick Ebright, Gladys Ely, James A. Emanuel, Richard Curry Esler, Chana Faerstein, John Fandel, William Henry Fanning, Norma Farber, Ruth Feldman, Arthur Davison Ficke, Edsel Ford, Frances Frost, Zulfikar Ghose, Elsie Gibbs, Douglas Gibson, William Gibson, Yetza Gillespie, Robert Gittings, Mary Goldman, Ruth Tumarkin Goodman, William Goodreau, Ralph Gordon, Darcy Gottlieb, Rosamond Haas, Horace E. Hamilton, Andras Hamori, Christopher Hampton, John Hay, Sara Henderson Hay, Howard Healy, Edith Henrich, William Heyen, Charles Higham, Philip Hobsbaum, David Holbrook, Raymond Holden, Barbara D. Holender, Edwin Honig, Diana der Hovanessian, Po Fei Huang, Daniel Hughes, Joan Hutton, Mary L. Inman, Ethel Jackbson, Geoffrey Johnson, Rosemary Joseph, Menke Katz, Ruth Douglas Keener, Lysander Kemp, Gerta

Kennedy, Anthony Kerrigan, James Kirkup, Aaron Kramer, Ernest Kroll, Dilys Laing, Ruth Lechlitner, Michael Leech, Philip Legler, Geoffrey Lehmann, Jo Ann Leichliter, Virginia Linton, David A. Locher, Katie Louchheim, Malcolm Lowry, Edward Lucie-Smith, Norman MacCaig, David McCord, Howard McCord, Lucie McKee, Francis Maguire, Charles Malam, Jack Matthews, Jane Mayhall, Jerome Mazzaro, Gerard Previn Meyer, Heather Ross Miller, James L. Montague, Marion Montgomery, George H. Moorse, John Richard Moreland, Samuel French Morse, W. R. Moses, Richard Murphy, George Murray, Neil Myers, Leonard E. Nathan, Israel Newman, Frederick Nicklaus, John Nixon, Jr., Leslie Norris, Mary Oliver, Rose O'Neil, Paul Oppenheimer, Garrett Oppenheim, Anthony Ostroff, Winthrop Palmer, Ross Parmenter, Michael Parr, Louise D. Peck, Eric Pfeiffer, Roger Pfingston, J. Phoenice, Ruth Pitter, Harriet Plimpton, Stanley Plumly, John Press, Arnold Price, Nancy Price, Glenn Pritchard, A. K. Ramanujan, Richard C. Raymond, Bryon Herbert Reece, A. I. Richards, Anne Ridler, Ralph Robin, W. W. E. Ross, David Russell, I. L. Salomon, F. R. Scott, Anderson M. Scruggs, Edith Shiffert, William Vincent Sieller, Ruth Silcock, J. Edgar Simmons, Leroy Smith, Jr., A. J. M. Smith, Richard Snyder, Walter Sorell, Raymond Souster, Barry Spacks, Jon Stallworthy, Irwin Stark, William F. Stead, Louis Stoddard, A. W. Sullivan, Emma Swan, Karen Swenson, Marie Syrkin, Sister M. Therese, R. S. Thomas, Judy Thurman, Charles Tomlinson, Florence Trefethen, C. A. Trypanis, Harold Vinal, Charles A. Wagner, William Walden, Ted Walker, Vernon Watkins, James L. Weil, Morris Weisenthal, Neil Weiss, N. G. Westerfield, John Hall Wheelock, John Hazard Wildman, Peter Williamson, Mary Winter.

LEARY, Paris; Robert Kelly. A Controversy of Poets: An Anthology of Contemporary Poetry. New York: Doubleday, 1965.
John Ashbery, Paul Blackburn, Robin Blaser, Gray Burr, Gregory Corso, Robert Creeley, Peter Davison, James Dickey, Edward Dorn, Larry Eigner, Theodore Enslin, Lawrence Ferlinghetti, Edward Field, Donald Finkel, Allen Ginsberg, Anthony Hecht, Daniel Hoffman, Theodore Holmes, LeRoi Jones, Robert Kelly, X. J. Kennedy, Galway Kinnell, Melvin Walker La Follette, Gerrit Lansing, Paris Leary, Denise Levertov, Laurence Liberman, Robert Lowell, Michael McClure, Georgia Lee McElhaney, Jackson Mac Low, Edward Marshall, Thomas Merton, W. S. Merwin, Vassar Miller, Frank O'Hara, Charles Olson, Joel Oppenheimer, Rochelle Owens, Robert Pack, Kenneth Pitchford, Ralph Pomeroy, Adrienne Rich, Jerome Rothenberg, Stephen Sandy, Frederick Seidel, Anne Sexton, W. D. Snodgrass, Gary Snyder, Jack Spicer, Nancy Sullivan, Robert Sward, Diane Wakoski, Theodore Weiss, John Wieners, Richard Wilbur, Jonathan Williams, John Woods, Louis Zukofsky.

LEE, Al. The Major Young Poets. New York: World, 1971.
Marvin Bell, Michael Benedikt, William Brown, Charles Simic, Mark Strand, James Tate, C. K. Williams, David P. Young.

LEE, Don L.; James A. Emanuel. Dynamite Voices I: Black Poets of Detroit. Detroit: Broadside Press, 1971.
    Margaret Danner, Ebon, Mari Evans, Julia Fields, Nikki Gi-
ovanni, Donald L. Graham, David Henderson, Everett Hoagland, Norman Jordan, Etheridge Knight, Eugene Perkins, Conrad Kent Rivers, Carolyn Rodgers, Sonia Sanchez.

LEGGETT, Glenn H. 12 Poets. New York: Holt, Rinehart &
Winston, 1966.
    T. S. Eliot, Robert Frost.

LEYLAND, Winston. Angels of the Lyre, A Gay Poetry Anthology.
San Francisco: Panjandrum, 1975.
    Hector Tito Alvarez, William Barber, Bruce Boone, Victor
Borsa, Joe Brainard, Perry Brass, Adrian Brooks, Ira Cohen,
Kirby Congdon, Ed Cox, Emilio Cubeiro, Tim Dlugos, Robert
Duncan, David Eberly, Jim Eggeling, Kenward Elmslie, R.
Daniel Evans, Gerald L. Fabian, Salvatoro Farinella, Edward
Field, Charles Henri Ford, James Giancarlo, Allen Ginsberg,
John Giorno, Robert Gluck, Paul Goodman, Steve Jonas, E.
A. Lacey, Michael Lally, Gerrit Lansing, Winston Leyland,
Gerard Malanga, Paul Mariah, Wayne McNeill, Taylor Mead,
Tom Meyer, James Mitchell, Harold Norse, Frank O'Hara,
Chuck Ortleb, Stan Persky, Robert Peters, Vincent Sacardi,
Ron Schreiber, Perry Scott, Charley Shively, Aaron Shurin,
David Emerson Smith, Jack Spicer, George Stanley, Richard
Tagett, Hunce Voelcker, John Wieners, Jonathan Williams,
Terence Winch, Ian Young.

LEYLAND, Winston. Orgasms of Light. San Francisco: Gay Sun-
shine, 1977.
    Edgar Austin, Tommi Avicolli, William Barber, F. D. Blanton,
Victor Borsa, Perry Brass, Stuart Byron, Ira Cohen, Kirby
Congdon, Dennis Cooper, Ed Cox, Emilio Cubeiro, Gavin Dil-
lard, David Eberly, Jim Eggeling, Larry Eigner, Kenward
Elmslie, Salvatore Farinella, Charles Henri Ford, Allen Gins-
berg, John Ciorno, Robert Gluck, Will Inman, Tom Kennedy,
Maurice Kenny, James Kirkup, E. A. Lacey, Thomas Meyer,
Royal Murdoch, Harold Norse, Robert Peters, Felice Pisano,
Robert F. Riordan, Michael Rumaker, Raymonde Saint-Pierre,
Ron Schreiber, Robert Sellman, Charley Shively, Aaron Shurin,
David Emerson Smith, Jack Spicer, John Wieners, Jonathan
Williams, Ian Young.

LIVINGSTON, Myra Cohn. A Tune Beyond Us. New York: Har-
court, Brace & World, 1968.
    W. H. Auden, Harry Behn, Gwendolyn Brooks, E. E. Cumm-
ings, Richard Eberhart, T. S. Eliot, James Emanuel, Fulia
Fields, Robert Fitzgerald, Robert Frost, Corrado Govoni,
Robert Graves, Frank Horne, Langston Hughes, Randall Jar-
rell, X. J. Kennedy, David McCord, Archibald MacLeish,
Marianne Moore, Pablo Neruda, Louise Townsend Nicholl,
Norman Nicholson, Ezra Pound, James Reeves, Kenneth Rex-

roth, Theodore Roethke, Carl Sandburg, Louis Simpson, Stephen Spender, May Swenson, J. R. R. Tolkien, Giuseppe Ungaretti, Andrei Voznesensky, William Carlos Williams, Yevgeny Yevtushenko.

LOMAX, Alan; Raoul Abdul. 3000 Years of Black Poetry. New York: Dodd, Mead, 1970.
Samuel Allen, George Awooner-Williams, Lawrence Benford, David Granmer T. Bereng, Julian Bond, Arna Bontemps, Kwesi Brew, Jean Briere, Gwendolyn Brooks, Sterling A. Brown, Roussan Camille, Victor Hernandez Cruz, Waring Cuney, Roland Tomlekai Dempster, Mbella Sonne Dipoko, Owen Dodson, Ray Durem, Michael Echeruo, Mari Evans, Carol Freeman, Nikki Giovanni, Bobb Hamilton, Robert Hayden, Aig Higo, Frank Horne, Langston Hughes, Z. N. Hurston, Yusef Iman, Antonio Jacinto, Ted Joans, Georgia Douglas Johnson, Joseph E. Kariuki, Bob Kaufman, Patrice Emery Lumumba, Agnes Maxwell-Hall, A. L. Milner-Brown, Gabriel Okara, Christopher Okigbo, Lenrie Peters, Oliver Pitcher, Richard Rive, Walter Adolphe Roberts, Emile Roumer, Wole Soyinka, Sam Duby R. Sutu, Harold Milton Telemaque, Melvin B. Tolson, Jean Toomer, Derek Walcott.

LORRIMER FILMS LTD. Wholly Communion: International Poetry Reading at the Royal Albert Hall, London, June 11, 1965. New York: Grove, 1965.
Gregory Corso, Harry Fainlight, Lawrence Ferlinghetti, Allen Ginsberg, Ernst Jondl, Christopher Logue, Alexander Trocchi.

LOURIE, Dick. Come to Power: Eleven Contemporary American Indian Poets. Trumansburg, N.Y.: Crossing Press, 1974.
Minerva Allen, Lew Blockcolski, Joseph Bruchac, Karoniaktatie, Duane Niatum, Winston Mason, Norman Russell S. Roberto Sandoval, Suzan Shown, Leslie Silko, Ray Young Bear.

LOWENFELS, Walter. Poets of Today: A New American Anthology. New York: International, 1966.
George Bass, Art Berger, Alvah Bessie, Millen Brand, George Bratt, Marion Buchman, Olga Cabral, Alvaro Cardona-Hine, Carlos Cortez, Richard Davidson, Walt Delegall, Ray Durem, Eileen Egan, Mari Evans, Vincent Ferrini, Gene Frumkin, David Gallatin, Estelle Gershgoren, Don Gordon, Leslie Woolf Hedley, Barbara Hinchcliffe, Carl Wendell Hines, Jr., Herschel Horn, Frank Horne, Charles Humboldt, Joe Johnson, Kay Johnson, Aaron Kurtz, Peter La Farge, Carl Larsen, Jack Lindeman, Richard Lyons, Stuart McCarrell, William J. Margolis, James Boyer May, Eve Merriam, May Miller, J. M. Murphy, Howard McCord, Myron O'Higgins, Raymond Patterson, Irene Paull, Anne Peters, William J. Pomeroy, Naomi Replansky, Harland Ristau, Lucy Smith, Ray Smith, Yuri Smith, Alan Swallow, Dalton Trumbo, Paul Vesey, Mel Weisburd, Nancy Westlake, Joseph White, Sarah E. Wright, Carl Yeargens, Curtis Zahn.

LOWENFELS, Walter. Where Is Vietnam? American Poets Re-
spond: An Anthology of Contemporary Poems. Garden City, N. Y. :
Doubleday, 1967.
  Etel Adnan, Elizabeth Bartlett, Marvin Bell, Art Berger,
  Sidney Bernard, Harvey Bialy, Paul Blackburn, Robert Bly,
  Non Braymer, Olga Cabral, Hayden Carruth, Leo Connellan,
  Robert Creeley, James Dickey, Alan Dugan, Richard Eberhart,
  Richard A. Falk, David Ferguson, Lawrence Ferlinghetti,
  David Gallatin, Serge Gavronsky, Dan Georgakas, Julie Gib-
  son, Allen Ginsberg, Donald Hall, Nhat Hanh, Leslie Woolf
  Hedley, David Henderson, Robert Hershon, George Hitchcock,
  John Hollander, David Ignatow, Will Inman, Larry Jacobs,
  Hans Juergensen, Donald Justice, Jonathan Kaplan, Allan
  Katzman, Robert Kelly, Galway Kinnell, Denis Knight, Stanley
  Kunitz, Denise Levertov, Harry Lewis, Jack Lindeman, Karen
  Lindsey, Robert Lowell, Walter Lowenfels, Thomas McGrath,
  Clarence Major, Marya Mannes, Morton Marcus, Leonore
  Marshall, Thanasis Maskaleris, Thomas Merton, Robert Mezey,
  John Morgan, Howard Nemerov, Joel Oppenheimer, Robert
  Pack, Robert Peterson, Allan Planz, Felix Pollak, David Ray,
  Ishmael Reed, F. D. Reeve, David Rogers, Jerome Rothen-
  berg, Vern Rutsala, Saint Geraud, James Schevill, Dennis
  Schmitz, Howard Schulman, G. W. Sherman, Ross Shideler,
  rjs (Robert Joseph Sigmund), Louis Simpson, D. V. Smith,
  William Stafford, George Starbuck, Clemens Stark, Ed Stone,
  Eleanor Struthers, Robert Sward, John Tagliabue, Evelyn
  Thorne, Seth Wade, William Wantling, Leonard Williams,
  James Wright.

LOWENFELS, Walter. In a Time of Revolution. New York: Ran-
dom House, 1969.
  Daisy Aldan, Bob Allen, Carole Berge, Art Berger, Paul
  Blackburn, Horace Julian Bond, Grace Butcher, Harold Car-
  rington, Len Chandler, Charlie Cobb, Kirby Congdon, Victor
  Hernandez Cruz, Wesley Day, Allen de Loach, Diane Di Prima,
  Ree Dragonette, Al Flowler, A. Frederic Franklyn, Carl
  Gardner, Serge Gavronsky, Barbara Gibson, Emilie Glenn,
  John Harriman, Eily Catharine Harris, Howard Hart, David
  Henderson, Calvin C. Hernton, Barbara Holland, Will Inman,
  Marvin Jackman, Gerald Jackson, Joe Johnson, Percy Edward
  Johnston, Leonore Kandel, Allen Katzman, Bob Kaufman, Joel
  Kohut, Tuli Kupferberg, Peter La Farge, Carl Larsen, Julius
  Lester, D. A. Levy, Bruce Lippincott, Worth Long, Clarence
  Major, Cleve Matson, David Meltzer, June Meyer, George
  Montgomery, John Morgan, Freda Norton, Joel Oppenheimer,
  Marge Piercy, Alan Planz, N. H. Pritchard, Margaret Ran-
  dall, Lennox Raphael, David Rasey, Ishmael Reed, Steven
  Richmond, Sonia Sanchez, Ed Sanders, Dan Saxon, Fred Sil-
  ber, Isiah Smith, Clee Snipe, Jr. , Jane Stembridge, Ronald
  Stone, Gloria Tropp, Stephen Tropp, Diane Wakoski, William
  Wantling.

LOWENFELS, Walter. The Writing on the Wall: 108 American
Poems of Protest. New York: Doubleday, 1969.

Bob Allen, Elizabeth Bartlett, John Beecher, Art Berger,
Alexander Bergman, Douglas Blazek, Robert Bly, Kay Boyle,
Millen Brand, Gwendolyn Brooks, Sterling Brown, Charles
Bukowski, Christopher Bursk, Olga Cabral, Hayden Carruth,
Kirby Congdon, Leo Connellan, Gregory Corso, E. E. Cumm-
ings, Ray Durem, Mari Evans, Kenneth Fearing, Lawrence
Ferlinghetti, Sol Funaroff, Barbara Gibson, John Gill, Allen
Ginsberg, Arturo Giovannitti, Michael Gold, Don Gordon,
Woody Guthrie, Tim Hall, Robert Hayden, Samuel Hazo, Les-
lie Woolf Hedley, Calvin C. Hernton, Hyacinthe Hill, Langston
Hughes, David Ignatow, LeRoi Jones, Donald Justice, Leonore
Kandel, Bob Kaufman, Millea Kenin, Alfred Kreymborg, Tuli
Kupferberg, Peter La Farge, Dilys Laing, Bert Lee, Julius
Lester, Denise Levertov, D. A. Levy, Jack Lindeman, Worth
Long, Walter Lowenfels, Thomas McGrath, Archibald MacLeish,
Clarence Major, Thomas Merton, Kenneth Patchen, Raymond
Patterson, Marge Piercy, Felix Pollak, Ezra Pound, Margaret
Randall, Mrs. Sam Reece, Ishmael Reed, Ettore Rella, Naomi
Replansky, Renee Resendez, Kenneth Rexroth, Randy Rhody,
Muriel Rukeyser, Vern Rutsala, Sonia Sanchez, Carl Sandburg,
Ruth Lisa Schechter, Delmore Schwartz, Peter Seeger, John
Sinclair, George Starbuck, Stan Steiner, Jane Stembridge, Ed
Stone, Yuri Suhl, Genevieve Taggard, Melvin Tolson, Bartolo-
meo Vanzetti, Anca Vrbovska, William Wantling, Nancy Wil-
lard.

LOWENFELS, Walter. From the Belly of the Shark: A New An-
thology of Native Americans: Poems by Chicanos, Eskimos, Ha-
waiians, Indians, Puerto Ricans in the U. S. A., with Related Poems
by Others. New York: Random House, 1973.
Etal Adnan, Alta, John Angaiak, Robert Bacon, Stephen Berg,
Duane Big Eagle, Dolly Bird, Lew (Short Feathers) Blockcol-
ski, Robert Bly, Millen Brand, Besmilr Brigham, Joseph
Bruchac, Olga Cabral, Gladys Cardiff, Edmund S. Carpenter,
Jaime Carrero, Hayden Carruth, William Childress, Carl
Concha, Robert J. Conley, Leo Connellan, Jefferson Davis,
Jose-Angel Figueroa, Doug Flaherty, John Gill, Donald Duane
Govan, John Haines, William Harmon, Michael S. Harper, J.
C. Holman, Colette Inez, Manuel Jauregui, Maurice Kenny,
Chiron Khanshendel, Larry Lindsay Kimura, Elizabeth A.
Konapacky, Philip Legler, June Leivas, Meridel Le Sueur,
Gabriel O. Lopez, Howard McCord, Thomas McGrath, Carmen
M. Martinez, Ramon Martinez, John Milton, N. Scott Moma-
day, Robert Nelson Moore, Jr., Michael Moos, Duane Niatum,
Michael R. Nicholas, Charles Olson, Simon J. Ortiz, Ronald
Overton, Guy Owen, Haihai Pawo Pawo, Marge Piercy, David
Ray, Fred Red Cloud, Benjamin H. Rogers, Jerome Rothen-
berg, Michael Rumaker, Norman H. Russell, Ricardo Sanchez,
Roberto Sandoval, Ruth Lisa Schechter, Armand Schwerner,
Boots Sireech, Ray Smith, William Stafford, Hugo Stanchi,
Piri Thomas, Quincy Troupe, Robert Vargas, Charlie Vermont,
Juan Villegas, Mark Vinz, Gerald Robert Vizenor, Marnie
Walsh, William Wantling, Ramona Weeks, James Welch, Tom

Whitecloud, Anna White Feather, Nancy Willard, Keith Wilson, Philip Wofford, Ray Young Bear.

LOWENFELS, Walter. For Neruda, For Chile: An International Anthology. Boston: Beacon, 1975.
Etel Adnan, Yusuf Al-khal, George Amabile, Bob Arnold, Eva Ban, Sharon Barba, John Barnes, Willis Barnstone, Lee Baxandall, Henry Beissel, Zoe Best, Alan Britt, Joseph Bruchac, Olga Cabral, Charles Cantrell, Neeli Cherry, Chinweizu, Syl Cheney Coker, John Robert Colombo, Jack Curtis, Margot De Silva, W. S. Di Piero, Mike Dobbie, Franz Douskey, Ann Ducille, Ronald Lee Emmons, Gary Esolen, Jose-Angel Figueroa, Serge Cavronsky, Allen Ginsberg, Michael Gizzi, Carlos Golibart, Darcey Gottlieb, Ida Cramcko, Susan Grathwohl, Steven Michael Gray, Eric Greinke, Eamon Grennan, Sean Griffin, William Harrold, Robert Hass, Charles Hayes, Barbara A. Holland, Anselm Hollo, Bob Honig, Elias Hruska-Cortes, Will Inman, L. M. Jendrzejczyk, Cayl Jones, June Jordan, Hans Juergenson, Bernard Kelly, Stephen Kessler, Steve Kowit, Linda Lizut, Duane Locke, Dick Lourie, Walter Lowenfels, Pat Lowther, Stuart McCarrell, Thomas McGrath, David Martinson, Antar Sudan Katara Mberi, D. H. Melhern, Christina Morris, Harvey Mudd, Alejandro Murguia, Ed Ochester, Tanure Ojaide, Emily Paine, Cecil Rajendra, David Ray, Ishmael Reed, Robert Reinhold, Geoffrey Rips, Maria Rival, Jose Rodeiro, Leo Romero, Robert Rosenberg, Muriel Rukeyser, Andrew Salkey, Ruth Lisa Schechter, Tom Schmidt, James R. Scrimgeour, James Scully, Nina Serrano, Jory Sherman, Ray Smith, Hugo Stanchi, Nico Suarez, Michael Szporer, John Tagliabue, Nathaniel Tarn, Lorenzo Thomas, Carol Tinker, Quincy Troupe, William Wantling, Tom Wayman, Ramona Weeks, Clarke Wells, Elena Wilkinson, Robert Zaller, Harriet Zinnes.

LUCIE-SMITH, Edward. Holding Your Eight Hands: An Anthology of Science Fiction Verse. Garden City, N. Y.: Doubleday, 1969.
Brian A. Aldiss, Michael Benedikt, Asa Benveniste, D. M. Black, John Brunner, John Ciardi, Barry Cole, John Roberto Colombo, Robert Conquest, John Cotton, Thomas M. Disch, Mike Evans, Ruth Fainlight, John Fairfax, Anthony Haden-Guest, John Heath-Stubbs, Adrian Henri, Ted Hughes, Ronald Johnson, David Kilburn, Kenneth Koch, Ruth Lechtliner, C. S. Lewis, Edward Lucie-Smith, George Macbeth, Edwin Morgan, Jeff Nutall, Kenneth Patchen, Brian Patten, Peter Porter, Tom Rawroth, Peter Redgrove, John Sladek, D. M. Thomas, Jonathan Williams.

McCULLOUGH, Frances Monson. Earth Air Fire & Water: A Collection of Over 125 Poems. New York: Coward, McCann & Geoghegan, 1971.
Samuel Allen, Yehuda Amichai, Coleman Barks, Samuel Beckett, Marvin Bell, Michael Benedikt, Ted Berrigan, Wendell Berry, John Berryman, Elizabeth Bishop, Robert Bly, Louise

Bogan, Richard Brautigan, David Bromige, Michael Braunstein,
Tom Clark, Clark Coolidge, Robert Creeley, Victor Hernandez
Cruz, E. E. Cummings, James Dickey, Diane Di Prima, John
Dimroff, Robert Duncan, Kathleen Fraser, Dick Gallup, Tom
Galten, Allen Ginsberg, Thom Gunn, Donald Hall, Ted Hughes,
Randall Jarrell, Ted Joans, LeRoi Jones, Allen Kaplan, Gal-
way Kinnell, Kenneth Koch, Ruth Krauss, Denise Levertov,
Robert Lowell, Lewis Macadams, Jr., Howard McCord, Jack
Marshall, Jerome Mazzaro, N. Scott Momaday, Marianne
Moore, Frank O'Hara, Simon Ortiz, Ron Padgett, Kenneth
Patchen, John Perreault, Sylvia Plath, Ezra Pound, Adrienne
Rich, Theodore Roethke, Saint Geraud, James Schuyler,
Charles Simic, Louis Simpson, W. D. Snodgrass, Gary Sny-
der, William Stafford, Mark Strand, Dabney Stuart, May Swen-
son, Tom Veitch, Diane Wakoski, Anne Waldman, Philip Whal-
en, Mason Williams, William Carlos Williams, James Wright,
Al Young, Paul Zweig.

McGOVERN, Robert; Richard Snyder. 60 on the 60's: A Decade's
History in Verse. Ashland, Ohio: Ashland Poetry Press, 1970.
    W. H. Auden, Lawrence Benford, Daniel Berrigan, Robert
Bly, George Bowering, Gwendolyn Brooks, Hayden Carruth,
Hale Chatfield, Louis Coxe, Jon Eckels, Harry Edwards, Wil-
liam Elliott, Donald Hall, Will Inman, X. J. Kennedy, David
Kevorkian, James C. Kilgore, Denise Levertov, Philip Levine,
Robert Lowell, Robert McGovern, James Edmund Magner, Jr.,
Charles Martell, Warren Lane Malton, Leonard E. Nathan,
Howard Nemerov, Harry W. Paige, Eugene Ruggles, Rhoza W.
Simmons, W. D. Snodgrass, Richard Snyder, George Starbuck,
Hollis Summers, John Beauchamp Thompson, Lewis Turco,
Reed Whittemore, Richard Wilbur, John Woods.

McMAHON, Michael. Flowering After Frost: The Anthology of
Contemporary New England Poetry. Boston: Branden Press, 1975.
    George Abbe, Dick Allen, Allan Block, T. Alan Broughton,
Joseph Bruchac, Constance Carrier, D. W. Donzella, Ted
Enslin, Mira Fish, Bruce Holsapple, Divid Kherdian, Diane
Kruchkow, Gary Lawless, Lyn Lifshin, Michael McMahon,
Wesley McNair, Helena Minton, Napoleon St. Cyr, Robert
Siegel, Floyd C. Stuart, John Stevens Wade, George M. Young,
Jr.

McMICHAEL, James; Dennis Saleh. Just What the Country Needs,
Another Poetry Anthology. Belmont, Calif.: Wadsworth, 1971.
    Ai, Michael Benedikt, Robert Bly, Richard Brautigan, Philip
Dacey, Glover Davis, Russell Edson, John Haines, Michael
Harper, Robert L. Jones, Galway Kinnell, Philip Levine,
Larry Levis, Lou Lipsitz, James McMichael, Paul Malanga,
W. S. Merwin, Bert Meyers, Robert Mezey, Dennis Saleh,
Herbert Scott, Charles Simic, Gary Snyder, William Stafford,
Mark Strand, James Tate, Peter Wild, John Woods, Charles
Wright, David Young.

MAJOR, Clarence. The New Black Poetry. New York: International Publishers, 1969.
S. E. Anderson, Russell Atkins, Laurence Benford, Lebert Bethune, Hart Leroi Bibbs, Austin Black, Edwin Brooks, F. J. Bryant, Ed Bullins, Len Chandler, Sam Cornish, Stanley Crouch, Victor Hernandez Cruz, Gloria Davis, Ray Durem, Harry Edwards, Julia Fields, Bob Fletcher, Nikki Giovanni, Charles F. Gordon, Donald D. Govan, Carole Gregory, John Hall, Albert Haynes, David Henderson, Calvin C. Hernton, Quentin Hill, Everett Hoagland, Elton Hill-Abu Ishak, Lance Jeffers, Alicia L. Johnson, Howard Jones, LeRoi Jones, Norman Jordan, Bob Kaufman, Etheridge Knight, Don L. Lee, Cy Leslie, Worth Long, Audre Lorde, Joseph Major, June Meyer, Ernie Mkalimoto, Joseph M. Mosley, Glenn Myles, Larry Neal, Michael Nicholas, Dt Ogilvie, Charles Patterson, Ray Patterson, Tom Poole, N. H. Pritchard, Helen Quigless, Dudley Randall, Lennox Raphael, Amir Rashidd, Niema Rashidd (Fuller), Eugene Redmond, Ishmael Reed, Ridhiana, Conrad Kent Rivers, Sonia Sanchez, Johnie Scott, Gerald L. Simmons, Jr., Herbert A. Simmons, John Sinclair, Welton Smith, A. B. Spellman, Nazzam Al Sudan, Quincy Troupe, Darwin T. Turner, Malaika Ayo Wangara, Ron Welburn, John A. Williams, Al Young.

MALLEY, Jean; Hale Tokay. Contemporaries. 28 New American Poets. New York: Viking, 1972.
Mindy Aloff, Alta, Johari Amini, James Atlas, Gus Bertha, Steve Binder, Charlie Bordin, Toni Brown, Daniella Giseffi, Judy Grahn, Gerald Hausman, Erik Kiviat, Mary Norbert Korte, Jean Malley, David Melnick, Michael Mesic, Judith Moffett, Daniel Moore, Rochelle Nameroff, Monica Raymond, Robert Serling, John Oliver Simon, John Thomson, Hale Tokay, William Donald Wandick, Andrea Wyatt, Ian Young.

MALLORY, Lee. 20 Times in the Same Place: An Anthology of Santa Barbara Poetry. Carpinteria, Calif.: Painted Cave Books, 1973.
Brett Barton, P. J. Blumenthal, Bob Brown, Sam Hamill, Jo Anne Lee, Lee Mallory, Ken Maytag, S. M. Paulsen, Jaime Robles, Linda Rolens, Ted Shulgin, Merisa Smith, David Snyder, Bob Thrasher, Bill Timberman, Carol Tinker, Tim Wandell, Ken Weston, Peter Whigham, Geoff Young.

MARSHALL, Shirley E. A Young American's Treasury of English Poetry. New York: Washington Square, 1967.
John Masefield.

MATILLA, Alfredo; Ivan Silen. The Puerto Rican Poets: Los Poetas Puertorriqueños. New York: Bantam, 1972.
Pedro Pietro.

MATTHIAS, John. Twenty-three Modern British Poets. Chicago: Swallow Press, 1971.

Gavin Bantock, Basil Bunting, John Daniel, Ian Hamilton Finlay, Roy Fisher, Harry Guest, Lee Harwood, Anselm Hollo, Ted Hughes, David Jones, Christopher Logue, George MacBeth, Hugh MacDiarmid, Mathew Mead, Christopher Middleton, John Montague, Tom Raworth, Ken Smith, Nathaniel Tarn, D. M. Thomas, Charles Tomlinson, Gael Turnbull, Peter Whigham.

MAUD, Ralph; Aneirin Talfan Davies. Dylan Thomas's Choice: An Anthology of Verse Spoken by Dylan Thomas. New York: New Directions, 1963.
Max Adeler, W. H. Auden, George Barker, John Betjeman, Laurence Binyon, Frances Cornford, Idris Davies, Lawrence Durrell, Richard Eberhart, T. S. Eliot, Padraic Fallon, Oliver St. John Gogarty, Harry Graham, Robert Graves, Glyn Jones, Patrick Kavanagh, Sidney Keyes, Alun Lewis, Robert Lowell, Louis MacNeice, John Manifold, Marianne Moore, Ogden Nash, Frank O'Connor, William Plomer, Ezra Pound, John Crowe Ransom, Henry Reed, James Reeves, W. R. Rodgers, John Short, Edith Sitwell, Vernon Watkins, Dorothy Wellesley.

MAZUR, Gail. The Blacksmith Anthology. A Second Collection of Poems from the Blacksmith House. Cambridge, Mass.: Blacksmith Press, 1976.
Ray Amorosi, Timothy Baum, Jay Boggis, Rosellen Brown, William Corbett, Sam Cornish, Helene Davis, Alan Dugan, David Ferry, Kinereth Gensler, Celia Gilbert, Barbara L. Greenberg, Donald Hall, Marie Harris, Stratis Haviaras, Phyllis Janowitz, James Kates, Estelle Leontief, Miriam Levine, Margo Lockwood, Thomas Lux, Gerard Malanga, Gail Mazur, Nina Nyhart, Carole Oles, Linda Pastan, Jean Pedrick, Jane Lunin Perel, Robert Pinsky, James Reiss, Lee Rudolph, Ira Sadoff, Ron Schreiber, Philip Schultz, Lloyd Schwartz, Betsy Sholl, Jane Shore, Kathleen Spivack, James Tate, Florence Trefethen, Jean Valentine, Ruth Whitman, Bill Zavatsky.

MERCATANTE, Anthony S. The Harper Book of Christian Poetry. New York: Harper & Row, 1972.
W. H. Auden, E. E. Cummings, Dale Driscoll, Robert Lowell, Vassar Miller, Stephen Spender.

MILLER, Adam David. Dices or Black Bones: Black Voices of the Seventies. Boston: Houghton Mifflin, 1970.
William Anderson, Lucille Clifton, Conyus, Victor Hernandez Cruz, Sarah Webster Fabio, DeLeon Harrison, David Henderson, Calvin C. Hernton, Etheridge Knight, Clarence Major, Adam David Miller, Glenn Myles, Patricia Parker, N. H. Pritchard, Ishmael Reed, A. B. Spellman, Al Young.

MILLER, James Edwin; Bernice Slote. The Dimensions of Poetry: A Critical Anthology. New York: Dodd, Mead, 1962.
W. H. Auden, E. E. Cummings, T. S. Eliot, Robert Frost,

Robinson Jeffers, Archibald MacLeish, John Masefield, Karl Shapiro, Stephen Spender.

MILTON, John R. Four Indian Poets. Vermillion, S. D. : Dakota Press, 1974.
Paula Gunn Allen, John Barsness, Todd Haycock, Jeff Saunders.

MOLLENKOTT, Virginia R. Adam Among the Television Trees: An Anthology of Verse by Contemporary Christian Poets. Waco, Texas: Word Books, 1971.
Daisy Aldan, Forrect Anderson, Prentice Baker, Verna Tomlinson Baker, Richard Bastian, Betty Ruth Bird, Robert Bloom, Marian Frances Brand, Albert Howard Carter, Grace Cavalieri, Henry Tim Chambers, Sallie Chesham, E. Margaret Clarkson, Paul Clause, E. R. Cole, Irene Dayton, Albert De Pietro, Sandra Ruth Duguid, Virginia Floyd, Wade Hall, David Sten Herrstrom, Colette Inez, Roderick Hartigh Jellema, John Leax, Jane Marie Luecka, Robert A. Martin, Richard Mathews, Merle Meeter, Peter Meinke, William R. Mitchell, James Nolan, Patricia Ramsey, Elisavietta Ritchie, Ethel Green Russell, Luci Shaw, Ruthe T. Spinnanger, Elmer F. Suderman, Barbara Earl Thomson, Lucille F. Travis, F. Eugene Warren, James E. Warren, Jr.

MOLLOY, Paul. Beach Glass and Other Poems. New York: Four Winds, 1970.
A. R. Ammons, John Ashbery, W. H. Auden, John Berryman, Elizabeth Bishop, Robert Bly, Louise Bogan, Julian Bond, Philip Booth, Elizabeth Coatsworth, E. E. Cummings, J. V. Cunningham, James Dickey, Alan Dugan, Kenneth Fearing, Lawrence Ferlinghetti, Robert Fitzgerald, Robert Francis, Robert Frost, Allen Ginsberg, Donald Hall, Robert Hayden, Langston Hughes, Rolfe Humphries, David Ignatow, Randall Jarrell, Robinson Jeffers, Ted Joans, Helene Johnson, X. J. Kennedy, Galway Kinnell, Kenneth Koch, Denise Levertov, Phyllis McGinley, Archibald MacLeish, James Merrill, W. S. Merwin, Josephine Miles, Marianne Moore, Howard Moss, Ogden Nash, John R. Nash, Howard Nemerov, Frank O'Hara, Sylvia Plath, Ezra Pound, John Crowe Ransom, Adrienne Rich, Theodore Roethke, Carl Sandburg, Karl Shapiro, Louis Simpson, L. E. Sissman, W. D. Snodgrass, Gary Snyder, William Stafford, Mark Strand, May Swenson, John Updike, David Wagoner, E. B. White, Reed Whittemore, Richard Wilbur, William Carlos Williams, Richard Wright.

MONACO, Richard. New American Poetry. New York: McGraw-Hill, 1973.
John Briggs, Edward Butscher, Christopher Collins, Clark Coolidge, Barbara Davis, Gene Fowler, David Galler, Dick Gallup, Mary Gordon, Richard Hugo, J. C. Jacobs, Richard Kostelanetz, J. T. Ledbetter, Philip Levine, Gary Livingston, Louis Phillips, David Posner, Dwight Robhs, Karen Swenson, Jean Valentine, Douglas Worth.

MONACO, Richard; John Briggs. The Logic of Poetry. New York: McGraw-Hill, 1974.
> John Ashbery, W. H. Auden, John Berryman, William Stanley Braithewaite, Gwendolyn Brooks, William Cassegrain, Helen Chasin, Christopher Collins, Robert Creeley, E. E. Cummings, James Dickey, Alfred Dorn, Richard Eberhart, T. S. Eliot, David Galler, Allen Ginsberg, Anthony Hecht, Robert Huff, Langston Hughes, Ted Hughes, Richard Hugo, Donald Justice, Galway Kinnell, Stanley Kunitz, Philip Larkin, Denise Levertov, Philip Levine, Robert Lowell, Archibald MacLeish, James Merrill, W. S. Merwin, Marianne Moore, Howard Nemerov, William Packard, Louis Phillips, Sylvia Plath, David Posner, Ezra Pound, Theodore Roethke, Muriel Rukeyser, Carl Sandburg, Anne Sexton, Karl Shapiro, W. D. Snodgrass, Stephen Spender, Karen Swenson, Judith Thurman, David Wagoner, Richard Wilbur, William Carlos Williams, Douglas Worth, James Wright.

MONTGOMERY, George; Erik Kiviat. Bluebeat: A Collection of Recent Sounds. New York: Bluebeat, 1964.
> Bob Blossom, Bonnie Bremser, Harold Carrington, Allen W. De Loach, Lynn Fisher, Stanley Fisher, Jerry Greenberg, Charles Guenther, Barbara Jarvik, Al Katzman, John Keys, Erik Kiviat, Jonas Kover, Tuli Kupferberg, Margo Love, Jack Micheline, George Montgomery, Barbara Moraff, Penrod, Szabo, Gloria Tropp, Stephen Tropp, Alex Wiener, R. C. Wilson.

MOORE, Lilian; Judith Thurman. To See the World Afresh. New York: Atheneum, 1974.
> A. R. Ammons, Margaret Atwood, Imamu Amiri Baraka, Robert Bly, Edwin Brock, Joseph Bruchac, Michael Casey, Lucille Clifton, Malcolm Cowley, James Dickey, Robert Frost, Paul Goodman, Jonathan Griffin, Langston Hughes, Ted Hughes, Randall Jarrell, June Jordan, Maxine Kumin, Philip Larkin, Denise Levertov, George Macbeth, W. S. Merwin, Robert Mezey, Marianne Moore, Charles Olson, Marge Piercy, Sylvia Plath, Kenneth Rexroth, Theodore Roethke, William Stafford, Adrien Stoutenberg, Brian Swann, John Updike, David Wagoner, Ruth Whitman, William Carlos Williams.

MOORE, T. Inglis; Douglas Stewart. Poetry in Australia: Volume I: From the Ballads to Brennan: Volume II: Modern Australian Verse. Univ. of California, 1965.
> Leslie Holdsworthy Allen, Thea Astley, Dorothy Auchterlonie, Albert Gordon Austin, Lex Banning, Ken Barratt, Bruce Beaver, Maurice Biggs, Peter Bladen, John Blight, Vincent Buckley, David Campbell, Nancy Cato, Robert Clark, Laurence Collinson, Alexander Craig, Zora Bernice May Cross, Kathleen Walker Dalziel, Bruce Dawe, Dulcie Deamer, James Martin Devaney, Rosemary de Brissac Dobson, Max Dunn, Mary Durack, Geoffrey Dutton, Mary Finnin, Robert David FitzGerald, Leon Maxwell Gellert, Edwin Gerard, Mary Jean Cameron

Gilmore, Paul Langton Grano, Henry Mackenzie Green, Judith Green, Rodney Hall, Edward Phillip Harrington, Max Harris, William Hart-Smith, Gwen Harwood, Ian Healy, Charles Higham, Alec Derwent Hope, Peter Hopegood, William Edward Horney, Flexmore Hudson, Eric Irvin, Margaret Irvin, Evan Jones, Nancy Keesing, Christopher Koch, Eve Langley, Sylvia Lawson, Geoffrey Lehmann, Jack Lindsay, Beryl Llywelyn Lucas, Noel Macainsh, Frederick Thomas Bennett Macartney, James McAuley, Ronald McCuaig, Nan McDonald, Isobel Marion Dorothea Mackellar, David Malouf, John Streeter Manifold, David Martin, Philip Martin, Ray Mathew, Harley Matthews, Don Maynard, Ernest G. Moll, T. Inglis Moore, Ian Mudie, R. D. Murphy, William Henry Ogilvie, Nettie Janet Gertrude Higgins Palmer, Hal Porter, Peter Porter, Elizabeth Riddell, Roland Edward Robinson, Eric Rolls, David Rowbotham, J. R. Rowland, Thomas William Shapcott, Winifred Maitland Shaw, R. A. Simpson, Kenneth Slessor, Vivian Smith, Douglas Stewart, Harold Stewart, Randolph Stow, Colin Thiele, John Thompson, Michael Thwaites, Val Vallis, Chris Wallace-Crabbe, Francis Webb, A. J. Wood, Judith Wright.

MORRISON, Lillian. Sprints and Distances: Sports in Poetry and the Poetry in Sports. New York: Crowell, 1965.
George Abbe, Franklin P. Adams, Samuel Allen, Patrick Anderson, Reginald Arkell, Richard Armour, W. H. Auden, Henry Charles Beeching, John Betjeman, Morris Bishop, Philip Booth, Milton Bracker, Gwendolyn Brooks, John Bruce, Constance Carrier, Joseph P. Clancy, Leonard Cohen, Gregory Corso, E. E. Cummings, David Daiches, John Davidson, Reuel Denney, Babette Deutsch, Conrad Dickmann, Alan Dugan, M. D. Feld, Robert Fitch, Robert Fitzgerald, Robert Francis, Walker Gibson, John Woodcock Graves, Robert Graves, Alexandra Grilikhes, Samuel Hazo, A. P. Herbert, Rolfe Humphries, Barney Hutchinson, Robinson Jeffers, John Kiernan, Maxine W. Kumin, Archibald Lampman, Andrew Lang, Philip Larkin, Irving Layton, Forbes Lindsay, David McCord, Phyllis McGinley, M. J. McMahon, K. L. Martin, Walt Mason, Lee Murchison, Robert Fuller Murray, Ogden Nash, Elder Olson, Edmund W. Peters, Ezra Pound, John Crowe Ransom, Martin Robbins, Wey Robinson, W. R. Rodgers, W. W. Eustace Ross, Carl Sandburg, William Jay Smith, John Tagliabue, Ernest Lawrence Thayer, Louis Untermeyer, Florence Victor, Robert Wallace, Neil Weiss, Winifred Welles, Thomas Whitbread, John Williams, Sheila Wingfield, E. A. Wodehouse, Andrew Young.

MORSE, David. Grandfather Rock: The New Poetry and the Old. New York: Delacorte Press, 1972.
Howard Blaikley, Eric Clapton, Leonard Cohen, Judy Collins, David Crosby, E. E. Cummings, Bob Dylan, John Fogerty, Robert Fripp, Jimi Hendrix, Robert Hunter, Paul Kantner, Donovan Leitch, John Lennon, Paul McCartney, Joni Mitchell, Tom Paxton, Mike Pinder, Keith Reid, Martin Sharp, Peter Sinfield, Stephen Stills, Bernie Taupin.

la MORTICELLA, Barbara. The Portland Poetry Festival. Portland Poetry Festival, 1976.
Mindy Aloff, Penny Avila, Michael Baker, John Beecher, Brian Boldt, Gwendolyn Brooks, H. Carr, Jan Clausen, Marty Cohen, Walt Curtis, Robert A. Davies, Susan Rives Denight, J. Denison, Gene Detro, Ingrid Eau, Willis Eberman, Carol Erdman, Geranna Fleming, Ethel Fortner, Rory Funke, Doreen Gandy, Doll Gardner, Chip Goodrich, Leanne Grabel, James Grabill, Leslie Grove, Sara Heide, Lois Lillian Heinlein, Anita Helle, Christopher Howell, Margaret Hoy, Julis Johnson, Jim Kaady, Barbara la Morticella, Donald Levering, Charlene Lowry, Stuart Lyman, John Marron, Jeffrey Scott Matthews, Leon Miller, Henry Morrison, S. E. Mossholder, Duane Niatum, Christina V. Pacosz, R. A. Reed, Carlos Reyes, Naomi Richman, Moshe Ross, Vern Rutsala, Carey Salisbury, Stuart Sandler, Randy Schroth, Tom Smario, Ken Smith, N. J. Stockman, R. A. Swanson, Ron Talney, Carol Tarlen, James Tate, George Venn, Richard Weinraub, Mo Whitney, Dan G. Wieden.

MURPHY, Beatrice M. Today's Negro Voices: An Anthology by Young Negro Poets. New York: Messner, 1970.
Barbara Baker, Yillie Bey, Donald E. Bogle, Townsend T. Brewster, Thelma Parker Cox, Gregory J. Ford, Nikki Giovanni, Bernette Golden, Roslyn Greer, Vera E. Guerard, Vernoy E. Hite, Marsha Ann Jackson, Yvette Johnson, David Llorens, Doc Long, Jr., Herman L. McMillan, Barbara Marshall, Beatrice M. Murphy, Carolyn J. Ogletree, Daniel W. Owens, Henrietta C. Parks, Dorothy C. Parrish, Antoinette T. Payne, Helen G. Quigless, Eugene Redmond, Robert Reedburg, Carolyn M. Rodgers, Linwood D. Smith, Charles Stewart, Robert J. Sye, Valerie Tarver, Austin D. Washington, Tommy Whitaker, Warner B. Wims.

MYERS, John Bernard. The Poets of the New York School. Philadelphia: Univ. of Pennsylvania, 1969.
John Ashbery, Joseph Ceravolo, Kenward Elmslie, Barbara Guest, Kenneth Koch, Frank Lima, Frank O'Hara, James Schuyler, Tony Towle.

NASH, Ogden. Everybody Ought to Know. Philadelphia: Lippincott, 1961.
Dorothy Aldis, E. C. Bentley, John Betjeman, Helen Bevington, Morris Bishop, Charles Edward Carryl, Marchette Chute, John Ciardi, Richard Corbet, E. E. Cummings, John Davidson, T. S. Eliot, Jake Falstaff, J. T. Fields, Robert Frost, Rose Fyleman, Robert Graves, A. P. Herbert, Ralph Hodgson, Samuel Hoffenstein, Heinrich Hoffman, Robert Lytton, William McConagall, John Masefield, Julia Moore, Ogden Nash, Keith Preston, John Crowe Ransom, Laura E. Richards, Carl Sandburg, William Bell Scott, John Skelton, Nancy Byrd Turner, William Carlos Williams.

NIATUM, Duane. Carriers of the Dream Wheel. New York: Harper & Row, 1975.

Liz Sohappy Bake, Jim Barnes, Joseph Bruchac, Gladys
Cardiff, Lance Henson, Roberta Hill, N. Scott Momaday, Dana
Naone, Duane Niatum, Simon J. Ortiz, Anita Endrezze Probst,
W. M. Ransom, Wendy Rose, Leslie Silko, James Welch, Ray
A. Young Bear.

OLSON, Elder. Major Voices: 20 British and American Poets.
New York: McGraw-Hill, 1973.
W. H. Auden, John Berryman, E. E. Cummings, T. S. Eliot,
Robert Frost, Robert Lowell, Archibald MacLeish, Marianne
Moore, Ezra Pound, Theodore Roethke, William Carlos Wil-
liams.

OPPENHEIMER, Joel. The Genre of Silence: A One-Shot Review.
New York: The Poetry Project, 1967.
Sam Abrams, Jack Anderson, Ted Berrigan, Ray Bremser,
Jim Brodey, Dan Clark, Robert David Cohen, Scott Cohen,
Robert Creeley, Fred Dorn, Clayton Eshleman, Jerrold Green-
berg, John Hopper, Robert Kelly, William McNeill, Jack Mar-
shall, Murray Mednick, Joel Oppenheimer, Frank Samperi,
Joel Sloman, Charles Stein, Anne Waldman, Lewis Warsh.

OPPENHEIMER, Joel. Advance Token to Boardwalk. 28 New Jer-
sey Poets. Scotch Plains, N. J.: Poets & Writers of New Jersey,
1977.
Madeline Tiger Bass, Penny Bihler, Ginger Brant, Kathleen
Chodor, Helen Cooper, Toi Derricotte, Bette Distler, Stephen
Dunn, Kate Ellis, Shaun Farragher, Mary Freericks, Lewis
Gardner, Dan Georgakas, William J. Higginson, Jon Klimo,
Alice Kolb, Tadashi Kondo, John Kriebel, Cleopatra Mathis,
Dawn O'Leary, Alicia Ostriker, Doris Radin, Vera Raynor,
Geraldine Saunders, Carole Stone, Rod Tulloss, Lois Van
Houten, Tom Weatherly.

OWEN, Guy. Southern Poetry Review: A Decade of Poems. Ra-
leigh, N. C.: Southern Poetry Review Press, 1969.
Betty Adcock, A. R. Ammons, Philip Appleman, James Apple-
white, Donald W. Baker, Wendell Berry, Van K. Brock,
Charles Bukowski, E. G. Burrows, Hayden Carruth, Fred
Chappell, John Ciardi, Louis Coxe, Joanne de Longchamps,
James Dickey, R. H. W. Dillard, Charles Edward Eaton, Ed-
ward Field, George Garrett, Jean Garrigue, Max Halperen,
O. B. Hardison, Leslie Woolf Hedley, Diana Hott, Will Inman,
Judson Jerome, X. J. Kennedy, Adrianne Marcus, William
Matthews, Vassar Miller, Ray Mizer, Robert Morgan, Herbert
Morris, Norman C. Moser, Howard Nemerov, Paul Baker
Newman, John Nixon, Jr., Guy Owen, John Pauker, Allen
Planz, Paul Ramsey, Julia Randall, Shreela Ray, William Pitt
Root, Gibbons Ruark, Larry Rubin, Gary Sange, Joseph Edgar
Simmons, Lucien Stryk, Dabney Stuart, Hollis Summers, Wil-
liam E. Taylor, John Unterecker, Robert Watson, Peter Wild,
Miller Williams, Harold Witt, John Woods, Charles David
Wright.

OWEN, Guy; Mary C. Williams. New Southern Poets: Selected Poems from Southern Poetry Review. Chapel Hill: Univ. of North Carolina Press, 1974.

Betty Adcock, A. R. Ammons, James Applewhite, Prentice Baker, Coleman Barks, Gerald W. Barrax, Scott Bates, D. C. Berry, Wendell Berry, Doris Betts, Van K. Brock, Catherine Savage Brosman, Turner Cassity, Fred Chappell, James Dickey, R. H. W. Dillard, Gerald Duff, Charles Edward Eaton, Julia Fields, George Garrett, Malcolm Glass, John Haines, O. B. Hardison, William Harmon, Eugene Hollahan, Josephine Jacobsen, Roderick Jellema, Donald Justice, David Madden, Adrianne Marcus, Heather Miller, Jim Miller, Vassar Miller, Robert Morgan, Harry Morris, Norman C. Moser, Paul Baker Newman, Preston Newman, John Nixon, Jr., Linda Postan, Louis Phillips, Allen Planz, Stanley Plumly, Sam Ragan, Paul Ramsey, Julia Randall, Campbell Reeves, Alfred Reid, Gibbons Ruark, Larry Rubin, George Scarbrough, James Seay, Joseph Edgar Simmons, Dave Smith, Frank Steele, Leon Stakesbury, John Stone, Robert Joe Stout, Dabney Stuart, Hollis Summers, Eleanor Ross Taylor, Henry Taylor, William E. Taylor, Robert Watson, Gail Brockett White, James Whitehead, Miller Williams, Emily Herring Wilson, Charles Wright, Charles David Wright.

PADGETT, Ron; David Shapiro. An Anthology of New York Poets. New York: Random House, 1970.

John Ashbery, Bill Berkson, Ted Berrigan, Jim Brodey, Michael Brownstein, Joseph Ceravolo, Tom Clark, Clark Coolidge, Edwin Denby, Kenward Elmslie, Dick Gallup, John Giorno, Kenneth Koch, Frank Lima, Lewis MacAdams, Harry Mathews, Bernadette Mayer, Frank O'Hara, Ron Padgett, John Perreault, Ed Sanders, Aram Saroyan, Peter Schjeldahl, James Schuyler, David Shapiro, Tom Veitch.

PALMER, Doug. Poems Read in the Spirit of Peace and Gladness. Berkeley, Calif.: Peace & Gladness Press, 1966.

Eileen Adams, Richard Barker, Marianne Baskin, Lennart Bruce, Dawn F. Carey, David Cole, Gail Dusenbery, Gene Fowler, Hilary Ayer Fowler, Luis Carcia, Morton Grinker, D. R. Hazelton, James Koller, Robert Lax, Lowell Levant, Thanasis Maskaleris, Stephen Mindel, Tove Neville, Mary Norbert, Kay Okrand, Doug Palmer, David Rich, David Sandberg, David Schaff, John Oliver Simon, Gary Snyder, James Spencer, Leon Spiro, Sam Thomas, Jim Thurber, Jim Wehlage, Matthew Zion.

PARKER, Elinor. 100 More Story Poems. New York: Crowell, 1960.

Young E. Allison, William Edmondstone Aytoun, George Henry Baker, Beatrice Curtis Brown, Phoebe Cary, John Cunningham, Charles Dalmon, John Davidson, Sebastian Evans, Samuel Ferguson, Wilfrid Gibson, Sara Henderson Hay, Oliver Herford, Ralph Hodgson, Mildred Howells, Jean Ingelow, Joseph Lauren,

George Macdonald, Ogden Nash, John Mason Neale, Henry Newbolt, John Godfrey Saxe, W. C. Sellar, Ann Taylor, Jeffreys Taylor, Edith M. Thomas, Frederick Whittaker, James Wilson, R. J. Yeatman.

PARKER, Elinor. Here and There: 100 Poems About Places. New York: Crowell, 1967.
Neilson Abeel, Hervey Allen, Witter Bynner, Elizabeth Coatsworth, Padraic Colum, Edwin Curran, Robert Frost, Eva Gore-Booth, Gerald Gould, Ralph Hodgson, Ford Madox Heuffer, Robinson Jeffers, Arthur Ketchum, Richard Le Gallienne, Robert Lowell, John S. McGroarty, John Masefield, Gustave Nadaud, John Myers O'Hara, Lynn Riggs, Thomas William Rolleston, Sagittarius, Francis Saltus, Carl Sandburg, Clinton Scollard, George Sterling, Eugene Fitch Ware, John Hall Wheelock, E. B. White.

PARKER, Elinor. Four Seasons Five Senses. New York: Scribner, 1974.
Mary Coleridge, Hilda Doolittle, Robert Frost, Robert Graves, Nora Hopper, Thomas Howell, Barbara Euphan Todd, Katherine Tynan.

PARKER, Elinor. Poets and the English Scene. New York: Scribner, 1975.
John Betjeman, Frederick C. Boden, Wilfred Rowland Childe, Richard Church, Frances Cornford, Vivian de Sola Pinto, John Masefield, Norman Nicolson, Herbert Palmer, A. L. Rowse, V. Sackville-West, Siegfried Sassoon, Sacheverell Sitwell.

PARKS, Edd Winfield. Southern Poets. New York: Phaeton, 1970.
Donald Davidson, Merrill Moore, Josephine Pinckney, Jesse Stuart, Allen Tate, Robert Penn Warren.

PATTERSON. Lindsay. A Rock Against the Wind: Black Love Poems. New York: Dodd, Mead, 1973.
Dolores Abramson, Jeanette Adams, Johari Amini, Gwendolyn B. Bennett, William Stanley Braithwaite, Gwendolyn Brooks, Helen Morgan Brooks, Jayne Cortez, Linda Cousins, Blanche Taylor Dickinson, David Diop, Jackie Earley, Mari Evans, Jessie Redmond Fauset, Julia Fields, Clarence Franklin, Bruce C. Geary, Lethonia Gee, Paula Giddings, Nikki Giovanni, Linda Goss, Sam Greenlee, Angelina Weld Grimke, Frances E. W. Harper, Donald Jeffrey Hayes, R. Ernest Holmes, Langston Hughes, Femi Funmi Ifetayo, Ted Joans, Georgia Douglas Johnson, Helene Johnson, Hershell Johnson, Alice H. Jones, June Jordan, Joseph Kariuki, Khajuka, Don L. Lee, Pearl Cleage Lomax, Doughtry Long, Dee Dee McNeil, John Frederick Mathews, Pauli Murray, E. Marie Newsome, G. C. Oden, Lindsay Patterson, Rob Penny, Flavien Ranaivo, Dudley Randall, S. Carolyn Reese, Carolyn M. Rodgers, Loretta Rodgers, Sandra H. Royster, Sonia Sanchez, Ruby C. Saunders, Aishah Sayyida, Johnnie Scott, Sandra Sharp, Mervyn Taylor,

Richard W. Thomas, Mali Toure, Quincy Troupe, Darwin T. Turner, Maami Verano, Alice Walker.

PEARSON, Norman Holmes. Decade: A Collection of Poems from the First Ten Years of the Wesleyan Poetry Program. Middletown, Conn.: Wesleyan Univ. Press, 1969.

Alan Ansen, John Ashbery, Robert Bagg, Michael Benedikt, Robert Bly, Gray Burr, Turner Cassity, Tram Combs, Donald Davie, James Dickey, David Ferry, Robert Francis, John Haines, Edwin Honig, Richard Howard, Barbara Howes, David Ignatow, Donald Justice, Chester Kallman, Philip Levine, Lou Lipsitz, Josephine Miles, Vassar Miller, W. R. Moses, Leonard Nathan, Donald Petersen, Hyam Plutzik, Vern Rutsala, Harvey Shapiro, Jon Silkin, Louis Simpson, James Wright.

PECK, Richard. Sounds and Silences. New York: Delacorte Press, 1970.

Russell Atkins, W. H. Auden, George Barker, The Beatles, Arna Bontemps, Philip Booth, Gwendolyn Brooks, William Childress, Leonard Cohen, Richard Corbin, Robert Creeley, E. E. Cummings, James Dickey, Sonya Dorman, Glenn W. Dresbach, Richard Eberhart, T. S. Eliot, Mari E. Evans, Kenneth Fearing, Lawrence Ferlinghetti, Robert Francis, Robert Frost, Wolcott Gibbs, Morton Grosser, Woody Guthrie, Donald Hall, Langston Hughes, Evelyn Tooley Hunt, Randall Jarrell, Robinson Jeffers, Brooks Jenkins, LeRoi Jones, Molly Kazan, Galway Kinnell, Philip Larkin, Ruth Lechlitner, Denise Levertov, R. P. Lister, Phyllis McGinley, Louis MacNeice, Merrill Moore, Mary Oliver, Tom Paxton, Richard Peck, Jonathan Price, John Crowe Ransom, Henry Reed, Malvina Reynolds, Theodore Roethke, Carl Sandburg, Pete Seeger, Karl Shapiro, Louis Simpson, W. D. Snodgrass, Stephen Spender, William Stafford, May Swenson, Louis Untermeyer, John Updike, Richard Wilbur, William Carlos Williams.

PECK, Richard. Mindscapes. Poems for the Real World. New York: Delacorte Press, 1971.

Jonathan Aaron, Herbert R. Adams, Richard E. Albert, Hailu Araaya, W. H. Auden, DeWitt Bell, Morris Bishop, Lennart Bruce, Charles Bukowski, Alistair Campbell, Charles Causley, John Ciardi, Ann Darr, James Dickey, Isak Dinesen, Alan Dugan, Richard Eberhart, Mari Evans, Kenneth Fearing, Lawrence Ferlinghetti, Robert Frost, Alvin J. Gordon, Phyllis Gotlieb, Donald Hall, Marcie Hans, Robert Hayden, Oliver Herford, Dick Higgins, Barbara Howes, Langston Hughes, David Ignatow, Randall Jarrell, Robinson Jeffers, M. K. Joseph, Donald Justice, Galway Kinnell, Ron Koertge, Philip Larkin, John Leax, Phyllis McGinley, Rod McKuen, Howard Moss, Richard Peck, Quandra Prettyman, Kenneth Rexroth, Carl Sandburg, Karl Shapiro, William Stafford, Adrien Stoutenberg, May Swenson, Louis Untermeyer, John Updike, David Wagoner, Mildred Weston, Reed Whittemore, Oscar Williams, William Carlos Williams, Richard Wright.

PERRINE, Laurence; James M. Reid. 100 American Poems of the Twentieth Century. New York: Harcourt, Brace & World, 1966.
Conrad Aiken, Elizabeth Bishop, Louise Bogan, John Malcolm Brinnin, Malcolm Cowley, E. E. Cummings, James Dickey, Richard Eberhart, T. S. Eliot, Kenneth Fearing, Robert Frost, Isabella Gardner, Donald Hall, Anne Halley, Anthony Hecht, Rolfe Humphries, Randall Jarrell, Robinson Jeffers, Robert Lowell, Phyllis McGinley, Archibald MacLeish, Marianne Moore, Ogden Nash, Howard Nemerov, John Frederick Nims, Ezra Pound, John Crowe Ransom, Theodore Roethke, Alan Ross, Muriel Rukeyser, Carl Sandburg, Delmore Schwartz, James Scully, Anne Sexton, Karl Shapiro, Louis Simpson, W. D. Snodgrass, Will Stanton, Jon Swan, May Swenson, Allen Tate, Peter Viereck, Robert Penn Warren, Richard Wilbur, William Carlos Williams.

PERRY, John Oliver. The Experience of Poems. New York: Macmillan, 1972.
Conrad Aiken, W. H. Auden, Elizabeth Bishop, William Collins, Abraham Cowley, Robert Creeley, E. E. Cummings, J. V. Cunningham, Richard Eberhart, T. S. Eliot, William Empson, Robert Frost, Allen Ginsberg, Thom Gunn, Anthony Hecht, LeRoi Jones, X. J. Kennedy, John Lennon, Denise Levertov, Robert Lowell, Archibald MacLeish, Josephine Miles, Marianne Moore, Sylvia Plath, Ezra Pound, John Crowe Ransom, David Ray, Theodore Roethke, Anne Sexton, Karl Shapiro, Edith Sitwell, William Carlos Williams, Yvor Winters, James Wright.

PERRY, Phil. Mad Windows. Notre Dame, Ind.: Lit Press, 1969.
E. R. Baxter III, Doug Blazek, Charles Bukowski, Clayton Eshleman, Will Inman, T. L. Kryss, Brad Lehman, D. A. Levy, Lyn Lifshin, J. Matthias, Peter Michelson, Phil Perry, Ottone M. Riccio, Diane Wakoski, Peter Wild, Willie, Wayne Zade.

PETERSON, R. Stanley. Poetry II. New York: Macmillan, 1962.
Elizabeth Bishop, Hilda Conkling, Malcolm Cowley, E. E. Cummings, Hilda Doolittle, Richard Eberhart, Robert Frost, Ralph Hodgson, Edwin Honig, Phyllis McGinley, John Crowe Ransom, Carl Sandburg, Karl Shapiro, Stephen Spender, Louis Untermeyer, E. B. White, William Carlos Williams.

PHILLIPS, Robert. Moonstruck: An Anthology of Lunar Poetry. New York: Vanguard, 1974.
Jack Anderson, W. H. Auden, John Berryman, Alastair Campbell, E. E. Cummings, Babette Deutsch, James Dickey, William Dickey, Hilda Doolittle, William Empson, Raymond Federman, Robert Francis, Robert Frost, Allen Ginsberg, Horace Gregory, John Hollander, Robert Kelly, X. J. Kennedy, Galway Kinnell, Maxine Kumin, Stanley Kunitz, R. D. Laing, Denise Levertov, Archibald MacLeish, Josephine Miles, Lisel Mueller, Ed Ochester, Sylvia Plath, William Plomer, Al Pur-

dy, J. D. Reed, Ernest Sandeen, Anne Sexton, W. D. Snodgrass, Gary Snyder, William Stafford, Terry Stokes, May
Swenson, Constance Urdang, Jean Valentine, Marya Zaturenska.

PILON, A. Barbara. Concrete Is Not Always Hard. Middletown,
Conn.: Xerox Ed. Pub., 1972.
    Linda Abdar, Ilene Adams, Scott Alexander, Judith White
    Arthur, Rebecca L. Ayers, Marcia Batteiger, Philip Booth,
    Bob Cobbing, E. E. Cummings, Alyson Davis, Reinhard Dohl,
    Rick Eckstein, Bob Evans, Jay Evans, Ian Hamilton Finlay,
    Michael Flanders, Larry Freifeld, Robert Froman, Beth Gaunt,
    Joan Hanson, David Heeb, John Hollander, Patsy Jones, Myra
    Cohn Livingston, Michaele Lundberg, David McCord, Sam
    McDonald, Richard J. Margolis, Eve Merriam, Ewart Milne,
    Lodislav Novak, A. Barbara Pilon, Jonathan Price, Peter
    Quinn, Alastair Reid, Regina Sauro, Diane Scott, Mary Ellen
    Solt, Bob Stewart, Pamela Swain, May Swenson, Tish Thomp-
    son, John Updike, Nancy Sax Wachter, Emmett Williams,
    Mason Douglas Williams.

PLOTZ, Helen. The Marvelous Light: Poets and Poetry. New
York: Crowell, 1970.
    Charles Causley, William Cory, Rae Dalven, Dudley Fitts,
    Thomas di Giovanni, Patrick Kavanagh, David McCord, Dom
    Moraes, Norman Nicholson, Herbert Read, Henry Reed, Ali-
    stair Reid, Elizabeth Sewell, James Kenneth Stephen, Henry
    Treece, Arthur Waley, Peter Whigham.

PLUMLEY, William. Poems from the Hills. Charleston, W. Va.:
Morris Harvey College Publications, 1971.
    Carl Bode, Jeanne Delamater Bonnette, Arthur C. Buck, Pearl
    S. Buck, Marale G. Davis, Muriel Miller Dressler, Kimberly
    Dunham, Richard Eberhart, Louise Marsk Gabriel, Joseph
    Garrison, Jr., Emilie Glen, Ivan Hunter, Judson Jerome,
    Hans Juergensen, X. J. Kennedy, Blanche Whiting Keysner,
    Wallace E. Knight, Suzanne Legron, Don S. McDaniel, Louise
    McNeill (Pease), Stuart Marks, Cecilia Parsons Miller, Doris
    C. Miller, Jim W. Miller, Ann Nau, Lee Pennington, Richard
    Ray, Norman H. Russell, Hazel Rector Smith, Janet Smith,
    Lucye Rider Snyder, Bradley J. Stone, Jesse Stuart, Hollis
    Summers, Ethel Sure, John Foster West, Peter D. Ziukovic.

POETRY. Poetry. San Francisco: 1963.
    David Omer Bearden, Robert Franaman, Allen Ginsberg, An-
    drew Hoyem, Thomas Jackrell, Michael McClure, Daniel
    Moore, Charles Plymell, Roxie Powell, Alan Russo, Philip
    Whalen, J. Richard White.

POETS of America. Three Contemporary Poets. New York: Poets
of America, 1960.
    Grace Gilombardo Fox, Delina Margot-Parle, Aaron Schmuller.

POULIN, A. Contemporary American Poetry. Boston: Houghton
Mifflin, 1975.

John Ashbery, Imamu Amiri Baraka, John Berryman, Robert
Bly, Gwendolyn Brooks, Robert Creeley, James Dickey, Alan
Dugan, Robert Duncan, Lawrence Ferlinghetti, Allen Ginsberg,
David Ignatow, Galway Kinnell, Kenneth Koch, Denise Levertov,
John Logan, Robert Lowell, W. S. Merwin, Frank O'Hara,
Charles Olson, Sylvia Plath, Adrienne Rich, Theodore Roethke,
Anne Sexton, Louis Simpson, W. D. Snodgrass, Gary Snyder,
William Stafford, Richard Wilbur, James Wright.

PURDUE Research Foundation. A Suite of Four. West Lafayette,
Ind.: Purdue Univ. Studies, 1973.
    A. L. Lazarus, Barriss Mills, Felix Stefanile, Bruce Wood-
ford.

PYGMALION Press. The Tinseltown Poets. Hollywood, Calif.:
Pygmalion Press, 1974.
    Fred Dorsett, Leonore Kouwenhoven, Tony Perez, Jeffrey
Powers, Grant Sanders, P. Schneidre, Adrian Turcotte.

RANDALL, Dudley. Black Poetry: A Supplement to Anthologies
Which Exclude Black Poets. Detroit, Mich.: Broadside, 1960.
    Ahmed Alhamisi, Samuel Allen, Arna Bontemps, Gwendolyn
Brooks, Countee Cullen, Margaret Danner, Ray Durem, Ebon,
James A. Emanuel, Nikki Giovanni, Robert Hayden, Langston
Hughes, LeRoi Jones, Etheridge Knight, Don L. Lee, Doughtry
Long, Naomi Long Madgett, Clarence Major, Dudley Randall,
Sonia Sanchez, Edward S. Spriggs, Melvin B. Tolson, Jean
Toomer, Margaret Walker.

RANDALL, Dudley; Margaret C. Burroughs. For Malcolm; Poems
on the Life and the Death of Malcolm X. Detroit: Broadside, 1969.
    Nanina Alba, Gwendolyn Brooks, Margaret Burroughs, Marcel-
la B. Caine, Margaret Danner, Mari Evans, Julia Fields,
Bill Frederick, Zack Gilbert, Carmin Auld Goulbourne, Le
Graham, Bobb Hamilton, David Henderson, Theodore H. Horne,
Ted Joans, Christine C. Johnson, LeRoi Jones, K. William
Kgositsile, Etheridge Knight, Oliver Lagrone, David Llorens,
James Rowser Lucas, Clarence Major, Lawrence P. Neal,
George E. Norman, Patricia (McIlnay), James Patterson, Ray-
mond Patterson, Helen G. Quigless, Dudley Randall, Edward
Richer, Conrad Kent Rivers, Sonia Sanchez, John Sinclair,
Edward S. Spriggs, Margaret Walker, Reginald Wilson, Joyce
Whitsitt, James Worley, Jay Wright.

RANDALL, James R.; David Leviten. Three New Poets. Cambridge,
Mass.: Pym-Randall Press, c. 1968-1975.
    Christopher Bursk, William Corbett, Paul Hannigan.

READING. Reading. Philadelphia: Folcroft Press, 1971.
    Robert Bernstein, Victor Bockris, Ruth Lepson, Andrew Wylie.

REEVES, James. The Cassell Book of English Poetry. New York:
Harper & Row, 1965.

Edmund Blunden, E. E. Cummings, T. S. Eliot, Robert Frost, Robert Graves, Ezra Pound, John Crowe Ransom, Arthur Waley, Andrew Young.

REXROTH, Kenneth. Four Young Women: Poems. New York: McGraw-Hill, 1973.
Jessica Tarahata Hagedorn, Alice Karle, Barbara Szerlip, Carol Tinker.

RIGSBEE, David; Ellendea Proffer. The Ardis Anthology of New A-merican Poetry. Ann Arbor, Mich.: Ardis, 1977.
Charlotte Alexander, Pamela Alexander, Keith Althaus, Mark Axelrod, Neil Baldwin, Ron H. Bayes, Bruce Bennett, D. C. Berry, Michael Berryhill, Hunter Brown, Michael Burkard, Charles Cantrell, Marisha Chamberlain, David Childers, Billy Collins, Philip Dacey, Ann Deagon, Doug Flaherty, Peter Frank, Carol Frost, Tess Gallagher, Emery George, Marga-ret Gibson, Daniela Gioseffi, Patricia Goedicke, Ryah Tumark-in Goodman, Linda Gregg, Rachel Hadas, Robert Hahn, Marie Harris, Charles O. Hartman, Susan Hartman, William Heath, William J. Higginson, Michael Hogan, Tom House, T. R. Jahns, Lemuel Johnson, Loring Johnson, Rodger Kamenetz, Jane Katz, Terrance Keenan, Rolly Kent, David Kirby, Peter Klappert, Binnie Klein, Ron Koertge, Herbert Krohn, Naomi Lazard, David Lehman, Sharon Leiter, William Logan, Thomas Lux, Cynthia MacDonald, Heather McHugh, David McKain, Ger-ard Malanga, Cleopatra Mathis, Dale Matthews, Peter Meinke, Gary Miranda, Judith Moffett, John Morgan, Ed Ochester, Tom O'Grady, Perry Oldham, Steven Orlen, David Perkins, Henry Petroski, Katha Pollitt, T. E. Porter, Amanda Powell, Kraft Rompf, Bart Schneider, Rudy Shackelford, Jonathan Sisson, John Skoyles, Arthur Smith, Jordan Smith, R. T. Smith, Susan Snively, Kirtland Snyder, Gary Soto, William Sprunt, Martin Steingesser, Harry Stessel, Lynn Strongin, Lynn Sukenick, Brian Swann, Thom Swiss, Ross Talarico, Virginia R. Terris, Peter Trias, Dennis Trudell, Ellen Bryant Voigt, Ronald Wal-lace, W. S. Wardell, Michael Waters, Laurance Wieder, Richard Williams, Yvonne, Alan Ziegler, Larry Zirlin, Ahmos Zu-Bolton.

ROSE, Brian W. Lines of Action: An Anthology to Narrative and Lyrical Verse. New York: St. Martin's, 1961.
Martin Armstrong, Patric Barrington, John Bayliss, Edmund Blunden, N. H. Brettell, Guy Butler, C. F. Dennis, John Drinkwater, Georges Duhamel, T. S. Eliot, Kingsley Fair-bridge, Tom Farnol, Kate Filson, Leonard Flemming, C. Fox-Smith, Somerville Galney, Adam Lindsay Gordon, Eva Gore-Booth, Reginald Griffiths, Alan Herbert, Ralph Hodgson, Henry Lawson, E. V. Lucas, Wilson Mac Donald, Irene R. McLeod, John Manifold, John Masefield, Herbert Palmer, E. V. Rieu, Peter Roberts, W. W. E. Ross, Sagittarius, Doro-thy Sayers, Joseph Schull, Ian Serraillier, Virginia Sheard, F. Carey Slater, J. K. Stephen, Edward Wyndham Tennant, Ernest Lawrence Thayer, M. Ray Willis.

ROSEN, Kenneth. Voices of the Rainbow: Contemporary Poetry by American Indians. New York: Viking, 1975.
   Carroll Arnett, Charles Ballard, Peter Blue Cloud, Anita Endrezze-Probst, Phil George, Janet Campbell, Patty L. Harjo, Lance Henson, Roberta Hill, King D. Kuka, Harold Littlebird, Thomas Peacock, A. K. Redwing, Carter Revard, Leslie Marmon Silko, Jim Tollerud, Gerald Vizenor, Anna Walters, Ray A. Young Bear.

ROSENBLUM, Martin J. Brewing: 20 Milwaukee Poets. Lyme Center, N. H.: Giligia Press, 1972.
   Antler, Mike Dereszynski, Susan Firer, Geoff Gajewski, Jim Gibbons, Morgan Gibson, James Hazard, Dawn Knight, Steven Lewis, Roger Matchell, Tom Montag, Jim Orvino-Sorcic, Jefry Poniewaz, Martin J. Rosenblum, L. Bruce Rowe, Bob Watt, Kathy Wiegner, Suzanne Woods, Celia Young, Karl Young.

ROSENTHAL, M. L. The New Modern Poetry: British and American Poetry Since World War II. New York: Macmillan, 1967.
   Dannie Abse, A. Alvarez, Kingsley Amis, Brother Antoninus, John Berryman, John Betjeman, Elizabeth Bishop, Paul Blackburn, Robert Bly, Edwin Brock, Hayden Carruth, Charles Causley, John Ciardi, Austin Clarke, Robert Conquest, Robert Creeley, J. V. Cunningham, Donald Davie, Denis Devlin, James Dickey, Alan Dugan, Robert Duncan, Richard Eberhart, D. J. Enright, Lawrence Ferlinghetti, Ian Hamilton Finlay, David Galler, Jack Gilbert, Allen Ginsberg, Paul Goodman, W. S. Graham, Horace Gregory, Thom Gunn, Ramon Guthrie, Donald Hall, Michael Hamburger, Anthony Hecht, Geoffrey Hill, John Holloway, Katherine Hoskins, Graham Hough, Ted Hughes, Randall Jarrell, Elizabeth Jennings, LeRoi Jones, Patrick Kavanagh, Galway Kinnell, Thomas Kinsella, Carolyn Kizer, Stanley Kunitz, Dilys Laing, Philip Larkin, Irving Layton, Denise Levertov, John Logan, Robert Lowell, George MacBeth, Norman MacCaig, Hugh MacDiarmid, Jay MacPherson, W. S. Merwin, Christopher Middleton, John Montague, Richard Murphy, Howard Nemerov, Desmond O'Grady, Charles Olson, Sylvia Plath, Peter Porter, Henry Rago, Peter Redgrove, Kenneth Rexroth, Anne Ridler, W. R. Rogers, Theodore Roethke, Jerome Rothenberg, Muriel Rukeyser, James Schevill, Delmore Schwartz, Winfield Townley Scott, Anne Sexton, Karl Shapiro, Jon Silkin, Louis Simpson, Robin Skelton, A. J. M. Smith, W. D. Snodgrass, Gary Snyder, William Stafford, George Starbuck, May Swenson, R. S. Thomas, Anthony Thwaite, Charles Tomlinson, John Wain, Richard Weber, Theodore Weiss, Reed Whittemore, Richard Wilbur, David Wright, James Wright, Marya Zaturenska.

ROSENTHAL, M. L. 100 Postwar Poems, British and American. New York: Macmillan, 1968.
   Dannie Abse, A. Alvarez, Brother Antoninus, John Berryman, Elizabeth Bishop, Paul Blackburn, Robert Bly, Hayden Carruth,

Austin Clarke, Robert Creeley, Donald Davie, James Dickey,
Robert Duncan, D. J. Enright, Lawrence Ferlinghetti, Ian
Hamilton Finlay, Allen Ginsberg, Paul Goodman, W. S. Graham,
Thom Gunn, Ramon Guthrie, Donald Hall, Michael Hamburger,
Ted Hughes, Randall Jarrell, Elizabeth Jennings, LeRoi Jones,
Patrick Kavanagh, Galway Kinnell, Thomas Kinsella, Philip
Larkin, Denise Levertov, Robert Lowell, George MacBeth,
Norman MacCaig, Hugh MacDiarmid, W. S. Merwin, Christo-
pher Middleton, John Montague, Richard Murphy, Howard
Nemerov, Charles Olson, Sylvia Plath, Peter Redgrove, Ken-
neth Rexroth, Theodore Roethke, Muriel Rukeyser, James
Schevill, Delmore Schwartz, Anne Sexton, Jon Silkin, Louis
Simpson, W. D. Snodgrass, Gary Snyder, William Stafford,
May Swenson, R. S. Thomas, Charles Tomlinson, Theodore
Weiss, Richard Wilbur, David Wright.

ROTHENBERG, Jerome; George Quasha. America a Prophecy: A
New Reading of American Poetry from Pre-Columbia Times to the
Present. New York: Random House, 1973.
David Antin, John Ashbery, Imamu Amiri Baraka, Jimmy Bell,
Ted Berrigan, Harvey Bialy, Paul Blackburn, Robert Bly,
George Brecht, Charles Bukowski, Gregory Corso, Robert
Creeley, E. E. Cummings, Hilda Doolittle, Harold Dicker,
Edward Dorn, Robert Duncan, George Economou, Russell Ed-
son, Larry Eigner, T. S. Eliot, Theodore Enslin, Clayton
Eshleman, Kenneth Fearing, Lawrence Ferlinghetti, Charles
Henri Ford, Allen Ginsberg, John Giorno, Jim Harrison,
Ernest Hemingway, David Henderson, Dick Higgins, Anselm
Hollo, John Lee Hooker, Langston Hughes, David Ignatow,
Kenneth Irby, Robinson Jeffers, Stephan Jonas, Robert Kelly,
Jack Kerouac, Galway Kinnell, James Koller, Frank Kuenstler,
Philip Lamantia, Gerrit Lansing, James Laughlin, Denise
Levertov, Walter Lowenfels, Mina Loy, Michael McClure,
Thomas McGrath, Archibald MacLeish, Jackson Mac Low,
Bernadette Mayer, David Meltzer, Thomas Merton, W. S.
Merwin, Marianne Moore, Lorine Niedecker, Frank O'Hara,
Charles Olson, George Oppen, Joel Oppenheimer, Simon Ortiz,
Rochelle Owens, Kenneth Patchen, Allan Planz, Ezra Pound,
George Quasha, Carl Rakosi, Ishmael Reed, Kenneth Rexroth,
Charles Reznikoff, M. C. Richards, Theodore Roethke, Jer-
ome Rothenberg, Muriel Rukeyser, Sonia Sanchez, Carl Sand-
burg, Ed Sanders, Santo Blanco, Armand Schwerner, Eli
Siegel, Charles Simic, Louis Simpson, Gary Snyder, Jack
Spicer, Charles Stein, Nathaniel Tarn, Melvin B. Tolson,
Jose Garcia Villa, Diane Wakoski, Tom Weatherly, Philip
Whalen, Emmett Williams, Jonathan Williams, William Carlos
Williams, Keith Wilson, James Wright, Louis Zukofsky.

ROTHENBERG, Jerome. Revolution of the Word: A New Gathering
of American Avant-Garde Poetry 1914-1945. New York: Seabury
Press, 1974.
E. E. Cummings, Hilda Doolittle, Marcel Duchamp, Robert
Duncan, Kenneth Fearing, Charles Henri Ford, Walter Lowen-

fels, Mina Loy, Jackson Mac Low, Marianne Moore, Charles Olson, George Oppen, Kenneth Patchen, Ezra Pound, Kenneth Rexroth, Charles Reznikoff, Laura Riding, Louis Zukofsky.

ROTTMANN, Larry; Jan Barry; Basil T. Paquet. Winning Hearts and Minds: War Poems by Vietnam Veterans. Brooklyn, N. Y.: 1st Casualty Press, 1972.
Jan Barry, Igor Bobrowsky, James Boyer, Stanley Brownstein, Robert D. Buster, Michael Casey, L. DeWitt Clinton, Frank A. Cross, Jr., Mark Downey, William D. Ehrhart, Mary Emeny, Larry Fries, Robert C. Hahn, Sue Halpern, Gustav Hasford, Stephen R. Hatch, Julian Knaster, Harrison Kohler, Herbert Krohn, John Lytle, Jack McLain, Basil T. Paquet, Stan Platke, Charles M. Purcell, Don Receveur Jr., Larry Rottmann, Sergio, William J. Simon, Steven P. Smith, John Stulett, Tan, Landon Thorne, Michael Uhl, Burrows Younkin.

RUBIN, Louis Decimus. The Hollins Poets. Charlottesville: Univ. Press of Virginia, 1967.
John Alexander Allen, R. H. W. Dillard, Jean Farley, Julia Randall, William Jay Smith.

SALISBURY, Ralph. 3 Northwest Poets. Madison, Wisc.: Quixote Press, 1970.
Albert Drake, Lawson Inada, Douglas Lawden.

SALKEY, Andrew. Breaklight: The Poetry of the Caribbean. New York: Doubleday, 1972.
Michael Als, Elliott Bastien, Louise Bennett, Edward Brathwaite, Wayne Brown, George Campbell, H. D. Carberry, Jan Carew, Martin Carter, Charles Faustin, Sebastian Clarke, Gloria Escoffery, Wilson Harris, C. L. Herbert, Slade Hopkinson, Emmanuel Jean-Baptiste, Frank John, Evan Jones, Rudolph Kizerman, Knollys La Fortune, John La Rose, Syl Lowhar, Claude Lushington, Wordsworth McAndrew, Ian McDonald, Tony McNeill, Michael Abdul Malik, Jagdip Maraj, Tony Matthews, Marina Maxwell, Judy Miles, Mervyn Morris, Arthur Raymond, E. M. Roach, Dennis Scott, Clifford Sealy, Samuel Selvon, A. J. Seymour, Basil Smith, Ivan Van Sertima, Derek Walcott, Milton Williams.

SANDERS, Gerald DeWitt; John Herbert Nelson; M. L. Rosenthal. Chief Modern Poets of Britain and America. New York: Macmillan, 1964.
British: W. H. Auden, John Betjeman, Austin Clarke, Cecil Day Lewis, William Empson, Robert Graves, Thom Gunn, Ted Hughes, Patrick Kavanagh, Thomas Kinsella, Philip Larkin, Hugh MacDiarmid, Louis MacNeice, John Masefield, Siegfried Sassoon, Edith Sitwell, Stephen Spender, Charles Tomlinson. American: Conrad Aiken, Hilda Doolittle, Robert Duncan, Richard Eberhart, T. S. Eliot, Kenneth Fearing, Robert Frost, Randall Jarrell, Robinson Jeffers, Robert Lowell, Archibald MacLeish, Marianne Moore, Howard Nemerov, Charles Olson,

Sylvia Plath, Ezra Pound, John Crowe Ransom, Theodore
Roethke, Carl Sandburg, Karl Shapiro, Richard Wilbur, William Carlos Williams.

SARGENT, Genevieve. The Other Poetry Book. Big Fork, Minn.:
Northwoods Press, 1974.
Tilda S. Akers, Billie Allen, Josephine Austin, Mildred W.
Bradley, Emelie H. Burch, Bella Cameron, Gilbert Carvalho,
Myrtle E. Costello, Myrtle D. Danewalia, Mukund R. Dave,
Margaret Dovery, Helena Chase J. Drea, Raymond C. Emery,
Gregory Fontain, Truth Mary Fowler, Judith Ann Green, Nel-
son L. Haggerson, Merrie L. Hagopian, Freddie Phelps Han-
son, Dorothy D. Harris, Emmett L. Heaster, Louise Butts
Hendrix, Connie Hodges, Gertrude M. Houch, Rex Hudson,
Karl-Heinz Knauff, Ida Krangel, Ruth Latta, Iris Meads,
Geoff. Mwanja, Miriam Rose Paisley, Raghunath Pandit, Gauri
Pant, Edna G. Purviance, Virginia Rodas, Sylvia Rosenbaum,
Genevieve Sargent, Timothy Shaughnessy, Susan Shields, Colin
Simms, Lautaro Vergara, Ida Ruth Voss, Constance Walker,
Mary L. Wantner, Roi Yanez.

SATURDAY PRESS. Letters Stacked to Be Mailed: 4 New Poets.
Brooklyn, N.Y.: Saturday Press, 1975.
Howard Levy, Charlotte Mandel, Elizabeth Lynn Schneider,
Janet Sternburg.

SCHEFTEL, George. Poets of America: Anthology. Poets of A-
merica Pub. Co., 1966.
Lee Bain, Sylvia Bandyke, Mary Jane Barnes, Francesco
Bivona, Caroline Clark Marshall, Darrell L. Bolender, Miner
W. Brock, Emma Crobaugh, Edith M. Darby, Earle J. Grant,
Lillian Hammer, Etta Caldwell Harris, M. V. Holdsworth,
Hollis Koster, Roy Lisker, Helen Pisarelli Lombardi, William
J. Noble, Liboria Romano, George Scheftel, Charles B. Tink-
ham, Jake Trussell, Terrence R. Witt.

SCHNEIDER, Elisabeth W.; Albert L. Walker; Herbert E. Childs.
The Range of Literature: Poetry. New York: Van Nostrand, 1973.
Samuel Allen, A. R. Ammons, Brother Antoninus, W. H.
Auden, George Barker, Arna Bontemps, Gwendolyn Brooks,
Sterling A. Brown, Gregory Corso, E. E. Cummings, Hilda
Doolittle, T. S. Eliot, James A. Emanuel, Abbie Huston
Evans, Lawrence Ferlinghetti, Robert Frost, Allen Ginsberg,
Thom Gunn, William J. Harris, Robert Hayden, Langston
Hughes, Ted Hughes, Robinson Jeffers, Philip Larkin, Robert
Lowell, Archibald MacLeish, Louis MacNeice, N. Scott Moma-
day, Marianne Moore, Sylvia Plath, Ezra Pound, John Crowe
Ransom, Theodore Roethke, Carl Sandburg, Edith Sitwell,
Stephen Spender, Alan Stephens, May Swenson, Reed Whitte-
more, Richard Wilbur, William Carlos Williams.

SCHREIBER, Ron. 31 New American Poets. New York: Hill and
Wang, 1969.
Jack Anderson, G. Bishop-Dubjinsky, Besmilr Brigham, Victor

Contoski, Gail Dusenbery, Dave Etter, Gene Fowler, Dan
Georgakas, John Gill, John Haines, Phyllis Harris, Jim Har-
rison, Robert Hershon, William M. Hoffman, Emmett Jarrett,
Mary Norbert Korte, Robert Lax, Ethel Livingston, Dick
Lourie, Clive Matson, Jason Miller, Doug Palmer, Marge
Piercy, Alex Raybin, Joel Sloman, Lynn Strongin, John Un-
terecker, John Stevens Wade, Nancy Willard, Keith Wilson,
Jay Wright.

SEGNITZ, Barbara; Carol Rainey. Psyche: The Feminine Poetic
Consciousness: An Anthology of Modern American Women Poets.
New York: Dial, 1973.
Margaret Atwood, Besmilr Brigham, Mari Evans, Nikki Gio-
vanni, Patricia Goedicke, Erica Jong, Carolyn Kizer, Denise
Levertov, Lyn Lifshin, Marianne Moore, Rochelle Owens,
Marge Piercy, Sylvia Plath, Adrienne Rich, Anne Sexton, May
Swenson, Diane Wakoski.

SHAPIRO, Karl. American Poetry (American Literary Forms).
New York: Crowell, 1960.
Conrad Aiken, John Berryman, Elizabeth Bishop, John Ciardi,
E. E. Cummings, Richard Eberhart, T. S. Eliot, Kenneth
Fearing, Robert Frost, Allen Ginsberg, Randall Jarrell, Rob-
inson Jeffers, Robert Lowell, Archibald MacLeish, Marianne
Moore, Ezra Pound, John Crowe Ransom, Carl Sandburg,
Delmore Schwartz, Karl Shapiro, Allen Tate, Peter Viereck,
Robert Penn Warren, Richard Wilbur, William Carlos Williams.

SHERMAN, Susan; Dan Georgakas. Only Humans with Songs to Sing.
New York: Smyrna/Ikon Press, 1969.
Sam Abrams, Eleandor Aranson, Bob Auerback, Art Berger,
George Bowering, Diane Di Prima, David Gallatin, Dan
Georgakas, Saul Gottlieb, Will Inman, C. G. Johnson, Ed
Kissma, Richard Krech, Tsantah Lazky, Jack Lindeman, Dick
Lourie, Walter Lowenfels, Joe McClellan, Tom McGrath,
George Montgomery, Anis Nassar, Jeff Nutall, Jerry Parrott,
Marge Piercy, Margaret Randall, Haj Razavi, Dennis Redman,
Pat Robinson, John Oliver Simon, Susan Sherman, D. V.
Smith, Robert Sward, William Santling.

SHORE Publications. Six Eyes Open. Milwaukee: Shore Pub. Co.,
1972.
Hanley Elliott, Ken Kwint, Jeff Woodward.

SHUMAN, R. Baird. Nine Black Poets. Durham, N.C.: Moore,
1968.
Charles Cooper, Kattie M. Cumbo, Julia Fields, Carole
Gregory, William J. Harris, Lance Jeffers, Alicia Loy Johnson, James Arlington Jones, Richard W. Thomas.

SIMMONS, Ted. The Venice Poetry Company Presents. Los Angeles: Venice Poetry Company Assn., 1972.
Hilary Ayer, R. Tevis Boulware, Alan Brilliant, Charles Bu-

kowski, Samuel A. Eisenstein, Stuart Frieberg, Marguerite
Harris, Jack Hirschman, Michael Horovitz, Bill Jackson,
Ronald Koertge, Arthur Lerner, Gerald Locklin, Helen Luster,
K. Curtis Lyle, William J. Margolis, Deena Metzger, John
Montgomery, Eugene Redmond, Ted Simmons, John Thomas,
Quincy Troupe, David Vajalo, Emmett Williams.

SIMPSON, Louis. An Introduction to Poetry. New York: St. Martin's, 1967.
> W. H. Auden, Robert Creeley, E. E. Cummings, James Dickey,
> T. S. Eliot, Robert Frost, Allen Ginsberg, Thom Gunn, John
> Haines, Donald Hall, David Ignatow, Denise Levertov, Robert
> Lowell, Hugh MacDiarmid, Ezra Pound, Theodore Roethke,
> Louis Simpson, Gary Snyder, Richard Wilbur, William Carlos
> Williams.

SIXTIES. The Lion's Tail and Eyes. Madison, Minn.: Sixties
Press, 1962.
> Robert Bly, William Duffy, James Wright.

SKELTON, Robin. Five Poets of the Pacific Northwest. Seattle:
Univ. of Washington, 1964.
> Kenneth O. Hanson, Richard Hugo, Carolyn Kizer, William
> Stafford, David Wagoner.

SKLAR, Morty; Darrell Gray. The Actualist Anthology. Iowa City:
The Spirit That Moves Us Press, 1977.
> John Batki, Darrell Gray, Sheila Heldenbrand, David Hilton,
> Anselm Hollo, Allan Kornblum, Cinda Kornblum, George
> Mattingly, Chuck Miller, Dave Morice, Jim Mulac, John
> Sjoberg, Morty Sklar, Steve Toth.

The SMITH. The Immanentist Anthology: Art of the Superconscious. New York: The Smith, 1973.
> Steve Barfield, Ray Boxer, Alan Britt, Oscar Campa, Douglas
> Campbell, Damon Fazio, Charles Hayes, Duane Locke, Bill
> Lustig, James Macqueen, Elizabeth Fairclough Mahoney,
> Myrna Martinez, J. W. Noble, Jose Rodeiro, Paul Roth,
> Silva Scheibli, Mary Anne Steflik, Nicodemes Suarez, Salvatore
> Tagliarino, Charles Wyatt.

SMITH, A. J. M. The Oxford Book of Canadian Verse in English
and French. New York: Oxford, 1960.
> Patrick Anderson, Margaret Avison, Alfred Goldsworthy Bailey,
> Earle Birney, Arthur S. Bourinot, Elizabeth Brewster, Charles
> Bruce, Leonard Cohen, Roy Daniels, Alfred Des Rochers,
> Kildare Dobbs, Louis Dudek, Robert Finch, John Glassco,
> Alain Grandbois, Ralph Gustafson, Ronald Hambleton, Daryl
> Hine, Leo Kennedy, A. M. Klein, Frederick E. Laight,
> Irving Layton, Douglas Le Pan, Kenneth Leslie, Norman
> Levine, Dorothy Livesay, L. A. Mackay, Floris Clark
> McLaren, Jay MacPherson, E. W. Mandel, Anne Marriott,
> P. K. Page, E. J. Pratt, James Reaney, W. W. E. Ross,

F. R. Scott, A. J. M. Smith, Kay Smith, Raymond Souster, Heather Spears, Pierre Trottier, Myra Von Riedemann, Miriam Waddington, Wilfred Watson, Phyllis Webb, Anne Wilkinson.

SMITH, A. J. M. 100 Poems. New York: Scribner, 1965.
W. H. Auden, T. S. Eliot, Robert Frost, Ezra Pound, William Carlos Williams.

SMITH, Arthur James Marshall. Seven Centuries of Verse, English and American, from the Early English Lyrics to the Present Day. New York: Scribner, 1967.
W. H. Auden, E. E. Cummings, Richard Eberhart, T. S. Eliot, William Empson, Robert Frost, Robert Graves, Ralph Hodgson, Randall Jarrell, Robinson Jeffers, Robert Lowell, Archibald MacLeish, Louis MacNeice, John Masefield, Marianne Moore, John Crowe Ransom, Henry Reed, Theodore Roethke, Karl Shapiro, John Skelton, Stephen Spender, Allen Tate, Richard Wilbur, William Carlos Williams.

SMITH, Harry. The Smith Poets. New York: The Smith, 1971.
Sam Cornish, Gene Fowler, Jonathan Morse, Irene Schram, Theodore Sloane, Karen Swenson, Charles Wyatt.

SOLLID, Karen; John Sollid. The Musician Plays for Richard. Seattle: Spring Rain Press, 1972.
Richard Blackburn, August Kleinzabler, Jeffrey John Luke, Gerald McCarthy, Joanne M. Riley, Bruce Saari, Thomas Lee Smith, Patrick White.

SOLLID, Karen. Concrete Phoenix: A Collection of Eight Poets. Seattle: Spring Rain Press, 1973.
Jon Bracker, Betty Healy, Marc Hudson, Marjorie Luckmann, Byron Moffett, Paul Ruffin, Thomas Lee Smith, O. Howard Winn.

SOLLID, Karen; John Sollid. One Summer: An Anthology of Sixteen Poets. Seattle: Spring Rain Press, 1973.
Richard Blackburn, Susanne Dyckman, Raymond Federman, John Haines, Diane Hueter, August Kleinzahler, Marjorie Luckmann, Wayne Luckmann, Michael Madigan, Chong Yeh Parmeter, Joanne Riley, Michael Robinson, Thomas Lee Smith, William Stafford, Eve Triam, Patrick White.

SOLT, Mary Ellen. Concrete Poetry: A World View. Bloomington: Indiana Univ. Press, 1970.
Louise Bogan, Robert Creeley, E. E. Cummings, Carl Fernbach-Flarsheim, John Furnival, Peter Greenham, Dick Higgins, Dom Sylvester Houedard, Ronald Johnson, Robert Lax, Edwin Morgan, B. P. Nichol, Aram Saroyan, Mary Ellen Solt, Emmett Williams, Jonathan Williams, Louis Zukofsky.

STALLWORTHY, Jon. A Book of Love Poetry. New York: Oxford, 1974.

Fleur Adcock, Michael Alexander, W. H. Auden, John Berryman, John Betjeman, Austin Clarke, Tony Connor, Robert Creeley, E. E. Cummings, Donald Davie, Cecil Day Lewis, Paul Dehn, Lawrence Durrell, T. S. Eliot, Harry Fainlight, Lawrence Ferlinghetti, Robert Graves, Thom Gunn, John Heath-Stubbs, Anthony Hecht, A. D. Hope, Ted Hughes, Elizabeth Jennings, Donald Justice, Stanley Kunitz, Philip Larkin, Laurie Lee, Christopher Logue, Robert Lowell, Edward Lucie-Smith, Hugh MacDiarmid, Patrick MacDonogh, Archibald MacLeish, Louis MacNeice, Derek Mahon, W. S. Merwin, Robert Mezey, James Michie, Edwin Morgan, Brian Patten, Ezra Pound, John Press, Jonathan Price, F. T. Prince, John Crowe Ransom, Henry Reed, Kenneth Rexroth, W. R. Rodgers, Theodore Roethke, Alan Ross, Louis Simpson, Stevie Smith, W. D. Snodgrass, Stephen Spender, Jon Stallworthy, R. S. Thomas, Richard Weber, Hugo Williams.

STANFORD, Ann. The Women Poets in English. New York: McGraw-Hill, 1972.
Leonie Adams, Bernice Ames, Margaret Atwood, Louise Bogan, Kay Boyle, Gwendolyn Brooks, Jean Burden, Constance Carrier, Nancy Cato, Brenda Chamberlain, Lucille Clifton, Elizabeth Daryush, Babette Deutsch, Hilda Doolittle, Joan Finnigan, Hildegard Flanner, Janet Frame, Isabella Gardner, Jean Garrigue, Barbara Guest, Gwen Harwood, Ruth Herschberger, Frances Minturn Howard, Barbara Howes, Josephine Jacobsen, Elizabeth Jennings, Shirley Kaufman, Carolyn Kizer, Maxine Kumin, Eve Langley, Denise Levertov, Janet Lewis, Mina Loy, Phyllis McGinley, Marcia Lee Masters, Josephine Miles, Vassar Miller, Marianne Moore, Mary Oliver, Marge Piercy, Ruth Pitter, Sylvia Plath, Kathleen Raine, Julia Randall, Adrienne Rich, Anne Ridler, Muriel Rukeyser, Vita Sackville-West, May Sarton, Anne Sexton, Edith Shiffert, Edith Sitwell, Stevie Smith, Helen Sorrells, Ann Stanford, Ruth Stone, May Swenson, Mona Van Duyn, Celeste Turner Wright, Judith Wright, Marguerite Young, Marya Zaturenska.

STEELE, Frank. Poetry Southeast 1950-70. Martin, Tenn.: Univ. of Tennessee, 1968.
Scott Bates, Kenneth Beaudoin, Wendell Berry, Robert Canzoneri, Stephen Cox, James Dickey, R. H. W. Dillard, Edsel Ford, George Farrett, Andrew Glaze, Edwin Godsey, Stephen Malin, William Matthews, Marion Montgomery, Stephen Mooney, Paul Baker Newman, Guy Owen, Paul Ramsey, Julia Randall, Larry Rubin, George Scarborough, Frank Steele, William E. Taylor.

STEUBEN GLASS. Poetry in Crystal. New York: Spiral Press, 1963.
Conrad Aiken, Sara Van Alstyne Allen, W. H. Auden, Louise Bogan, Witter Bynner, Melville Cane, Gustav Davidson, Thomas Hornsby Ferril, Jean Garrigue, Horace Gregory, Donald Hall, Cecil Henley, Robert Hillyer, John Holmes, Robinson Jeffers,

Denise Levertov, Marianne Moore, Louise Townsend Nicholl, Kenneth Rexroth, Theodore Roethke, Delmore Schwartz, Karl Shapiro, W. D. Snodgrass, A. M. Sullivan, Hollis Summers, May Swenson, Joseph Tusiani, Mark Van Doren, John Hall Wheelock, Richard Wilbur, William Carlos Williams.

STEVENSON, Lionel; Howard Sergeant; Waddell Austin; Hildegarde Flanner; Gertrude Claytor; Frances Minturn Howard; Gemma D'Auria. Best Poems of 1966. Borestone Mountain Poetry Awards 1967: A Compilation of Original Poetry Published in Magazines of the English-speaking World in 1966. Palo Alto, Calif.: Pacific, 1967.
Betty Adcock, Carroll Arnett, Sanora Babb, Beth Bentley, Sam Bradley, Harry Brown, Sharon Lee Brown, Alistair Campbell, Hayden Carruth, Charles Causley, John Ciardi, Padraic Colum, Stanley Cooperman, John Cotton, James Crenner, James Dickey, Ruth Fox, Norman Friedman, Maurice Gibbons, Jack Gilbert, Arthur Gregor, Suzanne Gross, Harry Guest, Charles Higham, William Hollis, Ted Hughes, Judson Jerome, Allen Kanfer, Shirley Kaufman, David Knight, Maxine Kumin, Joan LaBombard, William Latta, Christopher Levenson, Denise Levertov, Laurence Lieberman, Jack Lindeman, Lou Lipsitz, Gerald Locklin, George MacBeth, J. H. McCandless, Morton Marcus, R. D. Mathews, Raeburn Miller, John Montague, W. R. Moses, Stanley Moss, Howard Nemerov, Alden Nowlan, Mary Oliver, Robert Peters, William Plomer, Peter Redgrove, Kenneth Keidrych Rhys, Adrienne Rich, Anne Sexton, Clarice Short, Jon Silkin, Kay Smith, Alex. Spaulding, Ann Stanford, Felix Stefanile, Warren Stevenson, Adrien Stoutenburg, Mona Van Duyn, Michael Van Walleghen, David Wagoner, Ted Walker, Robert Penn Warren, Vernon Watkins, John Hall Wheelock, Joan White, Harold Witt.

STIBITZ, E. Earle. Illinois Poets. A Selection. Carbondale: Southern Illinois Univ. Press, 1968.
Maxwell Bodenheim, Gwendolyn Brooks, Paul Carroll, R. R. Cuscaden, George Dillon, Glenn Ward Dresbach, Isabella Gardner, Paul Scott Mowrer, Lisel Mueller, John Frederick Nims, Jessica Nelson North, Elder Olson, Henry Rago, Carl Sandburg, Marjorie Allen Seiffert, Marion Strobel, Lucien Stryk, Robert Sward, Mark Turbyfill, Mark Van Doren.

STRAND, Mark. The Contemporary American Poets: American Poetry Since 1940. New York: World, 1969.
A. R. Ammons, Alan Ansen, John Ashbery, Marvin Bell, Michael Benedikt, John Berryman, Elizabeth Bishop, Robert Bly, Philip Booth, Edgar Bowers, Tom Clark, Gregory Corso, Henri Coulette, Robert Creeley, J. V. Cunningham, James Dickey, William Dickey, Alan Dugan, Alvin Feinman, Edward Field, Donald Finkel, Isabella Gardner, Jack Gilbert, Allen Ginsberg, Louise Gluck, Paul Goodman, John Haines, Donald Hall, Kenneth Ol Hanson, Anthony Hecht, Daryl Hine, Daniel Hoffman, John Hollander, Richard Howard, Barbara Howes, Robert Huff, Richard Hugo, David Ignatow, Randall Jarrell,

LeRoi Jones, Donald Justice, X. J. Kennedy, Galway Kinnell, Carolyn Kizer, Kenneth Koch, Al Lee, Denise Levertov, Philip Levine, Laurence Lieberman, John Logan, Robert Lowell, William E. Matchett, E. L. Mayo, William Meredith, James Merrill, W. S. Merwin, Howard Moss, Stanley Moss, Lisel Mueller, Howard Nemerov, Frank O'Hara, Charles Olson, Robert Pack, Donald Petersen, Sylvia Plath, Adrienne Rich, Theodore Roethke, James Schuyler, Winfield Townley Scott, Anne Sexton, Karl Shapiro, Charles Simic, Louis Simpson, L. E. Sissman, William Jay Smith, W. D. Snodgrass, Gary Snyder, William Stafford, Mark Strand, Robert Sward, May Swenson, James Tate, Constance Urdang, Peter Viereck, David Wagoner, Diane Wakoski, Theodore Weiss, Reed Whittemore, Richard Wilbur, Charles Wright, James Wright.

STRYK, Lucien. Heartland: Poets of the Mideast. DeKalb: Northern Illinois Univ., 1967.
Robert Bly, Gwendolyn Brooks, Paul Carroll, R. R. Cuscaden, Bruce Cutler, Frederick Eckman, Paul Engle, Dave Etter, Isabella Gardner, James Hearst, Robert Huff, John Knoepfle, Joseph Langland, John Logan, Thomas McGrath, Parm Mayer, Lisel Mueller, John F. Nims, Mary Oliver, Elder Olson, Raymond Roseliep, Dennis Schmitz, Karl Shapiro, William Stafford, Robert Sward, James Tate, Chad Walsh, John Woods, James Wright.

STRYK, Lucien. Heartland II: Poets of the Midwest. DeKalb: Northern Illinois Univ., 1975.
James B. Allen, Michael Anania, Jon Anderson, Jenne Andrews, Jim Barnes, Marvin Bell, James Bertolino, James Bonk, Walter Bradford, Branklin Brainard, George Chambers, D. Clinton, Victor Contoski, Peter Cooley, David Curry, Philip Dacey, Robert Dana, A. A. Dewey, R. P. Dickey, Stephen Dunn, Harley Elliott, David Allan Evans, Doug Flaherty, Robert Flanagan, Dan Gerber, Gary Gildner, Albert Goldbarth, Keith Gunderson, Jim Harrison, William Harrold, Michael Heffernan, Tom Hennen, Thomas James, Louis Jenkins, John Judson, Stanley Kiesel, Ted Kooser, Norbert Krapf, Greg Kuzma, Laurence Lieberman, Richard Lyons, Tom McKeown, Robert L. McRoberts, Marcia Lee Masters, John Matthias, Peter Michelson, Ralph J. Mills, Judith Minty, G. E. Murray, Linda Parker-Silverman, Mark Perlberg, Stanley Plumly, Felix Pollak, Carl Rakosi, David Ray, James Reiss, John Calvin Rezmerski, Michael Ryan, Ernest Sandeen, Howard Schwartz, R. E. Sebenthall, Bruce Severy, Michael Sheridan, Mary Shumway, Warren Slesinger, Dave Smith, A. G. Sobin, David Steingass, James Tipton, Stephen Tudor, Alberta Turner, Michael Van Walleghen, Robert Vas Dias, Rex Veeder, Mark Vinz, James L. White, Nathan Whiting, Robley Wilson, Jr., Warren Woessner.

STUDENT Nonviolent Coordinating Committee. Freedom School Poetry. Atlanta, Ga.: Student Nonviolent Coordinating Committee, 1965.

Shirley Ballard, Airvester Bowman, Charlie Brown, Joyce
Brown, Wilma Byas, Elnora Fondren, Allan Goodner, Ida Ruth
Griffin, Sandra Ann Harris, Alice Jackson, Robert Lee, Lynda,
Mitchell M., Madeline McHugh, David Marsh, Arelya J.
Mitchell, Edith Moore, Sandra Jo-Ann O., M. C. Perry, Ruth
Phillips, Lillie Mae Powell, Roosevelt Redmond, Nettie Rhodes,
Cora Sanders, Florence Seymour, William Smith, Rosalyn
Waterhouse, Lorenzo Wesley, Mary Zanders.

SUMAC PRESS. Five Blind Men. Fremont, Mich.: Sumac, 1969.
Dan Gerber, Jim Harrison, George Quasha, J. D. Reed,
Charlie Simic.

SUMMERFIELD, Geoffrey. First Voices: The Fourth Book. New
York: Random House; Knopf, 1970.
Jack Anderson, W. H. Auden, Edwin J. Brett, Albert Drake,
Bob Dunn, Paul Engle, Paul Goodman, Ian Griffiths, Arthur
Grimble, Woodie Guthrie, John Haines, Kevan Hall, Ted
Hughes, Charles E. Ives, Valerie Lorraine Jones, Denise
Levertov, Lou Lipsitz, Norman MacCaig, Charles Malam,
John Manifold, Morton Marcus, Richard J. Margolis, Eve
Merriam, Edwin Morgan, Alastair Reid, Charles Reznikoff,
Theodore Roethke, Carl Sandburg, Vernon Scannell, Jon Stall-
worthy, May Swenson, Charles Tomlinson, Eric Torgersen,
Mark Van Doren, Ted Walker, Vernon Watkins, Graeme Wil-
son.

TALISMAN. A Western Sampler: Nine Contemporary Poets: Se-
lected by the Editors of Talisman. Georgetown, Calif.: Talisman
Press, 1963.
Howard Baker, Myron Broomell, George Elliott, Leonard
Nathan, William Stafford, Ann Stanford, Alan Stephens, Clinton
Williams, Harold Witt.

TAYLOR, Henry. Poetry: Points of Departure. Cambridge, Mass.:
Winthrop, 1974.
John Alexander Allen, W. H. Auden, Ben Belitt, John Berry-
man, John Betjeman, Robert Bly, Fred Barnhauser, John
Malcolm Brinnin, Gwendolyn Brooks, John Byrom, Fred Chap-
pell, Kelly Cherry, Tom Clark, Lucille Clifton, Tony Connor,
John William Corrington, Gregory Corso, Malcolm Cowley,
Louis Coxe, Ann M. Craig, Robert Creeley, E. E. Cummings,
J. V. Cunningham, C. Day Lewis, Melvin De Bruhl, James
Den Boer, James Dickey, R. H. W. Dillard, Alan Dugan,
Richard Eberhart, T. S. Eliot, Robert Francis, Robert Frost,
George Garrett, Brewster Ghiselin, Gary Gildner, Allen Gins-
berg, Edwin S. Godsey, Steven Graves, John Haines, Bruce
Haley, Jerry Hammond, Samuel Hazo, Anthony Hecht, Conrad
Hilberry, Ralph Hodgson, John Hollander, R. Ernest Holmes,
Ray Holt, A. D. Hope, Barbara Howes, David Ignatow, Ran-
dall Jarrell, Robinson Jeffers, Dan Johnson, Erica Jong, Don-
ald Justice, X. J. Kennedy, Edward Kessler, Bill Knott, Paul
Lawson, Philip Legler, Denise Levertov, Robert Lowell, Wil-

liam Matthews, William Meredith, James Merrill, W. S. Merwin, Josephine Miles, May Miller, Howard Moss, Valery Nash, Howard Nemerov, Bink Noll, William Packard, Kenneth Patchen, Sylvia Plath, Ezra Pound, Paul Ramsey, Julia Randall, John Crowe Ransom, Henry Reed, Thomas Reiter, Theodore Roethke, Norman Rosten, Carl Sandburg, May Sarton, James Seay, Clarice Short, Jon Silkin, Louis Simpson, David Slavitt, M. J. Smith, William Jay Smith, W. D. Snodgrass, Gary Snyder, Stephen Spender, William Stafford, Ann Stanford, James Tate, Henry Taylor, John Updike, John Vernon, David Wagoner, Dianne Wakoski, Robert Watson, John Hall Wheelock, Thomas Whitbread, Richard Wilbur, William Carlos Williams, James Wright, Al Young.

TAYLOR, Warren; Donald Hall. Poetry in English. New York: Macmillan, 1970.
> W. H. Auden, George Barker, Elizabeth Bishop, E. E. Cummings, J. V. Cunningham, Richard Eberhart, T. S. Eliot, William Empson, Kenneth Fearing, Robert Francis, Robert Frost, Robert Graves, Thom Gunn, Geoffrey Hill, Ralph Hodgson, Ted Hughes, Philip Larkin, Denise Levertov, Robert Lowell, Hugh MacDiarmid, Archibald MacLeish, Louis MacNeice, W. S. Merwin, Marianne Moore, Howard Nemerov, Ezra Pound, Kathleen Raine, John Crowe Ransom, Theodore Roethke, Carl Sandburg, Karl Shapiro, Louis Simpson, Stephen Spender, Allen Tate, R. S. Thomas, Charles Tomlinson, Vernon Watkins, Richard Wilbur, William Carlos Williams, Yvor Winters.

TEN POETS. Ten Poets. Seattle: 1962.
> Beth Bentley, Nelson Bentley, Carol Hall, Richard F. Hugo, Carolyn Kizer, William H. Matchett, Theodore Roethke, Arnold Stein, Eve Triem, David Wagoner.

THOMAS, R. S. The Penguin Book of Religious Verse. Baltimore: Penguin, 1963.
> Ronald Bottrall, Robert Frost, Robinson Jeffers, Hugh MacDiarmid, Charles Madge, Kathleen Raine, John Crowe Ransom, Anne Ridler, Terence Tiller, Vernon Watkins, Douglas Young.

THREE. Three Some Poems. Cambridge: 1976.
> Jeannine Dobbs, Kin Gensler, Eliz Knies.

TISDALE, Celes. Betcha Ain't: Poems From Attica. Detroit, Mich.: Broadside, 1974.
> Brother Amar, Hersey Boyer, L. Alexander Brooks, Daniel Brown, Chico, Bill Dabney, Sanford Harris, Jr. (Sanford X), Isaiah Hawkins, Charles Johnson, Joseph Kitt (Jamal Ali Bey Hassan), Theodore McCain, Jr., Marvin McQueen, Harvey A. Marcelin, Curtiss C. Marshall, Mshaka (Willie Monroe), John Lee Norris (Kamua), Harold Eugene Packwood (Inhara Asia), Clarence Phillips, Jamail Abdur Rahman (Sheridan R. Nesbitt; Robert Sims), Christopher Sutherland, Celes Tisdale, Sam Washington, Raymond Webster (X; Odire Mbarar).

TOTEM PRESS. Four Young Lady Poets. New York: Corinth
Books, 1962.
  Carol Berge, Barbara Moraff, Rochelle Owens, Diane Wakoski.

TRAPP, Jacob. Modern Religious Poems: A Contemporary Anthol-
ogy. New York: Harper & Row, 1964.
  Conrad Aiken, Maxwell Anderson, Brother Antoninus, W. H.
  Auden, Richard Church, Elizabeth J. Coatsworth, E. E.
  Cummings, Carleton Drewry, Richard Eberhart, T. S. Eliot,
  Abbie Huston Evans, Lawrence Ferlinghetti, Robert Frost,
  Herman Hagedorn, Edith Henrich, John Holmes, Rolfe Humph-
  ries, Randall Jarrell, Robinson Jeffers, Josephine W. Johnson,
  Stanley Kunitz, Kenneth Leslie, Archibald MacLeich, Earl
  Marlatt, John Masefield, Murilo Mendes, John Moffit, Howard
  Moss, Edwin Muir, Helene Mullins, Elder Olson, Edith Love-
  joy Pierce, Conrado Nale Roxlo, Muriel Rukeyser, Carl Sand-
  burg, May Sarton, Siegfried Sassoon, Delmore Schwartz, Karl
  Shapiro, Odell Shepard, Edith Sitwell, Stephen Spender,
  Roberta Teale Swartz, Sister M. Therese, Gilbert Thomas,
  Michael Thwaites, Cesar Tiempo, Mark Van Doren, Jose
  Garcia Villa, Margaret Walker, Vernon Watkins, Marie De L.
  Welch, John Hall Wheelock, Richard Wilbur, Oscar Williams,
  William Carlos Williams.

TURNER, Darwin T. Black American Literature: Poetry. Colum-
bus, Ohio: Merrill, 1969.
  Margaret Walker Alexander, Arna Bontemps, William Stanley
  Braithwaite, Gwendolyn Brooks, Sterling Brown, Owen Dodson,
  Robert E. Hayden, Langston Hughes, Georgia Douglas Johnson,
  LeRoi Jones, Etheridge Knight, Don L. Lee, Naomi Long
  Madgett, Dudley Randall, Melvin B. Tolson, Jean Toomer,
  Darwin T. Turner.

UNIVERSITY OF MASS. A Curious Quire: Poems. Amherst,
Mass.: Univ. of Massachusetts Press, 1962.
  Leon O. Barron, David R. Clark, Stanley Koehler, Robert G.
  Tucker.

UNIVERSITY PRESS OF VIRGINIA. Poems From the Virginia
Quarterly Review 1925-1967. Charlottesville: Univ. Press of Vir-
ginia, 1969.
  Conrad Aiken, George Barker, Ben Belitt, John Berryman,
  Philip Booth, Harry Brown, Hayden Carruth, H. D., Donald
  Davidson, C. Day Lewis, James Dickey, Richard Eberhart,
  T. S. Eliot, Paul Engle, Dudley Fitts, Robert Francis, Rob-
  ert Frost, Jean Carrigue, Donald Hall, Randall Jarrell, Rob-
  inson Jeffers, Lawrence Lee, William Meredith, Marianne
  Moore, Theodore Morrison, Samuel French Morse, Howard
  Nemerov, John Frederick Nims, Elder Olson, Ruth Pitter,
  Carl Sandburg, William Jay Smith, Allen Tate, Dorothy Brown
  Thompson, Ulrich Troubetzkey, Robert Penn Warren, Edward
  Weismiller, Reed Whittemore, Richard Wilbur, William Carlos
  Williams.

UNTERMEYER, Louis. Modern American Poetry: Modern British
Poetry: Combined New and Enlarged Edition. New York: Harcourt,
Brace & World, 1964.
Leonie Adams, James Agee, Conrad Aiken, Richard Aldington,
W. H. Auden, George Barker, John Berryman, Louise Bogan,
Joseph Campbell, Melville Cane, Elizabeth J. Coatsworth,
Padraic Colum, Alex Comfort, Frances Cornford, E. E.
Cummings, C. Day Lewis, T. S. Eliot, Kenneth Fearing,
Robert Frost, W. W. Gibson, Robert Graves, Horace Gregory,
Roy Helton, Robert Hillyer, Ralph Hodgson, Langston Hughes,
Richard Hughes, Randall Jarrell, Robinson Jeffers, Robert
Lowell, David McCord, Hugh MacDiarmid, Archibald MacLeish,
Louis MacNeice, John Manifold, John Masefield, Marianne
Moore, Merrill Moore, Ogden Nash, Norman Nicholson, Ken-
neth Patchen, Ruth Pitter, Ezra Pound, Peter Quennell, John
Crowe Ransom, W. R. Rodgers, Muriel Rukeyser, Carl Sand-
burg, Siegfried Sassoon, Delmore Schwartz, Karl Shapiro,
Edith Sitwell, Sacheverell Sitwell, Stephen Spender, Genevieve
Taggard, Allen Tate, Jean Starr Untermeyer, Louis Untermey-
er, Peter Viereck, Sylvia Townsend Warner, Robert Penn
Warren, John Hall Wheelock, William Carlos Williams, Marya
Zaturenska.

UNTERMEYER, Louis. Men and Women: The Poetry of Love.
New York: American Heritage, 1970.
Philip Appleman, Samuel Bishop, Francis William Bourdillon,
Clinch Calkins, Nancy Cardozo, Leonard Cohen, William
Corkins, Ormond de Kay, Jr., Bartholomew Griffin, A. D.
Hope, Laurence Hope, Denise Levertov, Amy Levy, Michael
Lewis, Archibald MacLeish, Peter Anthony Motteaux, Jean-
nette Nichols, John Payne, Clement Robinson, Anne Sexton,
Karl Shapiro, W. D. Snodgrass, Jon Stallworthy, Louis
Untermeyer, Judith Viorst, Winifred Welles.

UNTERMEYER, Louis. 50 Modern American and British Poets
1920-1970. New York: McKay, 1973.
Conrad Aiken, John Ashbery, W. H. Auden, Imamu Amiri
Baraka, Wendell Berry, John Berryman, Elizabeth Bishop,
John Malcolm Brinnin, Gwendolyn Brooks, E. E. Cummings,
James Dickey, Richard Eberhart, T. S. Eliot, Robert Frost,
Allen Ginsberg, Thom Gunn, Jim Harrison, Anthony Hecht, A.
D. Hope, Barbara Howes, Langston Hughes, Ted Hughes,
Randall Jarrell, LeRoi Jones, Erica Jong, Galway Kinnell,
Stanley Kunitz, Robert Lowell, Archibald MacLeish, W. S.
Merwin, Marianne Moore, Sylvia Plath, Ezra Pound, Adrienne
Rich, Theodore Roethke, Muriel Rukeyser, Anne Sexton, Wil-
liam Jay Smith, Louis Simpson, W. D. Snodgrass, Stephen
Spender, May Swenson, Mona Van Duyn, Derek Walcott, Rich-
ard Wilbur, William Carlos Williams, James Wright.

VAN DEN HEUVEL, Cor. The Haiku Anthology: English Language
Haiku by Contemporary and Canadian Poets. Garden City, N.Y.:
Doubleday, 1974.

Mary Acosta, Eric Amann, Jack Cain, L. A. Davidson, Frances Drivas, Bernard Lionel Einbond, Larry Gates, James William Hackett, William J. Higginson, Gary Hotham, Clement Hoyt, Foster Jewell, Leroy Kanterman, Julia Rankin King, Elizabeth Searle Lamb, Geraldine Clinton Little, David Lloyd, Michael McClintock, Mabelsson Norway, Alan Pizzarelli, Marjory Bates Pratt, Sydell Rosenberg, Michael Segers, Ron Seitz, Robert Spiess, Bonnie Squires, Jan S. Streif, Tom Tico, James Tipton, Cor van den Heuvel, Anita Vigil, Nicholas Virgilio, Gerald Robert Vizenor, Larry Wiggin, Rod Willmot, John Wills, Kenneth Yasuda, Virginia Brady Young.

VINCENT, Jean Anne. Patriotic Poems America Loves: 125 Poems Commemorating Stirring Historical Events and American Ideals. Garden City, N. Y.: Doubleday, 1968.

Laurence Altgood, Maxwell Anderson, J. A. Armstrong, Edward Bangs, Arlo Bates, Katherine Lee Bates, Rosemary Benet, Henry Halcomb Bennett, William E. Brooks, H. C. Bunner, Katherine Garrison Chapin, Thomas Curtis Clark, Robert Peter Tristram Coffin, John Daly, Thomas Osborn Davis, John Williams De Forest, Sydney Dobell, Joseph Rodman Drake, Thomas Dunn English, Arthur Gordon Field, Francis Miles Finch, William Dudley Foulke, Robert Frost, Patrick Sarsfield Gilmore, Edmund L. Gruber, Edward Everett Hale, Felicia Dorothea Browne Hermans, Josiah Gilbert Holland, Joseph Hopkinson, Arthur Nicholas Hosking, John Hall Ingham, Francis DeHaes Janvier, Laurence M. Jones, Walter Kittridge, Alfred Kreymborg, Elias Lieberman, R. W. Lilliard, Archibald MacLeish, Guy Humphreys McMaster, Mildred Meigs, John Mitchell, James Montgomery, Theodore O'Hara, John Oxenham, William Ordway Partridge, John Pierpont, Jeremiah Eames Rankin, Grantland Rice, Daniel C. Roberts, Billy Rose, Carl Sandburg, Kate Brownlee Sherwood, Samuel Francis Smith, Frank L. Stanton, Burton Egbert Stevenson, Will Henry Thompson, Nancy Byrd Turner, Henry Van Dyke, V. B. Wilson, Francis Brett Young.

VINCENT, Stephen. Five on the Western Edge. San Francisco: Momo's Press, 1977.

Beau Beausoleil, Steve Brooks, Larry Felson, Hilton Obenzinger, Stephen Vincent.

VIOLET PRESS. We Are All Lesbians: A Poetry Anthology. New York: Violet Press, 1973.

Jeri Berc, Brooke, Jennifer Cloud, Helen Conrads, Susan Daily, Diane Devennie, Edith Dobell, Bobbie Geary, Elsa Gidlow, Deborah J. Glick, B. Goldberg, Judy Greenspan, Laura Hanna, Heather, Lee Lally, Alicia Langtree, Sasa Malzone, Judith Moss, Morgan Murielchild, Pan, Patty One Person, Ann Pollon, Vittoria Repetto, Judy Rosen, Rachel Rubin, Morgan Sanders, P. J. Schimmel, Sheel, Karen Snow, Teresa, Lilli Vincenz, Emily Rubin Wiener, Lucy Wilde, Fran Winant, Dana Wordes.

VRBOVSKA, Anca: Alfred Dorn, Robert Lundgren. The New Orlando
Poetry Anthology: Volume II. New Orlando Publications, 1963.
Frederika Blankner, Kate Brackett, Harold Briggs, Miner
Brock, Nathaniel Burt, Alvaro Cardona-Hine, Robert Clair-
mont, William Leo Coakley, Dorothy Dalton, Richard David-
son, Rose Davison, Joanne de Longchamps, Alfred Dorn, Ree
Dragonette, Leah Bodine Drake, Norma Farber, Annette B.
Feldmann, Dorothy Ellin Flax, David Gallatin, Gladys Wilmot
Graham, Lisa Grenelle, Orella D. Halstead, Leona Hamilton,
Leslie Woolf Hedley, Hyacinthe Hill, Carolyn Hoggins, Will
Inman, Kaja, Richard Kelly, Margaret M. Lavin, Robert Lay-
zer, James E. Lewisohn, Thelma Spear Lewisohn, Lawrence
Lipton, Lilith Lorraine, Louise Louis, Robert Lundgren, Rosa
Zagnoni Marinoni, Joseph Martinek, Alice Clear Matthews,
James Boyer May, Barriss Mills, Elizabeth Randall Mills,
Helene Mullins, Louis Newman, Edith Ogutsch, Guy Owen,
Edmund Pennant, John Peter, Henry Picola, Loker Raley,
Morris Reyburn, Liboria E. Romano, Larry Rubin, H. L.
Van Brunt, Anca Vrbovska, Mary Boyd Wagner, Rozana Webb,
Curtis Whittington, Jr. , Curtis Zahn.

VRBOVSKA, Anca: Alfred Dorn, Robert Lundgren. The New Orlando
Poetry Anthology: Volume III. New Orlando Publications, 1968.
Philip Appleman, Willis Barnstone, Sylvia Berry, Frederika
Blankner, Charles A. Brady, Marietta R. Clarke, William Leo
Coakley, Leo Connellan, Rose Davison, Richard Davidson, Al-
fred Dorn, Charles Edward Eaton, RobertOh Farber, Norma
Farber, Ruth Feldman, Annette B. Feldmann, Edsel Ford,
Kinereth Gensler, Emilie Glen, Patricia Goedicke, Katherine
Gorman, Leona Hamilton, Leslie Wollf Hedly, Suzanne Henig,
Hyacinthe Hill, Frances Minturn Howard, Maxine Kumin, James
Lewisohn, Lawrence Lipton, Robert Lundgren, Madeline Mason,
Anne Marx, James Boyer May, Edward L. Meyerson, Barriss
Mills, Clark Mills, Helene Mullins, Nicoli, Edith Ogutsch,
William Packard, Jennie M. Palen, Edmund Pennant, Henry
Picola, Julian Raeder, Liboria E. Romano, Eugeneia E. Shel-
ley, Thelma Spear Lewisohn, Margaret Tauss, Anca Vrbovska,
Mildred Wiackley.

WAGNER, Linda W. : C. David Mead. Introducing Poems. New
York: Harper and Row, 1976.
Margaret Atwood, W. H. Auden, Imamu Amiri Baraka, Wen-
dell Berry, John Berryman, Paul Blackburn, Robert Bly, Arna
Bontemps, Philip Booth, Richard Brautigan, Edwin Brock,
Gwendolyn Brooks, Robert Creeley, E. E. Cummings, Hilda
Doolittle, Richard Eberhart, Frederick Eckman, T. S. Eliot,
Joan Finnigan, Robert Frost, Sadamu Fujiwara, Allen Ginsberg,
Nikki Giovanni, Jim Harrison, Robert Hayden, Daniel Hoffman,
Langston Hughes, David Ignatow, Josephine Jacobsen, Randall
Jarrell, Robinson Jeffers, Bob Kaufman, X. J. Kennedy, Gal-
way Kinnell, Joseph Langland, James Laughlin, Don L. Lee,
Denise Levertov, Gordon Lightfoot, Phyllis McGinley, Archi-
bald MacLeish, George Meredith, Eve Merriam, Joni Mitchell,

Marianne Moore, Ogden Nash, Joyce Carol Oates, Kenneth
Patchen, Marge Piercy, Sylvia Plath, Ezra Pound, David Ray,
Ishmael Reed, Theodore Roethke, Muriel Rukeyser, Carl Sand-
burg, Anne Sexton, Jon Silkin, Louis Simpson, A. J. M.
Smith, Gary Snyder, Stephen Spender, William Stafford, Jules
Supervielle, May Swenson, David Wagoner, Diane Wakoski,
Reed Whittemore, William Carlos Williams, John Woods,
James Wright.

WALDMAN, Anne. The World Anthology: Poems from the St.
Mark's Poetry Project. New York: Bobbs-Merrill, 1969.
Sam Abrams, Jack Anderson, John Ashbery, Bill Berkson,
Ted Berrigan, Paul Blackburn, Joe Brainard, Jim Brodey,
Michael Brownstein, Steve Carey, Jim Carroll, Joseph Cera-
volo, Tom Clark, Andrei Codrescu, Scott Cohen, Clark
Coolidge, Jonathan Cott, Harlan Dangerfield, Edwin Denby,
Diane Di Prima, Kenward Elmslie, Larry Fagin, Dick Gallup,
Allen Ginsberg, John Giorno, Charles Goldman, Lee Harwood,
David Henderson, George Kimball, Ruth Krauss, Jonathan
Kundra, Joanne Kyger, Gerard Malanga, Frank O'Hara, Joel
Oppenheimer, Ron Padgett, John Perreault, Carter Ratcliff,
Rene Ricard, Iris Rifkin, Harris Schiff, Peter Schjedahl,
James Schuyler, Joel Sloman, Johnny Stanton, Charles Stein,
M. G. Stephens, Sotere Torregian, Tom Veitch, Anne Wald-
man, Lewis Warsh, Tom Weatherly.

WALDMAN, Anne. Another World: A Second Anthology of Works
from the St. Mark's Poetry Project. Indianapolis: Bobbs-Merrill,
1971.
Keith Abbott, John Ashbery, Bill Bathurst, Bill Berkson, Ted
Berrigan, Paul Blackburn, Ebbe Borregaard, Joe Brainard,
Richard Brautigan, Ray Bremser, Jim Brodey, Michael Brown-
stein, Steve Carey, Jim Carroll, Tom Clark, Andrei Codrescu,
Scott Cohen, Clark Coolidge, Robert Creeley, Diane Di Prima,
Thomas M. Disch, Kenward Elmslie, Larry Fagin, Mary
Ferrari, David Franks, Dick Gallup, Merrill Gifillan, Allen
Ginsberg, John Giorno, John Godfrey, Charles Goldman, Jon-
athan Gott, Ted Greenwald, Barbara Guest, Robert Harris,
David Henderson, Ed Kissam, Kenneth Koch, John Koethe,
James Koller, Ruth Krauss, Jonathan Kundra, Joanne Kyger,
Joseph Le Sueur, Frank Lima, Lewis MacAdams, Jr. , Jamie
MacInnis, Gerard Malanga, Bernadette Mayer, Catherine
Murray, Kathleen Norris, Charles North, Frank O'Hara, Joel
Oppenheimer, Ron Padgett, Carter Ratcliff, Lou Reed, Charles
Reznikoff, Ed Sanders, Aram Saroyan, Harris Schiff, Peter
Schjedahl, James Schuyler, Joel Sloman, Patti Smith, Gary
Snyder, Johnny Stanton, Kathleen Teague, Lorenzo Thomas,
John Thorpe, Sotere Torregian, Tony Towle, Tom Veitch,
Anne Waldman, Lewis Warsh, Philip Whalen, John Wieners,
Rebecca Wright.

WALLACE, Robert; James G. Taaffe. Poems on Poetry; The
Mirror's Garland. New York: Dutton, 1965.

Dannie Abse, Alan Ansen, W. H. Auden, Elizabeth Bishop,
John Ciardi, Robert Conquest, J. V. Cunningham, Donald
Davie, James Dickey, D. J. Enright, David Ferry, Edward
Field, Robert Francis, Robert Frost, Roy Fuller, Walker
Gibson, Jack Gilbert, Michael Hamburger, Anthony Hecht,
Daniel G. Hoffman, John Holmes, Ted Hughes, David Ignatow,
Robinson Jeffers, Elizabeth Jennings, X. J. Kennedy, Galway
Kinnell, James Kirkup, Kenneth Koch, Richmond Lattimore,
Denise Levertov, Thomas McGrath, Archibald MacLeish, Louis
MacNeice, William Meredith, James Merrill, W. S. Merwin,
Marianne Moore, Howard Moss, Howard Nemerov, Sylvia
Plath, Hyam Plutzik, Ezra Pound, Alastair Reid, Kenneth
Rexroth, Carl Sandburg, Karl Shapiro, Louis Simpson, Iain
Crichton Smith, W. D. Snodgrass, Stephen Spender, George
Starbuck, Peter Viereck, Jose Garcia Villa, John Wain, Rob-
ert Wallace, Vernon Watkins, David Wevill, Reed Whittemore,
Richard Wilbur, Oscar Williams, William Carlos Williams,
James Wright.

WALSH, Chad. Today's Poets: American and British Poetry Since
the 1930's. New York: Scribner, 1972.
      George Barker, Patricia Beer, John Bennett, John Berryman,
Carl Bode, John Ciardi, Robert Creeley, James Dickey, Law-
rence Durrell, William Everson, Lawrence Ferlinghetti, Roy
Fuller, Allen Ginsberg, Thom Gunn, Robert Hayden, Ted
Hughes, Philip Larkin, Don L. Lee, Laurie Lee, Denise
Levertov, Robert Lowell, George MacBeth, Vassar Miller,
Richard Murphy, Howard Nemerov, Bink Noll, Kenneth Patchen,
Brian Patten, Sylvia Plath, Theodore Roethke, Anne Sexton,
Karl Shapiro, W. D. Snodgrass, Gary Snyder, R. S. Thomas,
John Wain, Diane Wakoski, Derek Walcott, Chad Walsh, Rich-
ard Wilbur, James Wright.

WANG, Hui-ming. The Land on the Tip of a Hair: Poems in Wood.
Barre, Mass.: 1972.
      Duane Ackerson, Gregory W. Bitz, Robert Bly, Richard Deutch,
Siv Cedering Fox, Robert Francis, David Ignatow, Linda Pastan,
Tom Pickard, David Ray, Charles Simic, William Stafford,
James Tate, Tomas Transtromer, David Young.

WEIL, James L. Of Poem, An Anthology. New Rochelle, N. Y.:
Elizabeth Press, 1966.
      Carroll Arnett, Marvin Bell, Henry Birnbaum, Paul Blackburn,
Jon Bracker, Sam Bradley, Spencer Brown, Jerry H. Burns,
Cid Corman, Robert Creeley, R. R. Cuscaden, August Derleth,
Frederick Eckman, Theodore Enslin, Gena Ford, Marguerite
Harris, Joseph Joel Keith, Barriss Mills, Lorine Niedecker,
Ron Offen, George Oppen, Simon Perchik, Felix Pollak, Mar-
garet Randall, Tim Reynolds, Raymond Roseliep, William Staf-
ford, Felix Stefanile, James L. Weil, Frederic Will, Loring
Williams.

WEISHAUS, Joel. On the Mesa: An Anthology of Bolinas Writing.
San Francisco: City Light, 1971.

Bill Berkson, Michael Bond, Ebbe Borregaard, Bill Brown,
Tom Clark, Robert Creeley, Max Crosley, John Doss, Law-
rence Kearney, Joanne Kyger, Keith Lampe, Steven Lazar,
David Meltzer, John Thorpe, Lewis Warsh.

WESLEYAN UNIVERSITY. Spring Poetry Festival at Wesleyan 1960.
Middletown, Conn.: Wesleyan Univ., 1960.
Willis Barnstone, Philip Booth, Stuart Byron, Spike D'Arthenay,
Reuel Denney, Robert Duncan, David Ferry, Robert Francis,
Robert Frost, George Garrett, Eliot Glassheim, Donald Justice,
Stanley Kunitz, Muriel Ladenburg, R. H. McLaughlin, William
Meredith, Samuel French Morse, August Napier, Charles Ol-
son, Hyman Plutzik, Salvatore Quasimodo, Paul Ramsey,
Theodore Roethke, Wilbert Snow, Ruth Stone, Richard Wilbur,
William Carlos Williams, James Wright.

WHEELOCK, John Hall. Poets of Today VII. New York: Scribner,
1960.
James Dickey, Paris Leary, Jon Swan.

WHEELOCK, John Hall. Poets of Today VIII. New York: Scribner,
1961.
Albert Herzing, John M. Ridland, David R. Slavitt.

WHICHER, Stephen; Lars Ahnebrink. Twelve American Poets. New
York: Oxford, 1961.
E. E. Cummings, Robert Frost, Robinson Jeffers, Robert
Lowell, Ezra Pound, William Carlos Williams.

WIEBE, Dallas E. In the Late, Gnat Light. Cincinnati: Art Association of Cincinnati, 1965.
George Chambers, J. F. Hughes, David Lyttle, Joseph Margolis, Edward Morin, George Thompson, Dallas E. Wiebe.

WILDMAN, Eugene. Anthology of Concretism. Chicago: Swallow,
1969.
Alain Arias-Misson, Carlo Belloli, Jean Francois Bory, Klaus
Burkhardt, Henri Chopin, Carl Fernbach-Flarsheim, John
Furnival, Heinz Gappmayr, Bohumila Grogerova, Elizabeth
Herrmann, Dick Higgins, Josef Hirsol, Dom Sylvester Houedard,
Kitasono Katue, Arrigo Lora-Totino, Juliet McGrath, Jaroslav
Malina, Hansjorg Mayer, Edwin Morgan, Maurizio Nannucci,
Seiichi Niikuni, Decio Pignatari, Gerhard Ruhm, Aram Saroyan,
Mary Ellen Solt, Adriano Spatola, Maurigio Spatola, Timm
Uhlrichs, Jiri Valoch, Frans Vanderlinde, Emmett Williams,
Pedro Xisto.

WILENTZ, Elias. The Beat Scene. New York: Corinth, 1960.
Paul Blackburn, Ray Bremser, Marvin Cohen, Gregory Corso,
Robert Creeley, Richard Davidson, Diane DiPrima, Barbara
Ellen, Kenward Elmslie, Bruce Fearing, Lawrence Ferlinghetti,
John Fles, David Galler, Allen Ginsberg, Paul Goodman, James
Grady, Robert Hanlan, Howard Hart, Richard Higgins, Leonore

Jaffee, Ted Joans, LeRoi Jones, Jack Kerouac, Kenneth Koch,
Seymour Krim, Tuli Kupferberg, Philip Lamantia, Martin Last,
Joseph LeSueur, Michael McClure, Jack Micheline, William
Morris, Brigid Murnaghan, E. A. Navaretta, Robert Nichols,
Frank O'Hara, Peter Orlovsky, Dan Propper, Hugh Romney,
Albert Saijo, Marc D. Schleifer, Sally Stern, Lew Welch,
Philip Whalen, Jonathan Williams.

WILENTZ, Ted; Tom Weatherly. Natural Process: An Anthology
of New Black Poetry. New York: Hill and Wang, 1970.
    Conyus, Sam Cornish, Nikki Giovanni, Michael S. Harper,
William J. Harris, David Henderson, Audre Lorde, L. V.
Mack, Clarence Major, N. H. Pritchard, Lennox Raphael,
Carolyn M. Rodgers, Sonia Sanchez, Askia Muhammad Toure,
Tom Weatherly, Jay Wright, Al Young.

WILLIAMS, Emmett. An Anthology of Concrete Poetry. New York:
Something Else Press, 1967.
    Friedrick Achleitner, Alain Arias-Misson, H. C. Artman,
Ronaldo Azeredo, Stephen Bann, Carlo Belloli, Max Bense,
Edgard Braga, Claus Bremer, Augusto De Campos, Haroldo
De Campos, Henri Chopin, Carl Friedrick Claus, Bob Cobbing,
Reinhard Dohl, Torsten Ekbom, Oyvind Fahlstrom, Carl
Fernbach-Flarsheim, Ian Hamilton Finlay, Larry Friefeld,
Heinz Gappmayr, Ilse Garnier, Pierre Garnier, Matthias
Goeritz, Eugen Comringer, Ludwig Gosewitz, Bohumila
Grogerova, Jose Lino Grunewald, Brion Gysin, Al Hansen,
Vaclav Havel, Helmut Heissenbuttle, Josef Hirsal, Ake Hodell,
Dom Sylvester Houdedard, Ernst Jandl, Bengt Emil Johnson,
Ronald Johnson, Hiro Kamimura, Kitasono Katue, Jiri Kolar,
Ferdinand Kriwet, Franz Van Der Linde, Arrigo Lora-
Totino, Cavan McCarthy, Jackson Mac Low, Hansjorg Mayer,
Franz Mon, Edwin Morgan, Hansjorgen Nielsen, Seiichi Niikuni,
Lodislav Novak, Yuksel Pazarkaya, Decio Pignatori, Wlademir
Dias Pino, Luiz Angelo Pinto, Carl-Fredrik Reutersward,
Diter Rot, Gerhard Ruhm, Aram Saroyan, John J. Sharkey,
Edward Lucie-Smith, Mary Ellen Solt, Adriano Spatola, Daniel
Spoerri, Andre Thomkins, Enrique Uribe Valdivielso, Franco
Verdi, Paul De Vree, Emmett Williams, Jonathan Williams,
Pedro Xisto, Fujitomi Yasuo.

WILLIAMS, Miller. Contemporary Poetry in America. New York:
Random House, 1973.
    Ralph Adamo, Dick Allen, A. R. Ammons, Alvin Aubert, John
Berryman, John Biguenet, Elizabeth Bishop, Robert Bly, Gwen-
dolyn Brooks, Charles Bukowski, Robert Canzoneri, John
Ciardi, Jane Cooper, John William Corrington, Gregory Croso,
Robert Creeley, J. V. Cunningham, James Dickey, William
Dickey, R. H. W. Dillard, Alan Dugan, Richard Eberhart,
Dave Etter, William Everson, Lawrence Ferlinghetti, Donald
Finkel, Calvin Forbes, Gene Frumkin, George Garrett, Allen
Ginsberg, Donald Hall, James Harrison, Robert Hayden,
Anthony Hecht, John Hollander, Barbara Howes, Robert Huff,

Langston Hughes, Randall Jarrell, Judson Jerome, Donald Justice, X. J. Kennedy, Milton Kessler, Galway Kinnell, Maxine Kumin, Denise Levertov, Laurence Lieberman, John Logan, Robert Lowell, Gary Margolis, Dan Masterson, William Meredith, James Merrill, W. S. Merwin, Josephine Miles, Vassar Miller, William Mills, Howard Nemerov, John Frederick Nims, Joyce Carol Oates, Frank O'Hara, Charles Olson, Robert Pack, Kenneth Patchen, Sylvia Plath, Jonathan Price, Adrienne Rich, Theodore Roethke, Anne Sexton, Karl Shapiro, Stuart Silverman, Louis Simpson, David R. Slavitt, William Jay Smith, W. D. Snodgrass, Gary Snyder, Barry Spacks, William Stafford, David Steingass, John Stone, Mark Strand, Dabney Stuart, Hollis Summers, Lewis Turco, Peter Viereck, David Wagoner, Diane Wakoski, Robert Wallace, Robert Penn Warren, James Whitehead, Richard Wilbur, John Williams, Miller Williams, Charles Wright, James Wright, Al Young.

WILLIAMS, Oscar; Edwin Honig. The Mentor Book of Major American Poets. New York: New American Library, 1962.
W. H. Auden, E. E. Cummings, Robert Frost, Archibald MacLeish, Marianne Moore, Ezra Pound, John Crowe Ransom, William Carlos Williams.

WILLIAMS, Oscar. Master Poems of the English Language: Over One Hundred Poems Together with Introductions by Leading Poets and Critics of the English-speaking World. New York: Trident, 1966.
W. H. Auden, George Barker, E. E. Cummings, Richard Eberhart, T. S. Eliot, Robert Frost, Marianne Moore, Ezra Pound, John Crowe Ransom, William Carlos Williams.

WILLIAMS, Oscar. An Anthology of American Verse from Colonial Days to the Present. Cleveland: World, 1966.
Leonie Adams, Conrad Aiken, W. H. Auden, Joseph Bennett, John Berryman, Elizabeth Bishop, Louise Bogan, William Burford, Malcolm Cowley, E. E. Cummings, Reuel Denney, Richard Eberhart, T. S. Eliot, Robert Frost, Isabella Gardner, Brewster Ghiselin, Donald Hall, Anthony Hecht, Daniel G. Hoffman, Edwin Honig, Robert Horan, Robinson Jeffers, Josephine W. Johnson, V. R. Lang, David Lougee, Robert Lowell, Willard Mass, Claire McAllister, Archibald MacLeish, Esther Mathews, W. S. Merwin, Marianne Moore, Howard Moss, Ogden Nash, Howard Nemerov, Helen Neville, Elder Olson, Robert Pack, Ezra Pound, Frederic Prokosch, John Crowe Ransom, Theodore Roethke, Muriel Rukeyser, Carl Sandburg, Delmore Schwartz, Karl Shapiro, Hy Sobiloff, William Stafford, Ruth Stone, Allen Tate, Dunston Thompson, John Thompson, Jr., Parker Tyler, Mark Van Doren, Mona Van Duyn, Byron Vazakas, Robert Penn Warren, Edward Weismiller, John Hall Wheelock, Richard Wilbur, Oscar Williams, William Carlos Williams.

WILLIAMS, Oscar; Hyman J. Sobiloff. The New Pocket Anthology of American Verse from Colonial Days to the Present. New York: Washington Square, 1972.
> Leonie Adams, Conrad Aiken, John Ashbery, W. H. Auden, Joseph Bennett, John Berryman, Elizabeth Bishop, Robert Bly, Louise Bogan, William Burford, Malcolm Cowley, Robert Creeley, J. V. Cunningham, James Dickey, Hilda Doolittle, Alan Dugan, Robert Duncan, Richard Eberhart, Alvin Feinman, Edward Field, Robert Frost, Isabella Gardner, Brewster Ghiselin, Allen Ginsberg, Anthony Hecht, Daniel G. Hoffman, Edwin Honig, Langston Hughes, Randall Jarrell, Robinson Jeffers, Josephine W. Johnson, LeRoi Jones, Bill Knott, Kenneth Koch, Stanley Kunitz, Denise Levertov, John Logan, Robert Lowell, Archibald MacLeish, William Meredith, James Merrill, W. S. Merwin, Marianne Moore, Howard Moss, Ogden Nash, Howard Nemerov, Frank O'Hara, Charles Olson, Elder Olson, Robert Pack, Sylvia Plath, Ezra Pound, Frederic Prokosch, John Crowe Ransom, Charles Reznikoff, Theodore Roethke, Muriel Rukeyser, Carl Sandburg, James Schuyler, Delmore Schwartz, Anne Sexton, Karl Shapiro, Louis Simpson, William Jay Smith, W. D. Snodgrass, Hyman J. Sobiloff, William Stafford, Emma Swan, May Swenson, Allen Tate, Melvin B. Tolson, Mark Van Doren, Byron Vazakas, Robert Penn Warren, Edward Weismiller, John Hall Wheelock, Richard Wilbur, Jonathan Williams, William Carlos Williams, Yvor Winters, James Wright, Louis Zukofsky.

WINANS, A. D. California Bicentennial Poets Anthology. San Francisco: Second Coming Press, 1976.
> Pancho Aguila, Elizabeth Bartlett, Douglas Blazek, Luke Breitt, Charles Bukowski, Neeli Cherkovski, Naomi Clark, Geoffrey Cook, Elias Hruska Cortes, Louis Cuneo, Donald Eulert, William Everson, Paul F. Fericano, Lawrence Ferlinghetti, Kathleen Fraser, Paul Foreman, Gene Fowler, Sandra Gilbert, Rafael Jesus Gonzales, Ben Hiatt, Jack Hirshman, Barbara Hughes, Bob Kaufman, Leonard Keller, Sarah Kennedy, Mary Norbert Korte, Ronald Koertge, X. L. Lanners, Ross Laursen, Todd S. J. Lawson, Philip Levine, Ed "Foots" Lipman, Gerald Locklin, Glenna Luschei, Helen Luster, Kaye McDonough, Lee Mallory, Paul Mariah, Adrianne Marcus, Morton Marcus, Al Masarik, George Mattingly, David Meltzer, Herb Middleton, Anne Menebroken, Jack Micheline, Wayne Miller, Josephine Miles, Alejandro Murguia, Harold Norse, Joyce Odam, Robert Peters, Juan Gomez Quinomes, Ishmael Reed, Steve Richmond, Alfred Robles, Foster Robertson, Gene Ruggles, Dennis Saleh, Luis Omar Salinas, John Oliver Simon, Arthur Smith, Gary Soto, Ann Stanford, Lynn Sukenick, Ernesto Trejo, George Tsongas, Roberto Vargas, William Wantling, Shirley Williams, A. D. Winans, Gordon Kirkwood Yates, Al Young.

WINKLER, Anthony C. Poetry As System. Glenview, Ill.: Scott, Foresmen, 1971.

John Ashbery, Jean Francois Bory, George MacKay Brown, Lorena Bruff, Charles Bukowski, Neeli Cherry, Gregory Corso, Kenri Coulette, J. V. Cunningham, Freddie J. Dyer, Larry Eigner, T. S. Eliot, Robert Frost, Pierre Garnier, Allen Ginsberg, Eugen Gomringer, Anthony Hecht, Ernst Jandl, Stanley Kunitz, Philip Lamantia, Robert Lowell, Edward Lucie-Smith, Michael McClure, James Michie, Marianne Moore, Kenneth Patchen, Sylvia Plath, Ezra Pound, Theodore Roethke, Carl Sandburg, Louis Simpson, W. D. Snodgrass, May Swenson, Frans Venderlinde, Peter Viereck, David Wagoner, William Wantling, William Carlos Williams, Pedro Xisto.

WINTERS, Yvor; Kenneth Fields. Quest for Reality: An Anthology of Short Poems in English. Chicago: Swallow, 1969.
Louise Bogan, Edgar Bowers, J. V. Cunningham, Elizabeth Daryush, Catherine Davis, Charles Gullans, Thom Gunn, Janet Lewis, Mina Loy, N. Scott Momaday, Helen Pinkerton, Alan Stephens, William Carlos Williams, Yvor Winters.

WITT-DIAMANT, Ruth; Rikutaro Fukuda. 53 American Poets of Today. Folcroft, Pa.: Folcroft Library Editions, 1971.
Daisy Aldan, John Berryman, Elizabeth Bishop, Robin Blaser, Edgar Bowers, James Broughton, John Ciardi, Gregory Corso, Robert Creeley, James Dickey, Robert Duncan, Richard Eberhart, William Everson, Lawrence Ferlinghetti, Edward Field, Bernard A. Forrest, Jean Garrigue, Allen Ginsberg, Madeline Gleason, Barbara Guest, Gertrude Harris, Barbara Howes, Randall Jarrell, LeRoi Jones, Stanley Kunitz, Joseph Langland, Paris Leary, Denise Levertov, Robert Lowell, James Merrill, W. S. Merwin, Josephine Miles, Howard Nemerov, Frank O'Hara, Kenneth Patchen, Kenneth Rexroth, Theodore Roethke, Muriel Rukeyser, James Schevill, Delmore Schwartz, Winfield Townley Scott, Anne Sexton, Karl Shapiro, William Jay Smith, W. D. Snodgrass, Gary Snyder, Jack Spicer, William Stafford, Peter Viereck, Robert Penn Warren, Philip Whalen, Richard Wilbur, James Wright.

WOODS, Ralph Louis. A Third Treasury of the Familiar. New York: Macmillan, 1970.
Conrad Aiken, W. H. Auden, Karle Wilson Baker, T. S. Eliot, Robert Frost, Wilfrid Gibson, Ralph Hodgson, Langston Hughes, Elias Lieberman, Phyllis McGinley, Archibald MacLeish, John Masefield, Marianne Moore, Carl Sandburg, Stephen Spender.

YOUNG, Ian. The Male Muse. Trumansburg, N.Y.: Crossing Press, 1973.
Robert Adamson, William Barber, Oswell Blakeston, Perry Brass, Jim Chapson, Kirby Congdon, Robert Duncan, Jim Eggeling, Salvatore Farinella, Edward Field, John Gill, Allen Ginsberg, Paul Goodman, Walter Griffin, Thom Gunn, Michael Higgins, Brian Hill, Christopher Isherwood, Graham Jackson, Ronald Johnson, James Kirkup, Zdzislaw Kurlowicz, E. A. Lacey, John Lehmann, James Liddy, Paul Mariah, Paul Mau-

rice, James Mitchell, Edward Mycue, Harold Norse, Robert Peters, Ralph Pomeroy, Michael Ratcliffe, Jay Socin, Richard Tagett, Burton Weiss, John Wieners, Jonathan Williams, Tennessee Williams, Ian Young.

PART II

POETS

    After each poet's name, the anthologies in which his work appears are listed in alphabetical order. The particular book is described under the key reference word in the Anthologies section. If an editor is responsible for more than one book, the publication years are given to differentiate them.

    If the editor produced two books in the same year, they are differentiated by a reference to the publisher. If the year and the publisher both coincide, the title is indicated.

    The year given in parentheses immediately after the poet's name is his birth date, unless otherwise indicated.

    Only poets living as of 1960 are listed.

    Alternate spellings, abbreviations and pseudonyms of the poets' names are indicated in parentheses.

A

Jonathan AARON: Peck 1971
George ABBE (1911): Bates,
   Derleth, Lask, Lowenfels
   1966, McMahon, Morrison,
   Vrbovska 1963, 1968
Joanne ABBONIZIO: Brindle
Keith ABBOTT: Waldman 1971
Linda ABDAR: Pilon
Neilson ABEEL: Parker 1967
Peter ABRAHAMS (1919): Bre-
   man, Hopkins (Knopf),
   Hughes 1963
Robert J. ABRAMS (1924):
   Hughes, Pool
Sam ABRAMS: H. Jones,
   Oppenheimer 1967, Sherman,
   Waldman 1969
Dolores ABRAMSON: Patterson

L. Kristee ABRAHAMSON:
   Brindle
Dannie ABSE (1923): Brinnin
   1963, 1970; Ellmann 1973,
   Firmage, Greaves, Rosen-
   thal 1967, 1968; Wallace
Vito (Hannibal) ACCONCI
   (1940): Carroll (Young A-
   merican Poets)
Chinua ACHEBE (1930): Bre-
   man
Friedrich ACHLEITNER: E.
   Williams
Will W. ACKERLY: Jackson
Duane ACKERSON: Wang
Valentine ACKLAND (1906):
   Knowles
Milton ACORN: J. Gill
Mary ACOSTA (1922): Van
   den Heuvel

G. ADALI-MORTTI: Hughes
1963
Charles Foller ADAM: Jackson
Helen ADAM (1909): Allen
1960, Arts Festival 1963,
Derleth, Gross, Harris
1973, Howe, Kennedy 1973
Ralph ADAMO (1948): M.
Williams
Austin ADAMS: Jackson
Eileen ADAMS: Palmer
Franklin P. ADAMS: Morrison
Gerald ADAMS: Gallery 1970
Herbert R. ADAMS: Peck 1971
Ilene ADAMS: Pilon
James Barton ADAMS: Jackson
Jeanette ADAMS: Patterson
John Q. ADAMS: Krech
Leonie ADAMS (1899): Aiken,
Bogan, C. Brooks, Driver,
Engle, Gregory 1962, Jacobus,
Stanford, Untermeyer 1964,
O. Williams 1966 (World)
Robert ADAMSON: Young
Betty ADCOCK: Owen 1969,
1974; Stevenson
Fleur ADCOCK (1934): Stall-
worthy
Lloyd ADDISON (1931): Bre-
man, Pool
Harold ADLER: Krech
Lucile ADLER: Konek, Lask
Etel ADNAN (1925): Lowenfels
1973, 1975
Arnold ADOFF: Adoff 1969
Etel ADRAN: Lowenfels 1967
(Where Is Vietnam?)
Vonna Hicks ADRIAN: Lask
Jill Kelsey AESCHBACHER:
Hoffman
Cecilia AFRICA: Giovanni
Pancho AGUILA: Winans
Maureen Mongraw AGUZIN:
Brindle
AI: Halpern
Christina Ama Ata AIDOO
(1942): Breman, Kgositsile
Frank AIG-IMOUKHEUDE (1935):
Breman, Hughes 1963
Conrad AIKEN (1889): Aiken,
G. W. Allen, J. A. Allen,
Aloian, R. Bender, Bogan,
Brinnin 1963, 1970; Car-

ruth, Cole 1965, 1972;
Driver, Ellmann 1973,
1976; Engle, Gregory 1966,
Gwynn, Harlan, Holmes,
Jackson, McGinley, Perrine,
J. Perry, Sanders, Shapiro,
Steuben, Trapp, Univ.
Press of Va., Untermeyer
1964, 1973 (McKay), O.
Williams 1966 (World),
Woods
Tilda S. AKERS: Sargent
Nanina ALBA (1917-1968):
Adoff 1973, Hughes 1970,
D. Randall 1969
Richard ALBERT: Harlan
Richard E. ALBERT: Peck
1971
Jane A. ALBRITE: Brindle
Daisy ALDAN (1923): Chester,
Lask, Lowenfels 1969
(Random House), Mollen-
kott, Vrbovska 1968, Witt-
Diamant
Richard ALDINGTON (1892-
1962): Jacobus, Phillips,
Untermeyer 1964
Dorothy ALDIS (1896): Cole
1972, Nash
Brian ALDISS (1925): Baylor,
Lucie-Smith
Bailey ALDRICH: Jackson
Richard ALDRIDGE: Lask
Fernando ALEGRIA: Clay
Charlotte ALEXANDER: Rigs-
bee
Charlton A. ALEXANDER:
Jackson
Donald ALEXANDER: Clay
Floyce ALEXANDER (1938):
Bly 1970, Hewitt
Lewis ALEXANDER (1900):
Jordan
Margaret Walker ALEXANDER
(1915): Henderson, Turner
Michael ALEXANDER (1941):
Stallworthy
Pamela ALEXANDER: Rigsbee
Scott ALEXANDER: Pilon
Sidney ALEXANDER (1912):
Hughes 1970, Lask
Taylor ALEXANDER: Jackson
Carl ALEXY: Hanna 1960

Miguel ALGARIN: Algarin
Ahmed (Akinwale) ALHAMISI
(1940): Breman, P. Brown,
D. Randall 1960
Yusuf AL-KHAL: Lowenfels
1975
James Alexander ALLAN (1889):
T. Moore
John ALLCOCK (1952): Greaves
Billie ALLEN: Sargent
Bob ALLEN (1942): Lowenfels
1969 (Doubleday), 1969 (Ran-
dom House)
Dick ALLEN (1939): McMahon,
M. Williams
Edward ALLEN (1948): Kennedy
George ALLEN: Hanna 1960
James B. ALLEN (1931): Stryk
1975
John Alexander ALLEN: J. A.
Allen, M. Gibson, Rubin,
H. Taylor
Leslie Holdsworthy ALLEN
(1879): T. Moore
Minerva ALLEN: Lourie
Paul ALLEN: Jackson
Paula Gunn ALLEN: Dodge,
Milton
Samuel (W.) ALLEN (Paul Vesey)
(1917): Adoff 1968, 1973,
Bontemps 1963, 1974; Bre-
man, G. Brooks (Broadside
Treasury), P. Brown,
Greaves, Hayden, Henderson,
Hughes 1964, 1970; Jordan,
King 1975, Lomax, Lowen-
fels 1966, McCullough,
Morrison, D. Randall 1960,
Schneider
Sara Van Alstyne ALLEN:
Steuben
Blair H. ALLER: Crafts
Young E. ALLISON: Parker
1960
ALMA: Jihad
Bert ALMON: Crafts
Mindy ALOFF: De Loach 1976,
Malley, Morticella
Ern ALPAUGH (1914): Kennedy
Michael ALS: Salkey
ALTA (1942): Efros, Konek,
Krech, Lowenfels 1963,
Malley

Laurence ALTGOOD: J. A.
Vincent
Keith ALTHAUS: Rigsbee
ALURISTA: Clay
A. ALVAREZ (1929): Rosen-
thal 1967, 1968
Hector Tito ALVAREZ (1952):
Leyland 1975
Julia ALVAREZ (1950): Jordan
Ameen ALWAN: Bukowski
George (N.) AMABILE (1936):
Carroll (Young American
Poets), Lowenfels 1975
AMANI: Jihad
Eric AMANN (1938): Van den
Heuvel
Brother AMAR (1950): Tisdale
AMEENA: Jihad
Mark AMEN: Gallery 1973
Imamu AMEER (Amir) see
LeRoi JONES
Jackie AMERMAN: Brindle
Bernice AMES: Stanford
Nathanael AMES: Jackson
Yehuda AMICHAI (1924): Cole
1971, McCullough, Stall-
worthy
Johari AMINI see Jewel (C.)
LATTIMORE
Kingsley AMIS (1922): Baylor,
Brinnin 1963, Ellmann
1973, Engle, Hall 1962
(World), Kenseth, Rosen-
thal 1967
A. R. AMMONS (1926): Bach,
Brady, Brinnin 1970,
Carruth (Bantam), Cole
1972, Ellmann 1973, 1976;
Glikes, Harlan, Hollander,
Howard, Howard and Vic-
tor, Hurtik, Kennedy 1973,
1974; Kherdian 1973, Kos-
telanetz, Lask, L. Moore,
Owen 1969, 1974; Schneider,
Strand, M. Williams
Ray AMOROSI: Mazur
Karen Y. AMOS (Adesina
Ogunelese; Adesina
Ogunelese Akinwanile)
(1950): Giovanni
W. M. AMPT: Jackson
Michael ANANIA (1939): Anania,
Gallery 1970, Stryk 1975

ANASA: Jihad
Bill ANDERSON: Carruth (Bantam)
C. V. J. ANDERSON: Hadassah
Calvin ANDERSON: Dee
Charles L. ANDERSON (1938): Pool
Claudia ANDERSON: Giovanni
Forrest ANDERSON (1903): Mollenkott
Gwyneth ANDERSON (1907): Knowles
Jack ANDERSON (1935): Harris 1970, Oppenheimer 1967, Phillips, Schreiber, Summerfield, Waldman 1969
John Redwood ANDERSON (1883-1964): Knowles
Jon ANDERSON (1940): Carroll (Young American Poets), Halpern, Lask, Stryk 1975
Patrick ANDERSON (1915): Firmage, Morrison, A. J. M. Smith 1960
S. E. ANDERSON (1943): Adoff 1973, Coombs, King 1972, Major
Tom ANDERSON: Hallmark
William ANDERSON: A. Miller
Sally ANDRESEN: Dunnin
Jenne ANDREWS (1948): Stryke 1975
John ANGAIAK (1941): Lowenfels 1973
Maya (May) ANGELOU (1922): Gersmehl, Konek
Charles ANGOFF: Harris 1970
Marion ANGUS: Gregory 1966
Alan ANSEN (1922): Glikes, Pearson, Strand Wallace
Howard ANT (1927): Katzman
Susan Roe ANTHONY: Hoffman
David ANTIN (1932): Gross, Rothenberg 1973
Eleanor ANTIN: Gross
ANTLER: Rosenblum
Brother ANTONINUS see William EVERSON
Roger APLON: Carroll (Young American Poets)
Philip APPLEMAN: Owen 1969, Untermeyer 1970, Vrbovska 1968

James APPLEWHITE (1935): Carroll (Young American Poets), Evans, Owen 1969, 1974
Hailu ARAAYA: Peck 1971
Eleandor ARANSON: Sherman
A. J. ARBERRY (1905): Knowles
Myrtle ARCHER: Gallery 1973
Mrs. George ARCHIBALD: Jackson
John ARDEN: Cole 1967 (Macmillan)
David Hueschke ARGO: Krech
Alain ARIAS-MISSON: Wildman, E. Williams
Reginald ARKELL: Morrison
Sybil Leonard ARMES: Kauffman
Shelley ARMITAGE: Brindle
Richard (Willard) ARMOUR (1906): Aloian, Dunning, Morrison
J. A. ARMSTRONG: J. A. Vincent
Margaret D. ARMSTRONG: Kauffman
Martin ARMSTRONG (1882): Knowles, Rose
Carroll ARNETT (1927): Rosen, Stevenson, Weil
Bob ARNOLD: Lowenfels 1975
Lila ARNOLD: Konek
Judith White ARTHUR: Pilon
H. C. ARTMAN: E. Williams
John ASHBERY (1927): Allen 1960, Barnes, Brady, Brinnin 1963, Carroll (Poem in Its Skin), Carruth (Bantam), Ellmann 1973, 1976; Hall 1962 (Penguin), Harlan, Hollander, Howard, Howard and Victor, Koch, Leary, Monaco 1974, Myers, Padgett, Pearson, Poulin, Rothenberg 1973, Stepanchev, Strand, Untermeyer 1973 (McKay), Waldman 1969, 1971; Winkler
Margaret ASHMAN: Jackson
Edmond ASHTON: Cole 1971
Werner ASPENSTROM: Bly 1966

Sharon ASSELIN: Fox
Thea ASTLEY (1925): T.
  Moore
David ATAMIAN: Lask
Russell ATKINS (1926): Adoff
  1973, Bontemps 1963, 1974;
  Breman, Hughes 1970,
  Jordan, King 1975, Major,
  Peck 1970
R. H. ATKINSON (1932): Git-
  lin
Ron ATKINSON: Hausamn
James ATLAS: Malley
Margaret ATWOOD (1939):
  Beerman, Colley, De Roche,
  E. Gill, J. Gill, Howe,
  Konek, L. Moore, Segnitz,
  Stanford, Wagner
Alvin AUBERT (1930): M.
  Williams
Dorothy AUCHTERLONIE: T.
  Moore
W. H. AUDEN (1907-1973):
  Adams, J. A. Allen,
  Aloian, Arp, Banker,
  Barnes, Bates, Baylor, R.
  Bender, Bogan, Bold,
  Brady, Brinnin 1963, 1970;
  C. Brooks, Brower, Calder-
  wood, Chatman, Cole 1967
  (Macmillan), Colley, Crafts,
  Crane, Crang, Croft, De
  Roche, Drew, Driver, Ell-
  mann 1973, Engelberg,
  Engle, Felver, Gardner,
  J. Gibson, J. Gibson (Book
  Two), Glikes, Greaves,
  Gregory 1966, Gwynn, Hall
  1962 (Watts), Hannum Har-
  lan, Hieatt, Holmes, How-
  ard, Howard and Victor,
  Hurtik, Jackson, Jacobus,
  Kallich, Kennedy 1973,
  Kenseth, Livingston,
  McGovern, Mercatante,
  Monaco 1974, Morrison,
  Olson, Peck 1970, 1971; J.
  Perry, Phillips, Plotz,
  Sanders, Schneider, Simp-
  son, A. J. M. Smith 1965,
  1967; Stallworthy, Steuben,
  H. Taylor, W. Taylor,
  Trapp, Untermeyer 1964,

1973 (McKay); Wagner,
  Wallace, Williams and
  Honig, O. Williams 1966
  (Trident), 1966 (World);
  Woods
Bob AUERBACK: Sherman
Jane AUGUSTINE: Klonsky
AUSTIN (c. 1946): Gersmehl
Alan AUSTIN (1939): Gitlin
Albert Gordon AUSTIN (1918):
  T. Moore
Edgar (Allen) AUSTIN (d. 1974):
  Leyland 1977
Josephine AUSTIN: Sargent
Eleanor AVERITT: Dunning
Peter AVERY (1923): Stall-
  worthy
Tommi AVICOLLI (1951): Ley-
  land 1977
David AVIDAN (1934): Bold
Penny AVILA: Morticella
Margaret AVISON (1918): De
  Roche, Ellmann 1973, A.
  J. M. Smith 1960
AVOTCJA: Clay
Kofi AWOONER (1935): Adoff
  1969, Breman, Kgositsile
George AWOONER-WILLIAMS
  (1935): Lomax
Mark AXELROD: Rigsbee
Susan AXELROD (1944): Howe,
  Hewitt
Georgia AXTELL: Gallery
  1970
Ethan AYER: Derleth
Hilary AYER: Head, Simmons
Rebecca L. AYERS: Pilon
Vivian AYERS: Hughes 1964
Leo AYLEN: Crang
William Edmondstone AYTOUN:
  Parker 1960
Ronaldo AZEREDO (1937): E.
  William, Klonsky
AZIZI: Jihad

B

Ronald BAATZ: Gallery 1973
Sanora BABB: Stevenson
Donald C. BABCOCK: Lask
Maltbie D. BABCOCK: Kauff-
  man

Carey BACALAR: Gallery 1970
Forrest D. BACHTEL: Kiley
Robert BACON (1946): Lowen-
fels
Peggy BACON: Jackson
Jerry BADANES: Gross
Pamela BADYK: Gay
Kathryn BAER: Harlan
Robert BAGG (1935): Aiken,
Baylor, Brinnin 1963, Cole
1971, Jacobus, Pearson
Cherie A. BAGLEY: Brindle
Jenni L. BAGLEY: Brindle
Joyce M. BAGLEY: Brindle
Alfred Goldsworthy BAILEY
(1905): A. J. M. Smith
1960
Lee BAIN: Scheftel
Liz Sohappy BAKE: Niatum
Barbara (Anne) BAKER
(c. 1941): Murphy
Donald W. BAKER: Owen 1969
George Henry BAKER: Parker
1960
Howard BAKER (1905): Aiken,
Talisman
Karle Wilson BAKER (1878):
Woods
Michael BAKER: Morticella
Prentice BAKER (1925): Mol-
lenkott, Owen 1974
Robert A. BAKER: Baylor
Verna Tomlinson BAKER (1915):
Mollenkott
Richard BAKER-ROSHI: Fer-
linghetti
John BALABAN: Chace
Eleanor BALDWIN: Lask
Michael BALDWIN: Crang
Neil BALDWIN: Rigsbee
Charles BALLARD: Rosen
Charles G. BALLARD: Dodge
Shirley BALLARD: Student
Kate BALLEN: Adoff 1971
J. Q. BALLINGHAM: Jackson
James BALOIAN: Kherdian
1970
Eva BAN: Lowenfels 1975
Sylvia BANDYKE: Scheftel
Edward BANGS: Vincent
John Kendrick BANGS: Jackson
Carol BANKERD (1941): Klonsky
Harold BANN: Hadassah

Stephen BANN: E. Williams
Lex BANNING (1921): T.
Moore
Gavin BANTOCK (1939):
Matthias
Imamu Amiri (Ameer) BARAKA
see LeRoi JONES
Sharon BARBA: Bulkin, Chest-
er, Lowenfels 1975
Cal BARBER: Gay
William BARBER (1946): Ley-
land 1975, 1977; Young
Edwin BARCLAY: Hughes 1963
Sheppard BARCLAY: Jackson
Dubjinsky BAREFOOT: Gitlin
Steve BARFIELD: Fox, Smith
David BARKER: Jackson
Eric BARKER (1905): Firmage,
Lask
George BARKER (1913): Bay-
lor, R. Bender, Brinnin
1963, 1970; Cole 1967
(Macmillan), Crafts, Crang,
Engle, Firmage, Kallich,
Peck 1970, Schneider, W.
Taylor, Univ. Press of Va.,
Untermeyer 1964, Walsh,
O. Williams 1966 (Trident)
Richard BARKER (1929):
Glikes, Katzman, Palmer
Coleman BARKS (1937): Cole
1971, Colley, Evans,
Hewitt, Owen 1974, McCul-
lough
Jim BARNES (1933): Harris
1976, Niatum, Stryk 1975
John BARNES: Lowenfels 1975
Kate BARNES: Cole 1963
Keith BARNES: Cromie
Mary Jane BARNES: Scheftel
William D. BARNEY: Derleth
Willis BARNSTONE: Lowenfels
1975, Vrbovska 1968,
Wesleyan Univ.
Desiree A. BARNWELL:
Coombs, Giovanni
Gene BARO (1924): Derleth,
Driver, Hall 1962 (World)
Linda BARON: Dee
Ken BARRATT (1906): T.
Moore
Gerald W. (William) BARRAX
(1933): Adoff 1973, Car-

roll (Young American Poets),
Hayden, Henderson, Owen
1974
Eseoghene BARRETT (1941):
Breman
Patrick (Patric) BARRINGTON)
(1908): Cole 1963, Rose
Leon O. BARRON: Univ. of
Mass.
Anita BARROWS (1947): Chest-
er, Howe
Jan BARRY: Rottmann
John BARSNESS: Milton
Elizabeth BARTLETT (1911):
Lowenfels 1967, 1969
(Doubleday); Winans
Brett BARTON: Mallory
Paule BARTON-HAITI: De
Loach 1976
Gaston BART-WILLIAMS:
Greaves
Vasily BASHKIN: Cole 1963
Marianne BASKIN: Palmer
Ellen BASS (1947): Bulkin,
Howe
George BASS (1939): Lowen-
fels 1966
Madeline Tiger BASS: Oppen-
heimer 1977
Andrew BASTER (1945): Greaves
Richard BASTIAN (1941):
Mollenkott
Elliott BASTIEN: Salkey
Arlo BATES: Vincent
Katherine Lee BATES: Vincent
Scott BATES: Bates, Owen
1974, Steele
Thomas BATESON: Gregory
1962
Bill BATHURST: Waldman
1971
John BATKI: Sklar
Tom BATSON: Kiley
Marcia BATTEIGER: Pilon
Walton W. BATTERSHALL:
Jackson
Sol BATTLE: Battle
Timothy BAUM: Mazur
Lee BAXANDALL (1935): Git-
lin, Lowenfels 1975
Charles BAXTER: Bonazzi
1972
E. R. BAXTER III: P. Perry

Richard BAXTER: Kauffman
Taner BAYBARS: Lask
Ron H. BAYES: Rigsbee
John BAYLISS: Rose
Joseph Warren BEACH: Jack-
son
J. H. BEALE, Jr.: Jackson
David Omer BEARDEN: Poet-
ry San Francisco
Etta BEARDEN: Gallery 1970
The BEATLES: Peck 1970
Kenneth BEAUDOIN: Steele
Beau BEAUSOLEIL: S. Vincent
Laura BEAUSOLEIL: Efros
Phyllis BEAUVAIS (1940):
Howe, Konek
Bruce BEAVER (1928): T.
Moore
Francis BECENTI: Clay
Anne BECK: Brindle
Julian BECK: Gay
John BECKER: Cole 1963
Robin BECKER: Bulkin
Samuel BECKETT (1906): Ell-
mann 1973, McCullough
Frank BEDDO: Bates
Lucius BEEBE: Larrick
Audrey BEECHAM (1915):
Knowles
John BEECHER (1904): Gitlin,
Lowenfels 1966, 1969
(Doubleday); Morticella
Henry Charles BEECHING:
Morrison
Patricia BEER (1924): Crang,
Walsh
Barbra J. BEHM: Brindle
Harry BEHN (1898): Cole 1963,
1972; Livingston
Martha BEIDLER (1928): Bay-
lor
Ulli BEIER see David DIOP
Henry BEISSEL: Lowenfels
1975
Ken BELFORD: J. Gill
Sally BELFRAGE: Hecht
Ben BELITT (1911): H. Tay-
lor, Univ. Press of Va.
Fyodor BELKIN (1911): Cole
1963
Charles G. BELL (1916):
Brewton, Lask
DeWitt BELL: Peck 1971

Jimmy BELL: Rothenberg 1973
Marvin (Hartley) BELL: Carroll (Young American Poets),
Evans, Halpern, Howard,
Howard and Victor, Joseloff,
Al Lee, Lowenfels 1967,
McCullough, Strand, Stryk
1975, Weil
Vera BELL: Breman
Joe David BELLAMY: Gildner
Carlo BELLOLI: Wildman, E.
Williams
Robert Lawrence BELOOF
(1923): Aloian
Elchanan BEN-AMI: Banker
Margaret BENAYA: Lask
Michael BENEDIKT (1937):
Brinnin 1970, Carroll
(Young American Poets),
Gross, Halpern, Al Lee,
Lucie-Smith, McCullough,
Pearson, Strand
Rosemary (Carr) BENET (1898-
1962): Betts, Gannett
Lawrence (Laurence) BENFORD
(1946): Gross, Kramer,
Major, Lomax, McGovern
Lillie Kate Walker BENITEZ:
Henderson
Bruce BENNETT: Rigsbee
Gwendolyn B. BENNETT (1902):
Adoff 1973, Bontemps 1963,
1974; Hughes 1970, Patterson
Henry Holcolmb BENNETT:
J. A. Vincent
Joseph BENNETT: O. Williams
1966 (World)
John BENNETT (1920): Walsh
John BENNETT (1950): Fox,
Greaves, Lask
Lerone BENNETT (Jr.) (1928):
Adoff 1973, Baylor, Hughes
1964
Louise BENNETT: Salkey
Peggy BENNETT (1925): Cole
1963, 1967 (Macmillan)
Sherry BENNETT: Brindle
Sydna BENNETT: Adoff 1971
Max BENSE: E. Williams
Gerard BENSON: Cole
Beth BENTLEY: Stevenson, Ten
E. C. BENTLEY: Nash

Nelson BENTLEY: Ten
Wilder BENTLEY (1900):
Harvey
Walter BENTON: Cromie
Ted BENTTINEN: Harris 1976
Asa BENVENISTI: Lucie-Smith
Musu BER (1950): Breman
Jeri BERC: Violet
David Granmer T. BERENG:
Lomax
Leila BERG: Gersmehl
Stephen BERG (1934): Berg,
Lowenfels 1973
Carol BERGE (1928): Banker,
De Loach, E. Gill, Glikes,
Harris 1973, H. Jones,
Katzman, Lowenfels 1969
(Random House), Montgomery, Totem Press
Art BERGER (1920): Banker,
Lowenfels 1966, 1967,
1969 (Doubleday), 1969
(Random House); Sherman
Suzanne BERGER-RIOFF:
Freed
Alexander (F.) BERGMAN
(1912): Kramer, Lowenfels 1969 (Doubleday)
Marc BERGSCHNEIDER: Adoff
1971
George BERKE: Kiley
Constance E. BERKLEY (1931):
Dee, Giovanni
Martin BERKOVITZ: Kiley
Bill BERKSON (1939): Carroll
(Young American Poets),
Padgett, Waldman 1969,
1971; Weishaus
Bruce BERLIND: Harris 1976
Sidney BERNARD (1918): Bates,
Lowenfels 1967 (Where Is
Vietnam?)
Lynda BERNAYS: Brindle
Jeff BERNER (1940): Harvey
Robert BERNER: Hitchcock
Robert BERNSTEIN: Reading
R. C. BERRESFORD: Jackson
Daniel (Dan) BERRIGAN (1921):
Aiken, Breman, Crafts,
Gersmehl, Kennedy 1973,
McGovern, Plotz
Ted BERRIGAN (1934): Barnes,
Carroll (Young American

Poets), Clark, De Loach
1967, 1976, Dodge, Ell-
mann 1973, Friedman,
Harlan, McCullough, Mont-
gomery, Oppenheimer 1967,
Padgett, Rothenberg 1973,
Waldman 1969, 1971
Angel BERROCALES: Algarin
Chuck BERRY: Chace
D. C. BERRY: Owen 1974,
Rigsbee
Jan BERRY: Rottmann
Sylvia BERRY: Vrbovska 1968
Wendell BERRY: G. W. Allen,
Carruth (Bantam), (McCall);
De Roche, Hannum, Lask,
McCullough, Owen 1969,
1974; Steele, Untermeyer
1973, Wagner (McKay)
Helen BERRYHILL: Harlan,
Holmes
Michael BERRYHILL: Harris
1976, Rigsbee
John BERRYMAN (1914-1972):
G. W. Allen, Barnes, Bay-
lor, Brady, Berg, Brinnin
1963, 1970; Carruth (Ban-
tam), De Roche, Ellmann
1973, 1976; Engle, Glikes,
Harlan, Harris 1973,
Jacobus, Kennedy, McCul-
lough, Monaco 1974, Olson,
Phillips, Poulin, Rosenthal
1967, 1968; Shapiro, Stall-
worthy, Strand, H. Taylor,
Univ. Press of Va., Unter-
meyer 1964, 1973 (McKay),
Wagner, Walsh, M. Wil-
liams, O. Williams 1966
(World), Witt-Diamant
Mei BERSSENBRUGGE (1947):
Kherdian 1974
Gus BERTHA: P. Brown,
Malley
James BERTOLINO (1942):
Fox, Stryk 1975
Alvah BESSIE (1904): Lowen-
fels 1966
Zoe BEST: Lowenfels 1975
Lebert BETHUNE (1937):
Adoff 1973, Breman, Hen-
derson, Hughes 1970, Major

John BETJEMAN (1906): Bates,
Brinnin 1963, 1970; C.
Brooks, Calderwood, Cole
1967 (Macmillan), Crang,
Derleth, Ellmann 1973,
Engle, Gardner, Gwynn,
Kennedy, McGinley, Morri-
son, Nash, Parker 1975,
Rosenthal 1967, Sanders,
H. Taylor, Untermeyer
1964
Doris BETTS: Owen 1974
Robert BEUM (1929): Cromie,
Hearse
Helen BEVINGTON: Firmage,
Lask, McGinley, Nash
Yillie BEY (c. 1949): Murphy
William BEYER: Dunning
Harvey BIALY (1945): Harvey,
Krech, Lowenfels 1967,
Rothenberg 1973
Hart Leroi BIBBS (1930):
Major
Linda S. BICE: Brindle
E. H. BICKERSTETH: Kauff-
man
Frank BIDART (1939): Halpern
Beth BIDERMAN: Holmes
Linda L. BIELOWSKI: Brindle
Duane BIG EAGLE: Lowenfels
1973
Maurice BIGGS (1915): T.
Moore
John BIGUENET (1949): W.
Williams
Penny BIHLER: Oppenheimer
1977
BIMBO: Algarin
Steve BINDER: Malley
John BIRAM: Lask
Betty Ruth BIRD (1921):
Mollenkott
Dolly BIRD (1950): Lowenfels
1973
Laurel E. BIRD: Hallmark
George BIRDSEYE: Jackson
John BIRKBY (1950): Greaves
Henry BIRNBAUM: Weil
Earle BIRNEY (1904): Cole
1971, De Roche, Engle,
Larson, A. J. M. Smith
1960

Bobbie BISHOP: Bulkin
Elizabeth BISHOP (1911): Ad-
   ams, Aiken, G. W. Allen,
   J. A. Allen, Aloian, Beer-
   man, Bogan, Brady, C.
   Brooks, Brinnin 1968, 1970;
   Carruth (Bantam), Cole
   1963, Colley, De Roche,
   Driver, Ellmann 1973, 1976;
   Engle, Gregory 1966, Hall
   1962 (Watts), Hannum and
   Chase, Hopkins, Howard,
   Howard and Victor, Hughes
   1970, Jacobus, Kennedy
   1973, 1974; Koch, McCul-
   lough, McGinley, Perrine,
   J. Perry, Peterson, Plotz,
   Rosenthal 1967, 1968;
   Shapiro, Strand, W. Taylor,
   Untermeyer 1964, 1973
   (McKay); Wallace, M. Wil-
   liams, O. Williams 1966
   (World), Witt-Diamant
John Melville BISHOP III:
   Krech
Morris BISHOP: Aloian,
   Crafts, McGinley, Morrison,
   Nash, Peck 1971
Samuel BISHOP: Untermeyer
   1970
G. BISHOP-DUBJINSKY (1946):
   Schreiber
Richard BISSELL: Gildner
Ellen MARIE BISSERT: Bulkin
Gregory W. BITZ: Wang
Francesco BIVONA: Scheftel
Austin BLACK (1928): Major
D. M. BLACK (1941): Colley,
   Lucie-Smith
Peter BLACK: Greaves
Paul BLACKBURN (1926-1971):
   Banker, Carruth (Bantam),
   Cole 1967 (Macmillan),
   Crafts, Ellmann 1973, Freed,
   Harris 1973, Holmes, Kher-
   dian 1973, Lowenfels 1967,
   1969 (Random House); Ros-
   enthal 1967, 1968; Rothen-
   berg 1973, Wagner, Wald-
   man 1969, Weil, E. Wilentz
Richard BLACKBURN: Sollid
   1972, K. and J. Sollid
Thomas BLACKBURN: Lask

Emerson BLACKHORSE see
   Emerson Blackhorse
   "Barney" MITCHELL
Peter BLACKMAN (1909):
   Breman
Sherry BLACKMAN: Booker
R. (Richard) P. BLACKMUR
   (1904-1965): Aiken, J. A.
   Allen
Barbara BLACKWELL: Clay
Peter BLADEN (1922): T.
   Moore
Howard BLAIKLEY: Morse
Ed BLAIR: Banker
Francis C. BLAIR: Jackson
Jeff BLAIR: Adoff 1971
Whitney I. BLAIR: Kiley
Nora BLAKELY: P. Brown
Oswell BLAKESTON: Young
Santo BLANCO: Rothenberg
   1973
Frederika BLANKNER:
   Vrbovska 1963, 1968
F. D. BLANTON (1953): Ley-
   land 1977
Robin BLASER (1925): Allen
   1960, Arts Festival 1963,
   Barnes, Leary, Witt-
   Diamant
Randy BLASING: Carroll
   (Young American Poets)
Rena BLAUNER: Efros
Douglas BLAZEK: Fox, Krech,
   Lowenfels 1969 (Doubleday),
   P. Perry, Winans
Logan E. BLECKLEY: Jackson
John BLIGHT (1913): Knowles,
   T. Moore
Robert BLOCH: Derleth
Allan BLOCK: McMahon
Lew BLOCKCOLSKI (1943):
   Lourie, Lowenfels 1973
Jerry BLOEDOW (c. 1928):
   Hadassah, Katzman
Robert BLOOM (1925): Hadas-
   sah, Mollenkott
Harry A. BLOOMBERG: Jack-
   son
Bob BLOSSOM: Montgomery
Peter BLUE CLOUD (1933):
   Rosen
P. J. BLUMENTHAL: Mallory
Edmund BLUNDEN (1896-1974):

R. Bender, Bogan, Cole
1972, Croft, Engle, Reeves,
Rose, Untermeyer 1964
Robert BLY (1926): Adoff 1969,
Barnes, Baylor, Berg, Bly
1975, Bonazzi 1972, Brady,
Carruth (Bantam), Chace,
Cole 1965, 1967 (Macmil-
lan), 1971; Colley, Ellmann
1973, 1976; Fox, Hall 1962
(Penguin), Hannum, Hannum
and Chase, Harris 1973,
Heyen, Kennedy 1973, 1974;
Larrick, Lowenfels 1967,
1969 (Doubleday), 1973;
McCullough, McGovern, L.
Moore, Pearson, Poulin,
Rosenthal 1967, 1968; Rothen-
berg 1973, Strand, Stryk
1967, H. Taylor, Wagner,
Wang, M. Williams
Harry R. BLYTHE: Jackson
A. A. BOBLITZ: Jackson
Igor BOBROWSKY: Rottmann
Frederick BOCK: Lask
Layeh BOCK: Head
Bobbi BOCKETT: Brindle
Victor BOCKRIS: Reading
Carl BODE (1911): Plumley,
Walsh
Frederick C. BODEN (1902):
Parker 1975
Maxwell BODENHEIM: Stibitz
Jaime Torres BODET: Cromie
Louise BOGAN (1897-1970): J.
A. Allen, R. Bender, Brin-
nin 1963, 1970; Carruth
(Bantam), Chester, De
Roche, Engle, Harris 1973,
Howe, Kennedy 1973, Konek,
McCullough, Perrine, Solt,
Stanford, Steuben, Unter-
meyer 1964, O. Williams
1966 (World), Winters
Jay BOGGIS: Mazur
Nancy Jo BOGGS: Kiley
Dennis BOGIN: Bogin
Donald E. BOGLE (c. 1958):
Murphy
Diane BOGUS (c. 1946): Gio-
vanni
Curtis BOK: Jackson
Alan BOLD (1943): Baylor,
Bold

Brian BOLDT: Morticella
Darrel L. BOLENDER: Schef-
tel
Jody BOLZ: Hoffman
Horatius BONAR: Kauffman
Robert BONAZZI: Bonazzi 1972
Shorty BON BON: Algarin
Harold BOND (1939): Carroll
(Young American Poets),
Evans
(Horace) Julian BOND (1940):
Bontemps 1963, 1974;
Hughes 1964, 1970; Lomax,
Lowenfels 1969 (Random
House), Pool
Michael BOND: Weishaus
James BONK (1932): Stryk 1975
Jeanne Delamater BONNETTI:
Plumley
Arna (Wendell) BONTEMPS
(1902-1973): Adoff 1968,
1973; Bach, Bell, Bontemps
1963, 1974; Breman, Brew-
ton, Crafts, Hayden, Hughes
1970, King 1975, Lomax,
Peck 1970, D. Randall 1960,
Schneider, Turner, Wagner
Sue BOOKER: Booker
Bruce BOONE (1941): Leyland
1975
Sharon (Ida) BOONE: Booker,
Kohl
Philip BOOTH (1925): Brewton,
Brinnin 1963, 1970; Carruth
(Bantam), Dunning, Gwynn,
Hall 1962 (World), Hannum,
Hannum and Chase, Holmes,
Hurtik, Kennedy 1973,
Morrison, Peck 1970, Pilon,
Strand, Univ. Press of Va.,
Wagner, Wesleyan Univ.
Charlie BORDIN (1941): Gitlin,
Krech, Malley
Fred BORNHAUSER (1925): H.
Taylor
Ebbe BORREGAARD (1933):
Allen 1960, Waldman 1971,
Weishaus
Victor BORSA (1931): Leyland,
1975, 1977
Jean Francois BORY: Wildman,
Winkler
B. H. BOSTON: Kherdian 1970
Carol BOSWORTH: Hallmark

Ronald BOTTRALL (1906):
Firmage, Thomas
Sandy BOUCHER: Efros
R. Tevis BOULWARE: Sim-
mons
Francis (William) BOURDILLON:
Aloian, Untermeyer 1970
Cin BOURGEAULT: Hoffman
Arthur S. BOURINOT (1893):
A. J. M. Smith 1960
Sharon BOURKE: Henderson
Lord BOWEN: Rose
Robert T. BOWEN: Dee
George BOWERING (1938): J.
Gill, Gross, McGovern,
Sherman
Edgar BOWERS (1924): Cole
1967 (Macmillan), Engle,
Hall 1962 (Penguin), Lask,
Strand, Winters, Witt-
Diamant
Greg BOWERS: Adoff 1971
William BOWLES: Aloian
Airvester BOWMAN: Student
Geoffrey BOWNAS (1923):
Stallworthy
William BOX: Greaves
Ray BOXER: Smith
Aram BOYAJIAN: Blazek, J.
Gill
Arthur BOYARS (1925): Hall
1962 (World)
A. C. BOYD: Crang
Bruce BOYD (1928): D. M.
Allen 1960, 1964
Polly Chase BOYDEN: Gannett
Bill BOYDSTUN: Head
Hersey BOYER (1941): Tisdale
James BOYER: Rottmann
Kay BOYLE (1903): Chester,
Harvey, Howe, Hughes
1970, Lowenfels 1969
(Doubleday), Stanford
Rosalie BOYLE: Lask
Hugh Henry BRACKENRIDGE:
Jackson
Jon BRACKER: Sollid 1973,
Weil
Milton BRACKER (1909-1964):
Cole 1963, Lask, Morrison
Kate BRACKETT: Vrbovska
1963
Fred BRADFORD: Breman

Walter (W.) BRADFORD (1937):
G. Brooks 1971 (Broadside
Treasury), (Jump Bad); P.
Brown, Friedman, Stryk
1975
Juanita BRADLEY: Kohl
Mildred W. BRADLEY: Sar-
gent
Sam BRADLEY (1917): Der-
leth, Harris 1970, Steven-
son, Weil
Valerie Jo BRADLEY: Clay
Charles A. BRADY: Vrbovska
1968
Romola BRADY: Hoffman
Egard BRAGA: E. Williams
Franklin BRAINARD (1920):
Stryk 1975
Joe BRAINARD (1942): Fagin,
Leyland 1975, Waldman
1969, 1971
John G. C. BRAINARD: Jack-
son
Mary Gardner BRAINARD:
Kauffman
William Stanley BRAITHEWAITE
(1878-1962): Bontemps
1963, 1974; Hughes 1970,
Monaco 1974, Patterson,
Turner
Ellen BRAKE: Brindle
Berton BRALEY (1882-1966):
Kramer, Jackson
Robert BRANAMAN: Poetry
San Francisco
Daryl BRANCHE: Dee
Dollar BRAND (c. 1932): Bre-
man
Marian Frances BRAND (1915):
Mollenkott
Millen BRAND (1906): Lask,
Lowenfels 1966, 1969
(Doubleday), 1973
Irma BRANDEIS: Hecht
Kay BRANINE: Brindle
Ginger BRANT: Oppenheimer
1977
Perry BRASS (1947): Leyland
1975, 1977, Young
Edward BRATHWAITE (1930):
Breman, Lask, Salkey
George BRATT (1893): Lowen-
fels 1966

Richard Emil BRAUN (1934):
Ellmann 1973
Richard BRAUTIGAN (1935):
Arts Festival 1964, Fer-
linghetti, Harlan, Harvey,
Kennedy 1973, 1974;
Kherdian 1973, McCullough,
Waldman 1971
Nan BRAYMER (1895): Lowen-
fels 1967 (Where Is Viet-
nam?)
George BRECHT: Gross,
Rothenberg 1973
C. BREEZE: Clay
Luke BREITT: Winans
Claus BREMER (1924): Gross,
Klonsky, E. Williams
Bonnie BREMSER: De Loach
1976, Montgomery
Ray BREMSER (1934): D. M.
Allen 1960, De Loach 1976,
H. Jones, Montgomery,
Oppenheimer 1967, Wald-
man 1971, E. Wilentz
Eileen BRENNAN (1913):
Knowles
John Michael BRENNAN (1950):
Kennedy 1973
Joseph Payne BRENNAN (1918):
Derleth
Summer BRENNER: Chester
Cathy BRESHER: Adoff 1971
Gordon BRESSACK: Booker
Edwin J. BRETT: Summer-
field
N. H. BRETTELL: Rose
Kwesi BREW (1928): Breman,
Hughes 1963, Jacobus,
Lomax
Elizabeth BREWSTER (1922):
E. Gill, A. J. M. Smith
1960
Townsend T. BREWSTER (c.
1950): Murphy
Madeline S. BRIDGES: Kauff-
man
Shirley BRIDGES (1924): Han-
num
W. BRIDGES-ADAMS: J.
Gibson
Patrick BRIDGEWATER: Cole
1967 (Macmillan)
Jean BRIERE (1909): Lomax

Harold BRIGGS: Vrbovska 1963
John BRIGGS: Monaco 1973
Besmilr BRIGHAM (1923):
Chester, Konek, Lowenfels
1973, Schreiber, Segnitz
Alan BRILLIANT: Simmons
June BRINDEL: Gallery 1973
John Malcolm BRINNIN (1916):
Beerman, Brinnin 1963,
1970; Cromie, Ellmann
1973, Engle, Firmage,
Heyen, Howard, Howard
and Victor, Lask, Perrine,
H. Taylor, Untermeyer
1973 (McKay)
Alan BRITT: Fox, Gallery
1973, Lowenfels 1975,
Smith
Estelle D. BROADRICK: Gal-
lery 1970
William BROBST: Hanna 1960
Edwin BROCK (1927): Crang,
Cromie, Greaves, L.
Moore, Rosenthal 1967,
Wagner
Miner W. BROCK: Scheftel,
Vrbovska 1963
Van K. BROCK: Evans, Owen
1969, 1974
Jim (James) BRODEY (1942):
Montgomery, Oppenheimer
1967, Padgett, Waldman
1969, 1971
David BROMIGE: Gross, Har-
vey, McCullough
William BRONK: Carruth (Ban-
tam)
BROOKE: Violet
Christopher BROOKHOUSE:
Adoff 1969
Adrian BROOKS (1947): Ley-
land 1975
Audrey BROOKS: Adoff 1971
Edwin BROOKS (1918): Gross
Major
Eugene BROOKS: Lask
Gwendolyn BROOKS (1917):
Adoff 1968, 1969, 1970,
1973; Baylor, Bell, Bon-
temps 1963, 1974; Breman,
G. Brooks (Broadside
Treasury), (Jump Bad);
Carruth (Bantam), Chace,

Colley, De Roche, Ellmann 1973, 1976; Engle, Friedman, Giovanni, Greaves, Hannum, Harlan, Hayden, Hopkins (Knopf), (Nelson); Howe, Hughes 1970, Jacobus, Jordan, Kennedy 1973, 1974; King 1975, Konek, Livingston, Lomax, Lowenfels 1969 (Doubleday), McGovern, Monaco 1974, Morrison, Morticella, Patterson, Peck 1970, Poulin, D. Randall 1960, 1969; Schneider, Stanford, Stibitz, Stryk 1967, H. Taylor, Untermeyer 1973 (McKay), Wagner, M. Williams

Helen Morgan BROOKS: Hughes 1964, 1970; Patterson

Janet M. BROOKS: Black History

L. Alexander BROOKS: Tisdale

Phillips BROOKS: Kauffman

S. Marshall BROOKS, Jr.: Adoff 1971

Steve BROOKS: S. Vincent

William E. BROOKS: J. A. Vincent

Myron BROOMELL: Talisman

Catherine Savage BROSMAN: Owen 1974

John BROUGH (1917): Stallworthy

T. Alan BROUGHTON: McMahon

James BROUGHTON (1913): D. M. Allen 1960, Arts Festival 1964, Brewton, Harvey, Witt-Diamant

Ann BROWN: Giovanni

Beatrice Curtis BROWN: Parker 1960

Bill BROWN: Weishaus

Charlie BROWN: Student

Damian BROWN: Harlan

Daniel BROWN: Tisdale

Daryl BROWN: Booker

Dorothy Ann BROWN: Efros

Elaine BROWN: Dee

Ellen M. BROWN: Giovanni

Frank London BROWN (1927-1962): Hughes 1970

George Mackay BROWN (1927):

Hall 1962 (World), Windler

H. Rap BROWN: Henderson

Harry BROWN (1917): Stevenson, Univ. Press of Va.

Hunter BROWN: Rigsbee

Isabella Maria BROWN: Hughes 1964, 1970

Josephine Edith BROWN (1878-1964): Gildner

Joyce BROWN: Student

Julian BROWN: Derleth

Landa Loretta BROWN: Booker

Linda BROWN (1939): Pool

Marshall BROWN: Jackson

Michael Dennis BROWN (Browne) (1940): Gildner, Harris 1976, Jacobus

Nelson (Ameer) BROWN: Adoff 1971

Norman O. BROWN (1913): Gross, Rothenberg

Pam BROWN: Dee

Pete BROWN (1940): Cole 1972

Randy Meridith BROWN (randimeridethbrown): Gallery 1973

Richard BROWN: Clay

Rita Mae BROWN (1944): Bulkin, Howe, Konek

Rosellen BROWN: Mazur

Sharon Lee BROWN: Stevenson

Spencer BROWN: Weil

Sterling (A.) BROWN (1901): Adoff 1968, 1973; Bell, Bontemps 1963, 1974; Breman, Hayden, Henderson, Hughes 1970, Jordan, Kenseth, King 1975, Lomax, Lowenfels 1969 (Doubleday), Schneider, Turner

Toni BROWN: Malley

Wayne BROWN: Salkey

Willard L. BROWN: Jackson

William BROWN (1939): Hewitt, Al Lee

Irving BROWNE: Jackson

Michael Dennis BROWNE (1940): Halpern, Harris, 1973, 1976; Jacobus

William BROWNE (1930): Bontemps 1963, 1974

Henry Howard BROWNELL: Jackson

Alan BROWNJOHN (1931): Adoff 1969, Crang, Greaves, Lask
Michael BROWNSTEIN (1943): Carroll (Young American Poets), McCullough, Padgett, Waldman 1969, 1971
Stanley BROWNSTEIN: Rottmann
Charles BRUCE (1906): A. J. M. Smith 1960
John BRUCE: Morrison
Lennart BRUCE: Harvey, Palmer, Peck 1971
Mary Celinia BRUCE: Adoff 1971
Susan BRUCE: Brindle
Joseph BRUCHAC (1942): Lourie, Lowenfels 1973, 1975; McMahon, L. Moore, Niatum
Lorena BRUFF: Winkler
Laurel BRUMMET: Brindle
John BRUNNER (1934): Lucie-Smith
Thomas BRUSH (1941): Evans
Dennis BRUTUS: Kgositsile
F. J. BRYANT, Jr. (1942): Adoff 1973, Black History, Breman, P. Brown, Major
Tom BUCHAN (1931): Cole 1967 (Viking), 1971
Bonnie BUCHANAN: Crafts
Charles A. BUCHANAN (Imani Kujichangulia): King Pub.
Marion BUCHMAN: Harris 1970, Lowenfels 1966
Arthur C. BUCK: Plumley
Pearl S. BUCK (1892-   ): Plumley
Sharon BUCK: Crafts
Vincent BUCKLEY (1925): T. Moore
John BUCKNER: Blazek
David BUDBILL: Adoff 1969
Charles BUKOWSKI (1920): Blazek, Bukowski, De Loach 1976, Ferlinghetti, Gross, Kennedy 1973, Kherdian 1973, Lowenfels 1966, 1969 (Doubleday); Owen 1969, Peck 1971, P. Perry, Rothenberg 1973, Simmons, M. Williams, Winans, Winkler

Elly BULKIN: Bulkin
Amanda BULLINS: M. Gibson
Ed BULLINS (1935): Breman, Clay, Ferlinghetti, King 1972, Major
Jerald BULLIS: Hoffman
P. D. BULLOCK: J. Gibson
Elroy BUNDY: Head
H. C. BUNNER: J. A. Vincent
Basil BUNTING (1900): Cole 1971, Ellmann 1973, Gregory 1962, Matthias, Stallworthy
Emelie H. BURCH: Sargent
Carrie BURCHARDT: Adoff 1971
Boyd G. BURD: Kiley
Jean BURDEN (1914): Lask, Stanford
William (Skelly) BURFORD (1927): Bly 1970, Gersmehl, Lask, O. Williams 1966 (World)
Michael BURKARD: Rigsbee
Carl F. BURKE: Dee
Kenneth BURKE (1897): Aiken, Klonsky
Patrick R. BURKE: Kiley
Klaus BURKHARDT: Wildman
G. BURNET: Jackson
Dana BURNETT (1888-1962): Jackson, Kramer
Jesse BURNETT: Kohl
David BURNS: Harris 1970
Jerry H. BURNS: Weil
Jim BURNS (1936): Crang
Richard BURNS: Lask
Thom BURNS: Ferlinghetti
Stanley BURNSHAW (1906): Gregory 1966
Amelia Josephine BURR (1878): Jackson
Gray BURR: Leary, Pearson
Winifred Adams BURR: Derleth
Margaret BURROUGHS (1917): Dee, Giovanni, King 1975, D. Randall 1969
Abe BURROWS (1910): Cole 1967 (Viking)
E. G. BURROWS: Owen 1969
Christopher BURSK: Lowen-

fels 1969 (Doubleday), J.
R. Randall
Nathaniel BURT: Vrbovska 1963
Kevin BURVICK: Booker
Joanne BUSBY: Harlan
Frederick BUSCH: Hanna 1960
Joseph Bevans BUSH: Coombs
Pat J. BUSHONG: Brindle
Robert D. BUSTER: Rottmann
Grace BUTCHER (1934): Ash-
land, Chester, Efros,
Lowenfels 1969 (Random
House)
Gerald BUTLER (1942): Crafts,
Hewitt
Guy BUTLER: Rose
Lynn BUTLER: Konek
Edward BUTSCHER: Monaco
1973
St. John BUTTACI: Gallery
1973
Hezekiah BUTTERWORTH:
Kauffman
Tony BUZAN: Cole 1971
Wilma BYAS: Student
Witter BYNNER (Emanuel
Morgan) (1881-1968):
Cromie, Firmage, Hughes
1970, Jackson, Lask,
Parker 1967, Steuben
John BYROM: Kauffman, H.
Taylor
Stuart BYRON (1941): Leyland
1977, Wesleyan Univ.

C

Laurena CABANERO: Clay
Olga CABRAL (1910): Gross,
Kenseth, Kramer, Lowen-
fels 1966, 1967, 1969
(Doubleday), 1973, 1975
Emily CACHAPERO: Clay
Marilyn CADOGAN: Krech
Daniel L. CADY: Jackson
John CAGE (1912): Gross,
Harlan, Rothenberg
Jack CAIN (1940): Van den
Heuvel
Marcella B. CAINE (1915):
D. Randall 1969
David CALDER: Cole 1971

Ben CALDWELL: Baraka
Susan CALHOUN: Efros
Richard W. CALISCH: Gallery
1973
Clinch CALKINS: Untermeyer
1970
Amarette CALLAWAY: Hall-
mark
Noel CALLOW: Hoffman
Sandra CALTABIANO: Brindle
Bella CAMERON: Sargent
Roussan CAMILIE (1915-1961):
Lomax
James CAMP (1923): E.
Bender, R. Bender, Hope,
Kennedy 1973
Oscar CAMPA: Smith
Alastair (Alistair) CAMPBELL
(1926): Peck 1971, Phillips,
Stevenson
David CAMPBELL (1915):
Knowles, T. Moore
Douglas CAMPBELL: Smith
Frank CAMPBELL: Booker
George CAMPBELL: Salkey
Ian CAMPBELL (1933): Bold
Janet CAMPBELL (1946): T.
Allen, Dodge
Joseph CAMPBELL (1881):
Untermeyer 1964
Josie CAMPBELL: Booker
Malcolm CAMPBELL: Jackson
Melville CANE (1879): Adoff
1969, Jackson, Lash,
Steuben, Untermeyer 1964
Criss Ellen CANNADY: Hoff-
man
Terry CANNON (1940): Gitlin,
Gross
Ruthe D. CANTER: Bulkin
Charles CANTRELL: Lowen-
fels 1975, Rigsbee
Robert CANZONERI (1925):
Ashland, Steele, M. Wil-
liams
Ronald CAPLAN: H. Jones
Yvonne CARABALLO: Kohl
Doreen CARAHER: Harris
1973
H. D. CARBERRY: Salkey
Joseph CARDARELLI (1944):
Hewitt
Ramona CARDEN (1945): T.

Gladys CARDIFF (1942): Lowenfels 1973, Niatum
Alvaro CARDONA-HINE (1928): Lowenfels 1966, Vrbovska 1963
Nancy CARDOZO: Untermeyer 1970
Jan CAREW: Salkey
Jon CAREW (1922): Breman
Dawn F. CAREY: Palmer
Steve CAREY: Waldman 1969, 1971
Francis CARLET: Head
Sara King CARLETON: Derleth
Amy CARMICHAEL: Kauffman
Edmund S. CARPENTER (1922): Lowenfels 1973
John Randell CARPENTER: Lask
William Howard CARPENTER: Jackson
H. CARR: Morticella
Ray M. CARR: Banker
Jaime CARRERO (1931): Lowenfels 1973
Constance CARRIER (1908): McMahon, Morrison, Stanford
Graciela CARRILLO: Clay
Harold CARRINGTON (1939-1964): Gross, Lowenfels 1969 (Random House), Montgomery
Jim CARROLL: Waldman 1969, 1971
Paul CARROLL (1927): D. M. Allen 1960, Friedman, Stibitz, Stryk 1967
Hayden CARRUTH (1921): Brewton, Carruth (Bantam), (McCall); Lask, Lowenfels 1967, 1969 (Doubleday), 1973; McGovern, Owen 1969, Rosenthal 1967, 1968; Stevenson, Univ. Press of Va.
William Herbert CARRUTH: Jackson
Charles Edward CARRYL: Nash
Albert Howard CARTER (1913-1970): Mollenkott
Hodding CARTER (1907-1972): Hughes 1970, Kennedy 1973

Jimmie CARTER: Booker
Karin CARTER: Adoff 1971
Karl CARTER: Henderson
Lin CARTER: Derleth
Loleta CARTER: Booker
M. L. CARTER: Jackson
Martin CARTER (1927): Breman, Salkey
Gilbert CARVALHO: Sargent
Mabel MacDonald CARVER: Derleth
Raymond CARVER (1938): Evans, Gildner
Phoebe CARY: Parker 1960
Michael CASEY: L. Moore, Rottmann
Americo CASIANO: Algarin
William CASSEGRAIN (1945): Monaco 1974
Maxine CASSIN: Hearse
Turner CASSITY: Owen 1974, Pearson
Robert Clayton CASTO (1932): De Roche
Sophia CASTRO-LEON (c. 1932): Hewitt
Catherine CATER (1917): Bontemps 1963, 1974; Hughes 1970
Willa CATHER: McGinley
Lucy CATLETT: Ferlinghetti
Nancy CATO (1917): Brindle, T. Moore, Stanford
Don CAUBLE: Blazek, Fox
Charles CAUSLEY (1917): R. Bender, Bogan, Crang, Engle, J. Gibson (Book Two), Greaves, Hall 1962 (Watts), Hannum, Kenseth, Peck 1971, Plotz, Rosenthal 1967, Stevenson
Grace CAVALIERI (1932): Mollenkott
Catherine J. CAVIN: Brindle
Chris CAYER: Adoff 1971
G. F. CAYLEY: Cole 1967 (Macmillan)
G. J. CAYLEY: Cole 1972
Joseph CERAVOLO (1934): Meyers, Padgett, Waldman 1969
Georgette CERRUTTI: Bulkin
Margaret CESA: Harlan, Head

Brenda CHAMBERLAIN (1912-1971): Lask, Stanford
Marisha CHAMBERLAIN: Rigsbee
George CHAMBERS (1931): Stryk 1975, Wiebe
Henry Tim CHAMBERS (1903): Mollenkott
Jane CHAMBERS: Konek
Lorna Beers CHAMBERS: Derleth
Robert W. CHAMBERS: Jackson
Craig L. CHAMPION: Kiley
Len CHANDLER (1935): Gross, Lowenfels 1969 (Random House), Major
G. S. Sharat CHANDRA: Gildner
H. Gerald CHAPIN: Jackson
Katherine Garrison CHAPIN: Lask, J. A. Vincent
Ralph CHAPLIN (1887-1961): Bates, Cromie, Kramer
Arthur CHAPMAN: Jackson
Fred CHAPPELL (1936): Owen 1969, 1974; H. Taylor
Sean CHAPPELL: Kohl
Jim CHAPSON: Young
Martin Neil CHARET: Gallery 1973
Dorthi CHARLES (1950): Kennedy 1974
Beth CHASE: Brindle
Helen CHASIN (1938): Howe, Konek, Monaco 1974
Hale CHATFIELD: Ashland, McGovern
Cesar CHAVEZ (1928): Gersmehl
John CHENAULT: P. Brown, Clay
Elizabeth CHENEY: Kauffman
Neeli CHERKOVSKI: Winans
Maxine CHERNOFF: Friedman
Kelly CHERRY (1940): H. Taylor
Neeli CHERRY: Bukowski, Lowenfels 1975, Winkler
Sallie CHESHAM: Mollenkott
Elizabeth CHESLEY: Lask
Laura CHESTER: Chester Konek

Charlene CHESTNUT: Bonazzi 1972
Gail CHIARRELLO: Ferlinghetti
CHICO (c. 1948): Tisdale
Evans CHIGOUNIS: Harris 1976
Wilfred Rowland CHILDE (1890): Parker 1975
David CHILDERS: Rigsbee
William CHILDRESS (1933): Kennedy 1973, Kherdian 1970, Lowenfels 1973, Peck 1970
Delia CHILGREN: Chilgren
Lily CHILGREN: Chilgren
CHINWEIZU: Lowenfels 1975
Kathleen CHODOR: Oppenheimer 1977
Henri CHOPIN: Wildman, E. Williams
Martha CHOSA: Dodge
Curtis CHOY: Clay
Marcus B. CHRISTIAN (1900): Bontemps 1963, 1974; Hughes 1970
Saidi Mwanafunzi CHUMA: Jihad
Richard CHURCH (1893): J. Gibson, Parker 1975, Trapp
Miriam CHUSID: Brindle
Marchette CHUTE: Nash
John CIARDI (1916): Aiken, J. A. Allen, Brinnin 1963, 1970; Cole 1963, Crafts, Cromie, Driver, Dunning, Engle, Firmage, Gersmehl, Gwynn, Hine, Hurtik, Kennedy 1973, 1974; Lucie-Smith, Nash, Owen 1969, Peck 1971, Rosenthal 1967, Shapiro, Stevenson, Wallace, Walsh, M. Williams, Witt-Diamant
Lucy CHIENFUEGO: Algarin
Eugene CIRILLO: Kiley
William CIROCCO: De Loach 1976
William F. CLAIRE: Bonazzi 1972, Harris 1976
Robert CLAIRMONT: Vrbovska 1963
Joseph P. CLANCY: Morrison
Eric CLAPTON: Morse

Josephine CLARE: Gildner
Carl CLARK (1932): G. Brooks
(Jump Bad)
Charles Badger CLARK, Jr.:
Jackson
Dan CLARK: Oppenheimer 1967
David R. CLARK: Univ. of
Mass.
David CLARK (1920): Kenseth
J. K. CLARK: Lask
John Pepper (P.) CLARK (1935):
Adoff 1969, Breman, Hughes
1963, Jacobus, Kgositsile
John W. CLARK (1916): Fir-
mage
Naomi CLARK: Winans
Robert CLARK (1911): T.
Moore
Thomas A. CLARK (1944):
Klonsky
Thomas Curtis CLARK: J. A.
Vincent
Tom CLARK (1941): Barnes,
Carroll (Young American
Poets), Clark, Harlan,
McCullough, Padgett, Strand,
H. Taylor, Waldman 1969,
1971; Weishaus
Walter CLARK: Lask
Austin CLARKE (1896): Cole
1967 (Macmillan), Crang,
Ellmann 1973, Lask, Ros-
enthal 1967, 1968; Sanders,
Stallworthy
James Freeman CLARKE:
Kauffman
John Henrik CLARKE (1915):
Adoff 1973, Dee
Marietta R. CLARKE: Vrbovska
1968
Peter CLARKE: Hughes
1963
Sebastian CLARKE: Salkey
E. Margaret CLARKSON (1915):
Mollenkott
Sister CLAUDE OF JESUS:
Firmage
Paul CLAUSE (1939): Mollen-
kott
Andy CLAUSEN: Krech
Jan CLAUSEN: Bulkin, Morti-
cella
Buriel CLAY II: Clay

Gertrude CLAYTOR: Derleth
Pearl CLEAGE (1948): Booker,
Coombs
Sarah (N.) CLEGHORN: Aloian,
Jackson
Don CLELLAND: Kiley
Carole Gregory CLEMMONS
(1945): Adoff 1973, P.
Brown, Giovanni, Howe
François CLEMMONS: P.
Brown
Steve CLENDANIEL: Kohl
Elizabeth G. CLEPHANE:
Kauffman
Frank CLEVELAND (Clorox):
Booker
John CLIFFORD: Kauffman
Lucille CLIFTON (1936): Adoff
1973, 1974; Bell, Bontemps
1974, Brinnin 1970, Chace,
Chester, Cole 1971, Colley,
Halpern, Hopkins (Knopf),
Howe, Kennedy 1973, 1974;
A. Miller, L. Moore,
Stanford, H. Taylor
Michael CLIFTON: Kherdian
1970
Linda CLIMER: Brindle
D. CLINTON (1946): Stryk
1975
L. Dewitt CLINTON: Rottmann
Jennifer CLOUD: Violet
William Leo COAKLEY: Vrbov-
ska 1963, 1968
K. COASTON: Clay
Florence Earle COATES:
Kauffman
Elizabeth (J.) COATSWORTH
(1893): J. A. Allen, Cole
1963, 1972; Derleth, Dun-
ning, J. Gibson, J. Gibson
(Book Two), McGinley,
Parker 1967, Trapp, Unter-
meyer 1964
Charlie (Charles) COBB (1944):
Adoff 1973, Breman, Git-
lin, Lowenfels 1969 (Ran-
dom House)
Janice C. COBB: Clay
Bob COBBING: Pilon, E.
Williams
Catherine Cate COBLENTZ:
Kauffman

Stanton A. COBLENTZ: Derleth
Grant CODE: Derleth
Andrei CODRESCU: Waldman
1969, 1971
Robert P. Tristram COFFIN:
Dunning, Parker 1967, 1974
Richard M. COFFMAN: Kiley
Nevill COGHILL (1899): Knowles
F. H. COGSWELL: Jackson
Ira COHEN (1935): Leyland
1975, 1977
Joseph COHEN: Harris 1970
Leonard COHEN (1934): Adoff
1969, Baylor, Beerman,
Cole 1965, 1967 (Macmil-
lan), 1971, 1972; Crafts,
De Roche, Ellmann 1973,
Engle, Harlan, Joseloff,
Kennedy 1974, Morrison,
Morse, Peck 1970, A. J.
M. Smith 1969, Untermeyer
1970
Marty COHEN: De Loach
1976, Hoffman, Morti-
cella
Marvin COHEN: Harris 1973,
E. Wilentz
Richard COHEN: Hoffman
Robert COHEN: Harris 1973
Robert David COHEN: Banker,
Oppenheimer 1967
Scott COHEN: Oppenheimer
1967, Waldman 1969, 1971
Marty COHN: Brindle
Grey COHOE: T. Allen, Dodge
Rex Baker COILE: Banker
Syl Cheney COKER: Lowenfels
1975
Barry COLE: Lucie-Smith
David COLE: Palmer
E. R. (Eugene Roger) COLE
(1930): Mollenkott
William COLE: Cole 1967
(Macmillan), 1967 (Viking),
1971
Beverly E. (Elaine) COLEMAN
(1936): Giovanni
Catherine COLEMAN: Harris
1976
Jamie COLLAZO: Booker
Richard COLLIER: Fox
Billy COLLINS: Rigsbee
Christopher COLLINS (1936):
Monaco 1973, 1974

Fran COLLINS (Fatima): Gio-
vanni
Helen Johnson COLLINS (1918):
Hughes 1970
John COLLINS: Jackson
Judy COLLINS: Crafts, Morse
Leslie M. (Morgan) COLLINS
(1914): Bontemps 1963,
1974; Hughes 1970
Rufus COLLINS: Gay
Laurence COLLINSON (1925):
T. Moore
Frank A. COLLYMORE (1893):
Bogan
John Robert (Roberto) COLOMBO
(Columbo) (1936): Gross,
Hitchcock, Lowenfels 1975,
Lucie-Smith
Horatio COLONY: Aiken
Padraic COLUM (1881): Bogan,
Cole 1963, Colum, Knowles,
Parker 1967, Stevenson,
Untermeyer 1964
John Robert COLUMBO see
COLOMBO
Tram COMBS: Brinnin 1963,
1970; Pearson
Stephen R. COMER: Adoff
1971
Alex COMFORT (1920): Cole
1971, Cromie, Firmage,
Untermeyer 1964
Carl CONCHA: Lowenfels 1973
Carlos CONDE: Algarin
Kirby CONGDON (1924): De
Loach, Fox, Gross, Lask,
Leyland 1975, 1977; Lowen-
fels 1969 (Doubleday), 1969
(Random House), Montgom-
ery, Young
Hilda CONKLING (1910):
Aloian, Cole 1963, Peter-
son
Cynthia M. CONLEY (Zubena)
(c. 1946): Giovanni
Robert J. CONLEY (1940):
Lowenfels 1973
Leo CONNELLAN (1928): Low-
enfels 1967, 1969 (Double-
day), 1973; Vrbovska
Beverly CONNELLY: Derleth
Emma Reno CONNOR: Giovanni
Tony CONNOR (1930): Crang,
Greaves, Stallworthy, H.

Taylor
Robert CONQUEST (1917): Ell-
mann 1973, Lucie-Smith,
Rosenthal 1967, Wallace
Helen CONRADS: Violet
Anthony CONRAN (1931): Fir-
mage
Victor CONTOSKI (1936): Bay-
lor, Schreiber, Stryk 1975
Priscilla L. CONWAY: Giovan-
ni
CONYUS (Conys) (1942): Adoff
1973, Halpern, A. Miller,
E. Wilentz
Eliza COOK: Kennedy 1974
Geoffrey COOK: Winans
Gwendolyn COOK: Booker
Mike COOK (1939): G. Brooks
(Jump Bad)
Rose COOKE: Jackson
Sam COOKE: Chace
Sidney COOKSLEY: Lask
Peter COOLEY (1940): Evans,
Halpern, Stryk 1975
Clark COOLIDGE (1939): Car-
roll (Young American Po-
ets), Clark, Fagin, Harlan,
Hausman, McCullough,
Monaco 1973, Padgett,
Waldman 1969, 1971
Jerry COONLEY: Hadassah
Bonnie COOPER: Kohl
Charles COOPER (1948): Adoff
1970, 1973; Shuman
Dennis COOPER (1953): Ley-
land 1977
Helen COOPER: Oppenheimer
1977
Jane COOPER (1924): Hall
1962 (World), Howe,
Kessler, Knoek, M. Wil-
liams
Stanley COOPERMAN (1929):
Firmage, Joseloff, Steven-
son
Richard CORBET: Nash
William CORBETT: Mazur,
J. R. Randall
Alice CORBIN (1881): Hughes
1970
Lloyd (M.) CORBIN, Jr.
(Djangatolum) (1949):
Adoff 1970, 1973, 1974;
Jordan

Richard CORBIN: Peck 1970
Hilary CORKE (1921): Brinnin,
Cromie
William CORKINE: Untermeyer
1970
Cynthia M. CORLEY (c. 1946):
P. Brown
Cid CORMAN (1924): Carruth
(Bantam), De Loach 1976,
Harris 1973, Kennedy
1974, Weil
Philip CORNER: Gross
Frances CORNFORD (1886-
1960): Bogan, Cole 1963,
1965, 1967 (Macmillan),
1971, 1972; Holmes, Ken-
nedy 1974, Knowles,
Parker 1975, Untermeyer
1964
John CORNILLON: Blazek
Sam (Samuel James) CORNISH
(1938): Adoff 1973, 1974;
Breman, Evans, Fox,
Hausman, Major, Mazur,
H. Smith, T. Wilentz
Izora CORPMAN: Gildner
Joe CORRIE (1894-1968): Bold
John William CORRINGTON
(1932): Jacobus, Lowen-
fels 1966, H. Taylor, M.
Williams
Gregory CORSO (1930): Adams,
Adoff 1969, D. M. Allen
1960, Barnes, Baylor,
Beerman, Brady, Carruth
(Bantam), Chace, De
Loach 1976, Di Prima,
Dunning, Ellmann 1973,
Greaves, Harlan, Harris
1970, Hieatt, Hollander,
Hughes 1970, Hurtik,
Kennedy 1973, Kherdian
1973, 1974; Leary, Lorri-
mer, Lowenfels 1966,
1969 (Doubleday); Morrison,
Rothenberg 1973, Schneider,
Strand, H. Taylor, E.
Wilentz, M. Williams,
Winkler, Witt-Diamant
Elias Hruska CORTES (1943):
Winans
Mike CORTES: Harlan
Carlos CORTEZ (1923): Low-
enfels 1966

Jayne CORTEZ (1938): Adoff
1973, Coombs, Giovanni,
Patterson
William CORY: Plotz
Barbara CORYELL: Brindle
Myrtle E. COSTELLO: Sargent
Bill COSTLEY: Fox
Jonathan COTT: Carroll (Young
American Poets), Waldman
1969
John COTTON: Lucie-Smith,
Stevenson
Christopher COTTRELL:
Brindle
Henri COULETTE (1927):
Baylor, Engle, Hall 1962
(World), Kennedy 1973,
Kessler, Strand, Winkler
Mary Elizabeth COUNSELMAN:
Derleth
William COUNTESS: Hanna
1960
Martha COURTOT: Bulkin
Linda (S.) COUSINS (c. 1946):
Booker, Giovanni, Patter-
son
Mincy COWDERY: Black His-
tory
Joseph R. COWEN (1923):
Hughes 1970
Malcolm COWLEY (1898):
Aiken, L. Moore, Perrine,
Peterson, H. Taylor, O.
Williams 1966 (World)
Anne COX: Kiley
Carol COX: E. Gill
Ed COX (1946): Leyland 1975,
1977
Stephen COX: Steele
Thelma Parker COX (c. 1940):
Murphy
Louis (Osborne) COXE (1918):
Aiken, Cole 1963, Lask,
McGovern, Owen 1969, H.
Taylor
Gretchen CRAFTS: Crafts
Alexander CRAIG (1923): T.
Moore
Ann M. CRAIG (1952): H.
Taylor
Alan CRANG: Crang
Dan CRAWFORD: Hauffman
Max CRAWFORD (1938): Git-
lin

Tom CRAWFORD (1939): Evans
Frederick CRAWLEY: Dee
Patrick CREAGH (1930):
Knowles
Hubert CREEKMORE (1907-
1966): Bates
Robert CREELEY (1926): D.
M. Allen 1960, 1964; G.
W. Allen, J. A. Allen,
Barnes, Baylor, Berg, Bly
1970, Brady, Carroll (Po-
em in Its Skin), Carruth
(Bantam), Chace, Clark,
Cole 1965, 1967, 1971,
1972; Crafts, De Loach
1976, Di Prima, Ellmann
1973, 1976; Ferlinghetti,
Gross, Hall 1962 (Penguin),
Hannum, Harlan, Harris
1973, Heyen, Howard,
Howard and Victor, Hurtik,
Kennedy 1973, 1974; Kes-
sler, Kherdian 1973,
Leary, Lowenfels 1967,
McCullough, Monaco 1974,
Oppenheimer 1967, Peck
1970, J. Perry, Plotz,
Poulin, Rosenthal 1967,
Rosenthal 1967, Rothenberg
1973, Simpson, Solt, Stall-
worthy, Strand, H. Taylor,
Wagner, Waldman 1971,
Walsh, Weil, Weishaus,
E. Wilentz, M. Williams,
Witt-Diamant
James CRENNER (1938):
Stevenson
Jane CREWDSON: Kauffman
Judson CREWS (1917): Ferling-
hetti, Montgomery,
Vrbovska 1963
Stella CREWS (1950): Lane
Emma CROBAUGH: Scheftel
Wendy CROOKS: Head
Barbard (Ann) CROSBY (c.
1940): Giovanni
David CROSBY: Morse
Fanny J. CROSBY: Kauffman
Ranice Henderson CROSBY
(1952): Howe
Max CROSLEY (1936): Weis-
haus
Frank A. CROSS, Jr.: Rott-
mann

Hollace CROSS: Fox
Zora Bernice May CROSS
(1890): T. Moore
Kevin CROSSLEY-HOLLAND:
J. Gibson (Book Two)
Stanley CROUCH (1945): Adoff
1973, Breman, Coombs,
King 1972, Major
Doug CROW: Fox
Philip CROWDER: Kohl
Donald R. CROZIER: Kiley
Victor Hernandez CRUZ (1949):
Adoff 1969, 1973; Breman,
Chace, Clay, Colley, De
Loach 1976, Harvey, Ken-
nedy 1973, Kherdian 1973,
Lomax, Lowenfels 1969
(Random House), McCul-
lough, Major, A. Miller
George Paul CSICSERY (1948):
Gitlin
Emilio CUBEIRO (1947): Ley-
land 1975, 1977
Art CUELHO: Gallery 1970,
1973
Katherine L. CUESTAS (1944):
Jordan
Irene CULLEN: Brindle
Michael CULROSS: Bogin
Lawrence S. CUMBERBATCH
(1946): Coombs
Kattie M. CUMBO: Adoff
1970, Shuman
E. E. CUMMINGS (1894-1962):
Adams, G. W. Allen,
Aloian, Bach, Barnes,
Bates, Baylor, R. Bender,
Bogan, Brady, Brinnin
1963, 1970; G. Brooks,
Calderwood, Carruth (Ban-
tam), Cole 1963, 1965;
Colley, Colum, Corbett,
Crafts, Crane, Crang,
Croft, Cromie, De Roche,
Driver, Dunning, Ellmann
1973, 1976; Engle, Felver,
Gannett, Greaves, Gregory
1962, 1966; Gwynn, Hall
1962 (Watts), Hannum,
Harlan, Hieatt, Hine,
Holmes, Immaculate, Ja-
cobus, Kallich, Kennedy
1973, 1974; Kenseth,

Klonsky, Kramer, Living-
ston, Lowenvels 1969
(Doubleday), McCullough,
McGinley, Mercatante,
Monaco 1974, Morrison,
Morse, Nash, Olson, Peck
1970, Perrine, J. Perry,
Peterson, Phillips, Pilon,
Reeves, Rothenberg 1973,
1974; Schneider, Shapiro,
Simpson, A. J. M. Smith
1967, Wolt, Stallworthy,
H. Taylor, W. Taylor,
Trapp, Untermeyer 1964,
1973 (McKay); Wagner,
Whicher, Williams and
Honig, O. Williams 1966
(Trident), 1966 (World)
Parke CUMMINGS: Jackson
P. D. CUMMINS (1910):
Greaves
Louis CUNEO: Winans
Waring CUNEY (1906): Bon-
temps 1963, 1974; Breman,
Holmes, Kennedy 1973,
Lomax
J. V. CUNNINGHAM (1911):
Adams, Aiken, Arp, Bay-
lor, Carruth (Bantam),
Cole 1967 (Macmillan),
1971; Ellmann 1973, Engle,
Hall 1962 (Watts), Harlan,
Harris 1973, Howard,
Howard and Victor, Ken-
nedy 1973, 1974; Kostelan-
etz, Larson, Lask, J.
Perry, Rosenthal 1967,
Strand, H. Taylor, W.
Taylor, Untermeyer 1964,
Wallace, M. Williams,
Winkler
James CUNNINGHAM (1936):
G. Brooks (Jump Bad), P.
Brown
John CUNNINGHAM: Parker
1960
Tom CUNNINGHAM: Bogin
Waring CUREY (1906): Bon-
temps 1974
Allen CURNOW: Firmage
Edwin CURRAN: Parker 1967
Alvin Lewis CURRY, Jr.:
Kohl

David CURRY (1942): Stryk
1975
Linda CURRY (1953): Hopkins
(Knopf), Jordan
Jack CURTIS: Lowenfels 1975
Walt CURTIS: Morticella
Wesley CURTRIGHT (1910):
Hughes 1970
Lord CURZON: Cole 1971
Cyril CUSACK: Lask
R. R. CUSCADEN: Gildner,
Stibitz, Stryk 1967, Weil
Ralph Spaulding CUSHMAN:
Kauffman
Tom CUSON (c. 1945): Fer-
linghetti, Gitlin
Bruce CUTLER: Stryk 1967
Simon CUTTS (1944): Klonsky

D

Bill DABNEY: Tisdale
Philip DACEY (1939): Evans,
Halpern, Rigsbee, Stryk
1975
Bernard B. DADIE (1916):
Jacobus
Roald DAHL (1916): Cole 1963
David DAICHES: Jacobus,
Morrison
Susan DAILY: Violet
John DALEY: De Loach 1976
Elaine DALLMAN: Brindle
Charles DALMAN (1872): Cole
1963, 1971; Parker 1960
Dorothy DALTON: Vbrovska
1963
Rae DALVEN: Plotz, Stall-
worthy
John DALY: J. A. Vincent
Kathleen Walker DALZIEL
(1881): T. Moore
Vinnie-Marie D'AMBROSIO:
Konek
Kim DAMMERS: Gallery 1970
S. Foster DAMON (1893):
Kostelanetz
Jaledi DAMU: Jihad
Francis DANA: Jackson
Robert DANA (1929): Lask,
Stryk 1975
Walter (K.) DANCY (1946):
Coombs, Henderson

Myrtle D. DANEWALIA:
Sargent
Harlan DANGERFIELD: Wald-
man 1969
John DANIEL (1935): Gross,
Matthias
Roy DANIELS (1902): A. J.
M. Smith 1960
Deborah DANNER: Booker
Margaret (Essie) DANNER
(1915): Adoff 1973, Bell,
Bontemps 1963, 1974;
Breman, G. Brooks
(Broadside Treasury), P.
Brown, Hayden, Hender-
son, Hughes 1964, Hughes
1970, King, Al Lee, Don
L. Lee, Lowenfels 1966,
D. Randall 1960, 1969
Edith M. DARBY: Scheftel
Louise DARCY: Lask
Pegram DARGAN: Jackson
Ruben DARIO: Bly 1970
Hole K. DARLING: Jackson
Margaret Stanion DARLING:
Derleth
Ann DARR: Peck 1971
Spike D'ARTHENAY: Wesleyan
Univ.
Elizabeth DARYUSH (c. 1891):
Stanford, Winters
Tony DATER: Kiley
Mukund R. DAVE: Sargent
Russell W. DAVENPORT:
Jackson
Richard DAVID: Hanna 1960
Donald DAVIDSON (1893-1968):
C. Brooks, Cromie, Parks,
Univ. Press of Va.
Gustav DAVIDSON: Derleth,
Lask, Steuben
J. D. DAVIDSON: Jackson
John DAVIDSON: Cole 1967,
Nash, Parker 1960
L. A. DAVIDSON: Van den
Heuvel
M. E. DAVIDSON: Adoff 1971
Richard DAVIDSON (1929):
Gross, Lowenfels 1966,
Vrbovska 1963, 1968; E.
Wilentz
Donald DAVIE (1922): Bedient,
Engle, Hall 1962 (World),
Harris 1976, Hollander,

Lask, Pearson, Rosenthal
1967, 1968; Stallworthy,
Wallace
Robert A. DAVIES: Morticella
Alyson DAVIS: Pilon
Barbara DAVIS: Monaco 1973
Catherine DAVIS (1924): Win-
ters
Donald S. C. DAVIS: Dee
Frank Marshall DAVIS (1905):
Adoff 1969, 1973; Bell,
Bontemps 1963, 1974; Hay-
den, Henderson, Holmes,
Hughes 1970, King
Gene H. DAVIS: Kiley
Gloria DAVIS: Major
Glover DAVIS: Kherdian 1970
Guy DAVIS: Dee
Halsey DAVIS: Hausman
Helene DAVIS: Mazur
Jefferson DAVIS (1944): Lowen-
fels 1973
Karen DAVIS: Brindle
La Verne DAVIS: Dee
Marale G. DAVIS: Plumley
Mike DAVIS: Kohl
Nora DAVIS: Dee
Ossie DAVIS (1922): Dee,
Hughes 1970
Rik DAVIS: Blazek
Robert A. DAVIS (1917): Adoff
1968
Ronda (M.) DAVIS: G. Brooks
(Broadside Treasury),
(Jump Bad); King 1972
Thomas Osborn DAVIS: J. A.
Vincent
William M. DAVIS: Cole 1967
Peter DAVISON (1928): Brinnin
1970, Crafts, Harris 1976,
Kennedy 1974, Leary
Rose DAVISON: Vbrovska 1963,
1968
Bruce DAWE (1930): Cromie
Mitchell DAWSON: Jackson
Robert (Bob) DAWSON (1941):
Hollander, Krech
Mrs. Donald A. DAY: Kauff-
man
Gregory Alan DAY: Black
History
Wesley DAY (1935): Harris
1970, Lowenfels 1969
(Random House)

C. (Cecil) DAY LEWIS (1904-
1972): J. A. Allen, R.
Bender, Bold, Brinnin
1963, 1970; Croft, Driver,
Ellmann 1973, Engle,
Firmage, J. Gibson (Book
Two), Greaves, Hannum,
Hurtik, Sanders, Stall-
worthy, H. Taylor, Univ.
Press of Va., Untermeyer
1964
Irene DAYTON (1922): Gallery
1970, 1973; Mollenkott
Ann DEAGON: Rigsbee
Dulcie DEAMER (1890): T.
Moore
Geoffrey DEARMER (1893):
Cole 1963, J. Gibson,
Knowles
Ann DEBBAN: Harlan
Rosemary DE BRISSAC DOB-
SON (1920): T. Moore
Melvin DE BRUHL (1950): H.
Taylor
Augusto De CAMPOS: Gross,
E. Williams
Haroldo DE CAMPOS: Gross,
E. Williams
Voltarine DE CLEYRE: Jack-
son
Miriam DeFORD: Jackson
John Williams DE FOREST:
J. A. Vincent
(Mary) Madeline DE FREES
(1919): Chester, Howe,
Larson
Paul DEHN (1912): Cole 1971,
1972; Dunning, Knowles,
Stallworthy
Michael F. DEI-ANANG:
Hughes 1963
Ormond DE KAY, Jr.: Unter-
meyer 1970
Clarissa Scott DELANEY (1914):
Bontemps 1974
P. L. DELANO: Kiley
Walter (Walter) DELEGALL
(1936): Henderson, Lowen-
fels 1966
Mark D'ELIA: Adoff 1971
Sharon N. DELMAIN: Brindle
Allen DE LOACH: De Loach,
1968, 1976; Lowenfels
1969 (Random House),

Montgomery
Joan DE LOACH: De Loach 1976
Joanne DE LONGCHAMPS: J.
    A. Allen, Lask, Owen 1969,
    Vrbovska 1963
Leona McC. DE MERE: Jackson
Stephanie DE MARIA: Chilgren
Roland Tomlekai DEMPSTER:
    Hughes 1963, Lomax
Dale DE NARD: Battle
James D. DEN BOER (1937):
    Kennedy 1973, H. Taylor
Edwin (Orr) DENBY (1903):
    Cole 1965, Padgett, Wald-
    man 1969
Susan Rives DENIGHT:
    Morticella
Robert DE NIRO (1922):
    Klonsky
J. DENISON: Morticella
Mary Lou DENMAN: Crafts
Reuel (Nicholas) DENNEY
    (1913): Aiken, Crafts,
    Morrison, Wesleyan Univ.,
    O. Williams 1966 (World)
C. F. DENNIS: Rose
R. M. DENNIS: P. Brown
Tom (Thomas C.) DENT:
    Hughes 1964
Jim DENTON: Kohl
Wally DEPEW: Blazek
Albert DE PIETRO (1913):
    Mollenkott
Doris DERBY: Giovanni
Solomon DERESSA: Kgositsile
Mike DERESZYNSKI: Rosen-
    blum
Diana DER HOVANESSIAN:
    Lask
August DERLETH: Derleth,
    Jackson, Weil
Joseph DE ROCHE (1938): De
    Roche
Toi DERRICOTTE: Oppenheimer
    1977
Alvaro DE SA: Gross
Margot DE SILVA: Lowenfels
    1975
Vivian DE SOLA PINTO (1895-
    1969): Parker 1975
Alfred DES ROCHERS (1901):
    A. J. M. Smith 1960
Carl DE SUZE (1916): Gwynn

Peter M. DESY: Harris 1970
Gene DETRO: Morticella
Richard DEUTCH: Wang
Babette DEUTSCH (1895): J.
    A. Allen, Chester, Cole
    1967, Cromie, Dunning,
    Firmage, Hannum, Han-
    num and Chase, Hughes
    1970, Immaculate, Morri-
    son, Phillips, Stanford
Joel DEUTSCH: Fox
R. H. DEUTSCH: Harris 1976
James Martin DEVANEY (1890):
    T. Moore
Diane DEVENNIE: Violet
Denis DEVLIN: Rosenthal
    1967
William DeVOTI: Bonazzi
    1974, Hausman
Paul DE VREE: Wildman, E.
    Williams
A. A. DEWEY (1947): Stryk
    1975
Barbara L. DEXTER:
    Brindle
Mwanafunzi DHATI: Jihad
Harold DICKER (1925): De
    Loach 1968, Gross,
    Rothenberg 1973
James DICKEY (1923): Adams,
    G. W. Allen, J. A. Allen,
    Baylor, Brady, Brewton,
    Brinnin 1970, Carroll (Po-
    em in Its Skin), Carruth
    (Bantam), Chace, De Roche,
    Ellmann 1973, 1976, Engle,
    Hall 1962 (Penguin), 1962
    (World); Hannum, Hannum
    and Chase, Harlan, Hol-
    lander, Howard, Howard
    and Victor, Hughes 1970,
    Hurtik, Kennedy 1974,
    Kherdian 1973, Kostelanetz,
    Lask, Leary, Lowenfels
    1967, McCullough, Monaco
    1974, L. Moore, Owen
    1969, 1974; Pearson, Peck,
    Perrine, Phillips, Poulin,
    Rosenthal 1967, 1968;
    Simpson, Steele, Stevenson,
    Strand, H. Taylor, Univ.
    Press of Va., Untermeyer
    1964, 1973 (McKay); Wal-

lace, Walsh, Wheelock 1960,
M. Williams, Witt-Diamant
R. P. DICKEY (1936): Hall-
mark, Stryk 1975
William DICKEY (1928): Cole
1967, Phillips, Strand, M.
Williams
Blanche Taylor DICKINSON:
Patterson
Susan Lee DICKINSON: Gallery
1973
Conrad DICKMANN: Morrison
Alan DIENSTAG: Harvey
Alfred DIGGS: P. Brown
Thomas DI GIOVANNI: Plotz
Annie DILLARD: M. Gibson
Gavin DILLARD (1954): Ley-
land 1977
R. H. W. DILLARD (1937): J.
A. Allen, M. Gibson, Owen
1969, 1974; Rubin, Steele,
H. Taylor, M. Williams
George DILLON (1906): Cole
1965, Stibitz
John DIMOFF (1931): Larrick,
McCullough
Carol DINE: Brindle, Bulkin
Isak DINESEN (1885-1963):
Beerman, Bogan, Larrick,
Peck 1971
Birago DIOP (1906): Jacobus
David DIOP (Ulli Beier): Pat-
terson, Kgositsile
Raymond DiPALMA (1943):
Hewitt
Emanuel DI PASQUALE (1943):
Kennedy 1974
W. S. DI PIERO: Lowenfels
1975
Mbella Sonne DIPOKO (1936):
Breman, Lomax
Diane Di PRIMA (DiPrima)
(1934): Chester, De Loach
1968, 1976; Di Prima,
Durand, Ferlinghetti, Git-
lin, Howe, H. Jones,
Kherdian, Konek, Lowen-
fels 1969 (Random House),
McCullough, Sherman,
Waldman 1969, E. Wilentz
Thomas M; DISCH (1940):
Lucie-Smith, Waldman
1971

Stuart DISCHELL: Harris 1976
Bette DISTLER: Oppenheimer
1977
Mark DI SUVERO: Hauge
Alan DIXON: Cole 1971
DJANGATOLUM see Lloyd
M. CORBIN, Jr.
Zweli ed DLADLA: Kgositsile
Tim DLUGOS (1950): Leyland
1975
Mike DOBBIE: Lowenfels 1975
Jeannine DOBBS: Balazs,
James
Kildare DOBBS (1923): A. J.
M. Smith 1960
Edith DOBELL: Violet
Sydney DOBELL: J. A. Vin-
cent
Stephen DOBYNS: Gildner
Lee Wilson DODD: Jackson
Mary Mapes DODGE: Kauffman
Owen DODSON (1914): Adoff
1968, 1973; Bontemps 1963,
1974; Breman, Carruth
(Bantam), Hayden, Hender-
son, Hughes 1970, Jacobus,
Jordan, King, Lomax,
Turner
Reinhard DOHL: Pilon, E.
Williams
John DOLAN: Gallery 1973
Digby M. DOLBEN: Kauffman
Mary A. DOLL: Brindle
Gerard DOMBROWSKY: Fox
Maggie DOMINIC: Banker
Jack DONAHUE: Gallery 1970,
1973
Vickey DONALDSON: Giovanni
Pamela DONEGAN: Clay
Jim DONG: Clay
D. W. DONZELLA: McMahon
Ebon DOOLEY see EBON
Hilda DOOLITTLE (H. D.)
(1886-1961): Aloian, Bach,
Bogan, C. Brooks, Car-
ruth (Bantam), Chester,
De Roche, Ellmann 1973,
1976; Gregory 1962, 1966;
Howe, Jacobus, Kaplan,
Kennedy 1974, Parker
1974, Peterson, Phillips,
Rothenberg 1973, 1974;
Sanders, Schneider, Stan-

ford, Univ. Press of Va.,
Untermeyer 1964, Wagner
DORAN: Kauffman
Charles DORIA (1938): Anania,
De Loach 1976
Sonya DORMAN: Chester Peck
1970
Alfred DORN (1929): Derleth,
Monaco 1974, Vrbovska
1963, 1968
Edward DORN (1929): Aiken,
D. M. Allen 1960, Carruth
(Bantam), Clark, De Loach
1976, Ellmann 1973, 1976;
Kherdian 1973, Leary,
Rothenberg 1973
Fred DORN: Oppenheimer 1967
Fred DORSETT: Pygmalion
Vincent DORSETT: Booker
David DORSEY: Booker
John (R.) DOS PASSOS (1896-
1970): Kramer, Rothenberg
John DOSS (1923): Weishaus
Curil A. DOSTAL: Ashland
Mark DOTY: Gildner
Ruth DOTY: Gildner
Keith DOUGLAS: Crang
Rudolph DOUGLASS: Booker
Franz DOUSKEY: Lowenfels
1975
Rita DOVE (1952): Halpern
Margaret DOVERY: Sargent
Philip DOW (1937): Halpern,
Harvey, Hewitt
George DOWDEN: Blazek,
Gross
Mark DOWNEY: Rottmann
Kirby DOYLE (1932): D. M.
Allen 1960
Lynn DOYLE (1873-1961):
Knowles
Ree DRAGONETTE (1918):
Harris 1970, Lowenfels
1969 (Random House),
Vrbovska 1963
Albert DRAKE: Fox, Hitchcock,
Salisbury, Summerfield
Joseph Rodman DRAKE: Jack-
son
Leah Bodine DRAKE: Derleth,
Dunning, Vrbovska 1963
Helena Chase J. DREA:
Sargent

Glenn W. (Ward) DRESBACH
(1889-1968): Larrick,
Peck 1970, Stibitz
Muriel Miller DRESSLER:
Plumley
Ray DREW (1923): Kherdian
1973
Carleton DREWRY (1901):
Lask Trapp
Dale DRISCOLL (1939): Mer-
catante
Jack DRISCOLL: Hausman
Frances DRIVAS (1917): Van
den Heuvel
Will Allen DROMGOOLE:
Kauffman
Celia DROPKIN: Cole 1971
Sally Ann DRUCKER: Harlan
Helen DUBERSTEIN: Fox
Norman DUBIE (1945): Hal-
pern
William Edward (W. E.)
Burghardt (W. E. B.) DU
BOIS (1897-1963): Adoff
1973, Breman, Hughes
1970, Kramer
Gail DUBROW: Adoff 1971
Marcel DUCHAMP (1887-1968):
Rothenberg 1974
Ann DUCILLE: Lowenfels 1975
Alfred (A.) DUCKETT (1918):
Adoff 1973, Bontemps 1963,
1974; Dee, Hughes 1970,
Jordan
Louis DUDEK (1918): A. J.
M. Smith 1960
Nancy Kay DUDEK: Brindle
Richard DUERDEN (1927): D.
M. Allen 1960
Peter Kane DUFAULT (1923):
Cole 1963, Hannum and
Chase
Gerald DUFF: Colley, Owen
1974
Richard DUFFEE: Hoffman
Jessie DUFFEY: Adoff 1971
John DUFFY: Banker
Maureen DUFFY: Harris 1976
William DUFFY: Sixties
Alan DUGAN (1923): Adoff
1969, G. W. Allen, Bay-
lor, Brady, Brinnin 1963,
1970; Cole 1967, Ellmann

1973, Greaves, Gwynn,
Hannum, Howard, Howard
and Victor, Kennedy 1974,
Kostelantez, Lowenfels
1967, Mazur, Morrison,
Peck 1971, Poulin, Rosen-
thal 1967, Strand, H.
Taylor, M. Williams
Sandra Ruth DUGUID (1947):
Mollenkott
George DUHAMEL: Rose
Harold DULL: Gross
Henry DUMAS (1934-1968):
Adoff 1970, 1973; Breman,
Cole 1972, Gersmehl,
Gross, Henderson
Randy DUNAGAN: Colley, Kohl
Rea Lubar DUNCAN (1920):
Hughes 1970
Robert DUNCAN (1919): D. M.
Allen 1960, 1964; Arts
Festival 1963, Barnes,
Bly 1970, Brady, Carruth
(Bantam), Chace, De
Roche, Di Prima, Ellmann
1973, 1976; Gregory 1962,
Hall 1962 (Penguin), Har-
lan, Harris 1973, Leyland
1975, McCullough, Poulin,
Rosenthal 1967, 1968;
Rothenberg 1973, 1974;
Sanders, Wesleyan Univ.,
Witt-Diamant, Young
Kimberly DUNHAM: Gallery
1973, Plumley
Bob DUNN: Summerfield
Denis DUNN: Gross
Max DUNN (1895): T. Moore
Stephen DUNN (1939): Evans,
Halpern, Hoffman, Oppen-
heimer 1977, Stryk 1975
Mark DUNSTER: Lask
Elizabeth DU PREEZ: J. Gib-
son, J. Gibson (Book Two)
Mary DURACK (1913): T.
Moore
Robert DURAND: Durand
Ray DUREM (1915-1963):
Adoff 1968, 1970, 1973;
Breman, Colley, Hughes
1964, 1970; Jacobus, Jor-
dan, Kenseth, Kramer,
Lomax, Lowenfels 1966,
1969 (Doubleday); Major

Leslie DUREMBERG: Brindle
Sukey DURHAM: Bulkin
Lawrence DURRELL (1912):
Hannum, Stallworthy,
Untermeyer 1964, Walsh
Gail DUSENBERY (1939):
Kostelanetz, Palmer,
Schreiber
Geoffrey DUTTON (1922): T.
Moore
Sandra DUTTON: Brindle
Timothy DWIGHT: Jackson
Susanne DYCKMAN: K. and
J. Sollid
Freddie J. DYER: Winkler
Paul DYER: Fox
Bob DYLAN (1941): Chace,
Crafts, Kennedy 1973,
1974; Lowenfels 1966,
Morse
Clifford DYMENT (1914): J.
A. Allen, Cole 1963, J.
Gibson (Book Two),
Knowles
David R. DZWONKOSKI: Adoff
1971

E

Jacquelyn (Jaci) (Jackie)
(Jacqueline) EARLEY
(1939): Adoff 1974, Colley,
Coombs, Giovanni, Jordan,
King 1972, Patterson
R. (Rosalind) EARLY (c. 1949):
Giovanni
Annelle EASLIE: Banker
William EASTLAKE (1917):
Gersmehl
Mary EASTMAN: Brindle
Max EASTMAN (1883): Jack-
son
Charles Edward EATON (1916):
Derleth, Owen 1969, 1974;
Vrbovska 1968
Dorothy Burnham EATON:
Derleth
Ingrid EAU: Morticella
Jean EBBERT: Kilcy
Richard EBERHART (1904):
Aiken, J. A. Allen, Aloi-
an, Bates, Baylor, Brew-
ton, Brinnin 1963, 1970;

C. Brooks, Carruth (Bantam), Cole 1971, Colley, De Roche, Drew, Driver, Ellmann 1973, Engle, Gersmehl, Gwynn, Hall 1962 (Watts), Hannum, Hannum and Chase, Harlan, Harris 1970, Hieatt, Hopkins (Nelson), Hurtik, Immaculate, Kallich, Kennedy 1973, Knowles, Lask, Lowenfels 1967 (Watts), Monaco 1974, Peck 1970, 1971; Perrine, J. Perry, Peterson, Plotz, Plumley, Rosenthal 1967, Sanders, Shapiro, A. J. M. Smith 1967, H. Taylor, W. Taylor, Trapp, Univ. Press of Va., Untermeyer 1964, 1973 (McKay), Vrbovska 1963, 1968; Wagner, M. Williams, O. Williams 1966 (Trident), 1966 (World); Witt-Diamant

David EBERLY: Leyland 1975, 1977

Willis EBERMAN: Morticella

EBON (Thomas Dooley) (1942): Adoff 1973, G. Brooks (Broadside Treasury), Henderson, Lee 1971, D. Randall 1960

Fredrick EBRIGHT (1912): Hine, Lask

Michael ECHERUO (1937): Lomax

ECHNATON: Gay

Jon ECKELS: Brooks, P. Brown, McGovern

Frederick ECKMAN (1924): Stryk 1967, Wagner, Weil

Margaret ECKMAN: Colley, Kohl

Rick ECKSTEIN: Pilon

George ECONOMOU (1934): De Loach 1968, Gross, Harris, Rothenberg 1973

Elaine EDELMAN: Konek

Patience EDEN: McGinley

Mary S. EDGAR: Kauffman

Russell EDSON (1935): Bly 1975, Gross, Halpern, Klonsky, Rothenberg 1973

Harry EDWARDS (1942): Major, McGovern

Joyce EDWARDS: Kohl

Leta M. EDWARDS: Jackson

Soloman EDWARDS (1932): Hughes 1964, 1970

Lynda EFROS: Efros

Susan EFROS: Efros, Krech

Eileen EGAN: Lowenfels 1966

Jim EGGELING (1934): Leyland 1975, 1977; Young

William G. EGGLESTON: Bates

William (W.) D. EHRHART: Kiley, Rothmann

Robert J. EICHENBERG: Kiley

Douglas EICHHORN: Bogin

Larry EIGNER (1927): D. M. Allen 1960, Blazek, Carruth (Bantam), Gross, H. Jones, Leary, Leyland 1977, Rothenberg 1973, Winkler

Bernard Lionel EINBOND (1937): Van den Heuvel

Samuel A. EISENSTEIN: Simmons

Hugo EKBACK: Hoffman

Torsten EKBOM: E. Williams

Gunnar EKELOF: Cole 1971

Eileen ELIOT: Brindle

T. S. ELIOT (1888-1965): Adams, G. W. Allen, J. A. Allen, Aloian, Arp, Bach, Barnes, Baylor, Bogan, Brady, Brinnin 1963, 1970; C. Brooks, Brower, Calderwood, Carruth (Bantam), Chatman, Cole 1963, Colley, Colum, Crafts, Crang, Croft, De Roche, Drew, Driver, Ellmann 1973, 1976; Engelberg, Felver, Foster, Gannett, Gardner, J. Gibson, J. Gibson (Book Two), Greaves, Gregory 1962, 1966; Gwynn, Hall 1962 (Watts), Harlan, Hieatt, Hurtik, Jacobus, Kennedy 1973, 1974; Knowles, Leggett, Livingston, McGinley, Monaco 1974, Nash,

Olson, Opie, Peck 1970,
Perrine, J. Perry, Rose,
Rothenberg 1973, 1974;
Sanders, Schneider, Simp-
son, A. J. M. Smith 1965,
1967; Stallworthy, H. Tay-
lor, W. Taylor, Trapp,
Univ. Press of Va. , Unter-
meyer 1964, 1973 (McKay);
Wagner, O. Williams 1966
(Trident), (World); Winkler,
Woods
Barbara ELLEN: E. Wilentz
George (P.) ELLIOTT (1918):
Bogin, Kennedy 1973,
Talisman
Harley ELLIOTT (1940): J.
Gill, Shore, Stryk 1975
William ELLIOTT: McGovern
Colin ELLIS: Cole 1971,
Cromie
Kate ELLIS: Oppenheimer 1977
Richard ELLISON: Bates
Maxine Hall ELLISTON: P.
Brown
Kenward ELMSLIE (1929):
Carroll (Young American
Poets), Leyland 1975, 1977;
Myers, Padgett, Waldman
1969, 1971; E. Wilentz
Florence ELON: Chase, Hoff-
man
Gladys ELY: Lask
James (A.) EMANUEL (1921):
Adoff 1970, 1973, 1974;
Baylor, Bontemps 1963,
1974; Breman, G. Brooks
(Broadside Treasury),
Crafts, Hayden, Henderson,
Hughes 1964, 1970; Lask,
Livingston, D. Randall
1960, Schneider
Sister M. EMANUEL (1914):
Immaculate
Mary EMENY: Rottmann
Leatrice EMERUWA: Chester
Raymond C. EMERY: Sargent
Ronald Lee EMMONS: Lowen-
fels 1975
William EMPSON (1906): Arp,
Bach, C. Brooks, Ellmann
1973, Engle, Hurtik, Ken-
nedy 1974, Knowles, J.

Perry, Phillips, Sanders,
A. J. M. Smith 1967, W.
Taylor, Untermeyer 1964
Anita ENDREZZE-PROBST:
Rosen
Timothy ENGEL: Booker
Helen ENGELHARDT: Banker
John (David) ENGELS (1931):
Kennedy 1973
Paul ENGLE (1908): Adoff
1969, Brewton, Engle,
Gildner, Hurtik, Stryk
1967, Summerfield, Univ.
Press of Va.
Joseph Dunn ENGLISH: J. A.
Vincent
Maurice ENGLISH (1909):
Cromie
D. J. ENRIGHT (1920): Brin-
nin 1963, 1970; Crang,
Rosenthal 1967, 1968;
Wallace
Ted (Theodore) ENSLIN (1925):
De Loach 1968, 1976; Har-
ris 1973, Leary, McMahon,
Rothenberg 1973, Weil
Carol ERDMAN: Morticella
Max ERNST (1891): Rothenberg
Thomas ERSKINE: Cole 1971
Yetunde ESAN: Breman
Gloria ESCOFFERY: Salkey
Clayton ESHLEMAN (1935):
Banker, Carruth (Bantam),
Gross, Kennedy 1973, Op-
penheimer 1967, P. Perry,
Rothenberg 1973
Richard Curry ESLER: Lask
Gary ESOLEN: Lowenfels 1975
Martin ESSLIN: Cole 1967
(Macmillan)
Sandra Maria ESTEVES:
Algarin
Jim ESTRIN: Dee
Jane ESTY (1929): Firmage
Kendrick ETHERIDGE (1911):
Firmage
ETHNA: Giovanni
Dave ETTER (1928): Blazek,
Brewton, Cromie, Gildner,
Harris 1970, Kennedy 1973,
Schreiber, Stryk 1967, M.
Williams
Donald EULENT: Winans

David EVA: J. Gibson (Book
Two)
Abbie Huston EVANS (1881):
Cole 1972, Schneider,
Trapp
Bob EVANS: Pilon
David Allan EVANS (1940):
Evans, Gildner, Stryk 1975
Jay EVANS: Pilon
M. Sharon EVANS: Brindle
Mari (E.) EVANS (c. 1923):
Adoff 1968, 1970, 1973;
Bontemps 1963, 1974;
Coombs, Crafts, Giovanni,
Hayden, Henderson, Holmes,
Hopkins (Knopf), Howe,
Hughes 1964, King 1972,
Konek, Don L. Lee 1971,
Lomax, Lowenfels 1966,
1969 (Doubleday); Patter-
son, Peck 1970, 1971; D.
Randall 1969, Segnitz
Mike EVANS (1941): Lucie-
Smith
R. Daniel EVANS (1944): Ley-
land 1975
Sebastian EVANS: Parker 1960
James EVERHARD: M. Gibson
William EVERSON (Brother
Antoninus) (1912): D. M.
Allen 1960, Bates, Baylor,
Carruth (Bantam), (McCall);
Cromie, Ellmann 1973,
Harvey, Immaculate, Kos-
telanetz, Rosenthal 1967,
1968; Schneider, Trapp,
Walsh, M. Williams,
Winans, Witt-Diamant
Peter EVERWINE: Kherdian
1970
Gavin EWART: Cole, Firmage
Doris Amurr EZELL: Booker

F

RobertOh FABER: Banker
Gerald L. FABIAN (1924):
Leyland 1975
Mary FABILLI (1914): Konek
Sarah Webster FABIO (1928):
Adoff 1973, G. Brooks
(Broadside Treasury), P.

Brown, Henderson, A.
Miller
Chana FAERSTEIN: Harlan,
Lask
Charles FAGER: Gitlin
Larry FAGIN: Waldman 1969,
1971
Oyvind FAHLSTROM: E. Wil-
liams
Harry FAINLIGHT: Lorrimer,
Stallworthy
Ruth FAINLIGHT (1931): Howe,
Lucie-Smith
John FAIRFAX: Lucie-Smith
Ross FALCONER (1954):
Greaves
Adebayo FALETI: Hughes
1963
Richard A. FALK (1930):
Lowenfels 1967
Jake FALSTAFF: Cole, Nash
John FANDEL: Dunning, Lask
William Henry FANNING:
Lask
Norma FARBER: Derleth,
Lask, Vrbovska 1963,
1968
RobertOh FARBER: Vrbovska
1968
Salvatore FARINELLA (1940):
Leyland 1975, 1977; Young
Eleanor FARJEON (1881-1965):
Cole 1963, Knowles, Opie
Jean FARLEY: J. A. Allen,
M. Gibson, Rubin
Tom FARNOL: Rose
Shaun FARRAGHER: Oppen-
heimer 1977
FATIMA see Fran COLLINS
Jerry P. FAULKENBERRY:
Kiley
William FAULKNER (1897-
1962): Rothenberg
Dean FAULWELL: Bonazzi
1972
Jessie Redmond FAUSET
(1882-1961): Adoff 1973,
Patterson
Charles FAUSTIN: Salkey
W. M. L. FAY: Kauffman
Damon FAZIO: Smith
Bruce FEARING (1935): Cole
1963, Dunning

Kenneth FEARING (1902-1961):
Aloian, Baylor, Carruth
(Bantam), De Roche, Gwynn,
Hall 1962 (Watts), Hine,
Hurtik, Jackson, Jacobus,
Kennedy 1974, Lowenfels
1969 (Doubleday), Peck
1970, 1971; Perrine,
Rothenberg 1973, 1974;
Sanders, Shapiro, W. Tay-
lor, Untermeyer 1964, E.
Wilentz

Raymond FEDERMAN (1928):
Phillips, K. and J. Sollid

Cheri FEIN: Efros

Alvin FEINMAN (1929): Hollander, Strand

M. D. FELD: Morrison

Barbara FELDMAN: Bogin

Gary FELDMAN: Dee

Irving FELDMAN (1928):
Brinnin 1963, 1970; Ell-
mann 1974, Howard,
Howard and Victor,
Joseloff, Kessler, Lask

Ruth FELDMAN: Lask, Vbrovska 1968

Susan FELDMAN (1950): Halpern

Annette B. FELDMANN:
Vrbovska 1963, 1968

Morton FELIX: Gallery 1973

Peter FELLOWES (c. 1945):
M. Gibson, Hewitt

Larry FELSON: S. Vincent

B. FELTON: G. Brooks
(Broadside Treasury)

Lannon A. FENNER (Jr.):
Battle, Boombs

Elizabeth FENTON (1943):
Howe

David FERGUSON (1934):
Bates, Baylor, Lowenfels
1967

Kathleen FERGUSON (1945):
Klonsky

Samuel FERGUSON: Parker
1960

Dolores S. FERIA: Clay

Paul F. FERICANO: Winans

Lawrence FERLINGHETTI
(1919): Adoff 1969, D. M.
Allen 1960, 1964; Arts

Festival 1963, Baylor,
Brady, Carruth (Bantam),
Chace, Crafts, Crang, De
Roche, Dunning, Ellmann
1973, Engle, Ferlinghetti,
Harlan, Harvey, Holmes,
Hurtik, Kenseth, Kherdian
1973, Leary, Lorrimer,
Lowenfels 1966, 1967,
1969 (Doubleday); Peck
1970, 1971; Pilon, Plotz,
Poulin, Rosenthal 1967,
1968; Rothenberg 1973,
Schneider, Stallworthy,
Trapp, Walsh, M. Williams,
Winans, Witt-Diamant

Thelma P. FERNANDEZ-
Yarish: Brindle

Carl FERNBACH-FLARSHEIM:
Gross, Solt, Waldman, E.
Williams

Jaime FERRAN: Bogin

Mary FERRARI: Waldman 1971

Thomas Hornsby FERRIL
(1896): Brewton, Carruth
(Bantam), (McCall); Dunn-
ing, Larrick, Larson,
Steuben

Vincent FERRINI (1913):
Lowenfels 1966

David (Russell) FERRY (1924):
Cole 1972, Mazur, Pear-
son, Plotz, Wallace, Wes-
leyan Univ.

Thomas Greene FESSENDEN:
Jackson

Doug FETHERLING (c. 1947):
J. Gill

Robert W. FETT: Kiley

Joan FIATOR: Brindle

F. K. FIAWOO: Hughes 1963

Arthur Davison FICKE: Lask

Arthur Gordon FIELD: J. A.
Vincent

David Dudley FIELD: Jackson

Edward FIELD (1924): D. M.
Allen 1960, Chace, Colley,
De Roche, Holmes, How-
ard, Howard and Victor,
Kenseth, Leary, Leyland
1975, Lowenfels 1966,
Owen 1964, Strand, Wal-
lace, Witt-Diamant, Young

H. A. FIELD: J. Gibson
Michael FIELD: Hauffman
J. T. FIELDS: Nash
Julia FIELDS (1938): Adoff
    1969, 1970, 1973, 1974;
    Bell, Bontemps 1963, 1974;
    Breman, Hayden, Hughes
    1964, Don L. Lee, Living-
    ston, Major, Owen 1974,
    Patterson, D. Randall 1969,
    Skelton
Darlene FIFE: Fox
Ross FIGGINS: Gallery 1973
Jose-Angel FIGUEROA (1946):
    Algarin, Lowenfels 1973,
    1975
J. R. FIJI: Gallery 1970
Robert FILLIOU: Gross
Kate FILSON: Rose
Francis Miles FINCH: J. A.
    Vincent
Linda FINCH: Booker
Robert FINCH (1900): Cole
    1963, A. J. M. Smith 1960
Randolph FINGLAND: Gallery
    1973
Donald FINKEL (1929): Adams,
    J. A. Allen, Cole 1963,
    1967 (Macmillan), 1971;
    Dunning, Gildner, Hall
    1962 (World), Howard,
    Howard and Victor, Ken-
    nedy 1973, 1974; Kenseth,
    Leary, Strand, M. Williams
Ian Hamilton FINLAY (1925):
    Gross, Kennedy 1974,
    Klonsky, Matthias, Pilon,
    Rosenthal 1967, 1968; E.
    Williams
Hugh FINN (1925): Cale 1963
James FINNEGAN: Hanna 1960
Joan FINNIGAN (1925): Greaves,
    Stanford, Wagner
Mary FINNIN: T. Moore
Max FINSTEIN: D. M. Allen
    1964, Arts Festival 1964
Susan FIRER: Rosenblum
Mira FISH: McMahon
Lawrence FISHBERG: Booker
Lynn FISHER: Montgomery
Roy FISHER (1931): Colley,
    Harris 1976, Matthias
Stanley FISHER: Blazek, Mont-
    gomery

Robert FITCH: Morrison
Dudley FITTS (1903-1968):
    Gregory 1962, 1966; Plotz,
    Univ. Press of Va.
Robert David FITZGERALD
    (1902): T. Moore
Robert (Stuart) FITZGERALD
    (1910): Brinnin 1963,
    1970; Carruth (Bantam),
    Gregory 1962, 1966; Liv-
    ingston, Morrison, Plotz
Thomas FITZSIMMONS: Fox
Douglas (Doug) FLAHERTY
    (1939): Hallmark, Harris
    1976, Lowenfels 1973,
    Rigsbee, Stryk 1975
Robert FLANAGAN (1941):
    Freed, Stryk 1975
Michael FLANDERS: Pilon
Hildegaard FLANNER: Stan-
    ford
Dorothy Ellin FLAX: Vrbovska
    1963
Andrew FLEGE: Harlan
Ted FLEISCHMAN: Gallery
    1973
Geranna FLEMING: Morticella
Leonard FLEMMING: Rose
John FLES: E. Wilentz
Bob FLETCHER (1938): Major
Giles FLETCHER: Kauffman
John FLETCHER: J. Gibson
Annie Johnson FLINT: Kauff-
    man
Roland FLINT: Dunning
Nicholas FLOCOS (1936):
    Kherdian 1974
Virginia FLOYD (1927): Mol-
    lenkott
Tom FLUSTY: Head
George FLYNN: Gallery 1973
Javita G. FLYNN: Booker
Kathleen FOGARTY: Brindle
John FOGERTY: Morse
Jean FOLLAIN (1903): Cole
    1972
Jacinto FOMBONA-PACHANO:
    Bly 1970
Elnora FONDREN: Student
David FONG: Clay
Gregory FONTAIN: Sargent
Mary FONTAINE: Brindle
Calvin FORBES (1945): Adoff
    1973, Kennedy 1973, M.

Williams
Carolyn FORCHE (1950): Halpern
Charles Henri FORD (1909): Kenseth, Klonsky, Leyland 1975, 1977; Rothenberg 1973, 1974
Edsel FORD: Lask, Steele, Vrbovska 1968
Gena FORD: Konek, Weil
Gregory J. FORD (c. 1952): Murphy
Phyllis FORD: Gallery 1970, 1973
Wallace FORD: Booker
Wally FORD (1950): Coombs
Kent FOREMAN: G. Brooks (Broadside Treasury)
Paul FOREMAN: Harlan, Head, Winans
Morris D. FORKOSCH: Jackson
Nicole FORMAN (1945): Howe
Stephen FORMBY: Harlan
Bernard A. FORREST (1902): Witt-Diamant
Robert FORREY: Harris 1976
Ethel FORTNER: Morticella
Sam Walter FOSS: Jackson
Robert FOSTER: Bogin
William Dudley FOULKE: J. A. Vincent
Kingsley FOURBRIDGE: Rose
Al FOWLER (1939): Lowenfels 1969 (Random House)
Gene FOWLER (1931): Bly 1970, Gersmehl, Harlan, Harvey, Head, Monaco 1973, Palmer, Schreiber, H. Smith, Winans
Hilary Ayer FOWLER: Krech, Palmer
Lona M. FOWLER: Kauffman
Truth Mary FOWLER: Sargent
Gail FOX: Konek
Grace Gilombardo FOX: Poets of America
Hugh FOX: Fox, Gallary 1973, Krech
Ruth FOX: Stevenson
Siv Cedering FOX (1939): Chester, Evans, Wang
C. FOX-SMITH: Rose
Gretchen FRAELICH: Gallery 1970

Janet FRAME: Stanford
Peter FRANCE (1935): Stallworthy
Colin FRANCIS: Cole 1972
Robert (Churchill) FRANCIS (1901): Bogan, Brewton, Carruth (Bantam), (McCall); Cole 1967 (Macmillan), Cromie, Dunning, Engle, Gwynn, Hall 1962 (Watts), Holmes, Jacobus, Kennedy 1974, Kenseth, Larrick, Lask, Morrison, Pearson, Peck 1970, Phillips, H. Taylor, W. Taylor, Univ. Press of Va.
Robert FRANCOVIGLIA: Kiley
Florence Kiper FRANK (1890): Bates
Glen FRANK: Fox
Peter FRANK: Rigsbee
Lloyd FRANKENBERG (1907-1975): Cole 1965, Firmage
Charles FRANKLIN: Booker
Clarence FRANKLIN: Patterson
A. Frederic FRANKLYN (1927): Lowenfels 1969 (Random House)
David FRANKS: Waldman 1971
Carmen FRASER: Head
Kathleen FRASER (1937): Carroll (Young American Poets), Chester, Colley, Efros, Halpern, Harlan, Howe, Knoek, McCullough, Winans
Ray FRASER: J. Gill
Bill FREDERICK (1943): D. Randall 1969
Anne Hobson FREEMAN: Balazs
Arthur FREEMAN (1938): Brinnin 1970, Cromie
Carol (Carole) FREEMAN (1941): Adoff 1973, 1974; Colley, Giovanni, Howe, Lomax
T. J. FREEMAN: Crafts
Mary FREERICKS: Oppenheimer 1977
Larry FREIFELD: Pilon, E. Williams

Barbara FRENCH: Kiley
Stuart FRIEBERG: Simmons
Martha FRIEDBERG: Gallery
1973
Norman FRIEDMAN: Stevenson
Philip Allan FRIEDMAN: Gallery 1973
Richard FRIEDMAN: Friedman
Barbara FRIEND: Balazs
Larry FRIES: Rottmann
Richard H. FRIES: Jackson
Robert FRIPP: Morse
Bob FRISELL: Adoff 1971
Dennis FRITZINGER: Ferling-hetti
Robert FROMAN: Pilon
Carol FROST: Rigsbee
Frances FROST: Lask
Robert FROST (1874-1963):
Adams, G. W. Allen, J. A. Allen, Aloian, Arp, Barnes, Baylor, Beerman, R. Bender, Bogan, Brady, Brinnin 1963, 1970; C. Brooks, Brower, Cady, Calderwood, Carruth (Bantam), Chatman, Cole 1963, 1965, 1967 (Macmillan), 1971, 1972; Colley, Colum, Corbett, Crafts, Crang, Crane, Croft, De Roche, Drew, Driver, Dunning, Ellmann 1973, Engle, Felver, Gannett, J. Gibson, J. Gibson (Book Two), Greaves, Gregory 1962, 1966; Gwynn, Hall 1962 (Watts), Hannum, Hannum and Chase, Harlan, Hieatt, Hine, Hopkins (Nelson), Hurtik, Immaculate, Jacobus, Kallich, Kennedy 1973, 1974; Knowles, Larrick, Leggett, McGinley, L. Moore, Nash, Olson, Parker 1967, 1974; Peck 1970, 1971; Perrine, J. Perry, Peterson, Phillips, Reeves, Sanders, Schneider, Shapiro, Simpson, A. J. M. Smith 1965, 1967; H. Taylor, W. Taylor, Thomas, Trapp, Univ. Press of Va.,

Untermeyer 1964, 1973 (McKay); J. A. Vincent, Wagner, Wallace, Wesleyan Univ., Whicher, O. Williams 1966 (Trident), (World); Williams and Honig, Winkler, Woods
Gene FRUMKIN (1928): Bly 1970, Lowenfels 1966, M. Williams
Juan FUENTES: Clay
FUHARA: Jihad
Sharon FUHRMAN: Kiley
Sadamu FUJIWARA (1905): Wagner
Ethel Romig FULLER: Kauffman
Hoyt W. FULLER (1928): Adoff 1973, P. Brown
John FULLER (1937): Hall 1962 (World)
Roy FULLER (1912): J. A. Allen, Baylor, R. Bender, Cole 1967 (Macmillan), 1971; Ellmann 1973, Engle, Glikes, Knowles, Wallace
Robin FULTON: Cole 1972
Sol FUNAROFF: Lowenfels 1969 (Doubleday)
Wilfred J. FUNK: Jackson
Rory FUNKE: Morticella
John FURNIVAL (1933): Klonsky, Solt, Wildman
Rose FYLEMAN: Nash

G

W. E. G.: Banker
Louise Marsk GABRIEL: Plumley
Janice Marie GADSDEN (1952): Coombs
Farren GAINER: Gallery 1973
Albert W. GAINES: Jackson
Geoff GAJEWSKI: Rosenblum
Norman GALE: Cole 1967 (Macmillan)
John P. GALLAGHER: Kiley
Tess GALLAGHER (1943): Halpern, Hoffman, Rigsbee
David GALLATIN (1926): Lowenfels 1966, 1967;

Sherman, Vrbovska 1963
David GALLER (1929): Lask,
Monaco 1973, 1974; Rosen-
thal 1967, E. Wilentz
Menna GALLIE: Cole 1967
(Macmillan)
Philip GALLO: Gallery 1973
Dick (Richard John) GALLUP
(1941): Clark, McCullough,
Monaco 1973, Padgett,
Waldman 1969, 1971
Tom GALT: Gallery 1973
Tom GALTEN (1939): McCul-
lough
Christopher GAMBLE: Kohl
Doreen GANDY: Morticella
Roland GANT (1919): Greaves
Heinz GAPPMAYR: Wildman,
E. Williams
Isidro GARCIA: Algarin
Luis GARCIA (1939): Harvey,
Palmer
Rupert GARCIA: Clay
T. C. GARCIA: Algarin
Carl GARDNER (1931): Adoff
1973, Lowenfels 1969
(Random House), Hughes
1964
Doll GARDNER: Morticella
Fred GARDNER: Gitlin
Isabella (Stewart) GARDNER
(1915): J. A. Allen,
Carroll (Poem in Its Skin),
Chester, Cole 1963, 1967,
1971; Firmage, Harris 1973,
Perrine, Stanford, Stibitz,
Strand, Stryk 1967, O.
Williams 1966 (World)
Lewis GARDNER: Oppenheimer
1977
S. S. GARDONS (1929): Hall
1962 (World), Kessler
Angel Maria GARIBAY: Rothen-
berg
Alan GARNER (1934): Greaves
Ilse GARNIER: E. Williams
Pierre GARNIER: E. Williams,
Winkler
George (Palmer) GARRETT
(1929): J. A. Allen,
Bonazzi 1972, Hurtik, Owen
1969, 1974; Steele, H. Tay-
lor, Wesleyan Univ., M.
Williams

Kay GARRETT: Brindle
Jean GARRIGUE (1914): Aiken,
Brinnin 1963, 1970; Car-
ruth (Bantam), Cole 1967,
Ellmann 1976, Firmage,
Lask, Owen 1969, Stan-
ford, Steuben, Univ. Press
of Va., Vrbovska 1968,
Witt-Diamant
Joseph GARRISON (Jr.): M.
Gibson, Plumley
Phil GARRISON (1942): Durand
William Lloyd GARRISON:
Jackson
Crosbie GARSTIN (1877): Cole
1967
David GASCOYNE (1916):
Brinnin 1963, 1970; Cromie,
Gardner
Marina GASHE: Hughes 1963
Len GASPARINI (1941): Fox,
J. Gill
Betty GATES: Henderson
Larry GATES (1942): Van den
Heuvel
Tom GATES: Kiley
Beth GAUNT: Pilon
David S. GAUNTLETT: Kiley
Serge GAVRONSKY (1932):
Lowenfels 1967, 1969
(Random House), 1975
John GAWSWORTH (1912):
Firmage
Joyce GAYLES: Brindle
Bobbie GEARY: Violet
Bruce C. GEARY (Sayif
Shabazz): Patterson
Lethonia GEE: Patterson
Don FEIGER: J. A. Allen
C. F. GELLERT: Kauffman
Leon Maxwell GELLERT (1892):
T. Moore
Irene Haupel GENCO: Balazs
Kin (Kinereth) GENSLER:
James, Mazur, Vrbovska
1968
Jane GENTRY: J. A. Allen
Dan GEORGAKAS (1938):
Banker, Baylor, Gitlin,
Knight, Lowenfels 1967,
Oppenheimer 1977,
Schreiber, Sherman
Emery GEORGE: Rigsbee
Lloyd GEORGE: Harlan

Marguerite GEORGE: Derleth
Phil (Phillip William) GEORGE:
    T. Allen, Colley, Dodge,
    Rosen
Edwin GERARD (1891): T.
    Moore
Saint GERAUD see Bill KNOTT
Dan GERBER (1940): Stryk
    1975, Sumac
Estelle GERSHGOREN (1940):
    Lowenfels 1966
Karen GERSHON: Crang,
    Cromie
Glen GERSMEHL (1946):
    Gersmehl
Ira GERSHWIN (1896): Cole
    1965
A. Rasheed GHAZI: Camp
Brester GHISELIN (1903): J.
    A. Allen, Engle, Larson,
    H. Taylor, O. Williams
    1966 (World)
Zulfikar GHOSE: Crang, Lask
James GIANCARLO (1947):
    Leyland 1975
Jim GIBBONS: Rosenblum
Maurice GIBBONS: Stevenson
Stella GIBBONS (1902): Cole
    1963
Elsie GIBBS: Lask
Wolcott GIBBS: Peck 1970
E. K. GIBLIN: Jackson
Kahlil GIBRAN: Holmes
Barbara GIBSON (1930): Bay-
    lor, Lowenfels 1969
    (Doubleday), (Random
    House)
Douglas GIBSON: Lask
Julie GIBSON (1951): Lowen-
    fels 1967
Lydia GIBSON: Cole 1963
Margaret GIBSON: M. Gibson,
    Rigsbee
Morgan GIBSON (1929): Bay-
    lor, Rosenblum
Pamela GIBSON: Battle
Walker GIBSON (1880): Bay-
    lor, Cole 1967 (Macmillan),
    1967 (Viking), 1972;
    Dunning, Morrison, Unter-
    meyer 1964, Wallace
Wilfrid (Wilson) (W. W.)
    GIBSON (1878-1962):

Aloian, Cole 1963, 1967
    (Macmillan), 1967 (Viking);
    Colum, Cromie, J. Gibson,
    Knowles, Parker, Unter-
    meyer 1964, Woods
William GIBSON: Lask
Paula GIDDINGS: Coombs,
    Patterson
Elsa GIDLOW: Bulkin, Konek,
    Violet
Merrill GIFILLAN: Waldman
    1971
Celia GILBERT: Mazur
Dorothy GILBERT: Glikes
Jack GILBERT (1925): Crafts,
    Lowenfels 1966, Rosenthal
    1967, Stevenson, Strand,
    Wallace
Paul T. GILBERT: Cole 1972
Sandra GILBERT: Winans
Virginia GILBERT: Evans,
    Konek
Willie GILBERT: Booker
Zack GILBERT (1925): Adoff
    1973, P. Brown, D.
    Randall 1969
Richard Watson GILDER:
    Jackson
Gary GILDNER (1938): Cole
    1971, Gildner, Halpern,
    Kennedy 1974, Stryk 1975,
    H. Taylor
Alex GILDZEN: Fox
John GILL (1924): J. Gill,
    Lowenfels 1969 (Doubleday),
    1973; Schreiber, Young
T. H. GILL: Kauffman
Dan GILLESPIE (c. 1940):
    Hewitt
Robert GILLESPIE (1938):
    Evans
Yetza GILLESPIE: Lask
Leonard GILLEY: Gallery
    1970, 1973
Andrew GILLIES: Kauffman
Richard GILLMAN: Cromie
Charlotte Perkins GILMAN:
    Jackson
Dugan GILMAN: Bogin
Mary (Jean Cameron) GILMORE
    (1865-1962): Cole 1963,
    T. Moore
Patrick Sarsfield GILMORE:

J. A. Vincent
Somerville GILNEY: Rose
Charlotte Fox GINET: Brindle
Allen GINSBERG (1926): Adams,
D. M. Allen 1960, 1964;
Arts Festival 1963, Barnes,
Baylor, Berg, Bly 1970,
1975; Brady, Brinnin 1970,
Carroll (Poem in Its Skin),
Carruth (Bantam), Chace,
De Loach 1968, 1976; De
Roche, Di Prima, Ellmann
1973, 1976; Engle, Ferling-
hetti, Gitlin, Glikes, Har-
lan, Harvey, Harris 1970,
1973; Hollander, Howard,
Howard and Victor, Hurtik,
Jacobus, Kennedy 1973,
1974; Kessler, Kherdian
1973, Kostelanetz, Leary,
Leyland 1975, 1977; Lorri-
mer, Lowenfels 1966, 1967,
1969 (Doubleday), 1975;
McCullough, Monaco 1974,
J. Perry, Phillips, Poetry
San Francisco, Poulin,
Rosenthal 1967, 1968;
Rothenberg 1973, Schneider,
Shapiro, Simpson, Strand,
H. Taylor, Untermeyer
1964, 1973 (McKay); Wag-
ner, Waldman 1969, 1971;
Walsh, E. Wilentz, M.
Williams
Louis GINSBERG (1895-1976):
De Loach 1976, Harris 1970
John GIORNO (1936): De Loach
1976, Fagin, Gross,
Kostelanetz, Leyland 1975,
1977; Padgett, Rothenberg
1973, Waldman 1969, 1971
Nikki GIOVANNI (1943): Adoff
1969, 1970, 1973, 1974;
Bell, Bontemps 1974,
Breman, G. Brooks (Broad-
side Treasury), P. Brown,
Chester, Colley, Coombs,
Ellmann 1973, Giovanni,
Gross, Henderson, Hopkins
(Knopf), Howe, Jordan,
Kennedy 1974, King 1972,
Konek, Don L. Lee 1971,
Lomax, Major, Murphy,

Patterson, D. Randall
1960, Segnitz, Wagner, T.
Wilentz
Arturo GIOVANNITTI: Lowen-
fels 1969 (Doubleday)
Daniella GISEFFI: Chester,
Fox, Malley, Rigsbee
David GITIN (1941): Harvey,
Krech
David GITLIN: Head
Todd GITLIN (1943): Gitlin
Heidi GITTERMAN: Efros
Robert GITTINGS (1911): Lask,
Knowles
Dottie GITTLESON (1933):
Gersmehl
Michael GIZZI: Lowenfels
1975
Marty GLABERMAN: Harlan
Washington GLADDEN: Kauff-
man
Elton GLASER (1945): Evans
Malcolm GLASS: Owen 1974
Martin GLASS (1938): Gitlin
John GLASSCO (1909): A. J.
M. Smith 1960
Eliot GLASSHEIM (1938):
Crafts, Firmage, Wesleyan
Univ.
Jacob GLATSTEIN (1896):
Joseloff
Andrew GLAZE: Harris 1973,
Steele
Joe GLAZER: Hine
Lyle GLAZIER: Dunning
Madeline GLEASON (1913):
D. M. Allen 1960, J. A.
Allen, Harvey, Witt-
Diamant
Emilie GLENN (Glen) (1932):
Lowenfels 1969 (Random
House), Plumley, Vrbovska
1968
Deborah J. GLICK: Violet
Robert M. GLOVER: Kiley
Louise (Elizabeth) GLUCK
(1943): Carroll (Young
American Poets), Cole
1971, Evans, Halpern,
Strand
Robert GLUCK (1947): Ley-
land 1975, 1977
Rumer GODDEN: McGinley

John GODFREY: Waldman 1971
Edwin (S.) GODSEY (1930-1966):
Steele, H. Taylor
Patricia GOEDICKE (1931):
Rigsbee, Segnitz, Vrbovska
1968
Matthias GOERITZ: E. Williams
Lloyd GOLD: Gallery 1973
Michael GOLD (1893-1967):
Kramer, Lowenfels 1969
(Doubleday)
Albert GOLDBARTH (1948):
Evans, Stryk 1975
B. GOLDBERG: Violet
Reuben Lucius GOLDBERG
(1883-1970): Klonsky
Bernette GOLDEN (c. 1950):
Giovanni, Murphy
Elaine GOLDFEDER: Brindle
Charles GOLDMAN: Waldman
1969
Mary GOLDMAN: Lask
Mary Susan GOLDMAN: Brindle
Michael (Paul) GOLDMAN
(1936): Glikes, Hannum
and Chase
Ben GOLDSTEIN: Banker
Frances GOLFFING (1910):
Firmage
Carlos GOLIBART: Lowenfels
1975
Eugen (Eugene) GOMRINGER:
Gross, Harlan, Pilon, E.
Williams, Winkler
Joe GONCALVES (1937): P.
Brown, Colley
Irma CONZALEZ: Kohl
Rafael Jesus GONZALEZ
(Gonzales): Harvey, Winans
Joey GONZALVEZ, Jr.: Battle
Mrs. D. R. H. GOODALE:
Kauffman
Michael GOODE (1954): Jordan
W. T. GOODGE: Cole 1963
Mitchell GOODMAN: Carruth
(Bantam)
Paul GOODMAN (1911-1972):
Baylor, Carruth (Bantam),
Cole 1963, Gersmehl,
Gitlin, Glikes, Kennedy
1973, Leyland 1975, L.
Moore, Rosenthal 1967,
1968; Strand, Summerfield,
E. Wilentz, Young

Ryah Tumarkin GOODMAN:
Cole 1971, Derleth,
Rigsbee
Ruth Tumarkin GOODMAN:
Lask
Allan GOODNER: Student
William GOODREAU: Lask
Chip GOODRICH: Morticella
Christine GORA: Gallery 1970
Adam Lindsay GORDON: Rose
Alvin J. GORDON: Peck 1971
Charles F. GORDON (1943):
Major
Don GORDON: Lowenfels 1966,
1969 (Doubleday)
Henry GORDON: Adoff 1971
Mary GORDON: Konek,
Monaco 1973
Ralph GORDON: Glikes, Lask
Eva GORE-BOOTH: Parker
1967, Rose
Mindy GORLIN: Adoff 1971
Katherine GORMAN: Vrbovska
1968
Ludwig GOSEWITZ: E. Wil-
liams
Linda GOSS (1947): Coombs,
Giovanni, Patterson
Phyllis GOTLIEB: Peck 1971
Jonathan GOTT: Waldman
1971
Ann GOTTLIEB (1946): Howe
Darcey GOTTLIEB: Lask,
Lowenfels 1975
H. J. GOTTLIEB: Dunnin
Saul GOTTLIEB: Gay, Sher-
man
Theodore D. GOTTLIEB:
Jackson
Carmin Auld GOULBOURNE
(1912): D. Randall 1969
Elizabeth Porter GOULD:
Kauffman
Gerald GOULD: Parker 1967
Janice GOULD: Harlan
Mary S. GOULD: Kiley
Roberta GOULD: De Loach
1976
Donald D. (Duane) GOVAN
(1945): Lowenfels 1973,
Major
Oswald GOVAN: Henderson
Corrado GOVONI (1884):
Livingston

Leanne GRABEL: Morticella
James GRABILL: Morticella
James GRADY: E. Wilentz
A. C. GRAHAM: Knowles
Dan GRAHAM (1942): Kostelan-
etz
Don GRAHAM: Harlan
(Donald) D. L. GRAHAM (Dante)
(1944-1970): Adoff 1973,
Breman, Hayden, Henderson,
Don L. Lee 1971
Ernestine GRAHAM: Booker
Gladys Wilmot GRAHAM:
Vrbovska 1963
Harry GRAHAM: Cole 1971,
J. Gibson, McGinley
Le GRAHAM (1940): D. Randall
1969
W. S. GRAHAM (1921): Bedient,
Brinnin 1963, Rosenthal
1967, 1968
Judy GRAHN (1940): Bulkin,
Chester, Howe, Malley
Corney GRAIN: Cole 1971
Ida GRAMCKO: Lowenfels 1975
Alain GRANDBOIS (1900): A.
J. M. Smith 1960
Paul Langton GRANO (1894):
T. Moore
Earle J. GRANT: Scheftel
Otto GRANT: Booker
Sandy GRANT: Battle
Marcus J. GRAPES: Blazek
Susan GRATHWOHL: Lowenfels
1975
James GRAUERHOLZ: De
Loach 1976
Conrad GRAVES: Booker
John Woodcock GRAVES:
Morrison
Robert GRAVES (1895): Adams,
J. A. Allen, Arp, R.
Bender, Bogan, Brinnin
1963, 1970; C. Brooks,
Calderwood, Cole 1963,
1965, 1967 (Macmillan),
1971, 1972; Crafts, Crang,
Croft, Cromie, De Roche,
Ellmann 1973, Engle,
Felver, J. Gibson (Book
Two), Greaves, Gregory
1962, 1966; Hall 1962
(Watts), Hannum, Hannum

and Chase, Harlan, Hieatt,
Jacobus, Kennedy 1974,
Knowles, Livingston, Mor-
rison, Nash, Parker 1974,
Reeves, Sanders, A. J.
M. Smith 1967, Stallworthy,
W. Taylor, Untermeyer
1964
Steven GRAVES (1947): H.
Taylor
Alexander GRAY: J. Gibson
(Book Two)
Daniel Allen GRAY: Hoffman
Darrell GRAY: Hitchcock,
Sklar
Don GRAY: Fox
Frances Angevine GRAY: Der-
leth
Joycelyn GRAY: Booker
R. D. GRAY: Jackson
Steven Michael GRAY: Lowen-
fels 1975
Thomas GRAY: Cole 1971
William GRAY: Battle
Lynn GRAZNAK: Hallmark
Donald GREEN (c. 1947):
Coombs
Henry Mackenzie GREEN (1881-
1962): T. Moore
Judith GREEN (1936): T.
Moore
Judith Ann GREEN: Sargent
Alvin GREENBERG: Bonazzi
1972
Barbara L. GREENBERG
(1932): Chester, Hewitt,
Mazur
Jack GREENBERG: Jackson
Jerry (Jerrold) GREENBERG:
Montgomery, Oppenheimer
1967
Cathy GREENE: Brindle
Richard Leighton GREENE:
Cole 1971
Peter GREENHAM: Solt
David GREENHOOD: Jackson
Sam GREENLEE: Patterson
C. P. GREENOUGH: Jackson
Judy GREENSPAN: Violet
Florence GREENSTEIN:
Brindle
Ted GREENWALD: Waldman
1971

Roslyn GREER (c. 1952):
Murphy
Linda GREGG (1942): Halpern,
Rigsbee
Arthur GREGOR (1923): Carruth
(Bantam), Gregory 1962,
1966; Lask, Stevenson
Carole GREGORY (c. 1945):
Major, Shuman
Horace GREGORY (1898): Aiken,
Carruth (Bantam), Gregory
1962, 1966; Hannum, Phil-
lips, Rosenthal 1967, Steuben,
Untermeyer 1964
Yvonne GREGORY (1919):
Bontemps 1963, 1974
Eric GREINKE: Lowenfels 1975
Lisa GRENELLE: Derleth,
Vrbovska 1963
Eamon GRENNAN: Lowenfels
1975
R. H. GRENVILLE: Derleth
Christopher Murray GRIEVE
see Hugh MacDIARMID
Bartholomew GRIFFIN: Unter-
meyer 1970
Ida Ruth GRIFFIN: Kohl,
Student
Jonathan GRIFFIN: L. Moore
Sean GRIFFIN: Lowenfels 1975
Susan GRIFFIN (1943): Bulkin,
Chester, Efros, E. Gill,
Howe
Walter GRIFFIN: Gallery 1973,
Young
Ian GRIFFITHS: Summerfield
Reginald GRIFFITHS: Rose
Geoffrey GRIGSON (1905): Cole
1971
Alexandra GRILIKHES: Morri-
son
Arthur GRIMBLE: Summerfield
Naomi GRIMES: Giovanni
Angelina Weld GRIMKE: Patter-
son
Morton GRINKER: Head, Krech,
Palmer
Amy GROESBECK: Derleth
Bohumila GROGEROVA: Wild-
man, E. Williams
Antoni GRONOWICZ: Banker
Ronald GROSS (1935): Gross,
Hitchcock, Kennedy 1974

Suzanne GROSS: Stevenson
Morton GROSSER: Peck 1970
Allen GROSSMAN (1932):
Hollander
Kali GROSVENOR (c. 1962):
Adoff 1974, King 1972
Leslie GROVE: Morticella
Jon GRUBE: Krech
Major Edmund L. GRUBER:
J. A. Vincent
Bruce GRUND: Hadassah
Jose Lino GRUNEWALD: E.
Williams
John GUENTHER: Firmage
Vera E. GUERARD (c. 1944-
1967): Murphy
Bruce GUERNSEY: M. Gibson
Barbara GUEST (1920): D. M.
Allen 1960, Chester, Fer-
linghetti, Glikes, Kessler,
Myers, Stanford, Waldman
1971, Witt-Diamant
Harry GUEST (1932): Matthias,
Stevenson
Nicolas GUILLEN (1902):
Bates
Daniel GUILLORY: Hoffman
Charles GULLANS (1929):
Lask, Winters
Keith GUNDERSON (1935):
Stryk 1975
Thom GUNN (1929): J. A.
Allen, Arp, Baylor, R.
Bender, Brady, Brinnin
1973, 1970; C. Brooks,
Crang, De Roche, Ellmann
1973, Engle, J. Gibson
(Book Two), Gwynn, Hall
1962 (World), Hannum,
Hannum and Chase, Harvey,
Hollander, Holmes, Hurtik,
Larson, McCullough, J.
Perry, Plotz, Rosenthal
1967, 1968; Sanders,
Schneider, Simpson, Stall-
worthy, W. Taylor, Unter-
meyer 1964, 1973 (McKay);
Walsh, Winters, Young
Ralph GUSTAFSON (1909): A.
J. M. Smith 1960
A. B. GUTHRIE, Jr.: Dunning
Ramon GUTHRIE (1896-1973):
Rosenthal 1967, 1968

Woody GUTHRIE (1912-1967):
Chace, J. Gibson (Book
Two), Kennedy 1974,
Kramer, Lowenfels 1969
(Doubleday), Peck 1970,
Summerfield
Assia GUTMANN (1927-1970):
Stallworthy
Bernard GUTTERIDGE: Cole
1971
Jeanne Marie GUYON: Kauff-
man
Miguel GUZMAN: Battle
Brion GYSIN: E. Williams

H

H. D. see Hilda DOOLITTLE
Rosamond HAAS: Lask
Marilyn HACKER (1942):
Cromie, Halpern
J. (James) W. (William)
HACKETT (1929): Harlan,
Van den Heuvel
Rachel HADAS: Rigsbee
HADASSAH: Hadassah
Anthony HADEN-GUEST (c.
1938): Lucie-Smith
Hermann HAGEDORN (1882):
Trapp
Jessica Tarahata HAGEDORN:
Clay, E. Gill, Rexroth
Steven A. HAGERTH: Krech
Nelson L. HAGGERSON:
Sargent
James HAGOOD: Gallery 1970,
1973
Merrie L. HAGOPIAN: Sargent
Robert (C.) HAHN: Rigsbee,
Rottmann
John (M.) HAINES (1924): Cole
1971, 1972; De Roche,
Heyen, Kennedy 1974,
Larson, Lowenfels 1973,
Owen 1974, Pearson,
Schreiber, Simpson, K.
and J. Sollid, Strand,
Summerfield, H. Taylor
John HAISLIP (1925): Heyen
J. B. S. HALDANE (1892-
1966): Baylor
Edward Everett HALE: Kauff-
man, J. A. Vincent

Janet Campbell HALE (1947):
Clay, Rosen
Robert Beverly HALE (1901):
Cole 1963
Bruce HALEY (1933): H. Tay-
lor
A. Oakley HALL: Jackson
Carol HALL: Ten
Donald HALL (1928): Bates,
R. Bender, Bly 1970,
Brewton, Brinnin 1963,
1970; C. Brooks, Cole
1965, 1967 (Macmillan),
1967 (Viking), 1971, 1972;
Colley, Cromie, Dunning,
Engle, Glikes, Gwynn,
Hall 1962 (World), Han-
num, Hannum and Chase,
Hecht, Hope, Kennedy
1973, 1974; Lowenfels
1967, McCullough,
McGovern, Mazur, Peck
1970, 1971; Perrine,
Rosenthal 1967, 1968;
Simpson, Steuben, Strand,
Univ. Press of Va.,
Vrbovska 1963, M. Wil-
liams, O. Williams 1966
(World)
Eugene J. HALL: Jackson
Gary HALL: Kohl
John HALL (1943): Major
Kevan HALL: Summerfield
Prescott F. HALL: Jackson
Rodney HALL (1935): T.
Moore
Ted HALL: Bogin
Tim HALL: Gitlin, Lowenfels
1969 (Doubleday)
Tom HALL: Jackson
Wade HALL (1934): Mollenkott
Walter HALL: Durand
Fitz Greene HALLECK: Jack-
son
Anne HALLEY (1928): Howe,
Perrine
Max HALPEREN: Owen 1969
Daniel HALPERN (1945):
Gildner, Halpern
Sue HALPERN: Rottmann
Debbie HALPIN: Harlan
Charles G. HALPINE: Jack-
son
William HALSEY: Booker

Orella D. HALSTEAD: Vrbovska 1963
Ronald HAMBLETON (1917):
   A. J. M. Smith 1960
Michael HAMBURGER (1924):
   Baylor, Brinnin 1963,
   Engle, Gross, Hall 1962
   (World), Knowles, Rosenthal
   1967, 1968; Wallace
Sam HAMILL: Mallory
Alfred Starr HAMILTON (c.
   1915): Hewitt
Bobb HAMILTON (1928): Bre-
   man, G. Brooks (Broadside
   Treasury), Lomax, D.
   Randall 1969
Charles HAMILTON: Clay
Fritz HAMILTON: Gallery 1970,
   1973
Horace E. HAMILTON: Lask
Ian HAMILTON (1938): Ellmann
   1973
Leona HAMILTON: Vrbovska
   1963, 1968
Ruth HAMLIN: Banker
Annette HAMMER: Hoffman
Lillian HAMMER: Scheftel
Geraldine HAMMOND: Konek
Jerry HAMMOND (1923): H.
   Taylor
Sam HAMOD (1936): Kherdian
   1974
Andras HAMORI: Lask
Christopher HAMPTON: Lask
O. R. HANA: Baraka
Nhat HANH: Lowenfels 1967
Robert HANLON: E. Wilentz
Charles HANNA: Hanna 1960
Laura HANNA: Violet
Thomas HANNA (c. 1942):
   Hewitt
George HANNAH: Booker
Gregor HANNIBAL: Henderson
Paul HANNIGAN: Cole 1971,
   J. R. Randall
Marcie HANS: Dunning, Peck
   1971
Al HANSEN: E. Williams
Joyce HANSEN (1942): Giovanni
Freddie Phelps HANSON:
   Sargent
Joan HANSON: Pilon
Kenneth O. HANSON (1922):
   Larson, Skelton, Strand

C. G. HANZLICEK: Kherdian
   1970
E. Y. HARBURG: Dee
Walter HARD: Jackson
O. B. HARDISON: Owen 1969,
   1974
Joy HARJO (1951): Kherdian
   1974
Patty L. HARJO (1947): Dodge,
   Rosen
Mary HARLAN: Harlan
William HARMON (1938):
   Harris 1976, Hewitt,
   Lowenfels 1973, Owen 1974
Curtis HARNACK: Gildner
Frances E. W. HARPER:
   Patterson
Michael (Mike) (S.) HARPER
   (1938): Adoff 1973, P.
   Brown, Colley, Evans,
   Halpern, Harlan, Harvey,
   Henderson, Hopkins (Knopf),
   Lowenfels 1973, T. Wilentz
Barbara HARR (c. 1938):
   Anania, Harlan
John HARRIMAN (1940): Katz-
   man, Lowenfels 1969
   (Random House)
Edward (Phillip) HARRINGTON
   (1896): J. Gibson (Book
   Two), T. Moore
Dorothy D. HARRIS: Sargent
Emily Catharine HARRIS (1921):
   Lowenfels 1969 (Random
   House)
Ernestine HARRIS: Booker
Etta Caldwell HARRIS: Scheftel
Gertrude HARRIS (1914): Witt-
   Diamant
Howard HARRIS: Booker
Jana HARRIS: Efros
John HARRIS (1942): Kiley
John Sterling HARRIS (1929):
   Larson
Madelon HARRIS: Brindle
Marguerite HARRIS (1899-1978):
   De Loach 1968, Harris
   1970, 1973, 1976; Katzman,
   Simmons, Vrbovska 1963,
   1968; Weil
Marie HARRIS: E. Gill, Mazur,
   Rigsbee
Marla V. HARRIS: Booker
Marlene HARRIS: Kiley

Max HARRIS (1921): T. Moore
Phillip HARRIS: Kohl
Phyllis Masek HARRIS (1940):
Hannum, Schreiber
Robert HARRIS: Waldman 1971
Sandra Ann HARRIS: Student
Sanford HARRIS, Jr. (Sanford
X) (1939): Tisdale
William J. HARRIS (1942):
Adoff 1970, 1973, 1974;
Cole 1972, Colley, Schneid-
er, Shuman, T. Wilentz
Wilson HARRIS: Salkey
De Leon (DeLeon) HARRISON
(1941): Adoff 1973, A.
Miller
George HARRISON: Crafts,
Holmes
Jim (James) HARRISON (1937):
Carruth (Bantam), Ellmann
1973, Gross, Halpern,
Hannum and Chase, Lask,
Rothenberg 1973, Schreiber,
Stryk 1975, Sumac, Unter-
meyer 1973 (McKay),
Wagner, M. Williams
Tony HARRISON: De Loach
1976
William (E.) HARROLD (1936):
Foster, Lowenfels 1975,
Stryk 1975
Howard HART: Lowenfels 1969
(Random House), E. Wilentz
John HART (1948): Harvey
John HARTFORD (1937): Ken-
nedy 1973
Charles O. HARTMAN: Rigs-
bee
Hugh HARTMAN (1934): Felver
Susan HARTMAN: Rigsbee
William HART-SMITH (1911):
Cole 1971, 1972; Knowles,
T. Moore
Frances HARTWELL: Giovanni
Christopher HARVEY: Harlan
F. W. HARVEY: Cole 1963
Gwen HARWOOD: Stanford
Gwen HARWOOD (1920): T.
Moore
Lee HARWOOD (1939): Blazek,
De Loach 1976, Matthias,
Waldman 1969
Charles HASELOFF: Fox,
Harris 1976

Gustav HASFORD: Rottmann
Minnie Louise HASKINS:
Kauffman
Robert HASS (1941): Carroll
(Young American Poets),
Halpern, Lowenfels 1975
Christopher HASSALL: J.
Gibson
Donald HASSLER: Ashland
Umar Abd Rahim HASSON
(Tony Rutherford): G.
Brooks (Broadside Treas-
ury)
Marcia HASTIE: Hoffman
C. HATAKEYAMA: Knowles
Stephen R. HATCH: Rottmann
Jeanine HATHAWAY: Konek
William HATHAWAY (1944):
Hewitt
Bob HAUGE: Hauge
Gerald HAUSMAN: Hausman,
Malley
Vaclav HAVEL: E. Williams
Frances Ridley HAVERGAL:
Kauffman
Phil HAVEY (1930): Katzman
Stratis HAVIARAS: Mazur
Bobbie Louise HAWKINS:
Ferlinghetti
Isaiah HAWKINS: Tisdale
Walter Everette HAWKINS
(1883): Adoff 1973
Julian HAWTHORNE: Jackson
John HAY: Aloian, Jackson,
Lask
Sara Henderson HAY: Dunning,
Lask, Parker 1960
Susan Henderson HAY: Jack-
son
Todd HAYCOCK: Milton
Casey HAYDEN: Gitlin
Robert (E.) HAYDEN (1913):
Adoff 1968, 1969, 1973;
Bell, Bontemps 1963, 1974;
Brady, Breman, Brinnin
1970, G. Brooks (Broad-
side Treasury), Carruth
(Bantam), Chace, Colley,
Ellmann 1973, Harlan,
Hayden, Henderson, Hughes
1970, Jordan, Kennedy
1973, King, Lane, Lomax,
Lowenfels 1966, 1969
(Doubleday); Peck 1971,

D. Randall 1960, Schneider,
Turner, Wagner, Walsh,
M. Williams
Alfred HAYES (1911): Kramer
Charles HAYES: Lowenfels
1975, Smith
Donald Jeffrey HAYES (1904):
Adoff 1973, Bontemps 1963,
1974; Hughes 1970, Patterson
Lee Richard HAYMAN: Gallery
1973
Albert HAYNES (1936): Major
H. R. HAYS (1904): Cole 1971,
Hitchcock
Lee HAYS: J. Gibson, Kramer
Max HAYWARD (1924): Stallworthy
James HAZARD: Rosenblum
Robert HAZEL: Glikes
D. R. HAZELTON: Palmer
Anne HAZLEWOOD-BRADY:
Konek
Samuel (John) HAZO (1928):
Cole 1967 (Macmillan),
Lask, Lowenfels 1969
(Doubleday), Morrison,
H. Taylor
Robert HEAD: Blazek, Fox
Thomas HEAD: Ferlinghetti,
Harlan, Head
Betty HEALY: Sollid 1973
Howard HEALY: Lask
Ian HEALY (1919): T. Moore
Seamus HEANEY (1939):
Brinnin 1970, Cole 1971,
Crang, Ellmann 1973,
Greaves, Knowles
Marianne HEARN: Kauffman
James HEARST: Gildner,
Stryk 1967
Emmett L. HEASTER: Sargent
Curtis HEATH: Dunning
William HEATH: Rigsbee
HEATHER: Violet
John HEATH-STUBBS (1918):
J. A. Allen, R. Bender,
Brinnin 1963, 1970; Engle,
Hope, Kennedy 1974,
Knowles, Lucie-Smith,
Stallworthy
Carol HEBALD: Gildner
Reginald HEBER: Kauffman

Anthony (Evan) HECHT (1923):
Baylor, Brady, Brinnin
1963, 1970; Carruth (Bantam), Crang, Ellmann
1973, 1976; Engle, Hall
1962 (Penguin), (World);
Hannum, Hecht, Hollander,
Howard, Howard and Victor, Kennedy 1973, 1974;
Leary, Monaco 1974,
Perrine, J. Perry, Rosenthal 1967, Stallworthy,
Strand, H. Taylor, Untermeyer 1973 (McKay),
Wallace, M. Williams, O.
Williams 1966 (World)
Jenny HECHT: Gay
Roger HECHT: Harris 1976
Anne HEDLEY: Harlan, Head
Leslie Woolf HEDLEY (1918):
Kramer, Lowenfels 1966,
1967, 1969 (Doubleday);
Owen 1969, Vrbovska 1963,
1968
David HEEB: Pilon
Michael HEFFERNAN (1942):
Harris 1976, Stryk 1975
Jeff HEGLIN: Adoff 1971
Sara HEIDE: Morticella
John HEINEGG: Adoff 1971
Lois Lillian HEINLEIN:
Morticella
Helmut HEISSENBUTTEL: E.
Williams
C. H. HEJINIAN (1941):
Freed, Gallery 1970
Lyn HEJINIAN: De Loach 1976
Sheila HELDENBRAND: Sklar
Anita HELLE: Morticella
Anita HELLER: Harris 1976
Michael (Mike) HELLER:
Banker, Gross
Roy HELTON (1886): Untermeyer 1964
Felicia Dorothea Browne
HEMANS: J. A. Vincent
Ernest HEMINGWAY (1898-
1961): Rothenberg 1973
Cecil HEMLEY: Driver,
Steuben
Archibald HENDERSON:
Bonazzi 1972, Gallery
1973

David HENDERSON (1942):
Adoff 1970, 1973; Banker,
Breman, Clay, Colley, De
Loach 1968, Gross, Harlan,
Harvey, Hayden, Henderson,
Hopkins (Knopf), Hughes
1964, 1970; H. Jones,
Jordan, Kennedy 1973,
Kenseth, King 1972, Don L.
Lee, Lowenfels 1967, 1969
(Random House); A. Miller,
D. Randall 1969, Rothen-
berg 1973, Waldman 1969,
1971; T. Wilentz
Peggy HENDERSON (1949):
Howe
Philip HENDERSON (1906):
Knowles
Mary HENDLER: Kiley
Julie HENDON: Kohl
Sarah HENDON: Kohl
Susie HENDON: Kohl
Jimi HENDRIX: Morse
Louise Butts HENDRIX: Sar-
gent
Suzanne HENIG: Vrbovska 1968
Margot HENKELMANN: Brindle
Tom HENNEN (1942): Stryk
1975
Adrian HENRI (1932): Greaves,
Lucie-Smith
Edith HENRICH (1911): Lask,
Trapp
Lance HENSON: Niatum, Rosen
A. P. (Alan Patrick) HERBERT
(1890): Cole 1963, 1965;
Cromie, Morrison, Nash,
Rose
C. L. HERBERT: Salkey
Oliver HERFORD: Dunning,
Parker 1960, Peck 1971
Jacob HERMAN: Hitchcock
Jan HERMAN: Harvey
Shael HERMAN: Blazek
Ena HERNANDEZ: Clay
Calvin C. HERNTON (1932):
Adoff 1968, 1970, 1973;
Baylor, Bontemps 1974,
Breman, Gross, Hayden,
Hughes 1964, 1970; Jor-
dan, Lomax, Lowenfels
1969 (Doubleday), (Ran-
dom House); A. Miller

Elizabeth HERRMANN: Wild-
man
David Sten HERRSTROM (1946):
Mollenkott
Ruth (Margaret) HERSCHBERG-
ER (1917): Baylor, Dunn-
ing, Stanford
Sandi HERSCHEL: Gallery
William HERSCHELL: Jackson
Miriam HERSCHENSON:
Dunning
Marcie HERSHMAN: Bulkin
Robert HERSHON (1936): Bay-
lor, Colley, J. Gill, Ken-
nedy 1973, Lowenfels
1967, Schreiber
Roland HERWIG: Kiley
Albert HERZING: Wheelock
1961
Lawrence HETRICK (1940):
Hannum
Elizabeth HEWITT: Balazs
Geof HEWITT (1943): Cole,
J. Gill
John HEWITT (1907): Knowles
Philip HEY: Carroll (Young
American Poets), Evans,
Gildner
William HEYEN (1940): Cole
1971, Halpern, Harris
1970, Heyen, Lask
Ben (L.) HIATT: Blazek,
Krech, Winans
Evelyn HICKMAN: Foster
Philip S. HICKS: Battle
Alexandra L. HICKSON:
Brindle
Lori HIGA: Brindle
Annie HIGGINS: Cole 1967
(Macmillan)
Dewey HIGGINS: Booker
Dick (Richard) HIGGINS (1938):
Fox, Gross, Klonsky,
Peck 1971, Rothenberg
1973, Solt, Wildman, E.
Wilentz
Jo Fredell HIGGINS: Brindle
Michael HIGGINS: Young
William J. HIGGINSON (1938):
Oppenheimer 1977, Rigs-
bee
Charles HIGHAM (1931): Lask,
T. Moore, Stevenson

Aig HIGO (1929): Lomax
Conrad HILBERRY (1928): H.
    Taylor
Tim HILDEBRAND: Hitchcock
Brian HILL (1896): Young
Geoffrey HILL (1932): J. A.
    Allen, Ellmann 1973, Hall
    1962 (World), Rosenthal
    1967, W. Taylor
Hyacinthe HILL: Colley, Lowen-
    fels 1969 (Doubelday),
    Vrbovska 1963, 1968
Jeanne HILL: Bonazzi 1974
Leslie Pinckney HILL (1880-
    1960): Adoff 1973, Hughes
    1970, Kauffman
Pamela Woodruff HILL: Hender-
    son
Pati HILL (1921): Cole 1963
Roberta HILL: Niatum, Rosen
Quentin HILL (c. 1950): Major
Carol HILLE: Brindle
Robert (Silliman) HILLYER
    (1895-1961): J. A. Allen,
    Cole 1963, Dunning, Greg-
    ory 1962, Hopkins (Nelson),
    Steuben, Untermeyer 1964
David HILTON (1938): Hewitt,
    Sklar
Del HILYARD: Hallmark
Margery HIMEL: Konek
Sophie HIMMEL: Cromie
Barbara HINCHCLIFFE (1923):
    Lowenfels 1966
Gertrude HIND: Cole 1963
Al HINE (1915): Hine
Daryl (Darl) HINE (1936):
    Brinnin 1970, Ellmann
    1973, Hollander, Howard,
    Howard and Victor, Lask,
    A. J. M. Smith 1960,
    Strand
Edna HINER: Booker
Carl W. (Wendell) HINES (Jr.)
    (1940): Bontemps 1963,
    1974; Breman, Dunning,
    Hayden, Lowenfels 1966
Glenn HINES: Dee
C. J. HINKE: Banker
Henry HINTON: Black History
Jack HIRSCHMAN (1933):
    Bukowski, Durand, Simmons,
    Winans

Josef HIRSOL: Wildman, E.
    Williams
George (P.) HITCHCOCK (1914):
    Carruth (Bantam), (McCall);
    Fox, Glikes, Harvey,
    Hitchcock, Lowenfels 1966,
    1967
Vernoy E. HITE (c. 1951):
    Murphy
Everett HOAGLAND (1942): G.
    Brooks (Broadside Treas-
    ury), Lee 1971, Major
Russell HOBAN (1925): Cole
    1971, 1972
Philip HOBSBAUM: Lask
Christopher Z. HOBSON (1941):
    Gitlin
Sandra HOCHMAN (1936):
    Chester, Cole 1972, Howe,
    Jacobus, Vrbovska 1968
Ake HODELL: E. Williams
Connie HODGES: Sargent
Ralph HODGSON (1871-1962):
    Bogan, Cole 1963, 1971;
    Hall 1962 (Watts), Kenseth,
    Knowles, Nash, Parker
    1960, 1967; Peterson,
    Rose, A. J. M. Smith,
    H. Taylor, W. Taylor,
    Untermeyer 1964, Woods
Edwin A. HOEY: Dunning
Samuel HOFFENSTEIN: Cole
    1967, Jackson, Nash
Byrd HOFFMAN: Fagin
C. R. HOFFMAN: Harlan
Daniel (G.) HOFFMAN (1923):
    J. A. Allen, Beerman,
    Brinnin 1963, 1970; Car-
    ruth (Bantam), Cole 1967
    (Macmillan), Cromie,
    Engle, Howard, Howard
    and Victor, Kennedy 1973,
    Kostelanetz, Leary, Strand,
    Wagner, Wallace, O. Wil-
    liams 1966 (World)
Heinrich HOFFMAN: Harlan,
    Nash
William M. HOFFMAN (1939):
    Baylor, Schreiber
Judith HOGAN: Head
Michael HOGAN: Rigsbee
Robert HOGAN (1930): Baylor
Carolyn HOGGINS: Vrbovska

1963
Israel Kafu HOH (1912): Breman
David HOLBROOK (1923): Crang,
Hall 1962 (World), Lask
John Jarvis HOLDEN: Jackson
Molly HOLDEN: Cole 1971
Raymond HOLDEN: Lask
Raymond (P.) HOLDEN (1894):
Jackson, Knowles
M. V. HOLDSWORTH: Scheftel
Barbara D. HOLENDER: Lask
Eugene HOLLAHAN: Owens 1974
Barbara (A.) HOLLAND (1925):
Banker, De Loach 1968, Gallery 1973, Harris 1973, 1976;
Lowenfels 1969 (Random
House), 1975
Josiah Gilbert HOLLAND:
Kauffman, J. A. Vincent
John HOLLANDER (1929): Baylor, Brady, Brinnin 1963,
1970; Cole 1971, Ellmann
1973, Engle, Hall 1962
(World), Hecht, Hollander,
Howard, Howard and Victor, Kennedy 1974, Kessler,
Klonsky, Kostelanetz,
Lowenfels 1967, Phillips,
Pilon, Strand, H. Taylor,
M. Williams
Robert HOLLANDER: Glikes
Beth HOLLENDER: Dee
William HOLLIS: Stevenson
Anselm HOLLO (1934): Gildner,
Glikes, Gross, Lowenfels
1975, Matthias, Rothenberg
1973, Sklar
John HOLLOWAY (1920):
Knowles, Rosenthal 1967
Lucy Ariel Williams HOLLO-
WAY (1905): Hughes 1970
Nellie HOLLOWAY: Battle
Lee Anette HOLM: Brindle
Felice HOLMAN (1919): Larrick
J. C. HOLMAN: Lowenfels 1973
M. (Moses) Carl HOLMAN (1919):
Adoff 1973, Bontemps 1963,
1974; Hayden, Hughes 1970,
Jordan
Gwendolyn HOLMES (c. 1947):
Giovanni
John HOLMES (1904-1962):
Corbett, Engle, McGinley,

Steuben, Trapp, Wallace
R. Ernest HOLMES (1943):
Coombs, Patterson, H.
Taylor
Theodore HOLMES (1928):
Leary
Bruce HOLSAPPLE: McMahon
Spencer HOLST (1934): Rothenberg
Raz HOLT (1941-1970): H.
Taylor
Tim S. HOLT: Hadassah
Bernadette HOLTHIUS: Harlan
Rona Fogel HOLUB: Brindle
St. John HONEYWOOD: Jackson
Bob HONIG: Lowenfels 1975
Edwin HONIG (1919): Ellmann
1973, Lask, Pearson,
Peterson, O. Williams
1966 (World)
Margaret HONTON: Balazs
John Lee HOOKER (c. 1918):
Rothenberg 1973
Paul HOOVER: Friedman
A. D. HOPE (Alec Derwent)
(1907): J. A. Allen,
Brady, Ellmann 1973,
Hollander, Kennedy 1973,
T. Moore, Stallworthy,
H. Taylor, Untermeyer
1970, 1973 (McKay)
D. C. HOPE: Hope
Francis HOPE (1938): Greaves
Laurence HOPE: Untermeyer
1970
Peter HOPEGOOD (1891): T.
Moore
Kenneth HOPKINS (1914):
Cromie
Roy George HOPKINS: Clay
Woolsey R. HOPKINS: Jackson
Joseph HOPKINSON: J. A.
Vincent
Slade HOPKINSON: Salkey
John HOPPER: Oppenheimer
1967
Nora HOPPER: Parker 1974
Paul HOPPER: Hallmark
Robert HORAN (1922): Cole
1963, O. Williams 1966
(World)

John HORDER: Cole 1971
Paul HORGAN (1903): Cromie
Edward Newman HORN (1903):
    Cole 1967 (Macmillan),
    1971, 1972
Herschel HORN: Kenseth,
    Lowenfels 1966
Frank HORNE (1899): Bontemps
    1963, 1974; Crafts, Hayden,
    Hughes 1970, Livingston,
    Lomax, Lowenfels 1966
Theodore H. HORNE (1937):
    D. Randall 1969
William Edward HORNEY (1895-
    1963): T. Moore
Michael HOROVITZ (1935):
    Cole 1972, Crang, Simmons
Mary-Louise HORTON: Black
    History
Arthur Nicholas HOSKING: J.
    A. Vincent
Katherine de Montalant HOSKINS
    (1909): Rosenthal 1967
Gary HOTHAM (1950): Van den
    Heuvel
Diana HOTT: Owen 1969
Diane HOTTENDORF: Brindle
Gertrude M. HOUCK: Sargent
Dom Sylvester HOUEDARD:
    Solt, Wildman, E. Williams
Graham HOUGH: J. A. Allen,
    Rosenthal 1967
Lindy HOUGH: Konek
Tom HOUSE: Rigsbee
William Walsham HOW: Kauff-
    man
Ben HOWARD: Bogin
Earl E. HOWARD: Jackson
Frances Minturn HOWARD:
    Brewton, Stanford,
    Vrbovska 1968
Joan HOWARD: Bogin
Richard HOWARD (1929):
    Brinnin 1970, Ellmann 1974,
    Hecht, Hollander, Howard,
    Howard and Victor, Pear-
    son, Strand
Vanessa HOWARD (1955):
    Adoff 1974, Jordan
Vilma HOWARD: Hughes 1964
R. G. HOWARTH: Cole 1967
    (Macmillan), 1971
Fanny HOWE (1940): Hewitt

Christopher HOWELL: Morti-
    cella
Thomas HOWELL: Parker
    1974
Mildred HOWELLS: Parker
    1960
Barbara HOWES (1914): Bogan,
    Brewton, Brinnin 1963,
    1970; Chester, Cole 1963,
    Engle, Glikes, Hall 1962
    (Watts), Hannum, Konek,
    Lask, Pearson, Peck 1971,
    Plotz, Stanford, Strand,
    H. Taylor, Untermeyer
    1964, 1973 (McKay); W.
    Williams, Witt-Diamant
Margaret HOY: Morticella
Andrew HOYEM (1935): Arts
    Festival 1964, Harvey,
    Poetry San Francisco
Clement HOYT (1906-1970):
    Van den Heuvel
Elias HRUSKA-CORTES: Clay,
    Lowenfels 1975
Po Fei HUANG: Lask
John HUBBARD: Jackson
Lindley Williams HUBBELL
    (1901): Bates, Cromie
James Lee HUBERT: Chilgren
Frankie HUCKLENBROICH:
    Bulkin
George HUDDLESTON: Jack-
    son
Flexmore HUDSON (1913):
    Knowles, T. Moore
Marc HUDSON: Sollid 1973
Rex HUDSON: Sargent
Ford Madox HUEFFER:
    Parker 1967
Diane HUETER: K. and J.
    Sollid
Robert HUFF (1924): Hall
    1962 (World), Harris 1970,
    Monaco 1974, Strand,
    Stryk 1967, M. Williams
Ericka HUGGINS: Ferlinghetti
Barbara HUGHES (1939):
    Winans
Daniel HUGHES: Lask
J. F. HUGHES: Wiebe
Langston HUGHES (1902-1967):
    Adoff 1968, 1970, 1973,
    1974; Bach, Baylor, Bell,

Bold, Bontemps 1974, Breman, Carruth (Bantam), Cole 1972, Colley, Crafts, Cromie, De Roche, Dunning, Ellmann 1973, 1976; Engle, Gannett, Gersmehl, Greaves, Hannum, Harlan, Henderson, Holmes, Hopkins (Knopf), Hughes 1970, Jacobus, Jordan, Kennedy 1974, Kramer, Livingston, Lomax, Lowenfels 1969 (Doubleday), McGinley, Monaco 1974, L. Moore, Patterson, Peck 1970, 1971; D. Randall 1960, Rothenberg 1973, Schneider, Turner, Untermeyer 1964, 1973 (McKay); Wagner, M. Williams, Woods

Linda HUGHES: J. Gibson (Book Two)

Richard HUGHES (1900): Cole 1967 (Macmillan), Untermeyer 1964

Ted HUGHES (1930): Bedient, Brady, Brinnin 1963, 1970; Cole 1963, Crang, De Roche, Driver, Ellmann 1973, Engle, Foster, J. Gibson, J. Gibson (Book Two); Gregory 1966, Greaves, Hall 1962 (World), Hannum and Chase, Hollander, Hurtik, Jacobus, Kennedy 1973, 1974; Knowles, Larrick, Lucie-Smith, McCullough, Matthias, Monaco 1974, L. Moore, Rosenthal 1967, 1968; Sanders, Schneider, Stallworthy, Stevenson, Summerfield, W. Taylor, Untermeyer 1964, 1973 (McKay); Wallace, Walsh

Richard (F.) (Franklin) HUGO (1923): Adams, Glikes, Heyen, Howard, Howard and Victor, Kennedy 1973, Larson, Monaco 1973, 1974; Skelton, Strand, Ten

J. HUIZINGA: Harlan

Blair Ann HULL: Brindle

Dorothy Cope HULSE: Jackson

Charles HUMBOLDT (1910): Lowenfels 1966

Aletha HUMPHREYS: Derleth

Rolfe HUMPHRIES (1894): Jackson, Morrison, Perrine, Trapp

Evelyn Tooley HUNT: Peck 1970

Ted HUNT: Henderson

William HUNT: Carroll (Young American Poets)

Ivan HUNTER: Plumley

Robert HUNTER: Morse

Constance HUNTING: Harris 1970

Z. N. HURSTON: Lomax

Geraold HUSMAN: Malley

Barney HUTCHINSON: Morrison

Joan HUTTON: Lask

Aldous HUXLEY (1894-1963): Cole 1967 (Viking)

Douglas HYDE: McGinley

Evan HYDE: Booker

I

Reuben ICELAND: Cole 1971

Femi Funmi IFETAYO see Regina MICOU

Bruce IGNACIO: Dodge

David IGNATOW (1914): Adoff 1969, Baylor, Bly 1970, 1971; Brinnin 1970, Cole 1971, 1972; Carruth (Bantam), De Loach 1968, Glikes, Hannum, Harlan, Harris 1976, Heyen, Joseloff, Kennedy 1973, 1974; Kherdian 1973, Lask, Lowenfels 1967, 1969 (Doubleday); Pearson, Peck 1970, 1971; Poulin, Rothenberg 1973, Simpson, Strand, H. Taylor, Wagner, Wallace, Wang

Ron IKAN (1941): Evans

Yusef IMAN: Baraka, Dee, Lomax

Lawson (Fusao) INADA (1938): Clay, Halpern, Kherdian 1970, 1974; Larson, Salis-

bury
Colette INEZ (1931): Chester,
Gallery 1973, Harlan, Har-
ris 1973, Hewitt, Howe,
Konek, Lowenfels 1973,
Mollenkott
Jean INGELOW: Parker 1960
Oliver INGERSOLL (1912):
Foster
John Hall INGHAM: J. A.
Vincent
Forrest INGRAM: Bonazzi 1972
Mary L. INMAN: Lask
Will INMAN (1923): Banker, De
Loach 1968, 1976; Fox, Gitlin,
Glikes, Leyland 1977,
Lowenfels 1967, 1969 (Ran-
dom House), 1975; McGov-
ern, Owen 1969, P. Perry,
Sherman, Vrbovska 1963
Kenneth IRBY (1936): H. Jones,
Rothenberg 1973
Eric IRVIN (1908): T. Moore
Margaret IRVIN (1916): T.
Moore
Patricia IRVING: T. Allen
Wallace IRWIN: Jackson
Abraham C. ISAACSON: Jack-
son
Elton Hill-Abu ISHAK (1950):
Gross, Major
Christopher ISHERWOOD:
Young
Carlos ISLA: Bonazzi 1974
Michael Francis ITKIN: Banker
Charles E. IVES: Summerfield

J

Antonio JACINTO: Lomax
Marvin JACKMAN (1944):
Lowenfels 1969 (Random
House)
Thomas JACKRELL: Poetry
San Francisco
Alice JACKSON: Student
Angela JACKSON: Friedman
Aunt Molly JACKSON (1880):
Kramer
Bill JACKSON: Simmons
Eileen JACKSON: Kiley
Gerald JACKSON (1936): Bre-
man, Gross, Lowenfels
1969 (Random House)
Graham JACKSON (1949):
Young
Holiday JACKSON: Brindle
Linnie E. JACKSON: Kiley
James JACKSON (Gomui Malik):
King Pub.
Mae JACKSON (1946): Adoff
1970, 1973, 1974; Giovanni,
King 1972
Marsha A. JACKSON (c. 1947):
Murphy
Maurice Shelley JACKSON:
Booker, Hopkins (Knopf)
Percival E. JACKSON: Jack-
son
Robert George JACKSON:
Kohl
Sara JACKSON: Cole 1965
John JACOB: Fox
Elijah L. JACOBS: Brewton
J. C. JACOBS (1945): Monaco
1973
Larry JACOBS (1959): Lowen-
fels 1967
M. G. JACOBS: Gallery 1970
Josephine JACOBSEN (1908):
J. A. Allen, Immaculate,
Owen 1974, Stanford, Wag-
ner
Ethel JACOBSON: Lask
Don (Dan) JAFFE (1933):
Dunning
Leonore JAFFEE: E. Wilentz
David JAFFIN: Gallery 1973
Mick JAGGER (1943): Kennedy
1974
T. R. JAHNS: Rigsbee
Jamie JAMES: Hoffman
Thomas JAMES (1946-1973):
Halpern, Stryk 1975
Roberta JAMISON: Brindle
Ernst JANDL: E. Williams,
Winkler
Phyllis JANIK: Konek
Beatrice JANOSCO: Dunning
Phyllis JANOWITZ: Mazur
Francis de Haes JANVIER:
J. A. Vincent
Randall JARRELL (1914-1965):
G. W. Allen, J. A. Allen,
Aloian, Bates, Baylor,

Brady, Brinnin 1963, 1970;
C. Brooks, Carruth (Bantam), Chace, Cole 1967
(Macmillan), Corbett,
Cromie, Drew, Ellmann
1973, 1976; Engle, Foster,
Gwynn, Hannum, Harlan,
Holmes, Hughes 1970,
Hurtik, Immaculate, Kennedy 1973, 1974; Larrick,
Livingston, McCullough,
McGinley, Moore, Peck
1970, 1971; Perrine, Rosenthal 1967, 1968; Sanders,
Shapiro, A. J. M. Smith
1967, Strand, H. Taylor,
Trapp, Univ. Press of Va.,
Untermeyer 1964, 1973
(McKay); Wagner, M. Williams, Witt-Diamant
Emmett JARRETT (1939): J.
Gill, Kherdian 1973,
Schreiber
Barbara JARVIK: Montgomery
Sarah JARVIS (c. 1946):
Giovanni
Mauel JAUREQUI (1937): Lowenfels 1973
Emmanuel JEAN-BAPTISTE:
Salkey
John JEFFERE: J. Gibson
(Book Two)
Lance JEFFERS (1919): Adoff
1973, Breman, G. Brooks
(Broadside Treasury),
Gross, Henderson, King,
Major, Shuman
Robinson JEFFERS (1887-1962):
Aloian, Bach, Bates, Baylor, R. Bender, Bly 1970,
C. Brooks, Carruth (Bantam), (McCall); Cole 1963,
1965, 1967 (Macmillan),
1972; Corbett, Cromie, De
Roche, Driver, Ellmann
1973, 1976; Engle, Gannett,
Gregory 1966, Harlan,
Hurtik, Jackson, Kallich,
Kennedy 1973, Larson,
Morrison, Parker 1967,
Peck 1970, 1971; Perrine,
Rothenberg 1973, Sanders,
Schneider, Shapiro, A. J.

M. Smith 1967, Steuben,
H. Taylor, Thomas, Trapp,
Univ. Press of Va., Untermeyer 1965, Wagner, Wallace, Whicher, O. Williams
1966 (World)
Robert JEFFREY: Booker
Henry A. JEFFRIES: Jackson
Roderick (Hartigh) JELLEMA
(1927): Mollenkott, Murphy, Owen 1974
L. M. JENDRZEJCZYK:
Lowenfels 1975
Carol JENIFER: Black History
Brooks JENKINS: Dunning,
Peck 1970
Ellen JENKINS: Adoff 1971
Frank S. JENKINS: Dee
Louis JENKINS (1942): Stryk
1975
Elizabeth JENNINGS (1926):
Brinnin 1963, Cole 1971,
Crang, Driver, Engle,
Greaves, Hall 1962 (World),
Kennedy 1974, Rosenthal
1967, 1968; Stallworthy,
Stanford, Wallace
Kate JENNINGS: M. Gibson
Kevin JENNINGS: Booker
Leslie Nelson JENNINGS:
Derleth
Judson JEROME (1927):
Dunning, Larrick, Owen
1969, Plumley, Stevenson,
M. Williams
Foster JEWEL (1893): Van
den Heuvel
Bessie (Bess) JIGGETTS
(1933): Giovanni
Polly JOAN: Bulkin
Ted JOANS (1928): Adoff
1970, 1973, 1974; Bell,
Bontemps 1963, 1974;
Breman, G. Brooks
(Broadside Treasury),
Hayden, Henderson,
Holmes, Hughes 1964,
1970; Lomax, McCullough,
Patterson, D. Randall
1969, E. Wilentz
Amini JOHARI (1935): G.
Brooks (Jump Bad)
Frank JOHN (1941): Breman,

Salkey

Richard Johnny JOHN (1914):
Rothenberg

Alicia (L.) (Loy) JOHNSON
(1944): Adoff 1970, G.
Brooks (Broadside Treasury),
P. Brown, Coombs, Giovanni,
Gross, Major, Shuman

B. S. JOHNSON: Cole 1967,
Crang

Bergt Emil JOHNSON: E.
Williams

Bradlon JOHNSON: Booker

Bruce (C.) JOHNSON: Harlan,
Head

C. G. JOHNSON: Sherman

Charles JOHNSON (1937): Tisdale

Charles JOHNSON (1949):
Coombs

Christine C. JOHNSON (1916):
D. Randall 1969

Dennis (Denis) JOHNSON (1949):
Harris 1976, Hewitt

Don JOHNSON (1952): H. Taylor

Don Allen JOHNSON (1942):
Hughes 1964, 1970

Donald Farnham JOHNSON:
Gallery 1973

Fred JOHNSON (1940): Adoff
1973

Gary JOHNSON: Kherdian 1970

Gayle JOHNSON: J. A. Allen

Geoffrey JOHNSON: Derleth,
Lask

Georgia Douglas JOHNSON (1886-
1966): Adoff 1973, Bontemps
1963, 1974; Lomax, Patterson, Turner

Halvard JOHNSON: Bonazzi 1972,
Gross

Helen Armstead JOHNSON (1920):
Bontemps 1974

Helene JOHNSON (1907): Adoff
1973, Bontemps 1963, Pat-
terson

Henry J. B. JOHNSON (Tombora):
King Pub.

Hershell (Herschell) JOHNSON:
Booker, Coombs, Patterson

Honor JOHNSON: Efros

Joe JOHNSON (1940): Adoff 1973,
Gross, Lowenfels 1966, 1969
(Random House)

Josephine W. JOHNSON (1910):
Trapp, O. Williams 1966
(World)

Julie JOHNSON: Morticella

Kay JOHNSON: Lowenfels 1966

Lemuel JOHNSON: Rigsbee

Loring JOHNSON: Rigsbee

M. M. JOHNSON: Knowles

Margie JOHNSON: Fox

Mark JOHNSON: Gildner

Meg Sims JOHNSON: Brindle

Ronald JOHNSON (1935): Carroll (Young American Po-
ets), Carruth (Bantam),
Klonsky, Lucie-Smith,
Solt, E. Williams, Young

W. H. JOHNSON: Jackson

William "Butch" JOHNSON:
Black History

Yvette JOHNSON (c. 1943):
Murphy

Percy (Edward) JOHNSTON
(1930): Henderson, Lowen-
fels 1969 (Random House)

JOHNTHOMASON: Krech

George JONAS (1956): J. Gill

Stephen (Steve) JONAS (1927-
1970): Leyland 1975,
Rothenberg 1973

Ernst JONDL: Lorrimer

Alice H. JONES: Breman,
Coombs, Patterson

David JONES (1895): Ellmann
1973, Gross, Matthias

Donald L. JONES: Glikes

Elwood S. JONES: Jackson

Evan JONES (1931): T. Moore,
Salkey

Gayl JONES (1949): Jordan,
Lowenfels 1975

Gerald JONES: Cole 1971

Howard JONES (1941): Major

James Arlington JONES (1936):
Shuman

Jeanetta L. JONES (1947):
Harvey

Lawrence M. JONES: J. A.
Vincent

LeRoi (Le Roi) JONES (Imamu
Amiri Baraka) (1934):
Adoff 1968, 1970, 1973,
1974; D. M. Allen 1960,
1964; Bach, Baraka,
Barnes, Baylor, Bell,

Bold, Bontemps 1963, Brady, Breman, G. Brooks (Broadside Treasury), Carruth (Bantam), Colley, De Roche, Di Prima, Ellmann 1973, 1976; Gersmehl, Harlan, Hayden, Henderson, Hughes 1964, Hurtik, Jacobus, Jordan, Kennedy 1974, Kherdian 1973, King 1972, Leary, Lomax, Lowenfels 1966, 1969 (Doubleday); McCullough, Major, L. Moore, Peck 1970, J. Perry, Pool, Poulin, D. Randall 1960, 1969; Rosenthal 1967, 1968; Rothenberg 1973, Strand, Turner, Untermeyer 1973 (McKay), Wagner, E. Wilentz, Witt-Diamant

Pamela JONES: Booker

Patsy JONES: Pilon

Paulette JONES (1946): P. Brown, Giovanni

Robert L. JONES: Kherdian 1970

Rodney JONES: Hoffman

T. H. JONES (1921): Firmage

T. James JONES (1934): Firmage

Valeria Lorraine JONES: Summerfield

Winslow David JONES: Kiley

K. B. JONES-QUARTEY: Hughes 1963

Erica JONG (1942): Chester, Evans, E. Gill, Konek, Phillips, Segnitz, H. Taylor, Untermeyer 1973 (McKay)

A. C. JORDAN: Hughes 1963

June JORDAN (1936): Adoff 1973, Chester, Giovanni, Howe, Konek, Lowenfels 1975, Patterson

Norman JORDAN (1938): Adoff 1970, 1974; Breman, Dee, Hughes 1970, King 1972, Kramer, Don L. Lee 1971, Major

Beth Baruch JOSELOW: Balazs

M. K. JOSEPH: Peck 1971

Raymond A. JOSEPH: P. Brown

Rosemary JOSEPH: Lask

Ira JOYCE: Jackson

Mwanafunzi JUBA: Jihad

Adoniram JUDSON: Kauffman

Janice JUDSON: Banker

John JUDSON (1930): Gallery 1970, 1973; Gildner, Stryk 1975

Hans JUERGENSEN (Juergenson): Banker, Lowenfels 1967, 1975; Plumley

Suzanne JUHASZ: Balazs, Konek

Orvy JUNDIS: Clay

Donald JUNKINS (1931): Felver, Hausman

Donald JUSTICE (1925): Adams, Aiken, J. A. Allen, Baylor, Brady, Brinnin 1970, Brooks 1960, Carruth (Bantam), Cole 1971, De Roche, Dunning, Engle, Gildner, Hall 1962 (World), (Penguin); Hannum, Hitchcock, Holmes, Howard, Howard and Victor, Immaculate, Jacobus, Kennedy 1974, Kenseth, Larrick, Lowenfels 1967, 1969 (Doubleday); McGinley, Monaco 1974, Owen 1974, Pearson, Peck 1971, Stallworthy, Strand, H. Taylor, Wesleyan Univ., M. Williams

K

KK: Banker

Jim KAADY: Morticella

Jessie KACHMAR: Gallery 1970

Hannah KAHN: Holmes, Konek

Sy KAHN: Dunning

Regina KAHNEY: Brindle

Gylan KAIN: King 1972

KAJA: Blazek, Vbrovska 1963

KALI see Kali GROSVENOR

Chester KALLMAN (1921-1975): J. A. Allen, Pearson

Rodger KAMENETZ: Rigsbee

Hiro KAMIMURA: E. Williams

Charles KAMP: Hadassah

Jerry KAMSTRA: Ferlinghetti
Henry KANABUS: Friedman
Leonore (Lenore) KANDEL
(Kandell): Arts Festival
1964, Chester, Dunning,
Howe, Lowenfels 1969
(Doubleday), (Random
House); Montgomery
Julie KANE: Balazs
Allen KANFER: Stevenson
Leroy KANTERMAN (1923):
Van den Heuvel
Paul KANTNER: Morse
Allan KAPLAN: H. Jones,
McCullough
Bernard KAPLAN: Gildner
Gloria KAPLAN: Harris 1973
Jonathan KAPLAN (1949):
Gersmehl, Lowenfels 1967
Norman KAPLAN: Adoff 1971
Allan KAPROW: Gross
Joseph (E.) KARIUKI (1931):
Greaves, Lomax, Patterson
Alice KARLE: Rexroth
KARONIAKTATIE: Lourie
Walta KARSNER: Cole 1967
(Macmillan), 1972
Leo KARTMAN: Hadassah
James KATES: Mazur
Kitasono KATUE: Wildman,
E. Williams
Jane KATZ: Rigsbee
Menke KATZ: Lask
Milton KATZ: Bonazzi 1974
Vincent KATZ: Fagin
Al KATZMAN: Montgomery
Allen KATZMAN (1937): Banker,
De Loach 1968, 1976; Harris
1970, 1973; Lowenfels 1967,
1969 (Random House)
Don (Donald) KATZMAN (1937):
Banker, Katzman
Reginald Wright KAUFFMAN:
Jackson
Bob KAUFMAN (1925): Adoff
1969, 1970, 1973; Bell,
Breman, Brinnin 1970,
Carruth (Bantam), Chace,
Dee, Gross, Harvey,
Hayden, Henderson, Hughes
1970, Jacobus, Jordan,
Kherdian 1973, Lomax,
Lowenfels 1969 (Doubleday),

(Random House); Major,
Wagner, Winans
Shirley KAUFMAN (1923):
Chester, Harlan, Hewitt,
Hitchcock, Howe, Stanford,
Stevenson
Walter KAUFMANN: Glikes
Patrick KAVANAGH (1904-
1967): Cole 1967, 1971;
Ellmann 1973, Engle,
Plotz, Rosenthal 1967,
1968; Sanders, Untermeyer
1964
Ellen KAY (1931): Arp
Molly KAZAN: Peck 1970
Ellsworth McG. KEANE (1927):
Breman
Lawrence KEARNEY: Weishaus
Martha KEARNS: Gitlin
Eleanor KEATS: Balazs
John KEBLE: Kauffman
Stephen KEELY: Bonazzi 1974
Terrance KEENAN: Rigsbee
Ruth Douglas KEENER: Lask
William KEENS: Hoffman
Nancy KEESING (1923): T.
Moore
Bernard KEITH: Hope
Joseph Joel KEITH: Derleth,
Weil
George KEITHLEY (1935):
Felver, Gildner
Richard KELL: Cole 1967
(Macmillan)
John KELLEHER: Cole 1967
(Macmillan)
David KELLER: Harris 1976
Leonard KELLER (1927):
Winans
Martha KELLER: Brewton
Paul KELLER: Harlan
Walter R. KELLER: Bogin
Fleurette V. O. KELLEY:
Brindle
Reeve Spencer KELLEY:
Brewton
Bernard KELLY: Lowenfels
1975
Dave KELLY: Gildner
Richard KELLY: Vrbovska
1963
Robert KELLY (1935): Carroll
(Young American Poets),

Carruth (Bantam), De Loach 1968, 1976; Gross, H. Jones, Leary, Lowenfels 1967, Oppenheimer 1967, Phillips, Rothenberg 1973
Thomas KELLY: Kauffman
Walt KELLY (1913): Bogan
Jimmy KELSO: Harlan
Arnold KEMP: Coombs
Doris KEMP (c. 1952): Giovanni
Lysander KEMP: Lask
Delores KENDRICK: P. Brown
Millea KENIN: Lowenfels 1969 (Doubleday)
Dick KENNEDY (1932): Durand
Gerta KENNEDY: Lask
Leo KENNEDY (1907): A. J. M. Smith 1960
Mary KENNEDY: Cole 1963, 1965, 1971; Derleth
Sarah KENNEDY (c. 1960): Winans
Tom KENNEDY (1951): Leyland 1977
X. J. KENNEDY (1929): Adams, Baylor, E. Bender, R. Bender, Bogan, Brady, Brinnin 1970, Camp, Cole 1967 (Macmillan), 1971, 1972; De Roche, Engle, Gildner, Glikes, Gwynn, Hall 1962 (World), (Penguin); Harris 1973, Holmes, Hope, Immaculate, Jacobus, Lask, Leary, Livingston, McGinley, McGovern, Owen 1969, J. Perry, Phillips, Plumley, Strand, H. Taylor, Wagner, Wallace, M. Williams
Brendan KENNELLY (1936): Untermeyer 1964
Peggy KENNER (1937): G. Brooks (Jump Bad)
Dan KENNEY: Harvey
Jo KENNEY: Gersmehl
Maurice KENNY (1929): Leyland 1977, Lowenfels 1973
Louis KENT: Cole 1963
Rolly KENT: Rigsbee
Jean KENWARD (1920): Knowles
Judith KERMAN: De Loach 1976

Jack KEROUAC (1922-1969): Durand, Ferlinghetti, Hannum, Kherdian 1973, Rothenberg 1973, E. Wilentz
Walter H. KERR: Derleth
Anthony KERRIGAN: Lask
Edward KESSLER (1927): H. Taylor
Jascha (Frederick) KESSLER (1929): Kessler, Lask
Milton KESSLER (1930): Lask, M. Williams
Stephen KESSLER: Lowenfels 1975
Arthur KETCHUM: Parker 1967
David KEVORKIAN: McGovern
John KEYS: Katzman, Montgomery
Gustave KEYSER: Dunning
Blanche Whiting KEYSNER: Plumley
(W.) Keorapetse (William) (K. William) KGOSITSILE (1938): Adoff 1973, Bell, Breman, G. Brooks (Broadside Treasury), P. Brown, Henderson, H. Jones, Kgositsile, King 1972, D. Randall 1969
KHAJUKA see Don A. MIZELL
Chiron KHANSHENDEL (Bronwen E. Rose) (1948): Lowenfels 1973
David KHERDIAN (1931): Hausman, Kherdian 1970, 1973, 1974; McMahon
Vladislav KHODASEVICH: Aloian
KICHEKO: Jihad
Faye KICKNOSWAY (1936): Howe, Konek
Phil KIENHOLZ: Blazek
John KIERNAN: Morrison
Stanley KIESEL (1925): Stryk 1975
David KILBURN: Lucie-Smith
Frederick KILEY: Kiley
Crystal KILGORE: Hannum
James (C.) KILGORE (1928): Ashland, Kennedy 1974, McGovern

Carl KILLIBREW: G. Brooks
(Broadside Treasury)
Thalia KILRILAKIS: Efros
Willyce KIM: Bulkin
George KIMBALL: Waldman
1969
Harriet McEwn KIMBALL:
Kauffman
Larry Lindsay KIMURA (1946):
Lowenfels 1973
B. B. KING (1925): Kennedy
1973
Helen H. KING: P. Brown
Herman Stowell KING: Derleth
Julia Rankin KING (1939): Van
den Heuvel
Linda KING: Bukowski, Fer-
linghetti
Martha KING: De Loach 1976
Martin Luther KING, Jr. (1929-
1968): Lomax
Stoddard KING: Brewton
Charles KINGSLEY: J. Gibson
R. P. KINGSTON (1941): Evans
Eugene F. KINKEAD (1906):
Cole 1963
Galway KINNELL (1927): Adoff
1969, Aiken, Berg, Bogan,
Brinnin 1963, 1970; Carruth
(Bantam), (McCall); Cole
1967 (Macmillan), 1972; De
Roche, Driver, Ellmann
1976, Engle, Hall 1962
(Penguin), (World); Hannum,
Hannum and Chase, Harlan,
Harris 1973, Howard,
Howard and Victor, Kennedy
1973, 1974; Kenseth, Lar-
rick, Leary, Lowenfels 1967,
McCullough, Monaco 1974,
Peck 1970, 1971; Phillips,
Poulin, Rosenthal 1967,
1968; Rothenberg 1973,
Strand, Untermeyer 1973
(McKay), Wagner, Wallace,
M. Williams
Scott KINNEY: Crafts
J. Morley KINPORTS (1924):
Immaculate
Thomas KINSELLA (1928):
Adams, J. A. Allen,
Bedient, Brinnin 1970,
Cole 1967 (Macmillan), Ell-

mann 1973, Engle, Rosen-
thal 1967, 1968; Sanders,
Untermeyer 1964
David KIRBY: Rigsbee
Bertha KIRKENDALL: Gildner
James KIRKUP (1923): Aloian,
Knowles, Lask, Leyland
1977, Wallace, Young
Lincoln KIRSTEIN (1907): Ell-
mann 1973
Ed KISSAM: Sherman, Wald-
man 1971
Joseph KITT (Jamal Ali Bey
Hassan) (1940): Tisdale
Walter KITTREDGE: J. A.
Vincent
Philip G. KIVETT: Kiley
Erik KIVIAT: Malley, Mont-
gomery
Carolyn KIZER (1925): Adams,
Carruth (Bantam), Chester,
Hall 1962 (World), Harlan,
Howard, Howard and Vic-
tor, Howe, Kennedy 1973,
Konek, Rosenthal 1967,
Segnitz, Skelton, Stanford,
Strand, Ten
Rudolph KIZERMAN: Salkey
Peter KLAPPERT: Gildner,
Rigsbee
Edgar KLAUBER: Cole 1971
David KLEIMAN: Pilon
A. M. KLEIN (1909): Joseloff,
A. J. M. Smith 1960
Binnie KLEIN: Rigsbee
August KLEINZABLER: Sollid
1972, K. and J. Sollid
Irena KLEPFISZ: Bulkin
Mimi KLIMESH: Harlan
John KLIMO: Oppenheimer
1977
George KLINGLE: Jackson
Birgit KNABE: Gay
Julian KNASTER: Rottmann
Karl-Heinz KNAUFF: Sargent
Stillman F. KNEELAND: Jack-
son
Eliz KNIES: James
David KNIGHT: Stevenson
Dawn KNIGHT: Rosenblum
Denis KNIGHT (1921): Kramer,
Lowenfels 1967
Etheridge KNIGHT (1933):

Adoff 1969, 1970, 1973; Bell,
Breman, G. Brooks (Broad-
side Treasury), P. Brown,
Colley, Ellmann 1973,
Gersmehl, J. Gill, Gross,
Henderson, Jacobus, Don L.
Lee, Major, A. Miller, D.
Randall 1960, 1969; Turner
Holly KNIGHT: Brindle
James T. KNIGHT III: Kiley
Max KNIGHT: Cole 1967 (Mac-
millan)
Wallace E. KNIGHT: Plumley
John KNOEPFLE (1923):
Bonazzi 1972, Colley, Gildner,
Kennedy 1973, Stryk 1967
Zig KNOLL (1940): Durand
Bill (William Kilborn) KNOTT
(Saint Geraud) (1940): Bly
1966, 1975; Carroll (Young
American Poets), Gross,
Harris 1973, Kennedy 1973,
1974; Lowenfels 1967,
McCullough, H. Taylor
Alden A. KNOWLAN: Cole 1967
(Macmillan)
Alison KNOWLES: Gross
Frederic Lawrence KNOWLES:
Kauffman
Susanne KNOWLES (1911):
Knowles
Helena KNOX: Head
Hugh KNOX: Fox
Chris KOBAYASHI: Clay
Christopher KOCH (1932): T.
Moore
Kenneth KOCH (1925): D. M.
Allen 1960, Baylor, Brady,
Carruth (Bantam), Chace,
Ellmann 1973, Harlan, Har-
ris 1973, Hollander, Ken-
nedy 1974, Kessler,
Kherdian 1973, Lucie-Smith,
McCullough, Myers, Padgett,
Poulin, Strand, Waldman
1971, Wallace, E. Wilentz
(G.) Stanley KOEHLER: Glikes,
Univ. of Mass.
Laurie KOEL: Kohl
James KOENIG: Gallery 1973
Ronald (Ron) (B.) KOERTGE
(1940): Bukowski, Fox,
Haas, Peck 1971, Rigsbee,
Simmons, Winans

Richard I. KOETEEUW: Kiley
John KOETHKE: Waldman 1971
Harrison KOHLER: Rottmann
Joel KOHUT (1940): Gross,
Lowenfels 1969 (Random
House)
Jiri KOLAR: E. Williams
Alice KOLB: Oppenheimer
1977
Kathy KOLEDIN: Kohl
James KOLLER (1936): Har-
lan, Palmer, Rothenberg
1973, Waldman 1971
Ellis Ayitey KOMEY (1927):
Breman, Hughes 1963
Tadashi KONDO: Oppenheimer
1977
Carol KONEK: Konek
Elizabeth A. KONOPACKY
(1947): Lowenfels 1973
Vera Bishop KONRICK: Der-
leth
Ted KOOSER (1939): Gildner,
Harris 1976, Stryk 1975
Dennis KORAN: Head
Naoshi KORIYAMA: Dunning
Allan KORNBLUM: Fox, Sklar
Cinda KORNBLUM: Sklar
Vadim KOROSTYLEV: Cole
1963
Mary Norbert KORTE (1934):
Harvey, Konek, Malley,
Schreiber, Winans
Miriam KOSHLAND (1914):
Greaves, Patterson
Jocelyn KOSLOFSKY: Ferling-
hetti
Peter KOSTAKIS: Friedman
Richard KOSTELANETZ (1940):
Carroll (Young American
Poets), Harlan, Harris
1973, Klonsky, Kostelan-
etz, Monaco 1973
Hollis KOSTER: Scheftel
Leonore KOUWENHOVEN (c.
1955): Pygmalion
Diva Goodfriend KOVEN:
Booker
Jonas KOVER: Montgomery
Ana KOWALKOWSKY: Bulkin
John J. KOWALSKI: Kiley
Steve KOWIT: Lowenfels 1975
Peter L. KOZIK: Harris
1976

Aaron KRAMER (1921): Banker,
Kramer, Lask
Arthur (Axiphilis) KRAMER:
Jackson
Lawrence KRAMER: Gildner
Ida KRANGEL: Sargent
Norbert KRAPF (1943): Stryk
1975
Barbara KRASNOFF: Adoff
1971
L. N. KRAUSE: Gallery 1973
Ruth KRAUSS: Hausman,
McCullough, Waldman 1969,
1971
Richard (Rich) KRECH (1946):
Blazek, Fox, Gitlin, Krech,
Sherman
Alfred KREYMBORG (1883-1966):
Aiken, Cole 1963, 1965,
1967, 1972; Jackson,
Kramer, Lowenfels 1969
(Doubleday), J. A. Vincent
Seymour KRIM: E. Wilentz
Ann KRISCHON: Gallery 1973
Ferdinand KRIWET (1942):
Gross, Klonsky, E. Wil-
liams
Herbert KROHN: Rigsbee,
Rottmann
Silvia KROHN: Fox
Ernest KROLL (1914): Cole
1963, Gildner, Harris 1976,
Lask
Judith KROLL (1943): Gersmehl
Diane KRUCHKOW: Fox,
McMahon
T. L. KRYSS (1948): Blazek,
Fox, Gitlin, Gross, P.
Perry
Tom KRYSS: J. Gill
Geraldine KUDAKA: Clay
Frank KUENSTLER (1928):
Gross, Rothenberg 1973
King D. KUKA (1946): T.
Allen, Dodge, Rosen
Maxine (W.) KUMIN (1925):
Chester, Dunning, Evans,
Howe, Kennedy 1973,
Konek, Larrick, L.
Moore, Morrison, Phillips,
Stanford, Stevenson,
Vrbovska, M. Williams
Jonathan KUNDRA: Waldman
1969, 1971

Mazisi KUNENE (1930): Bre-
man, Kgositsile
Stanley KUNITZ (1905): Aiken,
J. A. Allen, Brinnin 1963,
1970; Carruth (Bantam),
Cole 1963, 1967 (Macmil-
lan), Ellmann 1973, Engle,
Howard, Howard and Vic-
tor, Joseloff, Kennedy
1973, Kenseth, Kostelanetz,
Lowenfels 1967, Monaco
1974, Phillips, Plotz,
Rosenthal 1967, Stallworthy,
Trapp, Untermeyer 1964,
1973 (McKay); Wesleyan U.,
Winkler, Witt-Diamant
Tuli KUPFERBERG (1923): De
Loach 1968, Gitlin, Lowen-
fels 1969 (Doubleday), (Ran-
dom House); Montgomery,
E. Wilentz
Zdzislaw KURLOWICZ (c.
1953): Young
Aaron KURTZ (1891-1964):
Kenseth, Lowenfels 1966
Markus KUTTER: Gross
Greg KUZMA (1944): Evans,
Fox, Hoffman, Kennedy
1973, 1974; Stryk
Stephen KWARTLER (1950):
Jordan
Ken KWINT: Shore
G. H. KWOCK (1920): Harvey
Kojo Gyinaye KYEI: Hopkins
(Knopf), Hughes 1963
Joanne KYGER (1934): D. M.
Allen 1964, Arts Festival
1964, Chester, Gross,
Harvey, Waldman 1969,
1971, Weishaus
Cho Sung KYUN: Cromie

L

Joan LaBOMBARD: Stevenson
E. A. LACEY: Leyland 1975,
1977; Young
Sid LA CHOLTER: Jackson
John LACHS: Colley
Earl E. LaCLAIR: Kiley
Muriel LADENBURG: Wesley-
an Univ.
Peter LA FARGE (1931-1965):

Kennedy 1973, Kramer, Lowenfels 1966, 1969 (Doubleday), (Random)
Melvin Walker LA FOLLETTE (1930): Hall 1962 (World), Lask, Leary, Vrbovska 1963
Knollys LA FORTUNE: Salkey
Oliver LA GRONE (Lagrone) (1915): Hughes 1964, 1970; King, D. Randall 1969
Frederick E. LAIGHT (1915): A. J. M. Smith 1960
Dilys LAING (1906-1960): Cole 1963, 1967 (Macmillan), 1972; Lask, Lowenfels 1969 (Doubleday), Rosenthal 1967
R. D. LAING (1927): Phillips
Amrit LAL: Hadassah
Lee LALLY: Violet
Michael LALLY (1942): Gitlin, Leyland 1975
Aquash LALUSH: Hughes 1963
Philip LAMANTIA (1927): D. M. Allen 1960, Carruth (Bantam), Ferlinghetti, Harlan, Kostelanetz, Rothenberg 1973, Vrbovska 1963, E. Wilentz, Winkler
Hazel Washington LA MARRE: Hughes 1970
Elizabeth Searle LAMB (1917): Van den Heuvel
Elizabeth LAMBERT (1925): Firmage
Barbara LA MORTICELLA: Morticella
Keith LAMPE (1931): Weishaus
Archibald LAMPMAN: Morrison
Louis LANDE: Jackson
Elizabeth LANDEWEER: Brewton
Hollis T. LANDRUM: Kiley
Carmella LANE: Bonazzi 1974
Patrick LANE: J. Gill
Pinkie Gordon LANE: P. Brown
William LANE: Harris 1973
Andrew LANG: Morrison
Deborah Paulin LANG: Brindle
V. R. LANG (1924): O. Williams 1966 (World)
Art LANGE: Friedman
Joseph (Thomas) LANGLAND (1917): Baylor, Brinnin

1963, Engle, Gildner, Hannum, Hannum and Chase, Jacobus, Kenseth, Stryk 1967, Vrbovska 1963, Wagner, Witt-Diamant
Eve LANGLEY (1908): T. Moore, Stanford
George LANGSTON: Crafts
Daniel (J.) LANGTON: Harvey, Hitchcock
Alicia LANGTREE: Violet
Frances Stoakley LANKFORD: Kauffman
LANNERS, X. L.: Winans
Gerrit LANSING (1928): H. Jones, Leary, Leyland 1975, Rothenberg 1973
Roberta Hickson LANTZ: Brindle
Fred LAPE (1900): Cole 1963, 1972
Carol Ann LAPEYROUSE: Brindle
Jaqueline LAPIDUS: Bulkin, Konek
Sharon Lee LAPLANTE: Brindle
Joan LARKIN: Bulkin
Philip LARKIN (1922): Adams, J. A. Allen, Arp, Baylor, Bedient, R. Bender, Brady, Brinnin 1963, 1970; C. Brooks, Cole 1967 (Macmillan), 1971, 1972; Crang, De Roche, Driver, Ellmann 1973, Engle, Greaves, Hall 1962 (World), Hannum and Chase, Hieatt, Hurtik, Kennedy 1973, 1974; Monaco 1974, L. Moore, Morrison, Peck 1970, 1971; Rosenthal 1967, 1968; Sanders, Schneider, Stallworthy, W. Taylor, Untermeyer 1964, Walsh
W. Livingston LARNED: Jackson
Beryle LA ROSE: Clay
John LA ROSE (1927): Breman, Salkey
Peter LAROUCHE: Blazek
Carl LARSEN (1935): Baylor,

Kenseth, Lowenfels 1966,
1969 (Random House)
Clinton F. LARSON (1919):
Larson
M. LA RUE (1944): Cole 1967
(Viking)
Martin LAST: E. Wilentz
Clara LASTER: Gallery 1973
Bette Darcie LATIMER (1927):
Adoff 1973, Hughes 1970
Richard LATTA: Gallery 1973
Ruth LATTA: Sargent
William LATTA: Stevenson
Jewel (C.) LATTIMORE (Johari
Amini): Adoff 1973, P.
Brown, Coombs, Giovanni,
Henderson, King 1972,
Malley, Patterson
Richard LATTIMORE (1906):
Aiken, Bates, Carruth
(Bantam), Engle, Hannum,
Harris 1976, Wallace
James LAUGHLIN (1914):
Carruth (Bantam), Durand,
Rothenberg 1973, Wanger
Joseph LAUREN: Parker 1960
Ross LAURSEN (1929): Winans
Robert LA VIGNE: De Loach
1976
Margaret M. LAVIN: Vrbovska
1963
Douglas LAWDER: Salisbury
Gary LAWLESS: McMahon
Van Ness LAWLESS: Jackson
Lynn LAWNER: Konek
Joyce Whitsitt LAWRENCE
see Joyce WHITSITT
William V. LAWRENCE: Jack-
son
David LAWSON: Carruth (Ban-
tam), Colley
Henry LAWSON: Rose
Paul LAWSON (1915): H. Tay-
lor
Sylvia LAWSON (1932): T.
Moore
Todd S. J. LAWSON: Winans
Robert LAX (1915): Gross,
Palmer, Schreiber, Solt
Irving LAYTON (1912): Cole
1963, Engle, J. Gill,
Kennedy 1973, 1974;
Morrison, Rosenthal 1967,
A. J. M. Smith 1960

Paul LAYTON: Adoff 1971
Robert LAYZER: Vrbovska
1963
Steven LAZAR (1948): Weis-
haus
Naomi LAZARD: Rigsbee
A. L. LAZARUS: Hunting,
Purdue
Tsantah LAZKY: Sherman
B. C. LEALE (1930): Knowles
Lonnie LEARD: Harlan, Head
Paris LEARY (1931): Harris
1976, Leary, Wheelock
1960, Witt-Diamant
John LEAX (1943): Mollenkott,
Peck 1971
Ruth LECHLITNER (1901):
Brewton, Dunning, Lask,
Lucie-Smith, Peck 1970
J. T. LEDBETTER: Monaco
1973
Al LEE (1938): Baylor, Strand
Bert LEE: Lowenfels 1969
(Doubleday)
Corrie L. LEE (Akili Sekou
Moyo): King Pub.
Don (L.) LEE (1942): Adoff
1969, 1970, 1973, 1974;
Baylor, Bell, Breman, G.
Brooks (Broadside Treas-
ury), (Jump Bad); P.
Brown, Chace, Colley,
Coombs, Ellmann 1973,
Gersmehl, J. Gill, Gross,
Henderson, Hopkins
(Knopf), Jacobus, Jordan,
King 1972, Major, Patter-
son, D. Randall 1960,
Turner, Wagner, Walsh
Jo Anne LEE: Mallory
Kenneth LEE: Clay
Laurie LEE (1914): Cole 1971,
Crang, J. Gibson (Book
Two), Greaves, Jacobus,
Stallworthy, Walsh
Lawrence LEE (1903): Univ.
Press of Va.
Mildred B. LEE: Jackson
Robert LEE: Student
Roger B. LEE: Booker
Michael LEECH: Lask
Jacob LEED (1924): Felver
Barbara F. LEFCOWITZ:
Harris 1976

Merrill LEFFLER: Harris 1976
Richard LE GALLIENNE:
Parker 1967
Philip LEGLER (1928): Lask,
Lowenfels 1973, H. Taylor
Suzanne LEGRON: Plumley
Brad LEHMAN: P. Perry
David LEHMAN: Rigsbee
Geoffrey LEHMANN (1940):
Cromie, Lask, T. Moore
John LEHMANN (1907): Brinnin
1963, Young
Jo Ann LEICHLITER: Lask
Jay LEIFER (1954): Kennedy
1973
Esther M. LEIPER: Gallery
1973
Donovan LEITCH: Morse
Sharon LEITER: Rigsbee
June LEIVAS (1950): Lowen-
fels 1973
J. R. LeMASTER: Ashland
Nancy LENAU: Gallery 1970
Andrew LENIHAN:. Booker
Florence Becker LENNON
(1895): Hughes 1970
John LENNON (1940): Crafts,
Holmes, Kennedy 1974,
Morse, J. Perry
George LEONG: Clay
Estelle LEONTIEF: Mazur
Douglas LE PAN: A. J. M.
Smith 1960
Ruth LEPSON: Reading
Eleanor LERMAN: Bulkin
Arthur LERNER: Simmons
Laurence LERNER (1925):
Baylor, Crang, Hall 1962
(World)
Cy LESLIE (1921): Major
Kenneth LESLIE (1892): A. J.
M. Smith 1960, Trapp
Julius LESTER (1939): Adoff
1973, Breman, Colley,
Hayden, Jordan, Lowenfels
1969 (Doubleday), (Random
House)
Joseph LE SUEUR: Waldman
1971, E. Wilentz
Meridel LE SUEUR (1900):
Lowenfels 1973
Reinhard LETTAU: Ferling-
hetti

W. (Winifred) M. LETTS
(1882): Cole 1963
Francis E. LEUPP: Jackson
Lowell LEVANT: Krech,
Palmer
Christopher LEVENSON: Cole
1971, Stevenson
Robert LEVERANT (1939):
Harvey
Ernest LEVERETT: Cole 1972
Don (Donald) LEVERING:
Gallery 1973, Morticella
Denise LEVERTOV (1923):
Adams, Adoff 1969, D. M.
Allen 1960, 1964; G. W.
Allen 1965, J. A. Allen,
Banker, Bates, Barnes,
Baylor, Berg, Brady,
Brinnin 1970, Carruth
(Bantam), (McCall); Chace,
Chester, Cole 1963,
Colley, Cromie, De Roche,
Ellmann 1973, 1976; Engle,
Gwynn, Hall 1962 (Penguin),
(World); Hannum, Hannum
and Chase, Harlan, Har-
ris 1973, Howard, Howard
and Victor, Howe, Jacobus,
Joseloff, Kennedy 1973,
1974; Kenseth, Kherdian
1973, Konek, Kramer,
Larrick, Leary, Lowenfels
1966, 1967, 1969 (Double-
day); McCullough, McGov-
ern, Monaco 1974, L.
Moore, Peck 1970, J.
Perry, Phillips, Plimpton,
Poulin, Rosenthal 1967,
1968; Rothenberg 1973,
Segnitz, Simpson, Stanford,
Steuben, Stevenson, Strand,
Summerfield, H. Taylor,
W. Taylor, Untermeyer
1964, 1970; Wagner, Wal-
lace, Walsh, M. Williams,
Witt-Diamant
Peter LEVI (1931): J. A.
Allen, Hall 1962 (World),
Knowles
Martin LEVINE: Adoff 1971
Miriam LEVINE: Mazur
Norman LEVINE (1924): A.
J. M. Smith 1960

Philip LEVINE (1928): Berg,
Brinnin 1970, Carruth
(Bantam), Ellmann 1973,
1976; Engle, Gitlin, Hall
1962 (World), Howard,
Howard and Victor, Ken-
nedy 1973, 1974; Kessler,
Kherdian, Larson,
McGovern, Monaco 1973,
1974; Pearson, Strand,
Winans
Stephen LEVINE (1937): Engle,
Gitlin
Nick LEVINSON: Booker
Larry LEVIS (1946): Evans,
Hoffman, Kherdian 1970
Peter LEVITT: De Loach
1976
Myron LEVOY: Glikes
Amy LEVY: Untermeyer 1970
D. A. LEVY (1942-1968):
Blazek, Fox, Gitlin, Lowen-
fels 1969 (Doubleday),
(Random House); P. Perry
Howard LEVY: Saturday Press
Newman LEVY (1888-1966):
Cole 1972
Emmanuel LEWIN: Jackson
Alun LEWIS: Cole 1967
(Macmillan)
Angelo LEWIS (1950): Adoff
1971, 1973
C. Day LEWIS see C. DAY
LEWIS
C. S. LEWIS (1898-1964):
Cole, Lucie-Smith
Franchon LEWIS: Efros
Harry LEWIS (1942): Lowen-
fels 1967
Janet LEWIS (1899): Cole 1971,
Stanford, Winters
Michael LEWIS: Untermeyer
1970
Steven LEWIS: Rosenblum
James (E.) LEWISOHN:
Vrbovska 1963, 1968
Landes LEWITIN: Hauge
Winston LEYLAND (1940):
Leyland 1975
John (Clarke) L'HEUREUX
(1934): Carroll (Young
American Poets), Cole
1971, Harlan

Sharon Mayer LIBERA: Konek
James LIDDY (1934): Young
Elias LIEBERMAN (1884-1969):
Jackson, J. A. Vincent,
Woods
Laurence LIEBERMAN (1935):
Leary, Stevenson, Strand,
Stryk 1975, M. Williams
Anne LIFSCHUTZ: Kramer
Lyn LIFSHIN: Chester, De
Loach 1976, E. Gill, J.
Gill, Konek, McMahon,
P. Perry, Segnitz
Gordon LIGHTFOOT: Wagner
R. W. LILLIARD: J. A.
Vincent
J. T. LILLIE: Cole 1963
Frank LIMA (1938): Hughes
1970, Myers, Padgett,
Waldman 1971
Robert LIMA (1935): Katzman
Abbey LINCOLN (Aminata
Moseka): Clay
Jack LINDEMAN (1924):
Lowenfels 1966, 1967,
1969 (Doubleday); Sherman,
Stevenson
Roger LINDLEY: J. Gibson
(Book Two)
J. A. LINDON (1914): Ken-
nedy 1974, J. Gibson, J.
Gibson (Book Two)
Forbes LINDSAY: Morrison
Jack LINDSAY (1900): Fir-
mage, T. Moore
Karen LINDSEY (1945):
Lowenfels 1967
Edith Willis LINN: Kauffman
Virginia LINTON: Lask
LINYATTA: G. Brooks (Jump
Bad)
Ed "Foots" LIPMAN (d. 1975):
Winans
S. John Mary LIPPERT:
Gallery 1970
Bruce LIPPINCOTT (1924):
Lowenfels 1969 (Random
House)
LIPSITZ: Harlan
Lou LIPSITZ (1938): Bonazzi
1972, Carroll (Young
American Poets), Carruth
(Bantam), Gitlin, Kennedy

1973, Pearson, Stevenson,
Summerfield
Lawrence LIPTON: Vrbovska
1963, 1968
Roy LISKER: Scheftel
R. P. LISTER (1914): Cole
1963, 1967 (Viking); Peck
1970
Jack LITEWKA: Harris 1976
Bill LITTLE: Banker, Freed
Deborah LITTLE: Black His-
tory
Harold LITTLEBIRD (1951):
Dodge, Rosen
Emanuel LITVINOFF (1915):
Firmage
A. J. LITWINIO: Hoffman
Dorothy LIVESAY (1909): A.
J. M. Smith 1960
Ethel LIVINGSTON (1947):
Schreiber
Gary LIVINGSTON: Monaco
1973
Myra Cohn LIVINGSTON (1926):
Larrick, Pilon
Taban Lo LIYONG: Jacobus
Linda LIZUT: Lowenfels 1975
Karl N. LLEWELLYN: Jackson
David LLORENS (1939): G.
Brooks (Broadside Treas-
ury), P. Brown, Murphy,
D. Randall 1969
A. L. LLOYD (1908): Stall-
worthy
David LLOYD (1930): Van den
Heuvel
Kenneth M. LLOYD: Kiley
L. Paul LLOYD (1949): Greaves
Amilcar LOBOS: Harvey
David A. LOCHER: Lask
Duane LOCKE: Fox, Gallery
1973, Lowenfels 1975,
Smith
Lawrence LOCKE: Hoffman
R. J. LOCKE: Jackson
Reginald LOCKETT: Clay
Tena LOCKETT (1945): Coombs
Timothy C. LOCKLEY: Kiley
Gerald LOCKLIN (1941):
Bukowski, Fox, Haas,
Simmons, Stevenson,
Winans
Margo LOCKWOOD: Mazur

Rachel LODEN: Efros
Michael S. LOEB: Jackson
Ron LOEWINSOHN (1937): D.
M. Allen 1960, J. A.
Allen, Arts Festival 1963,
Cole 1971, Kherdian 1973
Elouise LOFTIN (1950): Adoff
1973
C. A. LOFTON: Giovanni
John (Burton) LOGAN (1923):
Carroll (Poem in Its Skin),
Cole 1965, 1971; Crang,
Firmage, Gildner, Hall
1962 (Penguin), (World);
Harris 1973, Heyen, How-
ard, Howard and Victor,
Kessler, Kostelanetz,
Poulin, Rosenthal 1967,
Strand, Stryk 1967, M.
Williams
William LOGAN: Rigsbee
Christopher LOGUE (1926):
Bold, Lorrimer, Matthias,
Stallworthy
LOMAWYWESA (Michael
Kabotie): De Loach 1976
Bruce LOMAX: Black History
Pearl Cleage LOMAX (1948):
Adoff 1973, Patterson
Helen Pisarelli LOMBARDI:
Scheftel
Charles C. LONG: Dodge
Doc LONG (c. 1944): Murphy
Doughtry LONG (1942): Adoff
1973, 1974; G. Brooks
(Broadside Treasury),
Patterson, D. Randall
1960
Elizabeth-Ellen LONG: Brew-
ton
Frank Belknap LONG: Derleth
Worth LONG (1936): Lowen-
fels 1969 (Doubleday),
(Random House); Major
Samuel LONGFELLOW: Kauff-
man
Lynn LONIDIER: Fox
Michael LOPES: Harris 1976
Alonzo LOPEZ: T. Allen,
Dodge
Gabriel O. LOPEZ: Lowen-
fels 1973
Jorge LOPEZ: Algarin

Arrigo LORA-TOTINO: Wildman,
E. Williams
Audre LORDE (Lord) (1934):
Adoff 1973, Bell, Breman,
Bulkin, Colley, Henderson,
Howe, Hughes 1964, Jordan,
Major, T. Wilentz
Pare LORENTZ: Brewton
Lilith LORRAINE: Derleth,
Vrbovska 1963
Linda LORRAINE: Brindle
Katie LOUCHHEIM: Lask
David LOUGEE (1928): O. Wil-
liams 1966 (World)
Louise LOUIS: Vrbovska 1963
Dick (Richard) LOURIE (1937):
Anania, Banker, Colley,
J. Gill, Gitlin, Harris
1973, Lowenfels 1975,
Schreiber, Sherman
George LOVE: Adoff 1968,
Hughes 1964
Margo LOVE: Montgomery
Patricia LOW: Carruth (Bantam)
Robert LOWELL (1917-1977):
Adams, Adoff 1969, Aiken,
G. W. Allen, Aloian, Arp,
Bach, Bates, Baylor, Beer-
man, R. Bender, Berg,
Bly 1970, Brady, Brewton,
Brinnin 1963, 1970; C.
Brooks, Carruth (Bantam),
Chace, Chatman, De Roche,
Drew, Driver, Ellmann
1973, 1976; Engelberg,
Engle, Gregory 1966, Hall
1962 (Penguin), (Watts);
Hannum, Harlan, Harris
1976, Hieatt, Hine, Howard,
Howard and Victor, Hurtik,
Immaculate, Jacobus,
Kallich, Kennedy 1973,
1974; Kostelanetz, Leary,
Lowenfels 1967, McCullough,
McGovern, Mercatante,
Monaco 1974, Olson, Park-
er 1967, Perrine, J. Perry,
Poulin, Rosenthal 1967,
1968; Sanders, Schneider,
Shapiro, Simpson, A. J.
Smith 1967, Stallworthy,
Strand, H. Taylor, W.
Taylor, Untermeyer 1964,

1973 (McKay); Walsh,
Whicher, M. Williams, O.
Williams 1966 (World),
Witt-Diamant
Marilyn LOWEN (1944): Gitlin
Walter LOWENFELS (1897-1976):
Banker, De Loach 1968,
Gross, Harris 1973, Hughes
1970, Kenseth, Lowenfels
1966, 1967, 1969 (Double-
day), (Random House),
1975; Montgomery, Rothen-
berg 1973, 1974; Sherman,
Vrbovska 1968
Syl LOWHAR: Salkey
Charlene LOWRY: Morticella
Malcolm LOWRY: Lask
Pat LOWTHER: E. Gill,
Lowenfels 1975
Mina LOY (1883-1966): Car-
ruth (Bantam), Kennedy
1974, Rothenberg 1973,
1974; Stanford, Winters
Beryl Llywelyn LUCAS: T.
Moore
E. V. LUCAS: Rose
F. L. LUCAS: J. Gibson
(Book Two)
Heidi LUCAS: Kohl
James R. (Rowser) LUCAS
(1931): Coombs, Dee, D.
Randall 1969
Felipe LUCIANO (1947): Adoff
1973, King 1972
Edward LUCIE-SMITH (1933):
Brinnin 1970, Cole 1971,
1972; Colley, Greaves,
Gross, Hall 1962 (World),
Knowles, Lask, Lucie-
Smith, Stallworthy, E.
Williams, Winkler
Marjorie LUCKMANN: Sollid
1973, K. and J. Sollid
Wayne LUCKMANN: K. and
J. Sollid
Jane Marie LUECKA (1924):
Mollenkott
Edward LUEDERS (1923):
Dunning, Larson
LUKE (Joseph Brown) (1944):
Hewitt
Allen LUKE: Booker
Jeffrey John LUKE: Sollid 1972

Wing Tek LUM: Clay
Patrice Emery LUMUMBA (1926-
1961): Lomax
Denise LUNA: Brindle
Michaele LUNDBERG: Kohl,
Pilon
Robert LUNDGREN: Vrbovska
1963, 1968
Lennart LUNDH: Gallery 1973
Eileen LUNDIN: Kiley
Glenna LUSCHEI: Winans
Claude LUSHINGTON: Salkey
Helen LUSTER: Simmons,
Winans
Bill LUSTIG: Smith
Carol LUTHER: Black History
Gertrude May LUTZ: Dunning
Thomas LUX (1946): Evans,
Halpern, Mazur, Rigsbee
K. Curtis LYLE (1944): Adoff
1973, Simmons
Stuart LYMAN: Morticella
Annette LYNCH (1922): Baylor
Charles LYNCH (1943): Adoff
1973
Michael LYNCH: Harris 1976
Sylvia LYND: Knowles
LYNDA: Student
Sanford LYNE (c. 1946): Hewitt
Richard LYONS (1920): Lowen-
fels 1966, Stryk 1975
John LYTLE: Rottmann
Robert LYTTON: Nash

M

Willard MAAS: O. Williams
1966 (World)
Lewis MACADAMS, Jr.
(MacAdams): Carroll
(Young American Poets),
Padgett, Waldman 1971
Lewis (Perry) MacADAMS, Jr.
(1944): Cole 1971, McCul-
lough, Waldman 1971
Noel MACAINSH (1926): T.
Moore
Claire McALLISTER (1931):
Aiken, Gregory 1966, O.
Williams 1966 (World)
Wordsworth McANDREW:
Salkey

James McAULEY (1917): Im-
maculate, Knowles, T.
Moore
George MacBETH (1932): Ell-
mann 1973, Hall 1962
(World), Lucie-Smith,
Matthias, L. Moore, Rosen-
thal 1967, 1968; Stevenson,
Walsh
Angela McCABE (1951): Hal-
pern
Victoria McCABE: Gildner
Norman MacCAIG (1910):
Cole 1972, Knowles, Lask,
Rosenthal 1967, 1968;
Summerfield
Theodore McCAIN, Jr. (1945):
Tisdale
Ewan McCALL: J. Gibson
(Book Two)
James Edward McCALL (1880-
1963): Breman
J. H. McCANDLESS: Steven-
son
Lisa McCANN: Dee
Richard McCANN: M. Gibson
Stuart McCARRELL (1923):
Lowenfels 1966, 1975
Cavan McCARTHY: E. Wil-
liams
Eugene McCARTHY (1916):
Cole 1972, Colley
Gerald McCARTHY: Sollid
1972
Frederick Thomas Bennet
MACARTNEY (1887): T.
Moore
Paul McCARTNEY: Holmes,
Kennedy 1974, Morse
Diane McCARTY: Brindle
Ruth Rambo McCLAIN: Gio-
vanni
Joe McCLELLAN: Sherman
Winona McCLINTIC: Cole
1963
Michael McCLINTOCK (1950):
Van den Heuvel
Michael McCLURE (1932): D.
M. Allen 1960, Clark, Di
Prima, Ferlinghetti, Har-
lan, Harvey, Kherdian
1973, Leary, Lowenfels
1966, Poetry San Francisco,

Rothenberg 1973, E. Wilentz, Winkler
Ewan MacCOLL: Crang, J. Gibson
Judith McCOMBS: Konek
Frances McCONNEL: Colley
David McCORD (1897): Aloian, Bogan, Brewton, Cole 1963, Dunning, Larrick, Lask, Livingston, Morrison, Pilon, Plotz, Untermeyer 1964
Howard McCORD (1932): Carroll (Young American Poets), Lask, Lowenfels 1966, 1973; McCullough
Jane McCOY: Gallery 1970
Ronald McCUAIG (1906): Cole 1972
Ronald McCUAIG (1908): T. Moore
William McCURINE: Booker
Don S. McDANIEL: Plumley
Hugh MacDIARMID (1892): Bold, Cole 1967 (Macmillan), 1971; De Loach 1976, Ellmann 1973, Firmage, Gregory 1962, Hurtik, Kennedy 1974, Matthias, Rosenthal 1967, 1968; Sanders, Simpson, Stallworthy, W. Taylor, Thomas, Untermeyer 1964
Donagh MacDONAGH: Cole 1971
Cynthia MacDONALD (1932): Howe, Rigsbee
George MACDONALD: Kauffman, Parker 1960
Ian McDONALD: Salkey
Nan McDONALD (1921): T. Moore
Sam McDONALD: Pilon
Susan MacDONALD: Konek
Wilson MacDONALD: Rose
Patrick MacDONOGH: (1902-1962?): Cole 1963, 1965; Stallworthy
Kaye McDONOUGH: Ferlinghetti, Winans
Don MACE: Kiley
Georgia Lee McELHANEY: Leary
David McELROY (1941): Halpern
Gwendolyn MacEWEN: E. Gill

David McFADDEN: J. Gill
Roy McFADDEN (1922): Knowles
Jacqueline McFARLAND: Hitchcock
Basil C. McFARLANE (1922): Breman
Ernest McGAFFEY: Hine
Audrey McGAFFIN: Glikes
Jeanne McGAHEY: Brewton, Dunning, Harvey
Lawrence McGAUGH (1940): Adoff 1970
Patrick MacGILL (1890): Cromie
Phyllis McGINLEY (1905-1978): Aloian, R. Bender, Cromie, Dunning, Engle, Garrett, Hine, Holmes, Hopkins (Nelson), Howe, McGinley, Morrison, Peck 1970, 1971; Perrine, Peterson, Stanford, Untermeyer 1964, Wagner, Woods
Duane W. McGINNIS: Dodge
William McGONAGALL: J. Gibson (Book Two), Nash
Lawrence McGOUGH (1940): Adoff 1973
Roger McGOUGH (1937): Cole 1971, Ellmann 1937, Greaves, Kennedy 1974
Robert McGOVERN: Ashland, McGovern
Juliet McGRATH: Wildman
Thomas (M.) McGRATH (1916): Bly 1970, Bold, Carruth (Bantam), Cromie, Kenseth, Lowenfels 1966, 1967, 1969 (Doubleday), 1973, 1975; Rothenberg 1973, Sherman, Stryk 1967, Vrbovska 1963, 1968; Wallace
T. P. McGRIFF: Booker
John S. McGROARTY: Parker 1967
Mursalin MACHADO: Chilgren
Sioux McHARGUE: Kohl
Burns B. MACHOBANE: Kgositsile
Heather McHUGH (1948): Halpern, Hoffman, Rigsbee

Madeline McHUGH: Student
Vincent McHUGH (1904): Harvey
Patricia McILNAY (1934): D.
Randall 1969
Jamie MacINNIS: Waldman 1971
C. F. MacINTYRE: Gregory
1966
Charlotte Grant MacINTYRE:
Kauffman
Robert McINTYRE: Kauffman
Irwin L. McJUNKINS: Clay
L. V. MACK (1947): Adoff 1973,
T. Wilentz
David McKAIN: Rigsbee
L. A. MACKAY (1901): McGin-
ley, A. J. M. Smith 1960
Lucie McKEE: Lask
Isobel Marion Dorothea MACKEL-
LAR (1885): T. Moore
St. Clair McKELWAY (1905):
Hughes 1970
Ken McKEON: Head
Tom McKEOWN (1937): Evans,
Stryk 1975
Albert D. MACKIE (1904): Cole
1963
Rod McKUEN (1933): Adoff
1969, Hannum, Holmes,
Hurtik, Kennedy 1974, Peck
1971
Jack McLAIN: Rottmann
Floris Clark McLAREN (1904):
A. J. M. Smith 1960
Ken McLAREN: Banker
R. H. McLAUGHLIN: Wesleyan
Univ.
C. Marshall McLEAN: Kiley
William Alfred MacLEAN (1959):
Adoff 1970
William McLEAN: Kohl
William Alfred McLEAN, Jr.:
Adoff 1971
Archibald MacLEISH (1892):
Aiken, G. W. Allen, J. A.
Allen, Aloian, Baylor, R.
Bender, Bogan, Brady,
Brewton, Brinnin 1963,
1970; C. Brooks, Calderwood,
Carruth (Bantam), Crang,
De Roche, Drew, Ellmann
1973, 1976; Engle, Felver,
Gannett, Gregory 1962, 1966;
Gwynn, Hall 1962 (Watts),

Hannum, Harlan, Hieatt,
Hine, Hopkins (Nelson),
Hurtik, Jackson, Jacobus,
Kennedy 1973, 1974; Ken-
seth, Kramer, Livingston,
Lowenfels 1969 (Doubleday),
McGinley, Monaco 1974,
Olson, Perrine, J. Perry,
Phillips, Rothenberg 1973,
Sanders, Schneider,
Shapiro, A. J. M. Smith
1967, Stallworthy, W. Tay-
lor, Trapp, Untermeyer
1964, 1970, 1973 (McKay);
J. A. Vincent, Wagner,
Wallace, Williams and
Honig, O. Williams 1966
(World)
James H. McLEMORE: Booker
Irene (R.) Rutherford McLEOD
(1891): Cole 1963, Rose
Sharon McLEOD: Brindle
Jackson MAC LOW (1922):
Gross, Harris 1973, Katz-
man, Leary, Rothenberg
1973, 1974; E. Williams
M. J. McMAHON: Morrison
Michael McMAHON: McMahon
Guy Humphreys McMASTER:
J. A. Vincent
Jame McMICHAEL (1939):
Adams, Anania, Halpern
Herman L. McMILLAN (c.
1941): Murphy
Stanley McNAIL: Derleth
J. M. McNAIR: Jackson
Wesley McNAIR: McMahon
Salley Allen McNALL: Brindle
Tom McNAMARA: Blazek
(Frederick) Louis MacNEICE
(1907-1963): J. A. Allen,
Bates, R. Bender, Brin-
nin 1963, 1970; Cole 1971,
Croft, Cromie, De Roche,
Drew, Driver, Ellmann
1973, Firmage, Foster,
Gardner, Greaves, Greg-
ory 1966, Hall 1962
(Watts), Hannum, Hurtik,
Peck 1970, Sanders,
Schneider, A. J. M.
Smith 1967, Stallworthy,
W. Taylor, Untermeyer

1964, Wallace
Arona L. McNEIL (c. 1952):
   Giovanni
Dee Dee McNEIL: Patterson
Donald G. McNEIL: Jackson
Jean M. McNEILL: Giovanni
Louise McNEILL (Pease):
   Plumley
Tony McNEILL: Salkey
Wayne McNEILL (1953): Ley-
   land 1975
William McNEILL: Oppenheimer
   1967
Ron McNICOLL: Krech
A. MACONOCHIE: Jackson
Jay MacPHERSON (1931):
   Adams, Cole 1971, Engle,
   Hollander, Rosenthal 1967,
   A. J. M. Smith 1960
Sandra McPHERSON (1943):
   Chester, Cole 1972, Hal-
   pern, Howe, Larson
James MACQUEEN: Smith
Marvin McQUEEN (1939):
   Tisdale
John T. McRAE: Battle
Linda MACRAE: Brindle
Robert L. McROBERTS (1944):
   Stryk 1975
Margaret Phyllis MacSWEENEY:
   Dunning
John Albert MACY: Jackson
David MADDEN: Owen 1974
Charles MADGE (1912): Thomas
Naomi Long MADGETT (1923):
   Adoff 1973, Bell, G. Brooks
   (Broadside Treasury), Hay-
   den, Hopkins (Knopf), Hughes
   1964, 1970; Jordan, King,
   Konek, Kramer, Lane, D.
   Randall 1960, Turner
Haki R. MADHUBUTI (Don L.
   Lee): Friedman
Michael MADIGAN: K. and J.
   Sollid
Isaac MAEFIELD: Black History
Don MAGER: Bogin
Margo MAGID (1947): Howe
A. (Abraham) B. MAGIL (1905):
   Hughes 1970, Kramer
T. O. MAGLOW: Kennedy
   1974
James E. (Edmund) MAGNER,
   Jr.: Ashland, McGovern

Francis MAGUIRE: Lask
Othello MAHOME: Dee
Derek MAHON (1941): Colley,
   Stallworthy
Barbara MAHONE (1944):
   Adoff 1973, 1974; Giovanni
Elizabeth Fairclough MAHONEY:
   Smith
Norman MAILER (1923): Cole
   1967 (Macmillan)
Carolyn MAISEL: Konek
Clarence MAJOR (1936): Adoff
   1970, 1973; Bates, Baylor,
   Bell, Bontemps 1963, 1974;
   Breman, Colley, De Loach
   1976, Gross, Joran, King
   1972, Lowenfels 1967,
   1969 (Doubleday), (Random
   House); A. Miller, D.
   Randall 1960, 1969; T.
   Wilentz
Joseph MAJOR (1948): Major
Michael MAKOWSKY: Krech
Charles MALAM: Aloian,
   Dunning, Lask, Summer-
   field
Gerard MALANGA (1943):
   Carroll (Young American
   Poets), De Loach 1968, Haus-
   man, H. Jones, Leyland
   1975, Mazur, Montgomery,
   Rigsbee, Waldman 1969,
   1971
Barbara MALCOM: Breman
Pat MALCOM: Brindle
Myrna L. C. MALDONADO:
   Battle
Eugene T. MALESKA (1916):
   Hughes 1970
Michael Abdul MALIK: Salkey
Stephen MALIN: Steele
Jaroslav MALINA: Wildman
Judith MALINA: Gay
Jean MALLEY: Malley
Marianne MALLEY (1939):
   Gitlin
Douglas MALLOCH: Brewton
Anne MALLON: Brindle
Virginia Megeehan MALLON:
   Brindle
Lee MALLORY: Mallory,
   Winans
Louise MALLY: Harris 1970
Marvin MALONE: Fox

Walter MALONE: Jackson
David MALOUF (1934): T.
  Moore
Jude MALOUF: Adoff 1971
Sasa MALZONE: Violet
Mouloud MAMMERI: Kgositsile
Charlotte MANDEL: Saturday
  Press
E. W. MANDEL (1922): A. J.
  M. Smith 1960
Oscar MANDEL: Glikes
Elaine MANGER: Brindle
John (Streeter) MANIFOLD
  (1915): R. Bender, Bogan,
  Cole 1965, 1971; McGinley,
  T. Moore, Rose, Summer-
  field, Untermeyer 1964
Gregg MANIN: Adoff 1971
Paul MANN: Gitlin
Marya MANNES (1904): Bates,
  Lowenfels 1967
Pamela MANNING: Booker
Gianfranco MANTEGNA: Gay
Peter MANTI: Ferlinghetti
Jagdip MARAJ: Salkey
Harvey A. MARCELIN: Tisdale
Adrianne MARCUS: Efros, Fox,
  Owen 1969, 1974; Winans
Leonard MARCUS: Hoffman
Morton MARCUS (1936): Bates,
  Baylor, Carroll (Young
  American Poets), Evans,
  Gersmehl, Harlan, Harvey,
  Lowenfels 1967, Stevenson,
  Summerfield
Thea MARCUS: Hadassah
Herbert MARCUSE: Ferlinghetti
Gary MARGOLIS (1945): M.
  Williams
Joseph MARGOLIS: Wiebe
Richard J. MARGOLIS: Pilon,
  Summerfield
William J. MARGOLIS (1927):
  Lowenfels 1966, Simmons
Delina MARGOT-PARLE: Poets
  of America
Paul MARIAH (1937): Head,
  Krech, Leyland 1975,
  Winans, Young
Bayani J. MARIANO: Clay
Jeffrey MARIENTHAL: Gallery
  1970
Rosa Zagnoni MARINONI: Der-
  leth, Jackson, Vrbovska 1963

Jack MARION: Harlan
Karen MARKE: Brindle
Stuart MARKS: Plumley
Earl MARLATT (1892): Trapp
Daniel MARLIN: Head
Anne MARRIOTT (1913): A.
  J. M. Smith 1960
John MARRON: Morticella
David MARSH: Student
Barbara MARSHALL (c. 1945):
  Murphy
Caroline Clark MARSHALL:
  Scheftel
Curtiss C. MARSHALL (1925):
  Tisdale
Edward MARSHALL (1932): D.
  M. Allen 1960, Leary
Jack MARSHALL (1937):
  Carroll (Young American
  Poets), Glikes, McCullough,
  Oppenheimer 1967
Lee MARSHALL: Booker
Leonore MARSHALL: Banker,
  Lowenfels 1967
T. Dabney MARSHALL: Jack-
  son
Everett Lee MARSHBURN:
  Booker
Charles MARTELL: McGovern
Charles MARTIN: J. Gibson
  (Book Two)
David MARTIN (1915): T.
  Moore
Edward S. MARTIN: Jackson
Herbert (Woodward) MARTIN
  (1933): Adoff 1973, Lane
I. L. MARTIN: Morrison
Kathryn MARTIN: Balazs
Philip MARTIN (1931): T.
  Moore
Robert A. MARTIN (1931):
  Mollenkott
Joseph MARTINEK: Vrbovska
  1963
Marcel MARTINET: Cromie
Archie MARTINEZ: Algarin
Carmen MARTINEZ: Booker
Carmen M. MARTINEZ:
  Lowenfels 1973
David MARTINEZ: Dodge
Lucie MARTINEZ: Kohl
Lydia MARTINEZ: Booker
Maurice M. MARTINEZ (1934):
  Hughes 1970

Myrna MARTINEZ: Smith
Ramon MARTINEZ (1955):
    Lowenfels 1973
David MARTINSON: Lowenfels
    1975
Anne MARX: Derleth, Vrbovska
    1968
Arthur MARX: Harris
    1976
Mary MARY: Gay
Al MASARIK: Winans
Maria D. MASCARO (1949):
    Durand
John MASEFIELD (1878-1967):
    Aloian, R. Bender, Calder-
    wood, Cole 1967 (Viking),
    Colum, Croft, Ellmann
    1973, Gannett, J. Gibson,
    J. Gibson (Book Two),
    Knowles, Marshall, Nash,
    Parker 1967, 1975; Rose,
    Sanders, A. J. M. Smith
    1967, Trapp, Untermeyer
    1964, Woods
Thanasis MASKALERIS (1930):
    Lowenfels 1967, Palmer
Jean Denise MASON: Giovanni
Leo J. MASON (1947): Hender-
    son
Madeline MASON: Vrbovska
    1968
Mason Jordan MASON (Judson
    Crews): Hughes 1970
Walt MASON: Morrison
Winston MASON: Lourie
Marcia (Lee) MASTERS (1917):
    Dunning, Stanford, Stryk
    1975
Dan MASTERSON (1934): M.
    Williams
Marianne MASTERSON: Brindle
Florence Ripley MASTIN:
    Aloian
William E. MATCHETT:
    Strand
William H. MATCHETT (1923):
    Cole 1967 (Macmillan),
    1971; Hallmark, Hannum,
    Hannum and Chase, Ten
John Frederick MATHEUS:
    Patterson
Ray MATHEW (1929): T.
    Moore

Esther MATHEWS: O. Williams
    1966 (World)
Harry MATHEWS: Padgett
Jack MATHEWS (1925): Han-
    num, Hannum and Chase,
    Lask
John Frederick MATHEWS:
    Patterson
R. D. MATHEWS: Stevenson
Richard MATHEWS (1944):
    Harris 1976, Mollenkott
Cleopatra MATHIS: Oppen-
    heimer 1977, Rigsbee
Sharon Bell MATHIS (1937):
    Giovanni
Efrein MATOS: Dee
Clive MATSON (1941): De Loach
    1968, Harris 1973, Lowen-
    fels 1969 (Random House),
    Schreiber
Donald MATTAM: Cole 1967,
    1972
Fredric MATTESON: Gallery
    1973
Molly MATTFIELD: Hallmark
Alice Clear MATTHEWS:
    Vrbovska 1963
Dale MATTHEWS: Rigsbee
Harley MATTHEWS (1889): T.
    Moore
Jeffrey Scott MATTHEWS:
    Morticella
T. S. MATTHEWS: Cole 1967
    (Macmillan), Cole 1971
Tony MATTHEWS: Salkey
William MATTHEWS (1942):
    Bonazzi 1972, Cole 1971,
    Evans, Halpern, Harris
    1976, Heyen, Owen 1969,
    Steele, H. Taylor
John MATTHIAS (1941): Har-
    ris 1976, P. Perry,
    Stryk 1975
George MATTINGLY: Sklar,
    Winans
Edouard MAUNICK: Kgositsile
Sister M. MAURA: Firmage
Paul MAURICE: Young
Bob MAXEY: Coombs
Marina MAXWELL: Salkey
Agnes MAXWELL-HALL (1894):
    Lomax
James Boyer MAY (1904):

Lowenfels 1966, Vrbovska
1963, 1968
John W. MAY: Jackson
Bernadette MAYER (1945): Fagin,
Padgett, Rothenberg 1973,
Waldman 1971
Hansjorg MAYER (1943): Gross,
Klonsky, Wildman, E. Wil-
liams
Parm MAYER (1915): Harris
1970, Stryk 1972, Vrbovska
1968
Don MAYNARD (1937): T.
Moore
E. L. MAYO (1904): J. A.
Allen, Firmage, Gildner,
Plotz, Strand
Mary E. MAYO (1938): Katz-
man
Myra MAYO: Gildner
Welburn MAYOCK: Jackson
Ken MAYTAG (1945): Mallory
Gail MAZUR: Mazur
Jerome MAZZARO (1934):
Heyen, Lask, McCullough
Antar Sudan Katara MBERI:
Lowenfels 1975
Laura MEAD: Harlan
Mathew MEAD (1924): Matthias
Taylor MEAD: Leyland 1975
Iris MEADS: Sargent
Murray MEDNICK: Oppenheimer
1967
Alex B. MEEK: Jackson
Merle MEETER (1933): Mollen-
kott
Mildred MEIGS: J. A. Vincent
Peter MEINKE (1932): Harris
1976, Mollenkott, Rigsbee
William MELANEY: Adoff 1971
Jesus Papoleto MELENDEZ:
Algarin
D. H. MELHERN: Lowenfels
1975
David MELNICK: Krech, Malley
David MELTZER (1937): D.
M. Allen 1960, Arts Festi-
val 1964, De Loach 1976,
Durand, Harvey, Kherdian
1973, Lowenfels 1969 (Ran-
dom House), Rothenberg
1973, Weishaus, Winans
Susan MELTZER: Adoff 1971

Murilo MENDES (1902): Trapp
Consuelo MENDEZ: Clay
Ann (Anne) MENEBROKER:
Gallery 1973, Konek,
Winans
Helen MENKE: Brindle
Ifeanyi MENKITI: Gross,
Kgositsile
Susan MENNE: Brindle
George MEREDITH: De Roche,
Wager
William MEREDITH (1919):
C. Brooks, Cole 1971,
Ellmann 1973, Engle,
Hannum, Harris 1976,
Heyen, Howard, Howard
and Victor, Kennedy 1973,
Plotz, Strand, H. Taylor,
Univ. Press of Va., Wal-
lace, Wesleyan Univ., M.
Williams
William Tucker MEREDITH:
Hine
Sally MERLIN-JONES: Brindle
Susan MERNIT: Adoff 1971
Bob MERRILL (1922): Cole
1965
Eve MERRIAM (1916): Bates,
Colley, Dunning, Gersmehl,
Howe, Joseloff, Konek,
Larrick, Lowenfels 1966,
Pilon, Summerfield,
Wagner
Herbert MERRILL: Brewton
James MERRILL (1926):
Aiken, J. A. Allen, Brady,
Brinnin 1963, 1970; Car-
ruth (Bantam), Ellmann
1973, 1976; Engle, Hall
1962 (Penguin), (World);
Hecht, Hollander, Howard,
Howard and Victor, Ken-
nedy 1973, 1974; Lask,
Monaco 1974, Strand, H.
Taylor, Wallace, M. Wil-
liams, Witt-Diamant
Martha C. MERRILL: Brindle
Stuart MERRILL: Gregory
1966
Thomas MERTON (1915-1968):
J. A. Allen, Bonazzi 1972,
Carruth (Bantam), Corbett,
Firmage, Gross, Hitchcock,

Klonsky, Lowenfels 1967, 1969 (Doubleday), Rothenberg 1973

W. S. MERWIN (1927): Aiken, G. W. Allen, J. A. Allen, Baylor, Berg, Brady, Brinnin 1963, 1970; Carroll (Poem in Its Skin), Carruth (Bantam), (McCall); Chace, Cole 1971, 1972; De Roche, Driver, Ellmann 1973, 1976; Engle, Hall 1962 (Penguin), (World); Harris 1973, Hollander, Hopkins (Nelson), Howard, Howard and Victor, Kennedy 1973, 1974; Kessler, Leary, Monaco 1974, L. Moore, Poulin, Rosenthal 1967, 1968; Rothenberg 1973, Strand, H. Taylor, W. Taylor, Untermeyer 1973 (McKay), Wallace, M. Williams, O. Williams 1966 (World), Witt-Diamant

Michael MESIC: Malley

Patti MESNER: Brindle

Paula MESSINA: Brindle

Maurya METAL: Kohl

Rhonda METZ: Dee

Deena METZGER: Chester, Simmons

Diane MEUCCI: Ferlinghetti

Edna MEUDT: Derleth

Gerard Previn MEYER: Lask

June MEYER (1936): Lowenfels 1969 (Random House), Major

Thomas (Tom) MEYER (1947): Leyland 1975, 1977

Bert MEYERS (1928): Carruth (McCall), Cole 1963, 1967 (Macmillan), 1971; Kennedy 1973

Edward L. MEYERSON: Vrbovska 1968

E. H. W. MEYERSTEIN: Cole 1967 (Macmillan)

Leland S. MEYERZONE: Hadassah

Robert MEZEY (1935): Adams, J. A. Allen, Byalor, Berg, Cole 1967 (Macmillan),

Gildner, Gitlin, Hall 1962 (Penguin), Halpern, Hieatt, Joseloff, Kessler, Kherdian, 1970, Lowenfels 1967, L. Moore, Stallworthy

Frank MEZTA: Crafts

Mwanafunzi MFOLME: Jihad

Guy C. Z. MHONE: Kgositsile

Jack MICHELINE: De Loach 1976, Ferlinghetti, Montgomery, E. Wilentz, Winans

Peter MICHELSON (1937): Anania, Baylor, P. Perry, Stryk 1975

James MICHIE (1927): Hall 1962 (World), Stallworthy, Winkler

Regina MICOU (Femi Funmi Ifetayo): Patterson

Christopher MIDDLETON (1923): Brinnin 1970, Crang, Hall 1962 (World), Klonsky, Matthias, Rosenthal 1967, 1968

Herb MIDDLETON: Winans

Lynwood MIDDLETON: Kohl

Thomas MIDDLETON: Cole 1971

Ann MIKOLOWSKI: De Loach 1976

Ken MIKOLOWSKI: De Loach 1976

Patricia MILBURN: Brindle

Barbara MILES: Crafts

Josephine MILES (1911): J. A. Allen, Baylor, Carruth (Bantam), Chace, Chester, Cole 1967 (Macmillan), 1971; Ellmann 1973, Engle, Felver, Glikes, Harlan, Harvey, Head, Holmes, Hughes 1970, Jackson, Kennedy 1974, Konek, Larson, Pearson, J. Perry, Phillips, Stanford, H. Taylor, M. Williams, Winans, Witt-Diamant

Judy MILES: Salkey

Adam David MILLER (1922): Adoff 1973, A. Miller

Bill MILLER: Crafts

Brown MILLER: Blazek, Fox

Cecilia Parsons MILLER:
Plumley
Chuck MILLER: Sklar
Donna MILLER: Hauge
Doris C. MILLER: Plumley
Emily Huntington MILLER:
Kauffman
Heather (Ross) MILLER: Owen
1974
Jason MILLER: Schreiber
Jim MILLER: Owen 1974
Jim W. MILLER: Plumley
John MILLER: Harlan, Kohl
Kathy MILLER: Brindle
Leon MILLER: Morticella
Marcia Muth MILLER: Gallery
1970, 1973
Mary Britton MILLER (1883):
Cole 1963
May MILLER (1900): Lowenfels
1966, H. Taylor
Raeburn MILLER: Stevenson
Vassar MILLER (1924): Adams,
Bogan, Bonazzi 1972, Car-
ruth (McCall), Chester,
Driver, Engle, Hall 1962
(Watts), (World); Hannum,
Howe, Jacobus, Konek,
Lask, Leary, Mercatante,
Owen 1969, 1974; Pearson,
Stanford, Untermeyer 1964,
Walsh, M. Williams
Wayne MILLER (1939): Harvey,
Winans
Spike MILLIGAN (1918): Cole
1972
Alison MILLS: Clay
Barriss MILLS: Dunning,
Hunting, Purdue, Vrbovska
1963, 1968; Weil
Clark MILLS: Vrbovska 1968
Elizabeth Randall MILLS:
Vrbovska 1963
Ralph J. MILLS, Jr. (1931):
Stryk 1975
William MILLS (1935): M.
Williams
Ewart MILNE (1903): Cole
1963, Pilon
E. V. MILNER: Cole 1967
(Macmillan)
A. L. MILNER-BROWN:
Hughes 1963, Lomax

John MILTON (1924): Lowen-
fels 1973
Eugene MINARD: Hoffman
Khatchik MINASIAN: Kherdian
1970
Stevi MINCKLER: Brindle
Stephen MINDEL: Palmer
Cunthia MINDELL: Brindle
James MINOR: Gallery 1973
Helena MINTON: McMahon
Judith MINTY (1937): Harris
1976, Stryk 1975
L. Dean MINZE: Kiley
Marjorie MIR: Glikes
Gary MIRANDA: Rigsbee
Janice MIRIKITANI: Clay,
Harvey
Adrian MITCHELL (1932):
Baylor, Bold, Cole 1967
(Macmillan), Greaves
Arelya J. MITCHELL: Student
Emerson Blackhorse ("Barney")
MITCHELL (1945): T.
Allen, Dodge
James MITCHELL (1940):
Leyland 1975, Young
John MITCHELL: J. A.
Vincent
Joni MITCHELL (1943): Morse,
Wagner
Roger MITCHELL: Bonazzi
1972, Rosenblum
Ruth Comfort MITCHELL:
Jackson
William R. MITCHELL (1930):
Mollenkott
Don A. MIZELL (Khajuka) (c.
1949): Coombs, Black
History, Patterson
Ray MIZER: Owen 1969
Mwanafunzi MJANJA: Jihad
Ernie MKALIMOTO (1942):
Major
Bloke MODISANE: Hughes
1963
William MOEBIUS (1941):
Anania
Byron MOFFETT: Sollid 1973
Judith MOFFETT: Hoffman,
Malley, Rigsbee
John MOFFIT (1908): Dunning,
Larrick, Trapp
Ernest G. MOLL (1900): Cole

1967 (Macmillan), Knowles,
T. Moore
Kadia MOLLIN: J. Gill
Kadia MOLODOWSKY-LEW
(1894): Joseloff
Warren Lane MOLTON:
McGovern
N. Scott MOMADAY (1934):
Lowenfels 1973, McCullough,
Niatum, Schneider, Winters
Franz MON: E. Williams
Sergio MONDRAGON: Harris
1973
Paul MONETTE (1945): Halpern
Arthur W. MONKS: Hecht
Theodore MONOD: Kauffman
Arthur MONROE: Clay
Harold MONROE: Dunning,
McGinley
Tom MONTAG: Rosemblum
James L. MONTAGUE: Jack-
son, Lask
John MONTAGUE (1929): Gross,
Lask, Matthias, Rosenthal
1967, 1968; Stevenson,
Untermeyer 1964
George MONTGOMERY (1938): Ban-
ker, Blazek, De Loach 1968,
Lowenfels 1969 (Random House),
Montgomery, Sherman
James MONTGOMERY: Kauff-
man, J. A. Vincent
John MONTGOMERY: Simmons
Marion MONTGOMERY: Lask,
Steele
Jose MONTOYA (1932): Clay,
Harvey
Stephen MOONEY: Steele
Daniel MOORE (1940): Harvey,
Malley, Poetry San Fran-
cisco
Edith MOORE: Student
Jeannie Douglas MOORE (c.
1886): Giovanni
Judith MOORE: Colley
Julia MOORE: Nash
Marianne MOORE (1887-1972):
Adams, G. W. Allen,
Aloian, Arp, Bach, Baylor,
Beerman, Bogan, Brady,
Brinnin 1963, 1970; C.
Brooks, Brower, Carruth
(Bantam), Chace, Cole 1967

(Macmillan), 1971; Chester,
Crane, Croft, De Roche,
Drew, Driver, Ellmann
1973, Engle, Felver,
Gregory 1962, Hall 1962
(Watts), Hannum, Harlan,
Hieatt, Howe, Hughes
1970, Hurtik, Jacobus,
Kaplan, Kennedy 1974,
Koch, Livingston, McCul-
lough, McGinley, Monaco
1974, L. Moore, Olson,
Perrine, J. Perry, Roth-
enberg 1973, 1974; Sanders,
Schneider, Segnitz, Shapiro,
A. J. M. Smith 1967,
Stanford, Steuben, W. Tay-
lor, Univ. Press of Va.,
Untermeyer 1964, 1973
(McKay); Wagner, Wallace,
Williams and Honig, O.
Williams 1966 (Trident),
(World); Winkler, Woods
Merrill MOORE (1903): Colley,
Holmes, Parks, Peck 1970,
Untermeyer 1964
Richard MOORE (1927): Ken-
nedy 1973
Robert Nelson MOORE (Jr.)
(1943): Fox, Lowenfels
1973
Rosalie MOORE: Chester,
Dunning, Harvey
T. Inglis MOORE (1901): T.
Moore
George H. MOORSE: Lask
Michael MOOS (1949): Lowen-
fels 1973
Amus MOR: King 1972
Dom MORAES (1938): Ellmann
1973, Hall 1962 (World),
Plotz
Barbara MORAFF: Konek,
Montgomery, Totem Press
Carlos MORALES: Battle
Martita MORALES: Algarin
John Richard MORELAND:
Lask
Wayne MORELAND (1948):
Adoff 1973, Kohl
Dorinda MORENO: Clay
Donald MORGAN: Kohl
Edwin MORGAN (1920): Bay-

lor, Gross, Kennedy 1974,
Klonsky, Lucie-Smith, Solt,
Stallworthy, Summerfield,
Wildman, E. Williams
Emanuel MORGAN see Witter
BYNNER
G. R. MORGAN: Gallery 1970
John MORGAN (1946): Carroll
(Young American Poets),
Lowenfels 1967, 1969 (Ran-
dom House); Rigsbee
Robert MORGAN: Owen 1969,
1974
Robin MORGAN (1941): Gitlin,
Howe, Konek
William MORGAN: Head
Dave MORICE: Sklar
Edward MORIN: Wiebe
Anne MORKEN: Harlan
Alex MORRA: Blazek
Christina MORRIS: Lowenfels
1975
George P. MORRIS: Jackson
Harry MORRIS: Owen 1974
Herbert MORRIS: Harris 1976,
Owen 1969
James C. MORRIS (1920): P.
Brown
John MORRIS (1931): Hieatt
John N. MORRIS: Colley
Mervyn MORRIS: Salkey
Richard MORRIS: Bonazzi
1972, Fox, Head
Roberta MORRIS: Bogin
William MORRIS: J. Gibson
(Book Two), E. Wilentz
Henry MORRISON: Morticella
Jim MORRISON: Chace
Lillian MORRISON: Adoff
1969
Theodore MORRISON (1901):
Univ. Press of Va.
Ann MORRISSETT (1925): Cole
1965
Gloria MORROW: Booker
Jonathan MORSE: H. Smith
Samuel French MORSE (1916):
Immaculate, Lask, Univ.
Press of Va., Wesleyan
Univ.
Barbara La MORTICELLA:
Morticella
Frances McKinnon MORTON:
Kauffman

J. B. MORTON (1893-1970):
Cole 1972
Ernst MORWITZ: Gregory
1966
Aminata MOSEKA: Clay
Norman C. (Calvin) MOSER
(1931): Fox, Owen 1969,
1974
W. R. MOSES: Brewton,
Lask, Pearson, Stevenson
Joseph M. MOSLEY (1935):
Major
Howard MOSS (1922): Adoff
1969, Brewton, Brinnin
1963, 1970; Engle, Glikes,
Hall 1962 (World), Hannum
and Chase, Howard, How-
ard and Victor, Kennedy
1973, Peck 1971, Strand,
H. Taylor, Trapp, Wallace,
O. Williams 1966 (World)
Judith MOSS: Violet
Ralph MOSS: Harris 1970
Stanley MOSS (1935): Carruth
(Bantam), Cromie, Firmage,
Stevenson, Strand
S. E. MOSSHOLDER: Morti-
cella
Peter Anthony MOTTEAUX:
Untermeyer 1970
Eric MOTTRAM: De Loach
1976
H. L. MOUNTZOURES: Glikes
Geoffrey MOVIUS (1940): Ken-
nedy 1973
David MOWBRAY: J. Gibson
Paul Scott MOWRER: Cromie,
Stibitz
Ezekial MPHAHLELE (1919):
Breman, Hughes 1963,
Jacobus
Mwanafunzi Mayo MSEMAJI:
Jihad
MSHAKA (Willie Monroe):
Tisdale
Harvey MUDD: Lowenfels
1975
Ian MUDIE (1911): Greaves,
T. Moore
Lavonne MUELLER: Brindle
Lisel MUELLER (1924):
Chester, Cole 1971, Han-
num, Konek, Phillips,
Stibitz, Strand, Stryk 1967

A. MUIR: Cole 1963
Soshil MUKHERJEE: Hausman
Jim MULAC: Sklar
Helene MULLINS (1899): Cromie,
Gallery 1970, Jackson,
Trapp, Vrbovska 1963, 1968
Kelly MULLINS: Harlan
Patrick MULLINS: Ferlinghetti
Horace MUNGIN: Adoff 1970
Richard Kendall (R. K.)
MUNKITTRICK: Dunning,
Jackson
Amina MUNOZ: Algarin
Rukudzo MURAPA: P. Brown
Lee MURCHISON: Morrison
Royal MURDOCH (1898): Ley-
land 1977
Alejandro MURGUIA: Clay,
Lowenfels 1975, Winans
Morgan MURIELCHILD: Violet
Brigid MURNAGHAN: E.
Wilentz
Beatrice M. MURPHY: Hughes
1970, Murphy
Frank MURPHY: Banker
George MURPHY: Lask
J. M. MURPHY (1932): Lowen-
fels 1966
Richard MURPHY (1927): Lask,
Rosenthal 1967, 1968;
Walsh
R. D. MURPHY (1910): T.
Moore
Catherine MURRAY: Waldman
1971
Dan MURRAY (1938): Freed
G. E. MURRAY (1945): Stryk
1975
Pauli MURRAY (1910): Adoff
1973, Bates, Bontemps
1963, 1974; Howe, Hughes
1970, Patterson
Robert Fuller MURRAY:
Morrison
Susan MURRAY: Crafts
Pam MURTHA: Adoff 1971
Jessie Wilmore MURTON:
Brewton
David MUS: Carroll (Young
American Poets)
Douglas MUSELLA: Gallery
1973
Jack MUSGROVE: Gildner

Carol MUSKE (1945): Halpern
Mukhtarr MUSTAPHA (1943):
Breman
Norman Ogue MUSTILL (1931):
Harvey
Kuweka MWANDISHI: Black
History
Geoff. MWANJA: Sargent
Edward MYCUE (c. 1938):
Young
Frederic W. H. MYERS:
Kauffman
Jack MYERS (1941): Halpern
Neil MYERS: Gallery 1970,
Glikes, Lask
Glenn MYLES (1933): Major,
A. Miller

N

Gustave NADAUD: Parker 1967
Laura NAGAN: Adoff 1971
Rochelle NAMEROFF: Efros,
Malley
Berta Hart NANCE: Brewton
Maurizio NANNUCCI: Wildman
Dana NAONE: Niatum
Augustus NAPIER: Wesleyan
Univ.
Drew NASH: Head
H. C. NASH: Bonazzi 1972
James NASH: Banker
Ogden NASH (1902-1971):
Aloian, Bogan, C. Brooks,
Cole 1963, 1971, 1972;
Engle, Gannett, J. Gibson,
J. Gibson (Book Two);
Gwynn, Jackson, Jacobus,
Kennedy 1974, Knowles,
McGinley, Morrison, Nash,
Opie, Parker 1960, Perrine,
Untermeyer 1964, Wagner,
O. Williams 1966 (World)
Valery NASH (1932): H. Tay-
lor
Anis NASSAR: Sherman
Leonard (E.) NATHAN (1924):
Cole 1971, Harlan, Harvey,
Head, Lask, McGovern,
Pearson, Talisman
Ann NAU: Plumley
Anthony NAUMANN (1921):

Knowles
E. A. NAVARETTA: E. Wilentz
Bud NAVERO: De Loach 1976
Barbara D. NAZELROD: Brindle
Larry (Lawrence P.) NEAL
(1937): Bontemps 1974,
Breman, G. Brooks (Broad-
side Treasury), P. Brown,
Henderson, Jordan, King
1972, Major, D. Randall
1969
John Mason NEALE: Cole 1971,
Parker 1960
E. M. NEE (c. 1941): Freed
Judy NEELD: Balazs
N. P. NEILSON: Kauffman
Sasha NEJGEBAUER: Hitch-
cock
David NELSON: Dee, King
1972
Gordon NELSON: Dee
Jade NELSON: Brindle
Stanley NELSON: Fox
William A. NELSON: Hoffman
Howard NEMEROV (1920):
Aiken, J. A. Allen, Bates,
R. Bender, Brinnin 1963,
1970; Carruth (McCall),
Cole 1967 (Macmillan),
1972; De Roche, Driver,
Ellmann 1973, Engle,
Gwynn, Hall 1972 (Penguin),
Hannum, Hannum and
Chase, Hine, Howard,
Howard and Victor, Immac-
ulate, Joseloff, Kennedy
1973, 1974; Lask, Lowen-
fels 1967, McGinley,
McGovern, Monaco 1974,
Owen 1969, Perrine, Plotz,
Rosenthal 1967, 1968;
Sanders, Stevenson, Strand,
H. Taylor, W. Taylor,
Univ. Press of Va.,
Vrbovska 1963, 1968; Wal-
lace, Walsh, M. Williams,
O. Williams 1966 (World),
Witt-Diamant
Richard D. NESS: Kiley
Antonio Agostinho NETO:
Kgositsile
Peter G. NEUMANN: Gross
Helen NEVILLE: O. Williams
1966 (World)

Mary NEVILLE: Cole 1972
Tove NEVILLE: Palmer
Henry NEWBOLT: Parker
1960
Robert Henry NEWELL (Orphe-
us C. Kerr): Jackson
John NEWLOVE (1938): J.
Gill
C. J. NEWMAN: Hadassah
Felice NEWMAN: Bulkin
Israel NEWMAN: Lask
Louis NEWMAN (1895): Hughes
1970, Vrbovska 1963
Paul Baker NEWMAN: Carruth
(McCall), Owen 1969, 1974;
Steele
Preston NEWMAN: Owen 1974
Effie Lee NEWSOME (1885):
Adoff 1973, Bontemps
1963, 1974; Hughes 1970
(E.) Marie NEWSOME: Pat-
terson
Henry P. NEWTON: Ferling-
hetti
John NEWTON: Kauffman
Violette NEWTON: Harris
1970, 1973
Stelle NGATHO: Kgositsile
Thich NHAT-HANH (Nhat Hanh)
(1926): Gersmehl, Ken-
seth
Duane NIATUM (1938): Lourie,
Lowenfels 1973, Morticella,
Niatum
B. P. NICHOL (bpNichol)
(1944): Kostelanetz, Solt
A. X. NICHOLAS (1943):
Coombs
Michael (R.) NICHOLAS (1941):
Lowenfels 1973, Major
Louise Townsend NICHOLL:
Livingston, Steuben,
Vrbovska 1963
(Robert) Bob NICHOLS (1919):
Harris 1973, Katzman, E.
Wilentz
J. W. H. NICHOLS: Kauffman
Jeannette NICHOLS: Chester,
Untermeyer 1970
Starr Hoyt NICHOLS: Jackson
Martha Snell NICHOLSON:
Kauffman
Norman NICHOLSON (1914):
J. Gibson (Book Two),

Livingston, Parker 1975,
Plotz, Untermeyer 1964
Frederick NICKLAUS: Lask
Abioseh NICOL (1924): Breman,
Hughes 1963
NICOLI: Vrbovska 1968
Lorine NIEDECKER (1903-1970):
Carruth (Bantam), Chester,
Gross, Rothenberg 1973,
Weil
Hansjorgen NIELSEN: E. Wil-
liams
Veneta NIELSEN (1909): Larson
Seiichi NIIKUNI: Wildman, E.
Williams
John Frederick (F.) NIMS (1913):
J. A. Allen, R. Bender,
Corbett, Engle, Immaculate,
Kennedy 1973, 1974; McGin-
ley, Perrine, Stibitz, Stryk
1967, Univ. Press of Va.,
M. Williams
Anais NIN (1903-1977): Rothen-
berg
Lane NISHIKAWA: Clay
John NIST (1925): Firmage
NITAMAYO: Clay
John NIXON, Jr.: Lask, Owen
1969, 1974
Sallie NIXON: Hoffman
Thulani NKABINE: Clay
J. W. NOBLE: Smith
William J. NOBLE: Scheftel
James NOLAN (1947): Mollen-
kott
Bink (Blink) NOLL (1927):
Kennedy 1973, H. Taylor,
Walsh
J. M. NOLTE: Jack-
son
Mary NORBERT: Palm-
er
Charles NORMAN (1904):
Cromie
George E. NORMAN (1923):
D. Randall 1969
Kathleen NORRIS: Konek,
Waldman 1971
Leslie NORRIS (1921): Firmage,
Lask
Harold NORSE (1916): De
Loach 1976, Ferlinghetti,
Leyland 1975, 1977;
Winans, Young

Charles NORTH: Waldman
1971
Jessica Nelson NORTH:
Stibitz
Arthur K. NORTJE (1942):
Breman
Freda NORTON (1935): Lowen-
fels 1969 (Randon House)
Mabelsson NORWAY (c. 1912):
Van den Heuvel
Murray NOSS: Aloian
Alice NOTLEY: Clark, Fried-
man
Lodislav NOVAK: Pilon, E.
Williams
Robert NOVICK (1937-1968):
Gitlin
Alden (M.) NOWLAN: Cole
1971, Derleth, Stevenson
Wilfird NOYCE (1917-1962):
Knowles
George Rapall NOYES: Jack-
son
Ken NOYLE (1922): Baylor
Jeff (Jeffrey) NUTALL: De
Loach 1976, Lucie-Smith,
Sherman
Chuba NWEKE: Hughes 1963
Robert NYE (1939): Cole 1972
NYENYECKA: Jihad
Nina NYHART: Mazur

O

Andra Jo-Ann O: Student
W. OAKES: Banker
Joyce Carol OATES (1938):
Heyen, Konek, Wagner,
M. Williams
Johnson OATMAN, Jr.: Kauff-
man
Hilton OBENZINGER: S. Vin-
cent
Geoffrey O'BRIEN: Cole 1971,
Gross
Ed OCHESTER (1939): Lowen-
fels 1975, Phillips, Rigs-
bee
Tom OCKERSE (1940): Klonsky
Richard O'CONNELL: Glikes,
Gross
Barbara O'CONNELLY: Blazek,
Fox

Charles O'CONOR: Jackson
Joyce ODAM: Gallery 1970,
1973; Winans
Gloria (G. C.) ODEN (1923):
Adoff 1973, Bell, Bontemps
1963, 1973; Brady, Harlan,
Harris 1973, Hayden,
Hughes 1964, 1970; Konek,
Patterson
T. O'DONOGHUE: Knowles
Geoffrey A. OELSNER, Jr. :
Hallmark
Ron OFFEN: Blazek, Weil
Laim O'GALLAGHER (1917):
Kostelanetz
D. OGILBY: Banker
D. T. (Dt) OGILVIE: Breman,
Major
William Henry OGILVIE (1869-
1963): T. Moore
Carolyn (J.) OGLETREE (c.
1949): Clay, Murphy
Ned O'GORMAN: Aiken, Beer-
man, Felver
Desmond O'GRADY (1935):
Ellmann 1973, Rosenthal
1967
Tom O'GRADY: Rigsbee
Edith OGUTSCH: Derleth,
Vrbovska 1963, 1968
Frank O'HARA (1926-1966):
Barnes, Baylor, Brady,
Carroll (Poem in Its Skin),
Carruth (Bantam), Chace,
Ellmann 1973, 1976; Har-
lan, Hollander, Hughes
1970, Kherdian 1973, Koch,
Leyland 1975, McCullough,
Myers, Padgett, Poulin,
Rothenberg 1973, Strand,
Waldman 1969, 1971; E.
Wilentz, M. Williams
J. D. O'HARA (1931): Jacobus
John Myers O'HARA: Parker
1967
Theodore O'HARA: J. A.
Vincent
Myron O'HIGGINS (1918):
Adoff 1968, 1973; Bontemps
1963, 1974; Breman, Hay-
den, Hughes 1970, Kramer,
Lowenfels 1966
Tanure OJAIDE: Lowenfels 1975

Calvin O'JOHN (1946): T.
Allen, Dodge
Arthur OKAMURA (1932):
Rothenberg
Gabriel OKARA (1921): Bre-
man, Hughes 1963, Jacobus,
Kgositsile, Koch, Lomax
Christopher OKIGBO (1932-
1967): Breman, Hughes
1963, Kgositsile, Lomax
Kay OKRAND: Palmer
Claes OLDENBURG: Gross
Perry OLDHAM: Rigsbee
Dawn O'LEARY: Oppenheimer
1977
Carole OLES: Mazur
Jan OLIVER: Adoff 1971
Mary OLIVER (1935): Immac-
ulate, Lask, Peck 1970,
Stanford, Stevenson, Stryk
1967
Tejumola OLOGBONI: P.
Brown
Charles OLSEN: L. Moore
Tillie OLSEN: Efros
Charles OLSON (1910-1970):
D. M. Allen 1964, Betts,
Brady, Carruth (Bantam),
Chace, Di Prima, Ell-
mann 1973, 1976; Harlan,
Kennedy 1974, Kostelanetz,
Lowenfels 1973, Poulin,
Rosenthal 1967, 1968;
Rothenberg 1973, 1974;
Sanders, Strand, Wesleyan
Univ. , M. Williams
Elder OLSON (1909): Firmage,
Morrison, Stabitz, Stryk
1967, Trapp, Univ. Press
of Va. , O. Williams 1966
(World)
Lawrence E. OLSON: Kiley
Stephanie J. OLSON: Brindle
Ted OLSON: Colley
Toby OLSON: De Loach 1976,
Harris 1973
Cathy OLTMAN: Brindle
B. OMALADE: Giovanni
Bob O'MEALLY (1948): Adoff
1974
Michael ONDAATJE: Carruth
(McCall)
Rose O'NEIL: Lask

Maureen O'NEILL: Chilgren
Richard O'NEILL: Black History
Andrew Amankwa OPOKU: Hughes 1963
George OPPEN (1908): Gross, Harris 1973, Harvey, Rothenberg 1973, 1974; Weil
Garrett OPPENHEIM: Lask
Joel OPPENHEIMER (1930): Banker, Carruth (Bantam), Cole 1971, De Loach 1968, 1976; Di Prima, Harris 1973, H. Jones, Leary, Lowenfels 1966, 1967, 1969 (Random House); Oppenheimer 1967, Rothenberg 1973, Waldman 1969, 1971
Paul OPPENHEIMER: Lask
Ilo ORLEANS: Jackson
Steven ORLEN: Rigsbee
Gil ORLOVITZ (1918): Blazek, Vrbovska 1963
Peter ORLOVSKY (1933): D. M. Allen 1960, De Loach 1968, 1976; E. Wilentz
Gregory ORR (1947): Bly 1975, Halpern, Hewitt, Hoffman, Kennedy 1973
Thomas ORR: Harris 1970
Orlando ORTIZ: Dodge, Kohl
Simon (J.) ORTIZ (1941): De Loach 1976, Lowenfels 1973, McCullough, Niatum, Rothenberg 1973
Chuck ORTLEB (1950): Leyland 1975
Jim ORVINO-SORCIC: Rosenblum
Dennis C. OSADEBAY (1911): Breman, Hughes 1963
Edith D. OSBORNE: Brewton
Frances Sargent OSGOOD: Jackson
Steve OSTERLUND: Blazek
Martha OSTERSO: Foster
Fred OSTRANDER: Harvey
Alicia OSTRIKER: Oppenheimer 1977
Anthony OSTROFF (1923-1978): Crafts, Glikes, Harvey, Larson, Lask
Anne OSWALD: Gross

O. V.: Clay
Bonaro W. OVERSTREET: Holmes
Ronald OVERTON (1943): Lowenfels 1973
Sharlet OVERTON: Booker
Guy OWEN (1925): Kennedy 1974, Lowenfels 1973, Owen 1969, Steele, Vrbovska 1963
Daniel W. OWENS (c. 1949): Murphy
I. L. OWENS: Booker
Rochelle OWENS (1936): Chester, De Loach 1968, 1976; Gross, Howe, Leary, Rothenberg 1973, Segnitz, Totem Press
John OXENHAM: Kauffman, J. A. Vincent
Abiodun OYEWOLE: Dee
Cynthia OZICK: Glikes

P

Rosella PACE: Bukowski
Robert PACK (1929): J. A. Allen, Baylor, Brady, Driver, Firmage, Hall 1962 (World), Hannum, Kennedy 1973, Leary, Lowenfels 1967, Strand, M. Williams, O. Williams 1966 (World)
William PACKARD (1933): Monaco 1974, H. Taylor, Vrbovska 1968
Christina V. PACOSZ: Brindle, Morticella
Ron PADGETT (1942): Carroll (Young American Poets), Clark, McCullough, Padgett, Waldman 1969
Daphne Kiane PAGE: Henderson
P. K. PAGE (1917): A. J. M. Smith 1960
Elio PAGLIARANI: Cole 1971
Edgar PAIEWONSKY: Hewitt
Harry W. PAIGE: McGovern
Albert Bigelow PAINE: Brewton

Emily PAINE: Lowenfels 1975
Miriam Rose PAISLEY: Sargent
Jennie M. PALEN: Derleth, Vrbovska 1968
Grace PALEY (1922): Howe
Morton PALEY: Head
Jonathan PALLEY: Harlan
Ralph PALMA: Harris 1976
Ted PALMANTEER (1943): T. Allen
Doug PALMER (1941): Palmer, Schreiber
Herbert PALMER (1880-1961): Parker 1975, Rose
Miriam PALMER (1946): Chester, Howe
Nettie Janet Gertrude Higgins PALMER (1885): T. Moore
Robertson PALMER: Jackson
Timothy PALMER: Crang
Winthrop PALMER: Lask
PAN: Violet
Raghunath PANDIT: Sargent
Cunter PANNEWITZ: Gay
Gauri PANT: Sargent
Greg PAPE (1947): Halpern
Basil T. PAQUET: Rottmann
Dorothy PARKER (1893-1967): Aloian, Cole 1965, Cromie, Holmes, Kaplan, Kennedy 1974, McGinley
Patricia (Pat) (A.) PARKER (c. 1945): Bulkin, Colley, Harvey, Krech, A. Miller
Thomas L. PARKER: Booker
Linda PARKER-SILVERMAN (1942): Stryk 1975
Frank (Francis Ernest) Kobina PARKES (1932): Hughes 1963
Thomas PARKINSON (1920): Harvey
Cuba PARKS (c. 1944): Giovanni
Henrietta C. PARKS (c. 1951): Murphy
Frank J. PARMENTER: Jackson
Ross PARMENTER: Lask
Chong Yeh PARMETER: K. and J. Sollid
Michael PARR: Lask

Charles PARRIOTT: Hausman
Dorothy C. PARRISH (c. 1943): Clay, Murphy
Jean A. PARRISH: Giovanni
Viola PARRISH (1932): Giovanni
Jerry PARROTT: Sherman
William Ordway PARTRIDGE: J. A. Vincent
Paul PASCAL: Hecht
Pat PASSLOF: Hauge
Linda PASTAN (1932): Chester 1974, Cole 1971, Heyen, Mazur, Owen, Wang
Kenneth PATCHEN (1911-1972): J. A. Allen, Bates, Berg, Carruth (Bantam), (McCall); Colley, Crafts, Engle, Hannum, Hannum and Chase, Harlan, Holmes, Hughes 1970, Jacobus, Kherdian 1973, Klonsky, Kramer, Lowenfels 1969 (Doubleday), Lucie-Smith, McCullough, Rothenberg 1973, 1974; H. Taylor, Untermeyer 1964, Wagner, Walsh, M. Williams, Winkler, Witt-Diamant
Alan PATON (1903): Immaculate
PATRICIA see Patricia McILNAY
Brian PATTEN (1946): Adoff 1969, Baylor, Cole 1971, Greaves, Jacobus, Lucie-Smith, Stallworthy, Walsh
Mary PATTEN: Bulkin
Benjamin PATTERSON: Gross
Charles PATTERSON (1941): Major
Dorothy PATTERSON: Kohl
J. M. PATTERSON: Jackson
James PATTERSON (1933): D. Randall 1969
Lindsay PATTERSON: Patterson
Raymond (Ray) (Richard) PATTERSON (1929): Adoff 1968, 1969, 1970, 1973, 1974; G. Brooks (Broadside Treasury), Colley, Coombs, Heyen, Holmes,

Hopkins (Knopf), Hughes 1964, 1970; Jacobus, Jordan, Kramer, Lowenfels 1966, 1969 (Doubleday); Major, D. Randall 1969
Raymond R. PATTERSON (1942): Baylor
Charlie PATTON (1887): Rothenberg
John PAUKER: Owen 1969
Irene PAULL: Lowenfels 1966
S. M. PAULSEN: Mallory
Robert PAWLOWSKI: Hoffman
Haihai PAWO PAWO: Lowenfels 1973
Tom PAXTON (1937): Kenseth, Morse, Peck 1970
Antionette PAYNE (c. 1950): Murphy
John PAYNE: Untermeyer 1970
Yiiksel PAZARKAYA: E. Williams
Okot p'BITEK: Kgositsile
Jerry PEACE: Booker
D. PEACOCK: Brindle
Thomas PEACOCK: Rosen
Mervyn PEAKE (1911-1968): Greaves
Ellen PEARCE (1946): Konek
Darlene PEARLSTEIN: Friedman
Bernard PEARSON: Booker
PEASE see Louise McNEILL
Elisabeth PECK: Brewton
John PECK (1941): Halpern, Heyen
Louise D. PECK: Lask
Richard PECK: Peck 1970, 1971
Samuel Minturn PECK: Jackson
Jean PEDRICK: Mazur
Ronald E. PEDRO: Kiley
Claude PELIEU: Fox, Harvey
Dewey G. PELL (1917): Kennedy 1974
Oscar PENARANDA: Clay
Conrad PENDLETON: Derleth
Gerda PENFOLD: Bukowski
Edmund PENNANT: Vbrovska 1963, 1968
Lee PENNINGTON: Plumley
Rob PENNY (1940): Adoff 1973, 1974; Patterson

PENROD: Montgomery
Simon PERCHIK: Weil
Francesca Yetunde PEREIRA: Hughes 1963
Teresinha Alves PEREIRA: Clay
Jane Lunin PEREL: Mazur
Benjamin PERET: Harlan
Tony PEREZ (1935): Pgymalion
David PERKINS: Rigsbee
Eugene PERKINS (1932): Breman, P. Brown, Lee 1971
Stuart Z. PERKOFF (1930): D. M. Allen 1960, Bukowski
Mark PERLBERG (1929): Cole 1971, 1972; Stryk 1975
John PERREAULT (1937): Carroll (Young American Poets), Gross, McCullough, Padgett, Waldman 1969
Frederick Douglas PERRY: Kohl
Julianne PERRY (1952): Adoff 1973
M. C. PERRY: Student
Phil PERRY: P. Perry
Ronald (Peter Lee) PERRY (1932): Hall 1962 (World)
Stan PERSKY (1941): Leyland 1975
Patty One PERSON: Violet
Enid Rhodes PESCHEL: Gallery 1973
John PETER: Vrbovska 1963
Lord PETERBOROUGH: Cole 1971
Stuart PETERFREUND (c. 1946): Hewitt
Anne PETERS: Lowenfels 1966
Edmund W. PETERS: Morrison
Lenrie PETERS (1932): Breman, Lomax
Nancy PETERS: Ferlinghetti
Richard PETERS: Jackson
Robert (Louis) PETERS (1924): Bukowski, Gross, Hitchcock, Leyland 1975, 1977; Stevenson, Winans, Young

Donald PETERSEN (1928): De Roche, Hall 1962 (World), Pearson, Strand

Robert PETERSON (1924): J. Gill, Harvey, Hitchcock, Kenseth, Kramer, Lowenfels 1967

Ruth Delong PETERSON: Brewton

Dom Robert PETITPIERRE: Gross

Paul (Jones) PETRIE (1928): Cole 1963, Lask

Henry PETROSKI: Rigsbee

S. B. PETTINGILL, Jr. : Jackson

Daniel PETTIWARD (1913): Cole 1963

Andrew PEYNETSA (1904): Rothenberg

Eric PFEIFFER: Lask

Roger PFINGSTON: Lask

Arthur PFISTER (1949): G. Brooks (Broadside Treasury), Coombs, King 1972

Charles PHILBRICK: Aiken

Casper C. PHILLIPS: Jackson

Clarence PHILLIPS: Tisdale

David PHILLIPS: J. Gill

Frank Lamont PHILLIPS (1953): Bontemps 1974, Colley

Louis PHILLIPS (1942): Monaco 1973, 1974; Owen 1974

Patrice PHILLIPS (1949): Kennedy 1973

Ruth PHILLIPS: Student

J. PHOENICE: Lask

Donn PIATT: Jackson

Felice PICANO (1944): Leyland 1977

Tom PICKARD: Bly 1975, Wang

Henry PICOLA: Vrbovska 1963, 1968

Edith Lovejoy PIERCE (1904): Cromie, Trapp

Marge PIERCY (1934): Baylor, Brinnin 1970, Chester, Colley, Efros, E. Gill, J. Gill, Gitlin, Howe, Jacobus, Kennedy 1973, 1974; Konek, Lowenfels 1969 (Doubleday), (Random House), 1973; L. Moore, Schreiber, Segnitz, Sherman, Wagner

John PIERPONT: J. A. Vincent

Pedro PIETRI: Algarin

Decio PIGNATARI: Gross, Wildman, E. Williams

Jean Sophia PIGOTT: Kauffman

Albert G. PIKE: Kauffman

William PILLIN (1910): Bukowski, Lowenfels 1966

A. Barbara PILON: Pilon

Josephine PINCKNEY (1895): Parks

Mike PINDER: Morse

Dadi PINERO: Algarin

Miguel (Gomez) PINERO (1946): Algarin

PINK: Cole 1972

Helen PINKERTON (1927): Winters

Wlademir Dias PINO: E. Williams

Sanford PINSKER: Freed

Robert PINSKY: Mazur

Luiz Angelo PINTO: E. Williams

Oliver PITCHER (1923): Adoff 1973, Bontemps 1963, 1974; Hayden, Hughes 1964, Lomax

Kenneth PITCHFORD (1931): J. A. Allen, Gitlin, Leary

Ruth PITTER (1897): C. Brooks, Cole 1963, J. Gibson, J. Gibson (Book Two), Gregory 1962, 1966; Knowles, Lask, Stanford, Univ. Press of Va. , Untermeyer 1964

Herbert Lee PITTS (c. 1949): Coombs

Marie (Maere) M. PITTS (1948): Giovanni

Alan PIZZARELLI (1950): Van den Heuvel

Allen (Alan) PLANZ (1933): De Loach 1968, Lowenfels 1966, 1967, 1969 (Random House); Owen 1969, 1974; Rothenberg 1973

Sylvia PLATH (1932-1963):
Adams, J. A. Allen, Barnes,
Baylor, Berg, Brady, Brin-
nin 1963, 1970; Carruth
(Bantam), Chace, Chester,
De Roche, Driver, Ellmann
1973, 1976; Hall 1962
(World), Hannum, Harlan,
Harris 1973, Hollander,
Howe, Hurtik, Jacobus,
Kaplan, Kennedy 1973,
1974; Konek, Kostelanetz,
McCullough, Monaco 1974,
L. Moore, J. Perry,
Phillips, Poulin, Rosenthal
1967, 1968; Sanders,
Schneider, Segnitz, Stan-
ford, Strand, H. Taylor,
Untermeyer 1973 (McKay),
Wagner, Wallace, Walsh,
M. Williams, Winkler
Stan PLATKE: Rottmann
Francis T. P. PLIMPTON:
Jackson
Harriet PLIMPTON: Lask
William PLOMER (1903):
Brinnin 1963, Cole 1967
(Macmillan), Ellmann 1973,
Knowles, Phillips, Steven-
son
Harvey (M.) PLOTNICK: Gal-
lery 1970, 1973
David PLUMB: Head
Stanley PLUMLY (1939): Hal-
pern, Heyen, Lask, Owen
1974, Stryk 1975
Sterling (D.) PLUMPP (1940):
Adoff 1973, P. Brown
Hyam PLUTZIK (1911): J. A.
Allen, Carruth (Bantam),
Derleth, Felver, Joseloff,
Pearson, Wallace, Wesleyan
Univ.
Charles (Douglas) PLYMELL
(1935): Blazek, Fox, Har-
vey, Poetry San Francisco
John PODA: Jackson
Jaon POE (c. 1947): Giovanni
Michael POGLIANO: Crafts
Allen POLITE (1932): Hughes
1964
Marcella POLK (c. 1950):
Giovanni

Felix POLLAK (1909): Gallery
1970, Gross, Lowenfels
1967, 1969 (Doubleday);
Stryk 1975, Weil
Adelaide A. POLLARD: Kauff-
man
Katha POLLITT: Rigsbee
Ann POLLON: Violet
Edward POLS: Glikes
Stuart Kent POLZIN: Crafts
Marnie POMEROY (1932):
Cole 1963, 1971, 1972
Ralph POMEROY (1926): Adoff
1969, Cole 1967 (Macmil-
lan), Crafts, Holmes, Lask,
Leary, Young
William J. POMEROY (1915):
Lowenfels 1966
Jefry PONIEWAZ: Rosenblum
Marie PONSOT: Carruth (Ban-
tam)
Tom POOLE (1938): Adoff
1970, Colley, Major
Tom POOTS: Derleth
J. R. POPE: Cole 1967 (Mac-
millan)
Bern PORTER: Gross
Bill PORTER: Harris 1970
Hal PORTER (1917): T. Moore
Kenneth PORTER (1905):
Hughes 1970
Linda PORTER: Booker,
Hopkins (Knopf)
Peter PORTER (1929): Cole
1967 (Macmillan), Crang,
Kenseth, Lucie-Smith, T.
Moore, Rosenthal 1967,
Stallworthy
Ray PORTER: Jackson
T. E. PORTER: Rigsbee
Timothy L. PORTER (1946):
Coombs
David POSNER (1938): Monaco
1973, 1974
Charles POTTS: Krech
Jim POTTS: Clay
Ezra POUND (1885-1972):
Adams, Arp, Bach,
Barnes, Bates, Baylor,
R. Bender, Bly 1970,
Bogan, Brady, Brinnin
1963, 1970; C. Brooks,
Calderwood, Carruth (Ban-

tam), Chace, Cole 1965,
1967 (Macmillan), 1971,
1972; Croft, De Roche,
Dunning, Ellmann 1973,
1976; Gregory 1962, Gwynn,
Hall 1962 (Watts), Harlan,
Hieatt, Hine, Hurtik,
Jacobus, Kennedy 1974,
Kenseth, Klonsky, Monaco
1974, Morrison, Olson,
Perrine, J. Perry, Pound,
Reeves, Rothenberg 1973,
1974; Sanders, Schneider,
Shapiro, Simpson, A. J.
M. Smith 1965, Stallworthy,
H. Taylor, W. Taylor,
Untermeyer 1964, 1973
(McKay); Wagner, Wallace,
Whicher, Williams and
Honig, O. Williams 1966
(Trident), (World); Winkler

Blossom (F.) POWE: Dee
Amanda POWELL: Rigsbee
Ellie Mae POWELL: Kohl
Lillie Mae POWELL: Student
Roxie POWELL: Poetry San
Francisco
Kevin POWER: De Loach 1976
H. W. POWERS: Kiley
Jeffrey POWERS (1950):
Pygmalion
Jessica POWERS (1905): Corbett
Holly PRADO: Bukowski
Agnes (T.) PRATT (1945): T.
Allen, Dodge
E. J. PRATT (1883-1964):
Ellmann 1973, Engle,
Foster, A. J. M. Smith
1960
John Clarke PRATT: Kiley
Marjory Bates PRATT (1896):
Van den Heuvel
Paul PRENSKY: Banker
John PRESS (1920): Lask,
Stallworthy
Keith PRESTON: Nash
Richard PRESTON: Hoffman
Quandra PRETTYMAN (c.
1934): Adoff 1968, 1969,
1970, 1973; Hopkins
(Knopf), Peck 1971
Jacques PREVERT (1899-1977):

Adoff 1969, Cole 1971,
Stallworthy
Arnold PRICE: Lask
Jonathan PRICE (1941): Crang,
Peck 1970, Pilon, Stallworthy, M. Williams
Merle PRICE: Cromie
Nancy PRICE: Gildner, Konek,
Lask
Eric PRIESTLEY (1943):
Coombs
F. T. PRINCE (1912): Stallworthy, Untermeyer 1964
Daniel H. PRIOR: Jackson
Glenn PRITCHARD: Cole 1972,
Lask
N. H. PRITCHARD (Norman
Henry Pritchard II) (1939):
Adoff 1973, Breman,
Lowenfels 1969 (Random
House), Major, A. Miller,
T. Wilentz
Katherine Jo PRIVETT (1924):
Firmage
Anita Endrezze PROBST:
Niatum
Adelaide A. PROCTER: Kauffman
Frederic PROKOSCH (1908):
O. Williams 1966 (World)
Dan PROPPER: E. Wilentz
Joseph M. PROSKAUER: Jackson
John PUDNEY: Cole 1971
Harold Trowbridge PULSIFER:
Jackson
Charles M. PURCELL: Rottmann
A. W. (Al) PURDY (1918):
Blazek, De Roche, Ellmann 1973, Phillips
Elliot PURITZ: Hanna 1960
Edna G. PURVIANCE: Sargent
Linda PURRINGTON: Brindle
Frank PUTNAM: Jackson
Rodney PYBUS: Harris 1976
Craig Randolph PYES: Gitlin
A. Warnyeneh PYNE: Booker

Q

George QUASHA (1942): Gross,

Harris 1970, Rothenberg 1973, Sumac
Salvatore QUASIMODO: Wesleyan Univ.
Peter QUENNELL (1905): Knowles, Untermeyer 1964
Dorothy QUICK: Derleth
Helen (G.) QUIGLESS (1944): Major, Murphy, D. Randall 1969
Bernetta QUINN: De Loach 1976
Peter QUINN: Pilon
Juan Gomez QUINOMES: Winans
Cathleen QUIRK: E. Gill, Howe
Susan QUIST: De Loach 1976

R

Sun RA (c. 1928): Adoff 1973, Breman
Lawrence RAAB (1946): Halpern, Hausman, Hoffman
Marlene RACHMEIL: Hanna
Doris RADIN: Knight
Irma RADOVSKY: Brindle
Julian RAEDER: Vrbovska 1968
Burton RAFFEL: Colley, Dunning
Gerald RAFTERY: Brewton, Dunning
Sam RAGAN: Owen 1974
Henry RAGO (1915): Carruth (Bantam), Engle, Rosenthal 1967, Stibitz
Jamail Abdur RAHMAN (Sheridan R. Nesbitt; Robert Sims) (1932): Tisdale
De Wayne RAIL: Kherdian 1970
Kathleen RAINE (1908): Greaves, Stanford, W. Taylor, Thomas, Untermeyer 1964
RAKEMAN: Dee
Cecil RAJENDRA: Lowenfels 1975
Carl RAKOSI (1903): De Loach 1976, Rothenberg 1973, Stryk 1975

Hank RALEIGH: Hauge
Loker RALEY: Vrbovska 1963
A. K. RAMANUJAN: Lask
Sharon O. RAMIREZ: Harlan
Sussan RAMM (c. 1938): Giovanni
James G. RAMSAY, Jr.: Kiley
Patricia RAMSEY (1933): Mollenkott
Paul RAMSEY (1924): Cole 1971, Owen 1969, 1974; Steele, H. Taylor, Wesleyan Univ.
Flavien RANAIVO see Miriam KOSHLAND
Dorothy RANDALL: Dee
Dudley RANDALL (1914): Adoff 1968, 1970, 1973; Bell, Bontemps 1963, 1974; Breman, G. Brooks (Broadside Treasury), P. Brown, Ellmann 1973, Fox, Gersmehl, Hayden, Henderson, Hopkins (Knopf), Hughes 1964, 1970; Kennedy 1974, Major, Patterson, D. Randall 1960, 1969; Turner
James RANDALL (1938): Brooks, Lane
Jon RANDALL: Lane
Julia RANDALL (1923): J. A. Allen, M. Gibson, Howe, Owen 1969, 1974; Rubin, Stanford, Steele, H. Taylor
Margaret RANDALL (1936): Gitlin, Harris 1973, Lowenfels 1969 (Doubleday), (Random House); Sherman, Weil
randimeridethbrown see Randy Meredith BROWN
Innes RANDOLPH: Hine
Jeremiah Eames RANKIN: J. A. Vincent
John Crowe RANSOM (1888-1974): Adams, Aiken, G. W. Allen, J. A. Allen, Aloian, Arp, Bach, Barnes, Baylor, R. Bender, Brady, Brinnin 1963,

1970; C. Brooks, Brower, Calderwood, Carruth (Bantam), De Roche, Drew, Ellmann 1973, 1976; Engle, Gregory 1962, 1966; Gwynn, Hall 1962 (Watts), Hannum, Harlan, Hurtik, Immaculate, Jacobus, Kallich, Kennedy 1974, Kenseth, McGinley, Morrison, Nash, Parks, Peck 1970, Perrine, J. Perry, Peterson, Reeves, Sanders, Schneider, Shapiro, Stallworthy, H. Taylor, W. Taylor, Thomas, Untermeyer 1964, Williams and Honig, O. Williams 1966 (Trident), (World)

W. M. RANSOM: Niatum
Lennox RAPHAEL (1940): Adoff 1973, Gross, Lowenfels 1969 (Random House), Major, T. Wilentz
David RASEY (1935): Lowenfels 1969 (Random House)
Amir RASHIDD (1943): Major
Niema RASHIDD (Fuller): Major
Carter RATCLIFF: Waldman 1969, 1971
Michael RATCLIFFE (1941): Young
Greg RATHJEN: Harlan
Rochelle RATNER (1948): Hewitt, Harris 1973
John RAVER: G. Brooks (Broadside Treasury)
Isetta Crawford RAWLS (c. 1941): Giovanni
Tom RAWORTH (1934): Lucie-Smith, Matthias
David RAY (1932): Bonazzi 1972, Carruth (Bantam), Gildner, Glikes, Hall 1962 (World), Kennedy 1973, Lowenfels 1967, 1973, 1975; J. Perry, Stryk 1975, Wagner, Wang
Irvin RAY: Booker
Louise Crenshaw RAY: Jackson
Maude Louise RAY: Kauffman
Richard RAY: Plumley

Shreela RAY: Owen 1969
Alex RAYBIN (1945): Schreiber
Jesse Andrew RAYE: Booker
Arthur RAYMOND: Salkey
George Lansing RAYMOND: Jackson
Monica RAYMOND: Malley
Richard C. RAYMOND: Lask
Robert RAYMOND: Kiley
Bernard RAYMUND: Cole 1963
Vera RAYNOR: Oppenheimer 1977
Haj RAZAUI: Sherman
Herbert READ (1893-1968): Cole 1965, 1971, 1972; Cromie, Ellmann 1973, Kenseth, Knowles, Plotz
James REANEY (1926): Adams, A. J. M. Smith 1960
George REAVEY: Firmage
Don RECEVEUR, Jr.: Rottmann
Judith RECHTER (1937): Howe
Fred RED CLOUD (1928): Dodge, Lowenfels 1973
Otis REDDING: Chace
Peter REDGROVE (1932): Greaves, Hall 1962 (World), Lucie-Smith, Rosenthal 1967, 1968; Stevenson
Dennis REDMAN: Sherman
Eugene REDMOND (1938): Gersmehl, Gross, Henderson, Major, Murphy, Simmons
Roosevelt REDMOND: Student
Eugene REDMONT (1937): Adoff 1973
Thomas Dillon REDSHAW (1944): Kennedy 1973
A. K. REDWING (1948): Rosen
J. REDWOOD-ANDERSON: J. Gibson
Byron Herbert REECE (1918): Cole 1965, Lask
(Mrs.) Sam REECE: Lowenfels 1969 (Doubleday)
Alastair REED (1926): Engle
Clarence REED: King 1972
Cleave (Poncho) REED: Adoff 1971

Geinye REED: Giovanni
Henry REED (1914): Bates,
Baylor, Bogan, Brinnin
1963, Crang, Cromie, De
Roche, Gwynn, Harlan,
Holmes, Hurtik, Peck
1970, Plotz, A. J. M.
Smith 1967, Stallworthy,
H. Taylor
Ishmael REED (1938): Adoff
1973, Barnes, Breman,
Caly, Chace, Colley, Har-
vey, Heyden, Hughes 1970,
Jacobus, Jordan, Kennedy
1974, Lowenfels 1966,
1967, 1969 (Doubelday),
(Random House), 1975;
Major, Rothenberg 1973,
Wagner
Ivy Kellerman REED: Jackson
J. D. REED (1940): J. Gill,
Phillips, Sumac
Lou REED: Waldman 1971
R. A. REED: Morticella
Robert REEDBURG (c. 1941):
Murphy
A. A. REES: Kauffman
Gomer REES: Harris 1973
S. (Sarah) Carolyn REESE:
G. Brooks (Broadside
Treasury), Hughes 1970,
Patterson
F. D. REEVE (1928): Lowen-
fels 1967
Jean A. REEVE: Hoffman
Campbell REEVES: Owen 1974
Claude REEVES: Hine
James REEVES (1909): Cole
1963, 1967 (Viking), 1972;
J. Gibson, J. Gibson (Book
Two), Livingston
Katherine REEVES: Derleth
John Calvin REGMERSKI (1942):
Stryk 1975
Pat REH: Fox
Alastair (Alistair) REID (1926):
Brinnin 1970, Derleth,
Glikes, Hall 1962 (World),
Hannum, Hannum and
Chase, Pilon, Plotz,
Summerfield, Wallace
Alfred REID: Owen 1974
Keith REID: Morse

Evelyn Joyce REINGOLD: Clay
Paula REINGOLD: Konek
Robert REINHOLD: Lowenfels
1975
Robert REISNER: Klonsky
James REISS (1941): Ashland,
Halpern, Mazur, Stryk
1975
Thomas REITER (1940): H.
Taylor
Ettore RELLA: Lowenfels
1969 (Doubleday)
RENEE: Kohl
Vittoria REPETTO: Violet
Naomi REPLANSKY (1918):
Cole 1972, Howe, Lowen-
fels 1966, 1969 (Doubleday)
Renee RESENDEZ: Lowenfels
1969 (Doubleday)
Milton RESNICK: Hauge
Carl-Fredrik REUTERSWARD:
E. Williams
Carter REVARD: Rosen
Kenneth REXROTH (1905):
Adoff 1969, Berg, Bly
1970, Carruth (Bantam),
(McCall's); Crafts, Cromie,
Ellmann 1973, Firmage,
Harlan, Harvey, Kherdian,
1973, Kostelanetz, Larson,
Livingston, Lowenfels
1969 (Doubleday), L.
Moore, Peck 1971, Plotz,
Rosenthal 1967, 1968;
Rothenberg 1973, 1974;
Stallworthy, Steuben,
Stevenson, Wallace, Witt-
Diamant
Morris REYBURN: Vrbovska
1963
Carlos REYES (1935): Durand,
Morticella
Barbara A. REYNOLDS (1944):
P. Brown, Giovanni
Malvina REYNOLDS: Peck
1970
Tim REYNOLDS (1936): Ken-
nedy 1973, Lowenfels
1966, Weil
Philip REYS: Katzman
John Calvin REZMERSKI
(1942): Stryk 1975
Charles REZNIKOFF (1894-

1976): Adoff 1969, Carruth
(Bantam), Cole 1972, Greg-
ory 1966, Joseloff, Kennedy
1974, Kherdian 1973, 1974;
Rothenberg 1973, 1974;
Summerfield, Waldman 1971
Nettie RHODES: Student
Randy RHODY: Lowenfels 1969
(Doubleday)
Keidrych RHYS (1915): Steven-
son
Rene RICARD: Waldman 1969
Ottone (M.) RICCIO: Fox, P.
Perry
Cale Young RICE: Jackson
Grantland RICE: J. A. Vincent
Helen Stein RICE: Kauffman
Jo (Joe) Nell RICE: Booker,
Dee, Hopkins (Knopf)
Stan RICE (1942): Harvey,
Hewitt
Adrienne RICH (1929): Aiken,
Baylor, Brady, Bulkin,
Carruth (Bantam), Chace,
Chester, Crang, De Roche,
Ellmann 1973, 1976; Hall
1962 (Penguin), (World);
Hannum, Hannum and
Chase, Harris 1970, 1973;
Heyen, Hollander, Howard,
Howard and Victor, Howe,
Jacobus, Kennedy 1973,
1974; Konek, Leary, McCul-
lough, Plotz, Poulin,
Segnitz, Stanford, Stevenson,
Strand, Untermeyer 1973
(McKay), M. Williams
Dave RICH: Palmer
Keith RICHARD (1943): Kennedy
1974
Randall RICHARD: Adoff 1971
A. I. RICHARDS: Lask
Betsy RICHARDS: Crafts
Laura E. RICHARDS: Nash
M. C. RICHARDS (1916):
Rothenberg 1973
Nathan A. RICHARDS: Hender-
son
Justin RICHARDSON: Cole
1967 (Macmillan)
Donald R. RICHBERG: Jackson
Edward RICHER (1930): D.
Randall 1969

Naomi RICHMAN: Morticella
Steven (Steve) RICHMOND
(1941): Blazek, Bukowski,
Lowenfels 1969 (Random
House), Winans
Wendy G. RICKERT: Howe
Edgell RICKWORD: Cromie
Elizabeth RIDDELL (1909):
Greaves, T. Moore
Jesse C. RIDER: Kiley
RIDHIANA: Dee, Major
Laura RIDING (Jackson) (1901):
Ellmann 1973, Lask,
Rothenberg 1974
John RIDLAND (1933): Hitch-
cock, Kennedy
Anne RIDLER (1912): Brinnin
1963, Cole 1971, Greaves,
Lask, Rosenthal 1967,
Stanford, Thomas
E. V. RIEU (1887): Cole
1963, McGinley, Rose
Iris RIFKIN: Waldman 1969
John G. RIGGI: Brindle
Lynn RIGGS: Parker 1967
David RILEY: Head
Joanne M. RILEY: Sollid
1972, K. and J. Sollid
Martin RINKART: Kauffman
Suzanne Berger RIOFF (1944):
Howe
Robert F. RIORDAN (1951):
Leyland 1977
Geoffrey RIPS: Lowenfels
1975
Harland RISTAU (1927):
Lowenfels 1966
Elisavietta RITCHIE (1932):
Mollenkott
Maria RIVAL: Lowenfels 1975
Richard RIVE (1931): Hopkins
(Knopf), Hughes 1963,
Lomax
Conrad Kent (K.) RIVERS
(1933): Adoff 1968, 1970,
1973; Bell, Bontemps
1963, 1974; Breman, G.
Brooks (Broadside Treas-
ury), Hayden, Henderson,
Hughes 1964, 1970; Don
L. Lee 1971, Major, D.
Randall 1969
RJS (rjs) see Robert Joseph

SIGMUND
E. M. ROACH (1915): Breman,
Salkey
Martin ROBBINS (1931): Ken-
nedy 1973, Morrison
Susan ROBBINS: Dee
Dwight ROBBS (1940): Monaco
Ed ROBERSON (1939): Adoff
1973, Gildner, Hughes 1970
C. G. D. ROBERTS: J. Gibson
Daniel C. ROBERTS: J. A.
Vincent
Percival ROBERTS: Harris
1976
Peter ROBERTS: Rose
Roberta ROBERTS: Black
History
Walter Adolphe ROBERTS (1886-
1965): Hughes 1970, Lomax
Foster ROBERTSON: Harlan,
Head, Winans
Dwight ROBHS (1940): Monaco
1973
Ralph ROBIN: Lask
Clement ROBINSON: Untermeyer
1970
Edwin Meade ROBINSON: J.
Gibson (Book Two)
Kenneth Allan ROBINSON:
Brewton
Michael ROBINSON: K. and J.
Sollid
Pat ROBINSON: Sherman
Roland Edward ROBINSON (1912):
T. Moore
T. L. ROBINSON (1946):
Coombs
Wey ROBINSON: Morrison
Alfred ROBLES: Clay, Winans
Jaime ROBLES: Mallory
James Jeffrey ROCHE: Jackson
Margaret ROCKWELL (1921):
Bates, Kenseth
Virginia RODAS: Sargent
Jose RODEIRO: Lowenfels
1975, Smith
Rebecca L. RODES: Brindle
Carolyn (M.) RODGERS (1942):
Adoff 1973, 1974; Breman,
G. Brooks (Broadside
Treasury), (Jump Bad); P.
Brown, Coombs, Giovanni,
Gross, Howe, Kherdian

1974, King 1972, Don L.
Lee, Murphy, Patterson,
T. Wilentz
Loretta RODGERS: Patterson
W. R. RODGERS (1909-1969):
Barnes, Cole 1971, Ell-
mann 1973, Kenseth,
Morrison, Untermeyer
1964
Selden RODMAN (1909): Hughes
1970
Luz RODRIGUEZ: Algarin
Theodore ROETHKE (1908-
1963): Adams, G. W.
Allen, J. A. Allen,
Aloian, Bach, Barnes,
Baylor, Beerman, Berg,
Bly 1970, Bogan, Brady,
Brinnin 1963, 1970; C.
Brooks, Calderwood,
Carruth (Bantam), (McCall);
Chace, Cole 1963, 1965,
1967, 1971, 1972; Colley,
Crafts, De Roche, Drew,
Driver, Dunning, Ellmann
1973, 1976; Engle, Felver,
Firmage, Gersmehl,
Greaves, Gwynn, Hall
1962 (Watts), Hannum,
Hannum and Chase, Har-
lan, Hieatt, Holmes, Hur-
tik, Immaculate, Jacobus,
Kennedy 1973, 1974; Ken-
seth, Knowles, Kostelanetz,
Larrick, Larson, Living-
ston, McCullough, McGin-
ley, Monaco 1974, L.
Moore, Olson, Peck 1970,
Perrine, J. Perry, Poulin,
Rosenthal 1967, 1968;
Rothenberg 1973, Sanders,
Schneider, Simpson, A. J.
M. Smith 1967, Stallworthy,
Steuben, Strand, Summer-
field, H. Taylor, W. Tay-
lor, Ten, Untermeyer
1964, 1973 (McKay); Wag-
ner, Walsh, Wesleyan
Univ. , M. Williams, O.
Williams 1966 (World),
Winkler, Witt-Diamant
Benjamin H. ROGERS (1949):
Lowenfels 1973

Carolyn M. ROGERS: Henderson
David ROGERS (1932): Lowen-
fels 1967
Ronald ROGERS (1948): T.
Allen, Dodge
W. R. ROGERS (1911-1969):
Rosenthal 1967, Stallworthy
Alice ROGOFF: Head
Linda ROLENS: Mallory
Edwin ROLFE (1909): Hine,
Kenseth
Thomas William ROLLESTON:
Parker 1967
Eric ROLLS (1923): T. Moore
Edward ROMANO (1933): Gitlin
Liboria (E.) ROMANO: Derleth,
Scheftel, Vrbovska 1963,
1968
Leo ROMERO: Lowenfels 1975
Hugh ROMNEY: E. Wilentz
Kraft ROMPF: Rigsbee
William Pitt ROOT (1941):
Cole 1971, Evans, Owen
1969
Robert RORIPAUGH: Gallery
1973
Rose ROSBERG: Harris 1970
Don ROSCHER: Gallery 1973
Billy ROSE: J. A. Vincent
Chick ROSE: Morticella
Liz Farrell ROSE: Gitlin
Wendy ROSE: Clay, Niatum
Raymond (Francis) ROSELIEP
(1917): Derleth, Gallery
1973, Gildner, Glikes,
Harris 1970, 1976; Stryk,
Weil
Penelope ROSEMONT: Ferling-
hetti
Judy ROSEN: Violet
Kenneth ROSEN: Gildner,
Halpern
Sylvia ROSENBAUM: Sargent
Arthur E. ROSENBERG: Jack-
son
D. M. ROSENBERG: Freed
Dorothy ROSENBERG (1916):
Hughes 1970
Jim ROSENBERG (1947):
Barnes
Robert ROSENBERG: Lowenfels
1975
Sydell ROSENBERG: Van den
Heuvel

Martin J. ROSENBLUM:
Rosenblum
William ROSENFELD: Gallery
1970
M. L. ROSENTHAL (1917):
Heyen
Zoe ROSENTHAL: Brindle
Sunryu Suzuki ROSHI (1905-
1971): Rothenberg
Alan ROSS (1922): Baylor,
Cole 1971, Knowles,
Perrine, Stallworthy
Margaret Wheeler ROSS:
Jackson
Moshe ROSS: Morticella
(W.) W. E. (Eustace) ROSS
(1894-1966): Cole 1963,
Foster, Lask, Morrison,
Rose, A. J. M. Smith
1960
Michael ROSSMAN (1939):
Gitlin
Norman ROSTEN (1914):
Cromie, Kramer, H. Tay-
lor
Diter ROT: Gross, E. Wil-
liams
Dan ROTH: Dunning
Paul ROTH: Fox, Smith
Jerome ROTHENBERG (1931):
J. A. Allen, Bly 1975,
Cole 1967 (Macmillan),
De Loach 1968, 1976;
Glikes, Gross, Howard,
Howard and Victor,
Kherdian 1973, Leary,
Lowenfels 1967, 1973;
Rosenthal 1967, 1973
Larry ROTTMANN: Rottmann
Emile ROUMER (1903): Lomax
Colin ROWBOTHAM (1949):
Greaves
David ROWBOTHAM (1924):
T. Moore
L. Bruce ROWE: Rosenblum
J. R. ROWLAND (1925): T.
Moore
Martha Keller ROWLAND:
Derleth
A. L. ROWSE (1903): Parker
1975
Conrado Nale ROXLO (1898):
Trapp
Sandra H. ROYSTER: Patterson

R-P-O-P-H-E-S-S-A-G-R:
  Harlan
Gibbons RUARK (1941): Kennedy
  1973, Owen 1969, 1974
David (James D.) RUBADIRI
  (1930): Breman, Hughes
  1963, Kgositsile
Carol RUBENSTEIN: Banker
Jerry RUBIN (1938): Baylor
Larry (Jerome) RUBIN (1930):
  Derleth, Harris 1970, Lask,
  Owen 1969, 1974; Steele,
  Vrbovska 1963
Rachel RUBIN: Violet
Kathy RUDI: De Loach 1976
Mark RUDMAN: Hoffman
Raphael RUDNIK (1933): Ken-
  nedy 1974
Lee RUDOLPH: Hitchcock,
  Mazur
Paul RUFFIN: Sollid 1973
John M. RUGANDA: Jacobus
Eugene RUGGLES (1936): Har-
  vey, McGovern
Gene RUGGLES: Winans
Gerhard RUHM: Gross, Wild-
  man, E. Williams
Muriel RUKEYSER (1913):
  Aiken, J. A. Allen, Banker,
  Brinnin 1963, 1970; Carruth
  (Bantam), Chester, Cole
  1971, Colum, Hannum and
  Chase, Howard, Howard
  and Victor, Howe, Hughes
  1970, Immaculate, Jackson,
  Joseloff, Kennedy 1974,
  Konek, Kramer, Lowenfels
  1969 (Doubleday), 1975;
  Monaco 1974, Perrine,
  Rosenthal 1967, 1968; Roth-
  enberg 1973, Stanford,
  Trapp, Untermeyer 1964,
  1973 (McKay), Wagner, O.
  Williams 1966 (World),
  Witt-Diamant
Michael RUMAKER (1932):
  Ferlinghetti, Lowenfels 1973
William M. RUNYAN: Kauffman
Damon RUNYON: Jackson
Martin RUOSS: Hanna 1960
Francille RUSAN: Booker
Michael RUSH: Hoffman
Cassandre RUSSELL: Banker

David RUSSELL: Lask
Ethel Green RUSSELL (1890):
  Mollenkott
Greg RUSSELL: Dee
Norman (H.) RUSSELL (1921):
  Dodge, Gallery 1973, Ken-
  nedy 1973, Lourie, Lowen-
  fels 1973, Plumley
Sydney King RUSSELL: Der-
  leth, Dunning
A. P. RUSSO: Bukowski
Alan RUSSO: Poetry San
  Francisco
Lola Ingres RUSSO: Brewton
Tony RUTHERFORD see
  Umar Abd Rahim HASSON
Vern RUTSALA (1934): Colley,
  Harlan, Larson, Lowenfels
  1967, 1969 (Doubleday);
  Morticella, Pearson
Michael RYAN (1946): Halpern,
  Stryk 1975
Richard RYAN: Harris 1976
Therl RYAN: Colley
W. E. RYAN: Gallery 1973
Barbara C. RYBERG: Kauff-
  man
Sarah RYDER: Gallery 1970,
  1973
Anthony RYE: Knowles
Linda RZESNIOWIECKI:
  Brindle

S

Nina SABAROFF: Bulkin
Vincent SACARDI (d. 1972):
  Leyland 1975
Vita (Victoria) SACKVILLE-
  WEST (1892-1962): Kap-
  lan, Knowles, Parker
  1975, Stanford
Ira SADOFF (1945): Halpern,
  Mazur
SAGITTARIUS: Parker 1967,
  Rose
Albert SAIJO: E. Wilentz
Napoleon ST. CYR: McMahon
David ST. JOHN (1949): Hal-
  pern
Primus ST. JOHN (1939):
  Adoff 1973, Heyen, Larson

James ST. MARTIN: Clay
Raymonde SAINTE-PIERRE
(1951): Leyland 1977
Becky SAKELLARIOU: Brindle
Floyd SALAS: Head
Dennis SALEH (1942): Blazek,
J. Gill, Kennedy 1973,
Kherdian 1970, Winans
SALIMU: Jihad
Anthony SALINARO: Chilgren
(Luis) Omar SALINAS: Clay,
Kherdian 1970, 1974;
Winans
Raul SALINAS: Clay
Carey SALISBURY: Morticella
Ralph (J.) SALISBURY (1926):
Gildner, Larson
Andrew SALKEY: Lowenfels
1975
I. L. SALOMON: Lask
Louis B. SALOMON (1908):
Baylor
Francis SALTUS: Parker 1967
Eric SALZMAN: Hecht
Frank SAMPERI: Gross,
Oppenheimer 1967
Arthur M. SAMPLEY (1903):
Baylor, Dunning
Ann SAMS (c. 1938): Giovanni
Liz SAMUELSON: Brindle
Ricardo SANCHEZ (1941):
Lowenfels 1973
Sonia SANCHEZ (1935): Adoff
1970, 1973, 1974; Bell,
Breman, G. Brooks (Broad-
side Treasury), P. Brown,
Chace, Chester, Coombs,
Giovanni, Gross, Hender-
son, Jordan, King 1972,
Konek, Don L. Lee,
Lowenfels 1969 (Doubleday),
(Random House); Major,
Patterson, D. Randall
1960, 1969; Rothenberg
1973, T. Wilentz
David SANDBERG: Palmer
Carl SANDBURG (1878-1967):
G. W. Allen, J. A. Allen,
Aloian, Bach, Bates,
Beerman, Betts, Bold,
Corbett, Croft, Cromie,
De Roche, Dunning, Ell-
mann 1973, Foster, Gan-

nett, Gregory 1962, Han-
num, Hannum and Chase,
Harlan, Hopkins (Nelson),
Hughes 1970, Hurtik, Jack-
son, Kennedy 1974, Knowles,
Kramer, Larrick, Living-
ston, Lowenfels 1969
(Doubleday), Monaco 1974,
Morrison, Nash, Parker
1967, Peck 1970, 1971;
Perrine, Peterson, Roth-
enberg 1973, 1974;
Sanders, Schneider,
Shapiro, Stibitz, Summer-
field, H. Taylor, W. Tay-
lor, Trapp, Univ. Press
of Va. , Untermeyer 1964,
J. A. Vincent, Wagner,
Wallace, O. Williams
1966 (World), Winkler,
Woods
Helga SANDBURG (1918):
Konek, Vrbovska 1968
Ernest SANDEEN (1908): J.
A. Allen, Phillips, Stryk
1975
Cora SANDERS: Student
Ed SANDERS (1939): Clark, De
Loach 1968, Harris 1973,
Lowenfels 1969 (Random
House), Montgomery,
Padgett, Rothenberg 1973,
Waldman 1971
Glenn C. SANDERS: Booker
Grant SANDERS: Pygmalion
Morgan SANDERS: Violet
Zel SANDERS: Chace
Charles SANDFORD: Kauff-
man
Ernest SANDLEEN (1908):
Stryk 1975
Stuart SANDLER: Morticella
(S.) Roberto SANDOVAL (1950):
Lourie, Lowenfels 1973
Stephen SANDY (1934): Adoff
1969, Beerman, Kennedy
1973, Lask, Leary
Gary SANGE (1938): Evans,
M. Gibson, Owen 1969
Margaret E. SANGSTER:
Kauffman
Clive SANSOM (1910): J.
Gibson (Book Two), Greaves

Sherry SANTIFER: Giovanni
Lew SARETT: Brewton,
    Dunning
Genevieve SARGENT: Sargent
Aram SAROYAN (1943): Carroll
    (Young American Poets),
    Clark, Fagin, Harlan,
    Kennedy 1973, Montgomery,
    Padgett, Solt, Waldman
    1971, Wildman, E. Williams
May SARTON (1912): J. A.
    Allen, Bulkin, Chester,
    Stanford, H. Taylor, Trapp
Eileen SARUBBI: Brindle,
    Gallery 1970
Siegfried SASSOON (1886-1967):
    Aloian, Bates, R. Bender,
    Cole 1967 (Macmillan),
    1971, 1972; Croft, Cromie,
    De Roche, Ellmann 1973,
    Gardner, J. Gibson (Book
    Two), Greaves, Jacobus,
    Kallich, Kenseth, Knowles,
    McGinley, Parker 1975,
    Sanders, Trapp, Unter-
    meyer 1964
Roger SAULS: Fox
Geraldine SAUNDERS: Oppen-
    heimer 1977
J. Pamela SAUNDERS: Black
    History
Jeff SAUNDERS: Milton
Ruby C. SAUNDERS: Coombs,
    Patterson
Regina SAURO: Pilon
Minot J. SAVAGE: Jackson
John Godfrey SAXE: Jackson,
    Parker 1960
Alvin SAXON (Ojerke) (c. 1945):
    Adoff 1973
Dan SAXON (1939): De Loach 1968,
    Lowenfels 1969 (Random House)
Dorothy L. SAYERS: Rose
Aishah SAYYIDA: Patterson
Vernon SCANNELL (1922):
    Crang, Firmage, Summer-
    field
George SCARBOROUGH: Steele
George SCARBROUGH: Owen
    1974
Susan Fromberg SCHAEFFER:
    Konek
Vivianne SCHAFER: Adoff 1971

David SCHAFF (1943): Harvey,
    Palmer
Joleene SCHAN: Brindle
Barry SCHECHTER: Friedman
Danny SCHECHTER (1942):
    Gitlin
Ruth Lisa SCHECHTER:
    Banker, Chester, Lowen-
    fels 1969 (Doubleday),
    1973, 1975
George SCHEFTEL: Scheftel
Silva SCHEIBLI: Smith
Kathy SCHENKEL: Klonsky
James SCHEVILL (1920):
    Engle, Felver, Harlan,
    Harvey, Lask, Rosenthal
    1967, 1968; Witt-Diamant
Harris SCHIFF: Waldman
    1969, 1971
Alice SCHILZ: Kohl
Harold SCHIMMEL (1934):
    Stallworthy
P. J. SCHIMMEL: Violet
Peter SCHJEDAHL (1942):
    Carroll (Young American
    Poets), Padgett, Waldman
    1969, 1971
Marc D. SCHLEIFER: E.
    Wilentz
Tom SCHMIDT: J. Gill,
    Lowenfels 1975
William A. SCHMITT: Jackson
Dennis SCHMITZ (1937):
    Anania, Carroll (Young
    American Poets), Evans,
    Gildner, Lowenfels 1967,
    Halpern, Immaculate,
    Stryk 1967
Aaron SCHMULLER: Poets of
    America
Aaron SCHNEIDER: Hausman
Bart SCHNEIDER: Rigsbee
Elizabeth Lynn SCHNEIDER:
    Saturday Press
Isidor SCHNEIDER (1896-1977):
    Kramer
P. SCHNEIDRE: Pygmalion
Marion SCHOEBERLEIN: Gal-
    lery 1970, 1973
Irene SCHRAM: H. Smith
James L. SCHRARKEL: Kiley
Ron SCHREIBER (1934): De
    Loach 1976, Leyland 1975,

1977, Mazur
Randy SCHROTH: Morticella
Joseph SCHULL: Rose
Howard (Loeb) SCHULMAN:
Banker, Lowenfels 1967
Philip SCHULTZ: Mazur
Allan J. SCHURR: Harlan
James (Marcus) SCHUYLER
(1923): D. M. Allen 1960,
Chace, Clark, Ellmann
1973, Kennedy 1973,
McCullough, Myers, Pad-
gett, Strand, Waldman
1969, 1971
Antonia Y. SCHWAB: Derleth
Elaine SCHWAGER: Adoff
1969, 1971
Delmore SCHWARTZ (1913-
1966): Adams, J. A.
Allen, Brinnin 1963, 1970;
C. Brooks, Carruth (Ban-
tam), Cole 1967 (Macmil-
lan), Corbett, Driver,
Ellmann 1973, 1976; Engle,
Felver, Hannum and Chase,
Harlan, Hine, Hurtik,
Kostelanetz, Lowenfels
1969 (Doubleday), Perrine,
Rosenthal 1967, 1968;
Shapiro, Steuben, Unter-
meyer 1964, O. Williams
1966 (World), Witt-Diamant
Howard SCHWARTZ (1945):
Freed, Stryk 1975
Lloyd SCHWARTZ: Mazur
Teri J. SCHWARTZ: Brindle
Armand SCHWERNER (1927):
De Loach 1968, 1976, Gross,
Harris 1973, Kostelanetz,
Lowenfels 1973, Rothen-
berg 1973
Ilka SCOBIE: Brindle
Clinton SCOLLARD: Parker
1967
C. C. SCOTT: Adoff 1971
Robert Thomas SCOTELLARO
see SCOTTY
Dennis SCOTT (1939): Breman,
Salkey
Diane SCOTT: Pilon
Eddie SCOTT, Jr.: Booker
F. R. SCOTT (1899): Kenseth,
Lask, A. J. M. Smith 1960

Geoffrey SCOTT: Gregory
1966
Herbert SCOTT: Kherdian
1970
Johnie (Johnnie) (Harold)
SCOTT (1946): Breman,
Coombs, Major, Patterson
Linda Preston SCOTT: Brindle
Nancy SCOTT: De Loach 1976
Perry SCOTT: Leyland 1975
Sharon SCOTT (1951): G.
Brooks (Jump Bad); P.
Brown
Tom SCOTT (1918): Firmage
William Bell SCOTT: Nash
Winfield Townley SCOTT (1910):
J. A. Allen, Bogan, Brin-
nin 1963, Carruth (Ban-
tam), Cole 1967, 1971;
Dunning, Felver, Gregory
1962, Rosenthal 1967,
Strand, Witt-Diamant
SCOTTY (Robert Thomas
Scotellaro): Fox
E. J. SCOVELL (1907):
Knowles
James R. SCRIMGEOUR:
Lowenfels 1975
Anderson M. SCRUGGS: Lask
James SCULLY (1937):
Brinnin 1963, 1970; Han-
num, Hannum and Chase,
Lowenfels 1975, Perrine
Deri SEAGULL: Brindle
Clifford SEALY: Salkey
E. William SEAMAN: Hecht
James SEAY (1939): J. A.
Allen, Colley, Owen 1974,
H. Taylor
R. E. SEBENTHALL (1917):
Stryk 1975
John SECCOMBE: Jackson
Paul SECIC: Harlan
Malcolm M. SEDAM: Ashland
Pete (Peter) SEEGER: Chace,
J. Gibson, Lowenfels
1969 (Doubleday), Peck
1970
Edith SEGAL: Banker
Thomas D. SEGALL (1939):
Katzman
Michael SEGERS (1950): Van
den Heuvel

R. E. SEIBERT: Hitchcock
Frederick (Lewis) SEIDEL
(1936): Hollander, Leary
Hugh SEIDMAN (1940): Gross,
Halpern, Harris 1973
Marjorie Allen SEIFFERT:
Stibitz
Ron SEITZ (1935): Van den
Heuvel
W. C. SELLAR: Parker 1960
Robert SELLMAN (1955): Ley-
land 1977
Samuel SELVON: Salkey
Frank J. SERL: Kiley
Robert SERLING: Malley
Ian SERRAILLIER (1912): Cole
1963, 1965, 1967 (Macmil-
lan), (Viking); J. Gibson,
J. Gibson (Book Two),
Rose
Nina SERRANO (1934): Clay,
Harvey, Lowenfels 1975
Ivan Van SERTIMA: Salkey
Bruce SEVERY (1947): Dodge,
Stryk 1975
Jonathan M. SEWALL: Jackson
Elizabeth SEWELL: Plotz
Anne SEXTON (1928-1974):
Aiken, J. A. Allen, Baylor,
Brady, Brinnin 1963, 1970;
Carruth (Bantam), Chace,
Chester, Cole 1971, De
Roche, Driver, Ellmann
1974, Engle, Hall 1962
(World), Hannum, Hannum
and Chase, Heyen, Hieatt,
Howard, Howard and Vic-
tor, Hurtik, Jacobus, Ken-
nedy 1973, 1974; Konek,
Leary, McGinley, Monaco
1974, Perrine, J. Perry,
Phillips, Poulin, Rosen-
thal 1967, 1968; Segnitz,
Stanford, Stevenson, Strand,
Untermeyer 1964, 1970,
1973 (McKay); Wagner,
Walsh, M. Williams, Witt-
Diamant
A. J. SEYMOUR (1914):
Breman, Salkey
Florence SEYMOUR: Student
Rudy SHACKLEFORD: M.
Gibson, Rigsbee

Bertrand SHADWELL (1899):
Kramer
Elizabeth SHANE: Cole 1963
Ntozake SHANGE: Clay
Thomas William SHAPCOTT
(1935): T. Moore
David (Joel) SHAPIRO (1947):
Hollander, Kostelanetz,
Padgett
Harvey SHAPIRO (1924): Car-
ruth (Bantam), Cole 1971,
Crafts, Glikes, Harlan,
Kennedy 1973, Kostelanetz,
Pearson
Joan SHAPIRO: Balazs
Karl SHAPIRO (1913): Aiken,
G. W. Allen, Aloian,
Bach, Bates, Baylor,
Bogan, Brewton, Brinnin
1963, 1970; C. Brooks,
Carruth (Bantam), Crafts,
Drew, Dunning, Ellmann
1973, Engle, Felver,
Gwynn, Hall 1962 (Watts),
Hannum, Harlan, Hine,
Holmes, Hughes 1970,
Hurtik, Jackson, Joseloff,
Kallich, Kennedy 1974,
Larson, Monaco 1974,
Peck 1970, 1971; Perrine,
J. Perry, Peterson,
Rosenthal 1967, Sanders,
Shapiro, A. J. M. Smith
1967, Steuben, Strand,
Stryk 1967, W. Taylor,
Untermeyer 1964, 1970;
Wallace, Walsh, M. Wil-
liams, O. Williams 1966
(World), Witt-Diamant
Sid SHAPIRO: Blazek
Bill SHARI: Gay
Saidi SHARIFU: Jihad
John J. SHARKEY: E. Wil-
liams
Edith Shreiner SHARP:
Brindle
Martin SHARP: Morse
Sandra (Saundra) SHARP:
Coombs, Patterson
R. L. SHARPE: Kauffman
Timothy SHAUGHNESSY:
Sargent
Luci SHAW: Mollenkott

Robert B. SHAW: Hoffman
Winifred Maitland SHAW (1905):
　　T. Moore
Don SHEA (c. 1941): Hewitt
Virginia SHEARD: Rose
H. D. SHEDD, Jr.: Jackson
Walter SHEDLOFSKY: Derleth
Maureen SHEEDY: Adoff 1971
SHEEL: Violet
Loyal SHEGONEE: Dodge
Eugenia E. SHELLEY:
　　Vrbovska 1968
Martha SHELLEY: Bulkin
Richard SHELTON (1933):
　　Larson
Odell SHEPARD (1884): Trapp
Barbara Kitterman SHEPHERD:
　　Gallery 1973
Gerald SHEPHERD: Booker
Robert SHEPPARD: Crafts
Walt SHEPPERD: De Loach
　　1976
Michael SHERIDAN (1943):
　　Stryk 1975
Philip M. SHERLOCK (1902):
　　Breman
G. W. SHERMAN (1903):
　　Lowenfels 1967
Jory SHERMAN: Lowenfels
　　1975
Susan SHERMAN: Bulkin,
　　De Loach 1968, Sherman
Ruth Forbes SHERRY: Derleth
Judith Johnson SHERWIN (1936):
　　Banker, Ellmann 1973
John F. SHERWOOD: Jackson
Kate Brownie SHERWOOD: J.
　　A. Vincent
Ross SHIDELER (1936): Lowen-
　　fels 1967
Susan SHIELDS: Sargent
Edith (Marcombe) SHIFFERT:
　　Lask, Stanford
James SHIRLEY: Colley,
　　McGinley
Charley SHIVELY (1937): Ley-
　　land 1975, 1977
Martin Staples SHOCKLEY
　　(1908): Baylor
Betsy SHOLL: Mazur
Jane SHORE: Gildner, Mazur
Clarice SHORT (1910): Konek,
　　Larson, Stevenson, H. Taylor

John SHOWALTER: Harlan
Steve SHOWERS: Chilgren
Suzan SHOWN: Lourie
Stephen SHRADER (c. 1945):
　　Hewitt
Irene SHRAM: Banker
T. A. SHULGIN: Harlan,
　　Head
Ted SHULGIN: Mallory
Mary SHUMWAY (1926): Evans,
　　Stryk 1975
Aaron SHURIN (1947): Ley-
　　land 1975, 1977
Paul SHUTTLEWORTH: Chil-
　　gren
Eli SIEGEL (1902): Adoff
　　1969, Cole 1967 (Macmil-
　　lan), 1972; Firmage,
　　Rothenberg 1973
Eve SIEGEL: Gallery 1973
Robert SIEGEL: McMahon
William Vincent SIELLER:
　　Lask
Robert Joseph SIGMUND (rjs;
　　RJS) (1948): Kramer,
　　Lowenfels 1967
Lydia Huntley SIGOURNEY:
　　Brewton
Fred SILBER (1952): Lowen-
　　fels 1969 (Random House)
Alex SILBERMAN: Hoffman
Ruth SILCOCK: Lask
Jon SILKIN (1930): Brinnin
　　1970, Derleth, Driver,
　　Ellmann 1973, Hall 1962
　　(World), Hollander, Pear-
　　son, Rosenthal 1967,
　　1968; Stevenson, H. Taylor,
　　Wagner
Leslie (Marmon) SILKO:
　　Lourie, Niatum, Rosen
Ronald SILLIMAN: Krech
Louis SILLS: Jackson
Philip SILVER: Cole 1967
　　(Macmillan)
Miro SILVERA: De Loach
　　1976
Edward SILVERBUSH: Kiley
Stuart SILVERMAN (1933):
　　Harris 1970, M. Williams
Shel (Shelley) SILVERSTEIN
　　(1931): Cole 1963, 1965,
　　1967 (Macmillan), (Viking),

1971, 1972
Michael SILVERTON (1935):
Cole 1967 (Macmillan),
1971, 1972
Jack SIMCOCK (1929): Greaves
Charles SIMIC (1939): Bonazzi
1972, Carroll (Young Ameri-
can Poets), Chace, Cole
1971, Evans, Gross, Hal-
pern, Harlan, Kennedy
1973, Al Lee, McCullough,
Rothenberg 1973, Strand,
Sumac, Wang
Dan SIMMONS: Coombs
Gerald L. SIMMONS, Jr.
(1944): Major
Herbert A. SIMMONS (1930):
Major
James SIMMONS (1933): Ken-
nedy 1974
J. (Joseph) Edgar SIMMONS:
Owen 1969, 1974
Judy Dothard SIMMONS: Hen-
derson
Rhoza W. SIMMONS: McGovern
Ted SIMMONS: Harris 1970,
Simmons
Colin SIMMS: Sargent
Harold (L.) SIMON: Gallery
1970, 1973
Jess SIMON: Brindle
John SIMON: Cole 1967 (Mac-
millan), Head
John Oliver SIMON (1942):
Fox, J. Gill, Gitlin, Har-
vey, Krech, Malley,
Palmer, Sherman, Winans
Maurya SIMON: Brindle
Paul SIMON (1942): Baylor,
Chace, Kennedy 1974
William J. SIMON: Rottmann
Nina SIMONE (1933): Kennedy
1973
John SIMONITCH: Harlan
A. B. SIMPSON: Kauffman
Alan J. SIMPSON: Baylor
Carie SIMPSON (c. 1952):
Giovanni
Juanita SIMPSON: Booker
Louis SIMPSON (1923): Adams,
Bly 1970, Brady, Brewton,
Brinnin 1963, 1970; Car-
ruth (Bantam), Cole 1965,

1967 (Macmillan), 1971;
Colley, Cromie, De Roche,
Derleth, Ellmann 1973,
1976; Engle, Hall 1962
(Penguin), (Watts), (World);
Hannum, Heyen, Hine,
Hollander, Hopkins (Nel-
son), Howard, Howard and
Victor, Kennedy 1973,
Livingston, McCullough,
Pearson, Peck 1970, Per-
rine, Plotz, Poulin, Rosen-
thal 1973, 1974; Rothen-
berg 1973, Simpson, Stall-
worthy, Strand, H. Taylor,
W. Taylor, Untermeyer
1964, 1973 (McKay);
Vrbovska 1963, 1968;
Wagner, Wallace, M.
Williams, Winkler
Peter L. SIMPSON: Harris
1970
R. A. SIMPSON (1929): T.
Moore
Audrey M. SIMURDA: Brindle
David SINCLAIR (1945): Gitlin
John SINCLAIR (1941): Gitlin,
H. Jones, Lowenfels 1969
(Doubleday), Major, D.
Randall 1969
Peter SINFIELD: Morse
Burns SINGER (1928):
Firmage, Hall 1962 (World)
Billy SIPSER: Dee
Boots SIREECH (1952): Lowen-
fels 1973
Jeanne SIROTKIN: Efros
Leumas SIRRAH (1947): Bre-
man
L. E. SISSMAN (1928-1976):
Brinnin 1970, Cole, How-
ard, Howard and Victor,
Kennedy 1973, Strand
Jonathan SISSON: Rigsbee
Edith SITWELL (1887-1964):
Brinnin 1963, 1970; Croft,
Ellmann 1973, Engelberg,
Firmage, Foster, Gardner,
J. Gibson, J. Gibson
(Book Two), Gregory
1962, 1966; Immaculate,
McGinley, J. Perry,
Sanders, Schneider, Stan-

(Macmillan), 1971, 1972;
De Roche, Ellmann 1973,
J. Gibson, J. Gibson
(Book Two), Greaves,
Harris 1972, Kaplan, Kennedy 1974, Klonsky, Stallworthy, Stanford
Sydney Goodsir SMITH (1915):
Cole 1971, 1972
Thomas Lee SMITH: Sollid
1972, 1973; K. and J.
Sollid
Vivian SMITH (1933): T. Moore
Welton SMITH (1940): Adoff
1973, Hughes 1970, King
1972, Major
William SMITH: Student
William Jay SMITH (1918):
Adoff 1969, J. A. Allen,
Baylor, Bogan, Brinnin
1963, 1970; Cole 1963,
1965, 1967 (Viking), 1971;
Dunning, Engle, M. Gibson, Kennedy 1973, 1974;
Kenseth, Larrick, Lask,
McGinley, Morrison, Rubin,
Strand, H. Taylor, Univ.
Press of Va., Untermeyer
1964, 1973 (McKay); M.
Williams, Witt-Diamant
William R. SMITH: Jackson
Daniel SMYTHE (1908): Larrick
Stanley SNAITH (1903): Knowles
Barbara SNEAD: Kohl
Clayton SNEDEKER: Kiley
Roland SNELLING see Askia
Muhammad TOURE
Clee SNIPE, Jr. (1938):
Lowenfels 1969 (Random
House)
Susan SNIVELY: Rigsbee
W. D. SNODGRASS (1926):
Adams, G. W. Allen,
J. A. Allen, Baylor, R.
Bender, Bogin, Brinnin
1963, 1970; C. Brooks,
Carroll (Poem in Its Skin),
De Roche, Ellmann, Engle,
Gildner, Hall 1962 (Penguin), (World); Harlan,
Hieatt, Hollander, Hope,
Kennedy 1973, 1974;
Kessler, Kostelanetz,

Leary, McCullough,
McGinley, McGovern,
Monaco 1974, Peck 1970,
Perrine, Phillips, Poulin,
Rosenthal 1967, 1968;
Stallworthy, Steuben,
Strand, H. Taylor, Untermeyer 1964, 1970, 1973
(McKay); Wallace, Walsh,
M. Williams, Witt-Diamant
Linda SNORTON (c. 1950):
Giovanni
Karen SNOW: Violet
Wilbert SNOW: Wesleyan Univ.
Gary SNYDER (1930): D. M.
Allen 1960, 1964; J. A.
Allen, Arts Festival 1964,
Barnes, Baylor, Berg,
Bly 1970, 1975; Brady,
Carruth (Bantam), Chace,
Cole 1971, Colley, De
Roche, Di Prima, Durand,
Ellmann 1973, 1976;
Ferlinghetti, Gitlin, Hall
1962 (Penguin), Harlan,
Harvey, Hollander, Howard,
Howard and Victor, Kennedy 1973, 1974; Kherdian
1973, Kostelanetz, Larson,
Leary, Lowenfels 1966,
McCullough, McGovern,
Mallory, Phillips, Poulin,
Rosenthal 1967, 1968;
Rothenberg 1973, Simpson,
Strand, H. Taylor, Wagner, Waldman 1971, Walsh,
M. Williams, Witt-Diamant
Judith SNYDER: Brindle
Kirtland SNYDER: Rigsbee
Lucye Rider SNYDER: Plumley
Richard SNYDER: Ashland,
Gallery 1970, Lask
Thurmond L. SNYDER: Gross,
Hughes 1964
Hyman (Jordan) SOBILOFF
(1912): Aiken, Carruth
(Bantam), Vrbovska 1968,
O. Williams 1966 (World)
A. G. SOBIN (1944): Stryk
1975
Jay SOCIN (1914-1968): De
Loach 1968, Young

Andree SODENKAMP: Banker
Elda SODERQUIST: Brindle
Liz SOHAPPY (1947): T. Allen,
　Dodge
Marvin SOLOMON: Glikes
Philip SOLOMON (1954): Jordan
Mary Ellen SOLT (1920):
　Gross, Hewitt, Klonsky,
　Kostelanetz, Pilon, Solt,
　Wildman, E. Williams
Walter SORELL: Lask
James SORIC: Fox
Helen SORRELLS: Stanford
Gilbert SORRENTINO (1929):
　D. M. Allen 1960, H.
　Jones
Haron SOSNA: Crafts
Cleo SOTO: Brindle
Gary SOTO: Rigsbee, Winans
Judith SOUCEK: Hoffman
Raymond SOUSTER (1921):
　Cole 1963, 1967 (Macmil-
　lan), 1971; Lask
O. M. B. SOUTHARD: Harlan
Susan SOWARD: Giovanni
'Wole SOYINKA (1934): Bold,
　Breman, Greaves, Hughes
　1963, Kgositsile, Lomax
Barry SPACKS (1931): Glikes,
　Kennedy 1973, 1974; Lask,
　M. Williams
James SPADY: Black History
George SPARLING: Blazek
Adriano SPATOLA: Wildman,
　E. Williams
Maurigio SPATOLA: Wildman
Alex SPAULDING: Stevenson
Roberta SPEAR (1948): Hal-
　pern, Kherdian 1970
Heather SPEARS (1934): A. J.
　M. Smith 1960
(A.) (Alfred) B. SPELLMAN
　(1934): Adoff 1973, Bell,
　Breman, P. Brown, Hen-
　derson, Hughes 1964, H.
　Jones, Major, A. Miller
Skip (Alexander) SPENCE
　(1938): Kennedy 1973
Anne (Ann) SPENCER (1881):
　Adoff 1973, Bontemps
　1963, 1974; Crafts, Ell-
　mann 1973, Hayden
Bernard SPENCER (1909-1963):
　Cole 1971

James SPENCER: Palmer
Wade SPENCER: Booker
Stephen SPENDER (1909):
　Adams, J. A. Allen,
　Aloian, Bates, Baylor, R.
　Bender, Bogan, Brinnin
　1963, 1970; Calderwood,
　Colum, Crang, Croft,
　Drew, Ellmann 1973,
　Engle, Firmage, Gwynn,
　Hall 1962 (Watts), Hannum,
　Harlan, Hurtik, Immacu-
　late, Jacobus, Kenseth,
　Livingston, Mercatante,
　Monaco 1974, Peck 1970,
　Peterson, Sanders,
　Schneider, A. J. M.
　Smith 1967, Stallworthy,
　H. Taylor, W. Taylor,
　Trapp, Untermeyer 1964,
　1973 (McKay); Wagner,
　Wallace, Woods
Robert O. SPENGLER: Jack-
　son
Shalom SPERBER: Banker
Jack SPICER (1925-1965):
　Carruth (Bantam), Leyland
　1975, 1977; Rothenberg
　1973, Witt-Diamant
Robert SPIESS: Van den
　Heuvel
Ruthe T. SPINNANGER:
　Mollenkott
Leon SPIRO: Palmer
Carl J. O. SPITTA: Kauff-
　man
Kathleen SPIVACK (1938):
　Carroll (Young American
　Poets), Halpern, Konek,
　Mazur
Daniel SPOERRI (1930):
　Rothenberg, E. Williams
Ed (Edward S.) SPRIGGS
　(1934): Adoff 1969,
　Baraka, Breman, G.
　Brooks (Broadside Treas-
　ury), Colley, D. Randall
　1960, 1969
William SPRUNT: Rigsbee
Susan SQUIER: Hoffman
J. C. SQUIRE: Brewton
Bonnie SQUIRES: Van den
　Heuvel
Radcliffe SQUIRES (1917):

Larson
Wendell P. STAFFORD: Jackson
William STAFFORD (1914):
Adams, Adoff 1969, J. A.
Allen, Bates, Barnes,
Baylor, Berg, Bly 1970,
Brewton, Carruth (Bantam),
Chace, Cole 1967 (Macmillan), 1971; Crang, De
Roche, Dunning, Engle,
Gildner, Hall 1962 (Penguin), Hannum, Harris
1970, 1973; Heyen, Kennedy 1973, 1974; Kherdian
1973, Larrick, Larson,
Lask, Lowenfels 1967,
1973; McCullough, L.
Moore, Peck 1970, 1971;
Phillips, Plotz, Poulin,
Rosenthal 1967, 1968;
Skleton, K. and J. Sollid,
Strand, Stryk 1967, Talisman, H. Taylor, Wagner,
Wang, Weil, M. Williams,
O. Williams 1966 (World),
Witt-Diamant
D. A. STAHL: Crafts
Ginny STALEY: Head
Jon STALLWORTHY (1935):
Cole 1967, 1971; Ellmann
1973, Hannum, Lask,
Stallworthy, Summerfield,
Untermeyer 1970
Robert STALLWORTHY: Booker
Hugo STANCHI (1941): Lowenfels 1973, 1975
David STANDISH (1946): Gitlin
Ann STANFORD (1921): Hannum, Hannum and Chase,
Konek, Larson, Stanford,
Stevenson, Talisman, H.
Taylor, Winans
Nikos STANGOS (1936): Stallworthy
George STANLEY (1934): Arts
Festival 1964, Gross,
Harvey, Leyland 1975
Frank L. STANTON: J. A.
Vincent
Henry T. STANTON: Jackson
Johnny STANTON: Waldman
1969, 1971
Maura STANTON (1946): Halpern

Pat STANTON: Brindle
Will STANTON: Perrine
Shirley STAPLES: Coombs
George STARBUCK (1931):
Aiken, Baylor, Brinnin
1963, 1970; Carruth (Bantam), Cromie, Driver,
Gwynn, Hall 1962 (World),
Kennedy 1973, Kenseth,
Lowenfels 1967, 1969
(Doubleday); McGovern,
Wallace
Clemens STARK (1937):
Lowenfels 1967
Gary STARK: Harlan
Irwin STARK: Lask
Nancy L. STARK: Hecht
Chauncey C. STARKWEATHER:
Jackson
Vincent STARRETT (1886):
Aloian, Cromie, Derleth
William F. STEAD: Lask
Jordan STECKEL (1930):
Klonsky
Stuart STECKLER: Gallery
1970
Benjamin STEELE: Hausman
Frank STEELE: Owen 1974,
Steele
Timothy STEELE (1948):
Kennedy 1974
Felix STEFANILE (1920):
Derleth, Firmage, Hearse,
Hunting, Purdue, Stevenson, Weil
Mary Anne STEFLIK: Smith
Arnold STEIN: Ten
Charles STEIN (1944): Gross,
Oppenheimer 1967, Rothenberg 1973, Waldman
1969
Diane STEIN: Gallery 1973
Stan STEINER: Lowenfels
1969 (Doubleday)
Martin STEINGESSER: Rigsbee
David STEINGLASS (1940):
Cole 1971, Evans, Stryk
1975, M. Williams
Maris STELLA (1899): Corbett
Anthony M. STELMOK: Gallery 1970

Jane STEMBRIDGE (1939):
Gitlin, Lowenfels 1969
(Doubleday), (Random House)
Stephen STEPANCHEV (1915):
Harris 1970, 1976; Kher-
dian 1974, Lask
STEPHANY: G. Brooks (Broad-
side Treasury)
James Kenneth (J. K.) STEPHEN:
Cole 1971, Plotz, Rose
Alan STEPHENS (1925):
Schneider, Talisman, Win-
ters
M. G. STEPHENS: Waldman
1969
Tyrone STEPHENSON: Black
History
George STERLING: Parker
1967
Gerd STERN (1928): Kostelanetz
Sally STERN: E. Wilentz
Janet STERNBURG: Saturday
Press
Otto M. STERNFELD: Jackson
Craig STERRY (1943): Hewitt
Harry STESSEL: Rigsbee
Charles STETLER: Bukowski,
Haas
Catherine STETSON: Brindle
A. Wilber STEVENS (1921):
Larson
Lona STEVENS: Chace
Walt STEVENS: Gallery 1970
Wendy STEVENS: Bulkin
Anne STEVENSON (1933):
Cole 1971, Howe
Burton Egbert STEVENSON:
J. A. Vincent
Candace Thurber STEVENSON:
Brewton
Lionel STEVENSON: Brewton
Warren STEVENSON: Steven-
son
Bob STEWART: Pilon
Charles STEWART (c. 1945):
Murphy
Douglas STEWART (1913):
Knowles, T. Moore
Harold STEWART (1916): T.
Moore
Rose STEWART: Giovanni
Trumbull STICKNEY: Aiken,
Cole

James STILL: Brewton, Jack-
son
Stephen STILLS: Morse
Charles STILLWELL: Harlan
Robert STOCK: Head
Henry Jerome STOCKARD:
Kauffman
N. J. STOCKMAN: Morticella
Louis STODDARD: Lask
Glenn STOKES: Coombs
Terry STOKES (1943): Fox,
Gildner, Halpern, Phillips
Leon STOKESBURY (1944):
Evans, Owen 1974
Carolyn STOLOFF: Chester
Bradley J. STONE: Plumley
Carole STONE: Oppenheimer
1977
Ed STONE (1918-1977):
Lowenfels 1967, 1969
(Doubleday)
Joan STONE: Hoffman
John STONE (1936): Owen
1974, M. Williams
Le Roy (Leroy) STONE (1936):
Henderson
Ronald STONE (1937): Lowen-
fels 1969 (Random House)
Ruth STONE (1915): Aiken,
Cole 1963, Howe, Stanford,
Untermeyer 1964, Wesley-
an Univ., O. Williams
1966 (World)
Edward STOREY: Crang
Hester (G.) STORM: Head,
Krech
Joseph STORY: Jackson
Bob STOUT: Fox
Robert J. (Joe) STOUT:
Bonazzi 1974, Gallery
1973, Harlan, Owen 1974
Adrien STOUTENBURG (1916):
Bates, Brewton, Cromie,
Glikes, Hannum and
Chase, Hine, Larrick,
L. Moore, Peck 1971,
Stevenson, Vrbovska 1963
Randolph STOW (1935): T.
Moore
J. Anthony STOWERS: Head
Mark STRAND (1934): Brady,
Brinnin 1970, Carroll
(Young American Poets),

De Roche, Ellmann
1973, Evans, Harris
1973, Hollander, Howard,
Howard and Victor, Ken-
nedy 1973, Al Lee,
McCullough, Strand M.
Williams
Jean STREICH: Adoff 1971
Jan S. STREIF (1939): Van
den Heuvel
Marion STROBEL: Stibitz
Lynn STRONGIN (1939):
Bulkin, Chester, Har-
lan, Harvey, Head,
Howe, Knoek, Rigs-
bee, Schreiber
Jan STRUTHER: Brewton
Ann STRUTHERS: Gildner
Eleanor STRUTHERS (1930):
Lowenfels 1967
Lucien STRYK (1924):
Cromie, Heyen, Kal-
lich, Lask, Owen 1969,
Stibitz
Dabney STUART (1937):
Evans, M. Gibson,
Glikes, Lask, Owen
1969, 1974; McCul-
lough, M. Williams
Floyd C. STUART:
McMahon
Jane STUART: Derleth
Jesse STUART (1905): Brew-
ton, Derleth, Jackson,
Parks, Plumley
Maureen STUART: Kiley
Marcia STUBBS (1928): Ken-
nedy 1973
John STULETT: Rottmann
Nicodemes (Nico) SUAREZ:
Lowenfels 1975, Smith
Nazzam Al SUDAN (1944):
Major
Elmer F. SUDERMAN (1920):
Mollenkott
Yuri SUHL (1908): Banker,
Kenseth, Lowenfels 1966,
1969 (Doubleday)
Lynn SUKENICK (1937):
Chester, Howe, Rigsbee,
Winans
A. M. SULLIVAN (1896):
Corbett, Steuben

A. W. SULLIVAN: Lask
Nancy SULLIVAN (1929):
Leary
Debra E. SUMMERS: Black
History
Hal SUMMERS: Cole 1971,
J. Gibson
Hollis SUMMERS (1916):
Ashland, Lask, Owen
1969, 1974; McGovern,
Plumley, Steuben, M.
Williams
James E. SUMMERS:
Kiley
Tar Lee SUN: Gross
Robert SUND (1929): Cole
1972
Brenda Paik SUNOO: Clay
SUNSHINE: Krech
Jules SUPERVIELLE:
Wagner
Ethel SURE: Plumley
Lynn SURUMA (1943):
Giovanni
Susan SUTHEIM (1942):
Howe
Christopher SUTHERLAND:
Tisdale
Jan SUTHERLAND: Brindle
Sam Duby R. SUTU (d. 1965):
Lomax
Frank G. SWAIN: Jackson
Pamela SWAIN: Pilon
Alan SWALLOW (1915): Low-
enfels 1966
Emma SWAN: Lask
Jon SWAN: J. A. Allen,
Aloian, Hannum and Chase,
Larrick, Perrine,
Wheelock 1960
Brian SWANN (1940):
Halpern, L. Moore,
Rigsbee
R. A. SWANSON: Morticella
Robert (S.) SWARD (1933):
Carruth (Bantam), Cole
1967 (Macmillan), Gildner,
Glikes, Leary, Lowenfels
1967, Sherman, Stibitz,
Strand, Stryk 1967
Roberta Teale SWARTZ:
Trapp
John L. SWEENEY: Aiken

Karen SWENSON (1941): Banker,
Lask, Monaco 1973, 1974;
H. Smith
May SWENSON (1919): Adoff 1969,
Aiken, J. A. Allen, Aloian,
Baylor, Beerman, Brinnin
1963, 1970; Bulkin, Carruth
(Bantam), (McCall); Chester,
Cole 1963, Dunning, Glikes,
Hannum, Hannum and Chase,
Hollander, Howard, Howard
and Victor, Howe, Hurtik,
Kennedy 1973, 1974; Klonsky,
Konek, Larrick, Larson,
Lask, Livingston, McCul-
lough, Monaco, Peck 1970,
1971; Perrine, Phillips,
Pilon, Rosenthal 1967, 1968;
Schneider, Stanford, Stueben,
Strand, Summerfield, Unter-
meyer 1973 (McKay), Vrbov-
ska 1963, 1968; Wagner,
Winkler
Hildegarde Hoyt SWIFT: Brewton
Thom SWISS: Rigsbee
Robjert J. SYE (c. 1940):
Murphy
Velma West SYKES: Konek
David SYLVA: Kiley
Luis SYQUIA, Jr.: Clay
Serafin Malay SYQUIA: Clay
Marie SYRKIN: Lask
SZABO: Montgomery
Arthur SZE: Harlan, Head
Barbara SZERLIP: Rexroth
Michael SZPORER: Lowenfels
1975

T

John Banister TABB: Kauffman
Margo TAFT (1950): Howe
Sam TAGATAC: Clay
Richard TAGETT (1936): Ley-
land 1975, Young
Genevieve TAGGARD (1894):
Carruth (Bantam), Dunning,
Lowenfels 1969 (Double-
day), Untermeyer 1964
John TAGGART: Bogin
John TAGLIABUE (1923): Brew-
ton, Cole 1967 (Macmillan),

Glikes, Lowenfels 1967,
1975; Morrison
Salvatore TAGLIARINO: Smith
Ross TALARICO: Rigsbee
Margaret TALBOT: Brindle
Ron TALNEY: Morticella
Thomas TAMMARO: Adoff
1971
Tchikaya U TAM'SI: Kgositsile
TAN: Rottmann
Donna TANKERSLEY: Brindle
Robert TANNAHILL: Cole 1971
Stephen TAPSCOTT: Hoffman
Carol TARLEN: Morticella
Nathaniel TARN (1928): De
Loach 1976, Gross,
Joseloff, Lowenfels 1975,
Matthias, Rothenberg 1973
Valerie TARVER (c. 1956):
Murphy
Allen TATE (1899): Adams,
Aiken, G. W. Allen, Bach,
Baylor, R. Bender, Brin-
nin 1963, 1970; C. Brooks,
Carruth (Bantam), De
Roche, Driver, Ellmann
1973, 1976; Engle, Felver,
Hieatt, Howard, Howard
and Victor, Hughes 1970,
Immaculate, Jacobus,
Kallich, Parks, Perrine,
Plotz, Shapiro, A. J. M.
Smith 1967, W. Taylor,
Univ. Press of Va.,
Untermeyer 1964, O.
Williams 1966 (World)
James TATE (1943): Adams,
Baylor, Brinnin 1970,
Carroll (Young American
Poets), Colley, Ellmann
1973, Halpern, Hitchcock,
Kennedy 1973, 1974; Al
Lee, Mazur, Morticella,
Strand, Stryk 1967, H.
Taylor, Untermeyer 1964,
Wang
Betty E. TAUB: Katzman
Stephan TAUGHER: Holmes
Bernie TAUPIN: Morse
Roger TAUS: H. Jones
Margaret TAUSS: Vrbovska
1968
Ann TAYLOR: Parker 1960

Eleanor Ross TAYLOR: M.
Gibson, Owen 1974
Henry TAYLOR (1942): J. A.
Allen, M. Gibson, Kennedy
1973, 1974; Owen 1974,
H. Taylor
James O. TAYLOR (1949):
Greaves
Jeffreys TAYLOR: Parker
1960
Kent TAYLOR: Blazek, Fox
Mervyn TAYLOR: Patterson
Prentiss TAYLOR, Jr.: P.
Brown
Jerry TAYLOR: Booker
Rachel Annand TAYLOR (1876-
1960): Gregory 1966
Rod TAYLOR: Hoffman
Tom TAYLOR: Fox
W. Allen TAYLOR: Gallery
1970
William E. TAYLOR: Owen
1969, 1974; Steele
William H. TAYLOR, III:
Clay
TAZAMISHA: Jihad
M. M. TEAGER: Jackson
Kathleen TEAGUE: Ferling-
hetti, Harvey, Wald-
man 1971
Dennis TEDLOCK (1939): Gross,
Rothenberg
Miriam TEICHNER: Kauffman
Harold M. (Milton) TELEMAQUE
(1910): Breman, Lomax
John D. TELLER: Jackson
Anna TEMPLE: Kauffman
James W. TEMPLETON:
Gallery 1973
Edward Wyndham TENNANT:
Rose
James TENNEY: Gross
Jean TEPPERMAN (1945):
Gersmehl, Gitlin, Howe
TERESA: Violet
Robert L. TERRELL (c. 1942):
Coombs
Virginia R. TERRIS: Rigsbee
Rose Cooke TERRY: Jackson
Gerhard TERSTEEGEN: Kauff-
man
A. S. J. TESSIMOND (1902-
1962): Foster, J. Gibson

J. H. THACHER: Jackson
THANH HAI: Clay
Hole THATCHER: Gallery
1973
Ernest Lawrence THAYER:
Morrison
Richard Charles THAYER:
Gallery 1970, 1973
Emma Lou THAYNE (1924):
Larson
Luke THEODORE: Gay
Sister M. THERESE (1902):
Lask, Trapp
Colin THIELE (1920): T.
Moore
Charles (C.) THOMAS: Coombs,
Harlan
D. M. THOMAS (1935): Lucie-
Smith, Matthias
Edith M. THOMAS: Parker
1960
Gilbert THOMAS: Kauffman
John THOMAS: Bukowski,
Simmons
Linda THOMAS: Dee
Lorenzo THOMAS (1944):
Adoff 1973, Glikes, H.
Jones, Lowenfels 1975,
Waldman 1971
Piri THOMAS (1928): Lowen-
fels 1973
R. S. THOMAS (1913): Bedient,
Cole 1963, 1967 (Macmil-
lan), 1971, 1972; Crang,
Greaves, Harris 1973,
Knowles, Larrick, Lask,
Rosenthal 1967, 1968;
Stallworthy, W. Taylor,
Walsh
Richard THOMAS (1934): Lane
Richard (W.) THOMAS (1939):
Adoff 1973, Colley, Hughes
1970, King 1972, Patter-
son, Shuman
Ronald Stuart THOMAS (1913):
Gardner
Rosemary THOMAS: Brewton
Sam THOMAS: Palmer
Andre THOMKINS: E. Wil-
liams
Dorothy Brown THOMPSON
(1896): Brewton, Univ.
Press of Va.

Dunston THOMPSON (1918): O.
Williams 1966 (World)
George THOMPSON: Wiebe
Glenn THOMPSON (1955):
Jordan
James W. THOMPSON (1935):
Adoff 1973, Breman,
Coombs, King 1972
John THOMPSON (1907): T.
Moore
John THOMPSON (1930):
Firmage
John THOMPSON, Jr. (1918):
Kennedy 1973, O. Williams
1966 (World)
John Beauchamp THOMPSON:
McGovern
John R. THOMPSON: Jackson
Larry THOMPSON (1950):
Adoff 1970, 1971, 1973,
1974
Michael THOMPSON: J. Gib-
son, J. Gibson (Book Two)
Tish THOMPSON: Pilon
Will Henry THOMPSON: J. A.
Vincent
Barbara Earl THOMSON (1921):
Mollenkott
Everard THOMSON: Gallery
1973
John THOMSON: Malley
Evelyn THORNE: Kramer,
Lowenfels 1967
Landon THORNE: Rottmann
John THORPE: Waldman 1971,
Weishaus
Bob THRASHER: Mallory
James THURBER (1894-1961):
Gannett
Jim THURBER: Palmer
Judith (Judy) THURMAN (1947):
Lask, Monaco 1974
Anthony THWAITE (1930): Cole
1971, Crang, Hall 1962
(World), Kennedy 1974,
Rosenthal 1967, Stallworthy
Michael THWAITES (1915):
Knowles, T. Moore, Trapp
Tom TICO (1942): Van den
Heuvel
Cesar TIEMPO: Trapp
James H. TILLER, III: Kiley
Terence TILLER (1916): Thomas

Richard TILLINGHAST (1940):
Bates
Geoffrey TILLOTSON (1905):
Knowles
Bill TIMBERMAN (1943):
Mallory
Walasse TING (1939): Kennedy
1973
Carol TINKER (1940): Lowen-
fels 1975, Mallory, Rex-
roth
Charles B. TINKHAM: Scheftel
Bernadine TINNER: Black
History
James S. TIPPETT: Dunning
James (S.) (Sherwood) TIPTON
(1942): Fox, Hitchcock,
Stryk 1975, Van den Heuvel
Jim TIROFF: Gay
Celes TISDALE (1941): Tis-
dale
John TOBIAS: Dunning
Judith TOBIN: Brindle
Barbara Euphan TODD: Park-
er 1974
Ella TODD: Booker
Joe TODD: P. Brown
Ruthven TODD (1914): Firmage,
Harris 1976
Arthur TOEGEMANN: Adoff
1971
Hale TOKAY: Malley
J. R. R. TOLKIEN (1892-
1973): Livingston
Jim TOLLERUD: Rosen
Melvin B. (Beaunearus) TOL-
SON (1898-1966): Adoff
1973, Bell, Bontemps
1963, 1974; Hayden, Hen-
derson, Hughes 1970,
Kostelanetz, Lomax, Low-
enfels 1969 (Doubleday),
D. Randall 1960, Rothen-
berg 1973, Turner
Charles TOMLINSON (1927):
Bedient, Brady, Brinnin
1963, Crang, Ellmann
1973, Engle, Hall 1962
(World), Hollander,
Knowles, Lask, Matthias,
Rosenthal 1967, 1968;
Sanders, Stallworthy,
Summerfield, Untermeyer

1964, W. Taylor

William H. TOMPKINS: Jackson

Jean TOOMER (1893/4-1967):
Adoff 1968, 1973; Bell,
Bontemps 1963, 1974;
Brady, Breman, Ellmann
1973, Hayden, Hughes 1970,
Jordan, Kennedy, Lomax,
D. Randall 1960, Turner

Ali Sedat Hilmi TOREL (1930):
Camp

Eric TORGERSEN (c. 1944):
Cole 1971, Hewitt, Hitch-
cock, Summerfield

Sotere TORREGIAN (1941):
Carroll (Young American
Poets), Harvey, Waldman
1969, 1971

Steve TOTH: Sklar

William D. TOTTEN: Jackson

Shirley TOULSON: Crang

William TOUPONCE: Hausman

Askia Muhammad TOURE
(Roland Snellings): Adoff
1973, G. Brooks (Broadside
Treasury), Henderson,
Hughes 1970, King 1972,
T. Wilentz

Mali TOURE: Patterson

Saul TOUSTER: Hallmark

Tony TOWLE (1939): Carroll
(Young American Poets),
H. Jones, Myers, Padgett,
Waldman 1971

Tod TOWNLEY: Hoffman

George A. TOWNSEND: Jackson

Sage TRACK: Dodge

Joanne TRAMONTE: Brindle

Tomas TRANTROMER: Wang

Lucille F. TRAVIS (1931):
Mollenkott

Mark TRAYLOR: Black History

Grace TREASONE: Camp,
Kennedy 1974

Adriana TREDANARI: Brindle

Henry TREECE (1912): Cromie,
Plotz

Florence TREFETHAN: Lask,
Mazur

Ernesto TREJO (1950): Winans

Richard C. TRENCH: Kauffman

Lucia TRENT: Derleth

Neal TRENT: Kiley

Leonardo TREVIGLIO: Gay

Peter TRIAS: Rigsbee

Eve TRIEM: Harris 1970, K.
and J. Sollid, Ten

Alexander TROCCHI: Lorrimer

Gloria TROPP: Lowenfels 1969
(Random House), Montgom-
ery

Stephen TROPP (1930): Camp,
Kennedy 1974, Lowenfels
1969 (Random House),
Montgomery

Ulrich TROUBETZKOY
(1914): Univ. Press
of Va.

Perient TROTT (1910): Hughes
1970

Pierre TROTTIER (1925): A.
J. M. Smith 1960

Quincy TROUPE (1943):
Adoff 1973, Coombs,
Gersmehl, King 1972,
Kramer, Lowenfels
1973, 1975; Major, Patter-
son, Simmons

John T. TROWBRIDGE: Jack-
son

Grace E. TROY: Kauffman

Mike TRUDEAU: Fox

Dennis TRUDELL (1938):
Evans, Gildner, Hewitt,
Rigsbee

C. W. TRUESDALE: Bonazzi
1972

Marcela TRUJILLO: Clay

Dalton TRUMBO (1905): Lowenfels 1966

Gael TRUMBULL (1928):
Matthias

Chogyam TRUNGPA (1939):
Rothenberg

Jake TRUSSELL: Scheftel

Gloria TRUVIDO: Kohl

C. A. (A. Constantine)
TRYPANIS (1909): Cole
1967 (Macmillan), Cromie,
Lask

George TSONGAS: Winans

Margaret TSUDA: Larrick

TSUI Kit-fan: Clay

George F. TUCKER: Jackson

Harvey TUCKER: Banker, Gross

Robert (G.) TUCKER (1921):
Glikes, Kenseth, Univ. of
Mass.
Stephen TUDOR (1933): Stryk
1975
Mike TUGGLE: Harlan
Jun K. TUKITA: De Loach
1976
Rod TULLOSS: Oppenheimer
1977
Mark TURBYFILL: Stibitz
Lewis (Putnam) TURCO (1934):
Banker, Derleth, Glikes,
Heyen, McGovern, M.
Williams
Adrian TURCOTTE: Pygmalion
Gael TURNBULL: Cole 1971,
Matthias
Alberta TURNER (1919): Ash-
land, Stryk 1975
Darwin T. TURNER (1931):
Hughes 1970, Major, Pat-
terson, Turner
James TURNER (1909): Knowles
Nancy Byrd TURNER: Brewton,
Jackson, Nash, J. A.
Vincent
John TURPIN: Blazek
Joseph TUSIANI: Steuben
Ernest TYLER: Jackson
Parker TYLER (1907): O.
Williams 1966 (World)
Robert L. TYLER: Dunning
Katherine TYNAN: Parker
1974
Ian TYSON (1933): Rothenberg
John TYTELL: Harris 1970

U

Michael UHL: Rottmann
Timm UHLRICHS: Wildman
Ellen H. UNDERWOOD: Kauff-
man
Giuseppe UNGARETTI (1888):
Livingston
J. UNLAND: Harris 1970
John UNTERECKER (1922):
Owen 1969, Schreiber
Jean Starr UNTERMEYER
(1886): Untermeyer 1964
Louis UNTERMEYER (1885-
1977): Aloian, Bates,

Bogan, Cromie, Jackson,
Kramer, Morrison, Peck
1970, 1971; Peterson,
Stallworthy, Untermeyer
1964, 1970
John UPDIKE (1932): Adoff
1969, Cole 1967 (Macmil-
lan), (Viking), 1971, 1972;
Colley, Dunning, Hannum,
Hurtik, Kennedy 1974,
Knowles, L. Moore, Peck
1970, 1971; Pilon, H.
Taylor
Charles UPTON: Ferlinghetti,
Harvey
Michael UPTON: Krech
Constance URDANG (1922):
Kennedy 1973, Konek,
Phillips, Strand
B. A. URONOVITZ: Hadassah

V

David VAJALO: Simmons
Nanon VALAORITIS: Harvey
Enrique Uribe VALDIVIELSO:
E. Williams
Christopher VALENTINE:
Booker
Edward A. Uffington VALEN-
TINE: Jackson
Jean VALENTINE (1934):
Carruth (Bantam), Hannum,
Harris 1973, Mazur,
Monaco 1973, Phillips
Dorothy J. VALERLAN: Kiley
Carol VALHOPE: Gregory
1966
Val VALLIS (1916): T. Moore
Jiri VALOCH: Wildman
H. L. VAN BRUNT: Fox,
Vrbovska 1968
Cor VAN DEN HEUVEL (1931):
Van den Heuvel
Gerard VAN DER LEUN:
Blazek
Frans VANDERLINDE (Franz
Van Der Linde): Wildman,
E. Williams, Winkler
Mark VAN DOREN (1894-1972):
Bonazzi 1972, Carruth
(Bantam), (McCall); Cole
1965, 1967 (Macmillan);

Derleth, Engle, Gannett, Hannum, Hannum and Chase, Hopkins (Nelson), Howard, Howard and Victor, Immaculate, Jackson, Steuben, Stibitz, Summerfield, Trapp, Untermeyer 1964, O. Williams 1966 (World)

Mona VAN DUYN (1921): Chester, Howard, Howard and Victor, Howe, Jacobus, Konek, Stanford, Stevenson, Untermeyer 1973 (McKay), O. Williams 1966 (World)

Henry VAN DYKE: J. A. Vincent

Alex VAN GELDER: Hadassah

Paul VANGELISTI: Bukowski

Lois VAN HOUTEN: Oppenheimer 1977

VANISH: Krech

Allen VAN NEWKIRK: Carroll (Young American Poets)

Peter VAN TOORN (1944): Freed

Diana VAN TOSH: Gay

Michael VAN WALLEGHEN (1938): Stevenson, Stryk 1975

Bartolomeo VANZETTI: Lowenfels 1969 (Doubleday)

Maria VARELA: Gitlin

Robert VARGAS (1941): Lowenfels 1973

Roberto VARGAS: Clay, Winans

Suzanne VARGUS: Adoff 1971

Robert VAS DIAS (1931): Cole 1971, Colley, De Loach 1976, Gross, Stryk 1975

David K. VAUGHAN: Kiley

James (P.) VAUGHN (1929): Bontemps 1963, 1974; Hughes 1964, 1970

Suzanne VAUGHT: Brindle

Bryon VAZAKAS (1906): O. Williams 1966 (World)

Rex VEEDER (1947): Stryk 1975

Tom VEITCH (1941): McCullough, Padgett, Waldman 1969, 1971

George VENN: Morticella

Maami VERANO: Patterson

Franco VERDI: E. Williams

Lautaro VERGARA: Sargent

Charlie VERMONT (1945): Lowenfels 1973

Beatrice VERNE: Banker

John VERNON (1943): H. Taylor

Jones VERY: Kauffman

Paul VESEY see Samuel W. ALLEN

Quentin VEST: M. Gibson

Florence VICTOR: Glikes, Morrison

Peter (Robert Edwin) VIERECK (1916): J. A. Allen, Aloian, Baylor, Cromie, Engle, Gannett, Hine, Hurtik, Immaculate, Lask, Perrine, Plotz, Shapiro, Strand, Untermeyer 1964, Wallace, M. Williams, Winkler, Witt-Diamant

Anita VIGIL: Van den Heuvel

Jose Garcia VILLA (1914): Aiken, Firmage, Rothenberg 1973, Trapp, Wallace

Juan VILLEGAS (1954): Lowenfels 1973

Harold VINAL (1891): Derleth, Lask

Stephen VINCENT (1941): J. Gill, Harlan, S. Vincent

Lilli VINCENZ: Violet

Ngo VINH LONG: Gersmehl

Julia VINOGRAD: Carroll (Young American Poets), Efros, Head, Konek

Mark VINZ (1942): Lowenfels 1973, Stryk 1975

Judith VIORST: Untermeyer 1970

Xavier VIRAMONTES: Clay

Nicholas VIRGILIO (1928): Van den Heuvel

Gerald (Robert) VIZENOR (1934): Lowenfels 1973, Rosen, Van den Heuvel

Hunce VOELCKER (1940): Leyland 1975

Petra VOGT: Gay

Ellen Bryant VOIGT: Rigsbee

Jiri VOLOCH: Wildman
Alexis VON ADELUNG: Jackson
Myra VON RIEDEMANN (1935):
   A. J. M. Smith 1960
Julia VOSE: Efros
Ida Ruth VOSS: Sargent
Anca VRBOVSKA: Lowenfels
   1969 (Doubleday), Vrbovska
   1963, 1968

W

Richard WAARA: Ferlinghetti
Nancy Sax WACHTER: Pilon
Miriam WADDINGTON (1917):
   A. J. M. Smith 1960
Grace WADE: Efros
John Stevens WADE (1928):
   Lask, McMahon, Schreiber
Seth WADE (1928): Lowenfels
   1967
Charles A. WAGNER: Lask
D. R. WAGNER: Blazek, Fox,
   Krech
Geoffrey WAGNER: Gregory
   1966
Mary Boyd WAGNER: Vrbovska
   1963
David WAGONER (1926): Aiken,
   J. A. Allen, Carruth (Ban-
   tam), (McCall); Engle,
   Hall 1962 (World), Hannum,
   Harlan, Kennedy 1973,
   Kostelanetz, Larrick, Lar-
   son, Monaco 1974, L.
   Moore, Peck 1971, Skelton,
   Stevenson, Strand, H. Tay-
   lor, Ten, Wagner, M.
   Williams, Winkler
Joseph WAIGURU (1939):
   Breman
John WAIN (1925): J. A.
   Allen, Brinnin 1963, Cole
   1963, Cromie, Engle,
   Greaves, Hall 1962 (World),
   Hurtik, Rosenthal 1967,
   Wallace, Walsh
Jacques WAKEFIELD: Coombs
Diane WAKOSKI (1937): Bay-
   lor, Carroll (Young Ameri-
   can Poets), Carruth (Ban-
   tam), Chace, De Loach,

Ellmann 1973, Freed,
   Gross, Halpern, Harlan,
   Harris 1973, Howard,
   Howard and Victor, Katz-
   man, Kennedy 1973,
   Kherdian 1973, Konek,
   Leary, Lowenfels 1969
   (Random House), McCul-
   lough, P. Perry, Rothen-
   berg 1973, Segnitz, Strand,
   H. Taylor, Totem Press,
   Wagner, Walsh, M. Wil-
   liams
Sara WALBRIDGE: Brindle
Derek WALCOTT (1930):
   Bogan, Breman, Brinnin
   1970, Ellmann 1973,
   Knowles, Lomax, Salkey,
   Untermeyer 1973 (McKay),
   Walsh
William WALDEN: Lask
Franklin WALDHEIM: Jackson
Anne (Ann) WALDMAN (1945):
   Carroll (Young American
   Poets), Chester, De Loach
   1976, McCullough, Oppen-
   heimer 1967, Waldman
   1969, 1971
Joel WALDMAN: Krech
Constance WALDRON: Brindle
Keith WALDROP (1932): E.
   Bender, Jacobus, Kennedy
   1973, 1974
Rosmarie WALDROP (1935):
   Kennedy 1973
Arthur WALEY (1889-1966):
   Gregory 1966, Knowles,
   Plotz, Reeves, Stallworthy
Alice WALKER (1944): Adoff
   1973, Baylor, Evans,
   Halpern, Howe, Konek,
   Patterson
Constance WALKER: Sargent
Donald E. V. WALKER: Kiley
Kath WALKER: Konek
Margaret (Abigail) WALKER
   (1915): Adoff 1968, 1970,
   1973; Bell, Bontemps 1963,
   1974; Breman, G. Brooks
   (Broadside Treasury), P.
   Brown, Giovanni, Hayden,
   Howe, Hughes 1970, Jor-
   dan, King 1975, Konek,

D. Randall 1960, 1969;
Trapp
Mike WALKER: Booker
Ted WALKER (1934): Hannum
and Chase, Knowles, Lask,
Stevenson
Arnold WALL (1869-1966):
Knowles
Ann WALLACE: Dee
Emett "Babe" WALLACE: Dee
Robert WALLACE (1932): J.
A. Allen, Aloian, Cole
1963, Morrison, Wallace,
M. Williams
Ronald WALLACE: Rigsbee
Christopher (Chris) WALLACE-
CRABBE (1934): Hecht,
Hollander, T. Moore
Barry WALLENSTEIN: Freed
John Francis WALLER: Cole
1965
Gillian WALLINGTON: J.
Gibson
Karla WALLIS: Harlan
Ann WALSH: Harlan
Chad WALSH (1914): Colley,
Kenseth, Lask, Stryk 1967,
Walsh
Marnie WALSH: Dodge, Low-
enfels 1973
Martin De Porres WALSH:
Chilgren
Beecher W. WALTERMEIER:
Jackson
Beatrice WALTER (1948): Howe
Anna WALTERS (1946): Rosen
Dorothy WALTERS: Konek
Lila V. WALTERS: Kauffman
Winifred Fields WALTERS:
Dodge
Bruce WALTON (Mtu Weusi)
(1942): P. Brown
Tim WANDELL: Mallory
M. (William) D. (Donald)
WANDICK: P. Brown,
Malley
Donald WANDREI: Derleth
Malaika (Ayo) WANGARA see
Joyce WHITSITT
William WANTLING (1933-1974):
Blazek, Cole 1971, Fox,
Gross, Lowenfels 1967,
1969 (Doubleday), (Random

House), 1973, 1975; Sher-
man, Winans, Winkler
Mary L. WANTNER: Sargent
J. P. WARD: J. A. Allen
John A. WARD: Harlan
Val Gray WARD: P. Brown
W. S. WARDELL: Rigsbee
Darwin E. WARE: Jackson
Eugene Fitch WARE: Jackson,
Parker 1967
Rex WARNER (1905): Cole
1963, Crang, J. Gibson
(Book Two), Knowles
Sylvia Townsend WARNER
(1893): Untermeyer 1964
C. Henry WARREN (1895-
1966): Knowles
F. Eugene WARREN (1941):
Mollenkott
James E. WARREN, Jr.
(1908): Mollenkott
Robert Penn WARREN (1905):
Aiken, J. A. Allen, Beer-
man, Brady, Brinnin 1963,
1970; Carruth (Bantam),
Driver, Ellmann 1973,
1976; Engle, Howard,
Howard and Victor, Jack-
son, Parks, Perrine,
Shapiro, Stevenson, Univ.
Press of Va., Untermeyer
1964, M. Williams, O.
Williams 1966 (World),
Witt-Diamant
Lewis WARSH (1944): Carroll
(Young American Poets),
Oppenheimer 1967, Wald-
man 1969, 1971; Weishaus
Archie WASHBURN: Dodge
Austin D. WASHINGTON (c.
1943): Murphy
Dell WASHINGTON: Coombs
Sam (Samuel L.) WASHINGTON
(1952): Tisdale
Irma WASSALL (1908): Hughes
1970
Martin WASSERMAN: Banker
Rosalyn WATERHOUSE: Stu-
dent
Michael WATERS: Rigsbee
Martin A. WATKINS: Banker
Vernon WATKINS (1906-1967):
Brinnin 1963, 1970; C.

Brooks, Ellmann 1973,
Engle, Firmage, Glikes,
Immaculate, Knowles, Lask,
Stevenson, Summerfield,
W. Taylor, Thomas, Trapp,
Wallace
Patricia WATSON: Colley
Robert WATSON (1925): J. A.
Allen, Glikes, Kennedy
1973, Owen 1969, 1974;
H. Taylor
Ruth Jones WATSON: Giovanni
Wilfred WATSON (1911): Cole
1965, Firmage, A. J. M.
Smith 1960
Bob WATT: Rosenblum
W. W. WATT: Aloian
Tom WAYMAN: Lowenfels
1975
Tom WEATHERLY (Jr.) (1942):
Adoff 1973, De Loach 1976,
Oppenheimer 1977, Rothen-
berg 1973, Waldman 1969,
T. Wilentz
Miles WEAVER: Crafts
Roger WEAVER: Freed
Francis WEBB (1925): T.
Moore
Phyllis WEBB (1927): Engle,
Firmage, E. Gill, A. J.
M. Smith 1960
Rozana WEBB: Vrbovska 1963
Alfred K. WEBER: Crafts
Richard WEBER (1932): Ken-
seth, Rosenthal 1967,
Stallworthy
John WEBSTER: Cole 1971
Raymond WEBSTER (X) (Odire
Mbarar) (1941): Tisdale
Ramona WEEKS (1934): Lowen-
fels 1973, 1975
Robert Lewis WEEKS: Brewton
Jim WEHLAGE: Palmer
Dan G. WEIDEN: Morticella
Phil WEIDMAN: Fox
Henrietta WEIGEL: Gallery
1973
James L. WEIL (1929):
Brewton, Derleth, Dunning,
Glikes, Lask, Weil
Jules Alan WEIN (1918):
Joseloff
Eliot WEINBERGER: Gross

Emily Rubin WEINER: Violet
Hannah WEINER: Banker,
Gross, Hitchcock
John WEINERS: De Loach
1968, 1976
Roger WEINGARTEN (1945):
Halpern
Mary S. WEINKAUF: Brindle
Richard WEINRAUB: Morticella
Laurence WEISBERG: Ferling-
hetti
Mel WEISBURD (1927): Lowen-
fels 1966
Morris WEISENTHAL: Lask
Edward WEISMILLER (1915):
Univ. Press of Va. , O.
Williams 1966 (World)
Burton Ira WEISS (1946):
Gitlin, Young
Neil WEISS: Lask, Morrison
Ruth WEISS (1928): Efros,
Harvey
Theodore WEISS (1916): Adams,
Aiken, Brinnin 1970, Car-
ruth (Bantam), Ellmann
1973, Gregory 1966, Har-
ris 1970, Howard, Howard
and Victor, Leary, Rosen-
thal 1967, 1968; Strand
Carl WEISSNER: De Loach
1976
Ron WELBURN (1944): Adoff
1973, Breman, Major
James WELCH (1940): Carroll
(Young American Poets),
Chace, Colley, Halpern,
Kennedy 1973, Kherdian
1974, Larson, Lowenfels
1973, Niatum
Lew WELCH (1926): D. M.
Allen 1960, 1964; Arts
Festival 1963, Durand,
Harlan, Harvey, Kherdian
1973, E. Wilentz
Marie de L. WELCH: Knowles,
Trapp
Myra Brooks WELCH: Kauff-
man
Kathryn WELDY: Balazs
Cora J. WELLER: Brindle
Winifred WELLES: Morrison,
Untermeyer 1970
Wade WELLMAN: Derleth

Amos R. WELLS: Kauffman
Carolyn WELLS: McGinley
Clarke WELLS: Lowenfels
   1975
James WELSH: Dodge
Ingrid WENDT (1944): Howe
John WESLEY: Booker
Lorenzo WESLEY: Student
Don WEST (1909): Hughes 1970
John Foster WEST: Plumley
N. G. WESTERFIELD: Lask
Nancy WESTLAKE: Lowenfels
   1966
George H. WESTLEY: Jackson
Ken WESTON: Mallory
Mildred WESTON: Brewton,
   Cole 1967 (Macmillan),
   1971; Dunning, Holmes,
   Peck 1971
David WEVILL (1935): Brinnin
   1979, Wallace
Jerry WEXLER (1940):
   Gersmehl
John WEYMOUTH: Jackson
Philip WHALEN (1923): D. M.
   Allen 1960, Arts Festival,
   1963, Banker, Carruth
   (Bantam), Clark, Di Prima,
   Harlan, Kherdian 1973,
   McCullough, Poetry San
   Francisco, Rothenberg
   1973, Waldman 1971, E.
   Wilentz, Witt-Diamant
June D. WHALEY (1952): Lane
John WHEATCROFT: Harris
   1970
Beate WHEELER: Hauge
Charles Enoch WHEELER (1909):
   Bontemps 1963, 1974;
   Hughes 1970
Deborah WHEELER: Brindle
Edd WHEELER: Kiley
Joyce WHEELER: Giovanni
Ruth Winant WHEELER: Kauff-
   man
John Hall WHEELOCK (1886-
   1978): Aiken, Baylor,
   Cole 1965, 1972; Crafts,
   Cromie, Driver, Dunning,
   Engle, Hannum, Hannum
   and Chase, Howard, How-
   ard and Victor, Knowles,
   Lask, Parker 1967, Steuben,

Stevenson, H. Taylor,
   Trapp, Untermeyer 1964,
   O. Williams 1966 (World)
W. M. WHERRY, Jr.: Jack-
   son
William WHEWELL: Cole 1971
Peter WHIGHAM (1924): Mal-
   lory, Matthias, Plotz,
   Stallworthy
Lawrence WHISTLER (1912):
   Knowles
Hilda H. WHITAKER (c. 1921):
   Giovanni
Tommy WHITAKER (c. 1950):
   Murphy
Thomas (Bacon) WHITBREAD
   (1931): Glikes, Harlan,
   Lask, Morrison, H. Tay-
   lor
E. B. WHITE (1899): McGin-
   ley, Parker 1967, Peter-
   son
Edgar WHITE: Jackson
Franklin C. WHITE, Jr.:
   Kiley
Gail Brockett WHITE: Owen
   1974
Geoff WHITE: Harlan
J. Richard WHITE: Poetry
   San Francisco
James L. WHITE (1936):
   Stryk 1975
Jayne D. WHITE: Brindle
Joan WHITE: Stevenson
Joseph WHITE (c. 1934):
   Adoff 1968, 1973; Lowen-
   fels 1966
Lillian Zellhoefer WHITE:
   Brewton
Patrick WHITE: Sollid 1972,
   K. and J. Sollid
Tyner WHITE: Carroll (Young
   American Poets)
Vera WHITE: Brewton
Tom WHITECLOUD (d. 1971):
   Lowenfels 1973
Anna WHITE FEATHER (1938):
   Lowenfels 1973
James WHITEHEAD (1936):
   Owen 1974, M. Williams
Rita WHITEHEAD: Black
   History
Debbie WHITELY: Dee

Donna WHITEWING (1943): T.
Allen, Colley, Dodge
Nathan WHITING (1946): Stryk
1975
Seymour W. WHITING: Jackson
Ruth WHITMAN (1922): Chester,
Hausman, Kennedy 1973,
1974; Konek, Lask, Mazur,
L. Moore, Vrbovska 1963,
1968
J. D. WHITNEY: Evans
J. Stephen WHITNEY: Clay
Mo WHITNEY: Morticella
Joyce WHITSITT (Lawrence;
Malaika [Ayo] Wangara)
(1938): G. Brooks (Broadside Treasury), Major, D.
Randall 1969
Frederick WHITTAKER: Parker
1960
Reed WHITTEMORE (1919):
Adoff 1969, Bates, Brewton,
Cromie, Engle, Glikes,
Hall 1962 (Penguin), Kennedy 1974, Kenseth, McGovern, Peck 1971, Rosenthal
1967, Schneider, Strand,
Univ. Press of Va., Wagner, Wallace
Curtis WHITTINGTON, Jr.:
Vrobvska 1963
Franklin C. WHITWELL: Kiley
Frances WHYATT: Harris 1973
Mildred WIACKLEY: Vrbovska
1968
Michael WIATER (1944): Durand
Samuel Z. WICKS: Jackson
Margaret WIDDEMAR (1884-1978):
Derleth
Dallas (E.) WIEBE (1930):
Hope, Kennedy 1973, Wiebe
Wendy WIEBER (1951): Howe
Dan G. WIEDEN: Morticella
Laurence WIEDER: Rigsbee
Kathleen WIEGNER: E. Gill,
Rosenblum
Alex WIENER: Montgomery
John WIENERS (1934): D. M.
Allen 1960, Bly 1975,
Carruth (Bantam), De
Loach, Harvey, H. Jones,
Leary, Leyland 1975,

1977; Waldman 1971,
Young
Larry WIGGIN (1919): Van
den Heuvel
Richard WILBUR (1921):
Adams, Aiken, G. W.
Allen, J. A. Allen, Arp,
Bach, Baylor, R. Bender,
Bogan, Brady, Brinnin
1963, 1970; C. Brooks,
Calderwood, Carruth (Bantam), Chatman, Cole 1967
(Macmillan), 1971; Crafts,
Cromie, De Roche, Drew,
Driver, Ellmann 1973,
1976; Engle, Greaves,
Gwynn, Hall 1962 (Penguin), (Watts); Hannum,
Hannum and Chase, Harlan, Hieatt, Hopkins (Nelson), Howard, Howard and
Victor, Hurtik, Kennedy
1974, Knowles, Leary,
McGovern, Monaco 1974,
Peck 1970, Perrine, Plotz,
Poulin, Rosenthal 1967,
1968; Sanders, Schneider,
Shapiro, Simpson, A. J.
M. Smith 1967, Stallworthy,
Steuben, Strand, H. Taylor, W. Taylor, Trapp,
Univ. Press of Va.,
Untermeyer 1973 (McKay),
Wallace, Walsh, Wesleyan
Univ., M. Williams, O.
Williams 1966 (World),
Witt-Diamant
Peter WILD (1940): Halpern,
Harris 1970, Kennedy
1973, Larson, Owen 1969,
P. Perry
Lucy WILDE: Violet
Paul WILDERMANN: Fox
John Hazard WILDMAN: Lask
Hiram Ozias WILEY: Jackson
Anne WILKINSON (1910-1961):
A. J. M. Smith 1960
Elena WILKINSON: Lowenfels
1975
Florence WILKINSON: Kauffman
Frederic WILL (1928): Weil
Nancy WILLAND: Colley

P. Perry
M. Ray WILLIS: Rose
Rod WILLMOT: Van den Heuvel
John WILLS (1921): Van den
Heuvel
August WILSON (1945): Adoff
1973
E. V. WILSON: Jackson
Edmund WILSON (1895-1972):
Bogan, Jackson
Emily Herring WILSON: Owen
1974
Ernest J. WILSON, Jr. (1920):
Hughes 1970
Graeme WILSON: Summerfield
James WILSON: Parker 1960
Keith WILSON (1927): Hannum,
Hannum and Chase, Larson,
Lowenfels 1973, Rothenberg
1973, Schreiber
Omer WILSON: Hadassah
Pat WILSON (1926): Cole 1967
(Viking)
Philip WILSON: Kohl
R. C. WILSON: Montgomery
Reginald WILSON (1927): D.
Randall 1969
Robley WILSON, Jr. (1930):
Gildner, Stryk 1975
Ruth Anne WILSON: Brindle
Steve WILSON: Chilgren
V. B. WILSON: J. A. Vincent
John Augustus WILSTACK:
Jackson
Sigmonde (Kharlos) WIMBERLI
(Kharlos Tucker) (1938):
G. Brooks (Jump Bad), P.
Brown
Warner B. WIMS (c. 1946):
Murphy
A. D. WINANS: Fox, Winans
Fran (Francine) WINANT:
Bulkin, Gallery 1970, E.
Gill, Violet
Terence WINCH (1945): Ley-
land 1975
Neal WING: De Loach 1976
Bill WINGELL: Hanna
Sheila WINGFIELD (1906):
Cole 1965, Morrison
Josh WINK: Jackson
O. Howard WINN: Sollid 1973
Pete WINSLOW (1934): Cole
1971, Harvey, Krech

Helen WINTER: Gallery 1970,
1973
Henry WINTER: Jackson
Mary WINTER: Lask
Anne WINTERS: M. Gibson
Yvor WINTERS (1900-1968):
Aiken, Arp, Beerman, R.
Bender, C. Brooks, Car-
ruth (Bantam), Cole 1963,
1967 (Macmillan), 1972;
De Roche, Dunning, Ell-
mann 1973, 1976; Hall
1962 (Watts), Harris 1970,
Jackson, Kennedy 1974,
Larrick, Larson, Lask,
J. Perry, W. Taylor,
Untermeyer 1964, Winters
Allen WISNER: Harlan
Jonathan WITHERS: Kohl
Jill WITHERSPOON-BOYER
(1947): Lane
William WITHERUP (1935):
Hewitt
Harold WITT: Harris 1970,
Lask, Owen 1969, Steven-
son, Talisman
Terrence R. WITT: Scheftel
Joe WITTICH: Hallmark
E. A. WODEHOUSE: Morrison
Warren WOESSNER (1944):
Fox, Stryk 1975
Philip WOFFORD (1935):
Lowenfels 1973
Carl WOIDECK: Krech
Albert A. WOLDMAN: Jackson
Michael WOLFE: Hoffman
Helen WOLFERT: Chester
Fred WOLVER: Fox
Ko WON: Hallmark
S. P. WONDER: Hausman
Nanying Stella WONG: Clay
Okogbule WONODI (1936):
Breman
A. J. WOOD (1906): T. Moore
Charles Erskine WOOD: Jack-
son
Debi WOOD: Kiley
Sybil WOOD: Efros
William WOOD (1931): Cole
1965, 1967 (Macmillan),
1972
George Edward WOODBERRY:
Aloian
Bruce (P.) WOODFORD (1919):

Hunting, Kennedy 1973,
Purdue
A. R. M. (Maynor) WOODS:
Giovanni
D. C. WOODS: Jackson
Helen Gee WOODS: Gallery
1973
John (Warren) WOODS (1926):
Leary, McGinley, McGov-
ern, Owen 1969, Stryk
1967, Wagner
Nancy WOODS (1957): Larrick
Suzanne WOODS: Rosenblum
William WOODS: Cole 1971
Jeff WOODWARD: Shore
Martha WOODWARD: Gallery
1970
Dana WORDES: Violet
Romani (Romano) WORDLAW
(c. 1953): Giovanni
James WORLEY (1921): D.
Randall 1969
Elizabeth WORRAKER: J.
Gibson
Douglas WORTH (1940): Monaco
1973, 1974
Verna WOSKOFF: Banker
Ralph WOTHERSPOON (1897):
Cole 1963
Bruce (McM.) WRIGHT (1918):
Bontemps 1963, Adoff 1973,
Hughes 1970
Celeste Turner WRIGHT (1906):
Stanford
Charles (David) WRIGHT (1935):
Adams, Gersmehl, Glikes,
Halpern, Owen 1964, 1974;
Strand, M. Williams
David WRIGHT (1920): Brinnin
1963, Ellmann 1973,
Knowles, Rosenthal 1967,
1968
David WRIGHT (1926): Cole
1967 (Viking)
Frederick A. WRIGHT: Jack-
son
George T. WRIGHT: Glikes
James WRIGHT (1927): Adams,
Aiken, Berg, Bly 1970,
Bonazzi 1972, Brady,
Brewton, Brinnin 1970, C.
Brooks, Carroll (Poem in
Its Skin), Carruth (Bantam),

Chace, Cole 1967 (Mac-
millan), 1972; Derleth,
Ellmann 1973, 1976; Hall
1962 (Penguin), Hannum,
Harlan, Harris 1973,
Heyen, Hieatt, Hollander,
Hopkins (Nelson), Howard,
Howard and Victor, Ken-
nedy 1973, 1974; Kessler,
Kherdian, Kostelanetz,
Lask, Lowenfels 1967,
McCullough, Monaco 1974,
Pearson, J. Perry, Poulin,
Rosenthal 1967, 1968;
Rothenberg 1973, Sixties,
Strand, Stryk 1967, H.
Taylor, Untermeyer 1973
(McKay), Wagner, Wallace,
Walsh, Wesleyan Univ.,
M. Williams, Witt-Diamant
Jay WRIGHT (1935): Adoff
1973, Breman, Henderson,
Hughes 1964, Jordan, King
1975, D. Randall 1969,
Schreiber, T. Wilentz
Judith WRIGHT (1915): Bogan,
Cole 1971, Knowles, Stan-
ford, T. Moore, Unter-
meyer 1964
Keith WRIGHT: Lask
Rebecca WRIGHT: Waldman
1971
Richard WRIGHT (1908-1960):
Adoff 1968, 1973; J. A.
Allen, Bontemps 1963,
1974; Breman, Ellmann
1973, Holmes, Jacobus,
Jordan, Kramer, Peck
1971
Roxy Lavizzo WRIGHT (c.
1947): Giovanni
Sarah E. WRIGHT (1929):
Adoff 1973, Lowenfels
1966, Hughes 1970
Tom WRIGHT: Cromie
Elsebeth WULFF: Brindle
Audrey WURDEMANN: Jackson
Andrea WYATT: Malley
Charles WYATT: Smith, H.
Smith
Marvin WYCHE (1951): Bon-
temps 1974
William WYCHERLEY: Cole

1971
Andrew WYLIE: Reading

X

Ladele X (Leslie Powell):
Henderson
Marvin X (1944): Breman, G.
Brooks (Broadside Treas-
ury)
Paul XAVIER: Krech
Pedro XISTO (1901): Klonsky,
Wildman, E. Williams,
Winkler

Y

Kateb YACKINE: Kgositsile
Doug YAMAMOTO: Clay
Phyllis YAMPOLSKY: Hadassah
Roi YANEZ: Sargent
Mitsu YASHIMA: Clay
Kenneth YASUDA (1914): Van
den Heuvel
Fujitomi YASUO: E. Williams
Gordon Kirkwood YATES:
Winans
G. YAVORSKY (1950): Freed
Carl YEARGENS (1937): Lowen-
fels 1966
R. J. YEATMAN: Parker 1960
M. YEE: Clay
Samuel YELLEN (1906): Cromie,
Lask
Frank YERBY (1916): Bontemps
1963, 1974; Hughes 1970
Ruth Landshoff YORCK: Glikes
Lyle YORK: Brindle
Al YOUNG (1939): Adoff 1973,
Breman, Colley, Coombs,
De Roche, Evans, Harris
1973, Harvey, Kennedy
1973, Kherdian 1974, Krech,
Larrick, Don L. Lee,
McCullough, Major, A.
Miller, H. Taylor, T.
Wilentz, M. Williams,
Winans
Andrew YOUNG (1885): Bogan,
Cole 1963, 1967 (Macmil-
lan), 1971, 1972; J. Gibson,

J. Gibson (Book Two),
Knowles, Morrison, Reeves
Celia YOUNG: Rosenblum
David P. (Pollock) YOUNG
(1936): Gildner, Halpern,
Al Lee, Wang
Douglas YOUNG (1913): Cole
1972, Thomas
Edith L. YOUNG: Kauffman
Elsie YOUNG: Bulkin
Francis Brett YOUNG: Brew-
ton, J. A. Vincent
Frederic YOUNG: Harlan
Geoff YOUNG: Mallory
George M. YOUNG, Jr. :
Bonazzi 1974, McMahon
Ian YOUNG (1945): J. Gill,
Leyland 1975, 1977; Mal-
ley, Young
Karl YOUNG: Rosenblum
Leo YOUNG: Banker
Marguerite YOUNG: Bly 1975,
Stanford
Susan YOUNG: Booker
Sylvia YOUNG: Black History
Virginia Brady YOUNG: Van
den Heuvel
Ray (A.) YOUNG BEAR (Young-
bear) (1950): Barnes,
Dodge, Gildner, Lourie,
Lowenfels 1973, Niatum,
Rosen
Doug YOUNGBLOOD (1941):
Gitlin
Sarah YOUNGBLOOD: Konek
Burrows YOUNKIN: Rottmann
Gary YOUREE: Banker
YVONNE: Rigsbee

Z

Wayne ZADE: P. Perry
Curtis ZAHN: Lowenfels 1966,
Vrbovska 1963
Ed ZAHNISER: Harris 1976
Jan ZALESKI: Efros
Robert ZALLER: Lowenfels
1975
Virginia Dale ZAMOR: Brindle
Mary ZANDERS: Student
Boevi ZANKLI: Jacobus
Fred ZAPPALA: Banker

Cyn ZARCO: Clay
Marya ZATURENSKA (1902):
 Aiken, Gregory 1962, 1966;
 Hannum, Lask, Phillips,
 Rosenthal 1967, Stanford,
 Untermeyer 1964
Bill ZAVATSKY: Mazur
Raymond ZDONEK: Bly 1975
Yolande ZEALY: Booker,
 Hopkins (Knopf)
Aaron ZEITLIN (1898): Joseloff
Alan ZIEGLER: Rigsbee
Alison ZIER: Efros
Honora M. ZIMMER: Harris
 1970
Paul (J.) ZIMMER (1934):
 Carruth (Bantam), Cole
 1971, Felver, Heyen,
 Kennedy 1973
Edith ZIMMERMAN: Hanna
 1960
A. U. ZINKE: Jackson
Harriet ZINNES: Lask, Lowen-
 fels 1975
Matthew ZION: Palmer
Larry ZIRLIN: Rigsbee
Peter D. ZIVKOVIC: Plumley
Ahmos ZU-BOLTON: Rigsbee
Jack ZUCKER: Ashland
Louis ZUKOFSKY (1904-1978):
 Carruth (Bantam), De Loach
 1968, 1976; Ellmann 1973,
 Glikes, Gross, Harlan,
 Harris 1973, Kostelanetz,
 Lask, Leary, Rothenberg
 1973, 1974
Paul ZWEIG (1935): McCul-
 lough
Susan ZWINGER: Gildner